31.11
3/7/96

HENRY A. WALLACE

Henry A.
Wallace

HIS SEARCH FOR A NEW WORLD ORDER

GRAHAM WHITE AND JOHN MAZE

The University of North Carolina Press *Chapel Hill & London*

© 1995 The University of North
Carolina Press
Manufactured in the United States
of America

The paper in this book meets the
guidelines for permanence and durability
of the Committee on Production Guidelines
for Book Longevity of the Council on
Library Resources.

99 98 97 96 95   5 4 3 2 1

Library of Congress
Cataloging-in-Publication Data
White, Graham J.
Henry A. Wallace : his search for a
new world order
        p.   cm.
Includes bibliographical references
(p.   ) and index.
ISBN 0-8078-2189-6 (cloth : alk. paper)
1. Wallace, Henry Agard, 1888–1965.
2. Vice-Presidents — United States —
Biography.   3. United States — Politics
and government — 1933–1945.   4. United
States — Politics and government —
1945–1953.   I. Maze, J. R.
E748.W23W48   1995
973.917′092 — dc20
[B]   94-27199
        CIP

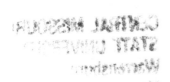

CONTENTS

ILLUSTRATIONS

PREFACE

Despite Henry Wallace's sober, reserved manner and his reluctance to engage in self-seeking politicking, his public career crystallized some of the most portentous choices in modern American and even world history. In domestic economics he stood for realistic altruism against aggressive self-interest, in international affairs for free trade and cooperation against isolationism. If he, rather than Harry Truman, had become president on Franklin Roosevelt's death, his policy of accommodation with the Soviet Union as against the Truman Doctrine of containment might have spared the world some forty years of cold war. Yet these worldly conflicts of attitude were in a way mirrored in his own personality. He was determined and steadfast in whatever he undertook but was certainly not a simple, single-minded person. Prominent among his internal conflicts was the contrast between his practical, empirical scientific thought, invaluable especially in his administration of the Department of Agriculture, and his fascination with mystical, theosophical conceptions of the perfectibility of humankind, which gave rise not only to his internationalism but also to quixotic adventurism and indiscretions that repeatedly threatened his public career.

Wallace's contemporaries sensed these contradictions. Whether they criticized his supposed failings or stressed, as many did, his achievements in scientific experimentation, his indestructible liberalism, and his originality of mind, they found him difficult to comprehend. "I understood him less than anyone I was associated with," former Farm Security Administration head Will Alexander said of Wallace, in an interview recorded in the early 1950s. Speaking of a tour of the South that he and Wallace made in 1936 to inspect the work being done to help the rural poor, Alexander recalled that the experience seemed to make no impression on Wallace whatsoever. "I never met his mind," he said, recalling their conversations. "I think he's better than what I saw in him," Alexander added apologetically. "I always knew I wasn't seeing the real fella." Samuel Bledsoe, an employee in Wallace's Department of Agriculture in the 1930s and his assistant for six weeks after Wallace became vice president in 1941, made similar observations. Henry Wallace possessed "a very good mind," and "had the makings of one of the great figures of American history," but "there [was] always something about him that you [didn't] quite understand." Members of the Senate, over whose deliberations Wallace presided, "didn't like him personally," Bledsoe recalled. The reason, aside from the vice president's tendency to walk past them with eyes averted and his reluctance to invite them to informal social occasions, was that "they didn't understand him." The remark became something of a commonplace. As Wallace's dispute with Reconstruction Finance Corporation chairman Jesse Jones reached its raucous climax in mid-1943, the *Akron Beacon Journal* noted that the vice president "ha[d] not become popular with the average politician," whether inside or outside of Congress. "They do not," the newspaper said, "understand him."[1]

We who attempt, now, to understand his thinking and assess the significance of this major player on the political stage during a critical period in the nation's history face a similar difficulty. It is a difficulty best explained by Samuel Bledsoe, who, of all those interviewed for the Columbia University Oral History Project, made the most serious attempt to come to terms with Wallace's enigmatic personality. Speaking of Russell Lord's 1947 book, *The Wallaces of Iowa*, Bledsoe complained that "it glossed over things." "It was obvious at the time," he said, "that Wallace was off on the wrong tangent." To Bledsoe, Lord had failed to discuss "the real Wallace." "He got a fictional character created there. Part of it is true, and lots of it isn't true. . . . The Wallace that puzzled his friends, the mystic, the Hamlet, the fellow who could be dominated, the introvert, that mixture of how can a man be a good politician who dislikes meeting people, and is shy in the presence of everybody, including his wife, I suppose, — those things aren't discussed." A longtime friend of the Wallace family and, for a period, one of Wallace's assistants in Washington, Lord had failed to answer the hard questions, or even to ask them.[2]

There are sharper questions to be asked about Henry Wallace, still unrecognized influences on his life that need to be identified and explored. How, for instance, was he able to reconcile scientific endeavor with theosophical belief? How was it that, so soon after coming to Washington, he could have associated himself with an international escapade whose true nature, had it been discovered, would have brought his dismissal from public office? What underlay his undoubted presidential ambitions? Why did he rashly challenge first Franklin Roosevelt and later Harry Truman, jeopardizing his political career? Why in

1948 did he run, and at such personal cost, in a race that he could not hope to win? What gave him the prescience to discern and the courage to try to forestall the growing perils of a nuclear world? How was it that Henry Wallace, who was not even a major executant of the nation's foreign policy, was able to enunciate perhaps the most humanely appealing and farsighted of blueprints for a new international order? The historical record now throws useful light on these and other questions, and on the man about whom they are asked. It can lead us now well beyond Bledsoe's despairing conclusion that "there is always something about [Henry Wallace] that you do not understand."

The emergence of perestroika and the subsequent events in the Soviet Union raises other poignant issues. Could Wallace have been right all along in believing that a constructive accommodation with the Soviet Union was possible? Did cold war proponents waste forty years in needless expenditure on weaponry, and in poisoning international relations with hatred and fear that may take another generation to fully dissipate? Has not history proved Wallace correct in forecasting that U.S. foreign policy would continue to be that of propping up reactionary and autocratic regimes in order to contain Soviet expansion? Or were the cold warriors correct in believing that only an unwavering confrontation could bring the Soviet Union to see the futility of its aggressive adventurism? The time is propitious to reexamine Wallace's grounds for the predictions and proposals he made: Were they based on a thoroughly realistic and practical understanding of the fundamentals of international economic relations or were they the by-product of a kind of romantic millennialism springing from his idiosyncratic religious convictions? Or did both strains of thought play some role here as they seem to have done in many other aspects of his political career? Evidence for each of these apparently incompatible tendencies has given rise to sharp, even bitter, divisions of opinion between those who have tried to assess the career of this extraordinary man.

We can begin our search for Henry Wallace by examining what he said about himself, about the influences on his life and the reasons for his behavior. This is so because he, like so many of his contemporaries, recorded an interview after he left public life. Wallace, in other words, has told what he wanted known of his own story. Moreover, he has done so at very great length — the transcript of this oral history, recorded in the early 1950s, covers more than five thousand pages.

Wallace's reminiscences stretch back to his childhood and forward past the end of his public career. In part, they were prompted by entries in his political diary, which he kept for part of 1935 and then (though with some significant gaps) from 1939 to 1945, and whose entries are often simply incorporated into the text of the oral history. At times, Wallace seems constrained by the diary, merely adding a brief and not very illuminating gloss to its often prosaic entries. But in other places, this is not so. By the time he reached 1942, he had begun to comment on the diary entries much more frequently, and often at considerable length, probably because the issues about which he spoke were more recent, but also because he was then embroiled in several rancorous controversies about which, at the time of the interviews, he still felt deeply. Toward the end of the oral history, with no diary entries to inhibit him, Wallace ranges freely over his whole life and career. He talks eagerly of the 1948 campaign, of his achievements as secretary of agriculture and vice president, of his vision of the "century of the common man," of his mysticism and religious beliefs. Here he offers "a brief analysis based on my observations in public life which might be of interest to the future historian"; there a homily on the purpose of our existence on Earth. He swings back to discuss the editorials and articles he wrote as a farm journalist in the 1920s, then moves to assess, frankly and judiciously, the persons with whom he most closely worked.

The oral history is full of revelations of Wallace's conscious, rational political thinking and ideology. So also is his diary — for the most part a political diary, many thousands of pages in length. These have formed the basis of our understanding and exposition of that thinking. But regarding his personal life he was extremely reserved, quite unlike his New Deal colleague and rival Harold Ickes. Ickes also left a voluminous political diary, but parallel with it ran an astonishingly frank private one, providing a highly colored backdrop to his public career.[3] Wallace felt that his personal life was none of posterity's business; it was not necessary to know about it in order to understand how he came to hold the doctrines he held. In his view, his political philosophy was a perfectly rational consequence of certain ethical principles that, like the drafters of the Declaration of Independence, he held to be self-evident. All were created equal, and along with their unalienable rights in life, liberty, and the pursuit of happiness went the right to a fair share of the potentially superabundant fruits of God's earth. What made some people see him as a dangerous radical or woolly-minded dreamer was that he wanted to extend these rights to all humankind, not just to white middle-class Americans.

No one arrives at a world view on perfectly rational grounds. In the steadfast stream of decent humanism and thoroughgoing empiricism that bore Wallace along throughout his life, there were some decidedly unusual eddies and cross-currents of thought. In the 1920s he began an unusual spiritual odyssey that in a sense he never abandoned. It significantly shaped his attitudes and gave a sense of transcendental purpose to his life. The major aim of this study is to explain, more fully than has been done before, this aspect of Henry Wallace's makeup, and to show how his eclectic spiritual beliefs and the social attitudes flowing from them made an impact on his public career. In doing so we have been greatly aided by two sets of letters, one from Wallace's personal papers and the other from those of Samuel Rosenman. The first set, written to Henry Wallace in the 1920s, helps us to trace his spiritual history during that time; the second, written by him in the 1930s, when placed alongside Agriculture Department and State Department records, tells a remarkable story of what can only be called, for some of that period, his double life. The diaries and memoirs of several of Wallace's contemporaries have allowed us to see him through their observant and perceptive eyes.

Henry Wallace's name, his career, and particularly his involvement in a campaign many saw as a major turning point in the history of the nation and even the world still evoke strong feelings. He has become a symbol—to some, of the kind of personal instability and political naïveté that can distort a nation's policies and imperil its survival, to others, of rare political courage and the sort of humane, expansive, beyond-consensus thinking that alone offers the promise of a new and better world. If his beliefs sometimes pushed him in injudicious, even potentially disastrous, directions, they also imparted a visionary quality to his thought that many found appealing, and a humanitarian bent to his practical policies that led him into sharp conflicts with other powerful figures in the Roosevelt and Truman administrations. The new world order that he envisioned was not like the one we have heard so much of in recent years. It did not involve the idea of a global police force manned and directed almost entirely by great powers, administering a conception of "justice" determined in significant measure by unadmitted national economic interests. What Wallace wanted to try was a world in which free trade, shared technological development, and international economic cooperation would remove the inequity and, he hoped, make obsolete the envy and greed that he saw as the main causes of war. What follows is our account of the sources of those dreams and their fate in one person's life.

We wish to record our gratitude to Richard Bosworth, Stephen Salsbury, and especially Shane White for their valuable criticism of early chapter drafts, to Kristine Garcia for her excellent assistance with our research, and to Richard Polenberg for his encouragement and support. The staffs of Fisher Library at the University of Sydney, the Library of Congress, the National Archives, the Herbert Hoover Library at West Branch, Iowa, and the University of Iowa Library helped us greatly, with Earl Rogers of the last-mentioned institution being exceptionally generous in this respect. Our thanks go also to Pamela Upton and Karin Kaufman of the University of North Carolina Press for their fine editorial work, and to the University of Iowa Library, the Associated Press, and Julius Lazarus for giving us permission to use photographic material. A financial contribution from the Department of History at the University of Sydney helped us prepare the manuscript for publication, and our research was greatly facilitated by a generous grant from the Australian Research Council.

HENRY A. WALLACE

1

THE EDUCATION OF
HENRY WALLACE

The interviewer had asked Henry Wallace about his childhood. His earliest recollections, Wallace said, were of a bobsled ride in a snowstorm and of staying the night in a hotel some distance from the family's Iowa farm and hearing noisy trains rush past. Once, at the farm, he had wandered into a cornfield and become lost; it was a long time before anxious searchers located him after hearing his plaintive cries. Beginning with these faint memories, Henry Wallace constructed the story of his life, explaining to himself and others what he had achieved and why, creating from the flux of experience an intelligible and purposeful tale.[1]

Wallace told his story in the early 1950s, when he was more than sixty years of age and well removed in time from the experiences he sought to portray. Much had happened to affect his interpretation of those experiences. He had risen high as secretary of agriculture and then as vice president, but there had been cruel disappointments too — his betrayal by Franklin Roosevelt, his sacking by Harry Truman. If he had been praised for his liberalism and farsighted statesmanship, he had also been criticized and maligned, dismissed as a mystic, denounced as a traitor. The disaster of 1948 must have been fresh in his mind, his mauling as a "Communist dupe" by a viciously hostile press a vivid memory. Perhaps the perspective of time gave a special kind of clarity as he sought to make sense of what had happened; and perhaps it superimposed structures that could not have been apparent at the time. Recollected from the 1950s, Henry Wallace's life was not as he had progressively understood it. His narrative is, however, the best place from which our quest for him may begin.

Henry A. Wallace was born on 7 October 1888, on a farm near the village of Orient, in Madison County, Iowa. His father was Henry C. Wallace, the son of another Henry Wallace, known as Uncle Henry, a former minister of the United Presbyterian church (from which he had to resign because of ill health) and since 1883, editor of the *Iowa Homestead*, a moderately influential agricultural paper. While studying dairying at the Iowa State College of Agriculture and Mechanical Arts, Henry C. met May Brodhead of Muscatine, Iowa, and when they agreed to marry, he discontinued his courses and moved onto a small farm near Orient, which his father, Uncle Henry, owned.[2] The following year, their first son, Henry A. Wallace, was born. But in a time of falling prices the farm did not prosper, and in 1892 the family moved to Ames, where, after rapidly completing the remainder of his course at the college, Henry C. Wallace became an assistant professor of dairying.

Henry A. Wallace's interest in the earth and its produce began very early. His mother, a dedicated gardener, encouraged in him a love of living things, especially plants. A few years after they had moved to Ames, when he was just eight years old, she supervised his first experiment in crossing flowers, and if the resulting strain of pansy was less beautiful than the parent plants, Wallace was still intrigued by the process and proud of its outcome. It was at Ames, too, that he became acquainted with George Washington Carver, then a student and research assistant at the college, who was a close friend of his father's and later became a famous Tuskegee chemist. Carver, whose "first love . . . was always plants," took Wallace on botany expeditions, the tall black man and the five-year-old boy wandering together in the woods and fields while Carver taught him to identify the parts of flowers. Pretending that the young boy's knowledge and powers of observation were greater than they were, Carver "incited" him to learn. Carver was "a very kindly person," Wallace said later. "I had a very great affection for him. . . . I suspect that he and my mother, between them, were responsible for my acquiring a love of plants at a very early age."[3]

Wallace's interest in agricultural experimentation began early, too, stimulated by his father but more particularly by his grandfather. In

1896 Henry C., in order to help run the rural paper the family had bought, resigned his professorship and moved the family to Des Moines. He became the business manager of *Wallaces' Farmer*, of which, he and his two brothers agreed, Uncle Henry should be the editor. As well as editing the paper, Uncle Henry farmed some land about ten miles southeast of Des Moines. He had already pioneered several agricultural improvements, including the introduction of bluegrass to the region, and on his farm he tried out new schemes and then wrote about them in *Wallaces' Farmer*. When his grandson visited, as he frequently did, the two of them would stroll through the fields inspecting the crops and discussing how yields might be improved. Because of these early influences, Wallace said, he had for a time "thought completely in terms of seeds, plants, and farming."[4]

For a time the Wallaces suffered severe hardship. The father's health was not robust—a typhoid attack in 1893 had almost taken his life—and his income from the paper was, at first, quite meager. Inevitably then, from a very early age, Wallace, as the eldest son, had to perform many burdensome tasks. Living in straitened circumstances on the poorer northern side of the city, he was made aware, too, of the hostility the local children felt toward the well-off children in west Des Moines, which left him with "a lifelong feeling of how it is that poor people feel toward rich people."[5] It is possible that such fragments of Wallace's remembered early life hold clues to his later attitudes. All his life, he would show a strong commitment to justice and a concern for equality of opportunity that took the form especially of opposition to economic discrimination. His childhood experience of hardship and poverty, and his early experience of the resentment the socially disadvantaged children felt toward those more fortunately placed, may have given an extra edge to these principled concerns.

As *Wallaces' Farmer* began to prosper, the family's circumstances improved, and in 1898 they were able to move to a ten-acre block on the west side of town. A couple of years later Henry C. built a substantial residence there, one of the best in the district. Even now, however, Wallace had to do a lot of hard physical work. His father planted an orchard on the block and kept some animals, and from the age of ten or so Wallace had to look after two cows, a horse, and some pigs. In winter, he had to prize the frozen sorghum loose with a pitchfork to keep the animals fed. In order to provide for the family's daily needs, he had to pump hard water from a well in the backyard and soft water from a cistern in the basement to separate tanks in the attic. He kept a vegetable garden and, having read in a catalog of "the wonders of strawberries," ordered six different varieties so that he could compare their yields. He loved this experimental work, but found the rest of his chores very arduous, and in these years he built up some resentment against his younger brothers, who seemed largely intent on having a good time. Only his sister Annabelle, closer to him in age, was sympathetic, remembering the hardship of former years.[6]

Wallace felt that his siblings were given preferential treatment by his parents, shown more lenience and indulgence, and he thought this unfair. Reflecting on this later, he observed that "the oldest [child] has to carry the brunt of the parents' enthusiastic but wrong ideas. So I was called Henry, that's all, with no nickname that I can remember." The point of that last sentence was that his mother endowed his younger brothers, John and James, with affectionate nicknames — "mother's sunshine boy" and "Wimpsie Wee" (after a favorite comic strip character), respectively — which evidently make him feel that they were more loved than he, plain Henry.[7] One characteristic of the mature Henry Wallace was his fervent adherence to the principle of universal justice — that is, an insistence on the absolute value of every human life, and on the basic rights of every human being. This belief must have come from many sources — his early religious training would be an obvious one — but may have gained added force from his childhood belief that his siblings were enjoying advantages that he was unfairly denied.[8]

He not only felt that the other children received more affection but also sensed that the affection he had been shown was limited and conditional on his doing well. As eldest son, he bore the name Henry Wallace and was expected to live up to it, something he grew to resent. He evidently reacted by suppressing his need for affection and determining to be sufficient to himself, independent, a loner who would compensate for that deprivation by becoming a superior person. His brothers may have been mainly interested in having a good time, but he was not. They may have been happy to accept the standards of the neighborhood boys, but he declined to do so. They did reasonably well at school, but he was determined to excel.[9] He consoled himself with the thought that personal achievement was more valuable than sentimental affection. There may be early clues here to the restless intellectual energy Wallace demonstrated all through his life, to his unrelenting drive to improve himself, to the independence he often exhibited in the political sphere, and to the sense of intellectual and moral superiority he frequently displayed, in relation to Franklin Roosevelt, for instance.

His chores and the rough way in which he continued to dress exposed him to a certain amount of ridicule, heightening the class consciousness of which he had earlier been made aware. "In high school I wasn't quite as happy because all through high school I had to take care of those two cows, and sometimes, I suspect, I didn't change my shoes, at any rate I remember my disquietude when I was a junior having another boy intercede with me 'For heaven's sake, don't make the girls so unhappy by smelling!' " Wallace felt somewhat out of place in this school, which enjoyed a much higher social status than those in the east or north ends of the city. Yet this was clearly not an intellectual failing; as a scholar, he usually distinguished himself.[10]

Despite feeling that he was being treated sternly, Wallace respected and admired his parents. He thought of his father as being very capable, a natural sportsman, a good businessman (probably, Wallace thought, because he was "distrustful of humanity," which "neither my grand-father nor myself were"), an instinctive politician, and as being strongly, though not narrowly, religious. But although he greatly admired his father for his many abilities, he did not feel close to him. Looking back, he commented that a "son never knows what his father is really like. I think it's impossible. . . . He was a very self-contained man."[11]

His mother had the greater influence, imbuing him not merely with her love of plants but also with her own austere moral code. Her parents having died of tuberculosis before she was four, she had been brought up in a strict religious manner first by her grandmother, the wife of a Methodist minister, and later by two aunts, one of whom was also the wife of a Methodist minister and the other whom Wallace remembered as being "excessively proper." With a large family to look after (eventu-ally there were five other children, two boys, John and James, and three girls, Annabelle, Mary, and Ruth), she had little time for social life and, Wallace recalled, "until I was twelve she had no use for salads because she thought they were some new-fangled notion that was being foisted on the American people by women's clubs." She was "old-fashioned New England American stock with all their prejudices, frugality, their ability to pinch pennies to the utmost," and from her Wallace learned not merely thrift but abstinence. She objected to smoking, so he did not smoke. She did not drink coffee or take any liquor and neither, for many decades, did he.[12]

It seems likely that one tenet of such a Puritan-style upbringing would have been that angry, hostile, or destructive impulses are evil. Looking back, he remembered a boyhood incident of his bursting out angrily with "Oh damn!" when he banged his head in a newly built, low-ceilinged chicken house on his father's ten-acre plot. It was the first time his mother had heard him swear and she beat him for it: "I'd committed the unforgivable sin."[13] Of course, when, as an adult, he referred to his action as an unforgivable sin he was mildly ridiculing his mother's concern over such a modest expletive, but the words he used may also have reflected his actual feeling at the time. Such a rebuke from a mother he loved and admired had sufficient effect for him to remember it after a lapse of some fifty years. It was part of a general training in self-restraint and nonaggression that was to have a lifelong effect on him, though his aggressive feelings sometimes could, as we shall see, find other forms of expression.

Religious influences on Wallace came not only from his parents but also through his attendance at the United Presbyterian Sunday school. His attitude there was serious and he accepted the teachings of the Bible in a personal and rather literal sense. But his interests were never narrowly focused, in part because of his close relationship with his grandfather, an intellectually vigorous and opinionated man, who readily dispensed ideas on subjects not only of religious but also of political and economic concern. Uncle Henry read the latest books, obtained periodicals from abroad, and sustained a lively correspondence with friends and associates within the United States and elsewhere. His practice of having his grandson read these letters to him after they had had lunch together, which they frequently did, must have exposed Wallace to a wide spectrum of information and ideas.

Though "truly devout," Uncle Henry interpreted the Bible broadly, setting it against a background of contemporary social, economic, and political issues. He adapted the Scriptures to people's immediate needs. Later, Wallace, too, would move in this direction, eventually leaving the United Presbyterian church (a move precipitated by his attempting to introduce the ideas of William James to the Sunday school class) and joining Episcopal church congregations, first in Des Moines, in 1930, and then in Washington.[14]

In high school and at Iowa State College in Ames, which he entered in 1906, Wallace read widely, studying the works of Emerson and becoming "profoundly interested" in William James's *Varieties of Reli-*

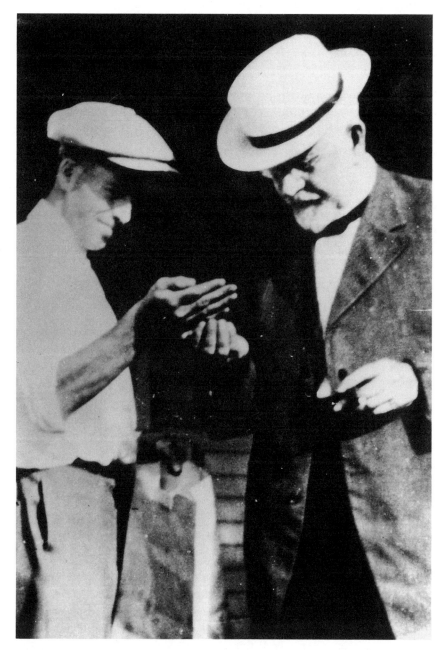

Henry A. Wallace and his grandfather, "Uncle Henry," examining corn yields. (Courtesy of the University of Iowa Library)

gious Experience. Certainly James's approach to theology must have been congenial to the interests that led to Wallace's long-term preoccupations. James wrote in a period when the opposition between a scientific, determinist view of the world, especially with regard to evolution, and the voluntarism of traditional religions, seemingly inseparable from the moral life, was at its intellectual height. What specially concerned James was that the fatalistic "scientism" of social Darwinism encouraged a complacent acceptance of social inequity. With his characteristic refusal to be impressed by supposedly conclusive universalistic arguments, James contended that for the most part the natural world ran on in the causal way science proposed, but that at crucial points inspired exertions of the human spirit could introduce novel factors leading to unprecedented physical and social developments. This reconciliation of evolution with a liberal approach to religion was what Henry Wallace had needed. He himself intervened in the evolutionary process, developing, among other things, new and more productive strains of corn and chickens, without ever turning away from his belief in the vital role of spiritual enlightenment in determining human destiny—as Uncle Henry had taught him.

The ability to change the physical world, James said, can come about through the phenomenon of "prayerful communion." "The appearance," he continued, "is that in this phenomenon something ideal, which in one sense is part of ourselves and in another sense is not ourselves, actually exerts an influence, raises our center of personal energy, and produces regenerative effects unobtainable in other ways."[15] This is not communion with a personal god, but a joining with some pervasive extrapersonal spiritual energy, best achieved through the individual's subconscious. If we can step over the boundary between conscious and subconscious, we may experience the identity of our personal spirit with that universal supernatural force, James believed.

The notion that the individual contains a spark of divine fire was a part of the Theosophical doctrine to which Wallace would give serious credence in later life, as we shall see. William James was also prepared to countenance the Buddhist belief in reincarnation and the concept of karma—the concept that if in life one strives toward the good, then in successive existences one will achieve higher and higher forms of existence and spiritual excellence. Wallace's belief in the possible present existence of such evolved individuals was, at its height, to lead him into a politically perilous adventure, partly motivated by the hope of finding their dwelling place.

Although bitter disappointments eventually caused Wallace to modify some of his more extreme Theosophical beliefs, he readily accepted less mystical aspects of James's thought. James's advocacy of the strenuous, "heroic" moral life seems directly reflected not merely in Wallace's lifelong devotion to physical fitness and sporting contests with his colleagues but also in the forlorn heroism, as we see it in retrospect, of his 1948 campaign as an independent presidential candidate. Again, James's criticism of imperialism on the ground that it devalued and crushed the traditional ideals of subject peoples, thus denying that they shared equally with the imperialists in the universal spirit and were equal before God, was precisely the belief that motivated Wallace in the field of foreign relations.

Another book, *In Tune with the Infinite*, by Ralph Waldo Trine, who, Wallace said later, may have been a type of mystic, posed for him the question of what was ultimately worthwhile. He combined the ideas of Trine with those of the shorter catechism of the United Presbyterian church, which his grandfather had urged him to memorize. "What is the chief end of man?" the catechism question read. "The chief end of man is to glorify God and enjoy him forever." But Wallace eventually formulated a different, and what would be for him a lasting, response. What is ultimately worthwhile, he concluded, is to promote "the long-time good of all mankind." [16]

During his college years, this interest in general human welfare manifested itself in a very practical way. Challenged by the problem of how to feed the world's people, he decided to experiment with diet. He had read a book entitled *Farmers for Forty Centuries* and been fascinated by its account of an economy that had little need of animals: "They could go direct to the plants and keep going for forty centuries." Working from the book, he calculated the minimum amount of land necessary to support himself, then tried to subsist on a diet based on the notional yield of such land. Eventually, however, he had to abandon the project because, as he later realized, the vitamin content of the diet was inadequate.[17]

In formal academic work, Wallace did outstandingly well, constrained, among other things, by the family expectation that the oldest son, the one who bore the name Henry Wallace, would distinguish himself, just as his grandfather, through his agricultural leadership, had done. From an early age he had been enjoined to "remember you're a Wallace," and, he explained later, "in our case that would mean an intellectual drive rather than a business drive because grandfather's contribution was essentially an intellectual contribution. That was the standard held up at any rate." At college he read Dickens, Washington Irving, the Waverley novels of Sir Walter Scott, and, in the field of philosophy, William James, Hegel, Herbert Spencer (whose universe he thought "cockeyed, non-human"), Plato, and Heraclitus. But his interests became increasingly scientific. He excelled in chemistry and mathematics and became particularly interested in the mathematical aspects of economics and in the possibility of using such knowledge for predictive purposes. He also became for a time, as the result of his studies, "quite a confirmed believer in evolution," though he later admitted to having some residual skepticism.[18] In 1910 he submitted his bachelor's thesis, "Relation Between Live Stock Farming and the Fertility of the Soil." In it, he stressed the problems attendant upon such farming and the critical importance of soil conservation. Even at that early period he was prepared to say that if individuals neglected their obligations in this regard, it was legitimate for the federal government to intervene — an attitude that would be anathema to the federal government itself and to most of the agricultural community for many years, but one that he was to promote throughout his life.[19] This feeling that there was a need for positive government involvement would lead him to support Theodore Roosevelt and the "Bull Moose" Party in 1912. Wallace graduated with honors in 1910, finishing first among the agricultural students, but instead of proceeding to postgraduate studies, he returned to work on *Wallaces' Farmer*, which had already printed many of his articles. He was to remain with the paper virtually until he entered public life.

In 1912, at the suggestion of his father and grandfather, he went on an agricultural tour of France, Germany, and England, visiting experiment stations and examining, among other things, the work being done with Indian corn, as well as inspecting many art galleries and cathedrals. From Europe, he traveled to the north of Ireland, to visit relatives and some close friends of Uncle Henry's — Sir Horace Plunkett and George W. Russell. The latter impressed Wallace greatly. Poet, editor, Theosophist, and a leader of the cooperative movement, Russell charmed him with his erudition and his knowledge of ancient Irish literature, which he was able effortlessly and melodiously to recite. The two men talked of agricultural subjects, with Russell "gravely question[ing] all cities," and stressing to his new friend that "strength came from the land." They spoke, too, of the ultimate purpose of our existence on Earth. Wallace later called Russell "one of the loveliest characters I ever knew," and it is not unlikely that the seeds of his later interest in Theosophy were sown here.[20]

Wallace had occasionally felt put upon in the name of family duty, but the value he placed on family life was manifested in his early, uncomplicated entry into matrimony. Not long after returning from his European trip he met Ilo Browne, of Indianola, Iowa, and their friendship developed quickly. She shared his great love of music and, as he said later, "tolerated my agricultural experiments [and] intellectual enthusiasms."[21] They were married on 30 May 1914 and moved into their own house in Des Moines. Their first child, born 18 September 1915, was a boy, Henry Browne Wallace, who in later life entered the crossbred poultry enterprise his father was to set up. This Henry was followed by another son, Robert, and a daughter, Jean. The family remained in Des Moines until Wallace entered the New Deal administration in 1933, and the marriage was stable and apparently happy until the end of his life.

The salary Wallace earned as assistant editor of *Wallaces' Farmer* was not large, and he endeavored to supplement it by farming some forty acres of land Ilo was able to buy after selling property that came to her as an inheritance. His father purchased an additional forty acres nearby and Wallace farmed both, running dairy cattle and growing corn. He rose each morning at 4 A.M. to milk the cattle, worked all day in the offices of *Wallaces' Farmer*, and often did more farmwork until well into the night. Soon after their marriage Ilo developed tuberculosis, from which she quickly recovered. In 1916 Wallace too was diagnosed by three doctors as having the disease. His weight dropped sharply and he had to live for four months at his mother's cottage at Green Mountain Falls, Colorado, while he recovered.[22]

As assistant editor of the family paper, Wallace applied scientific methods to the problems of agriculture. He used mathematics to establish the relationship between weather and corn yields, drawing on the work of Professor H. L. Moore of Columbia, but simplifying his methods. Intrigued with the concept of cycles, he attempted to work out a mathematical basis for them. He applied correlational methods to both livestock and crops and developed complex cost-of-production indexes for swine, taking account of labor costs, corn prices, shipping rates, and so on. Enabling farmers to see what they would need to receive for their swine if they were to make a reasonable profit, these corn-hog ratio charts, published in *Wallaces' Farmer* beginning in 1915, became very popular. Eventually Wallace discovered the existence of a seven-year cycle in these ratios, depending on delayed reactions to changes in supply and demand for both corn and hogs. He loved these mathematical and statistical studies, but their value was not just in the intellectual exploration; rather, this was the beginning of his recognition that individual farmers and individual segments of the rural industry could not operate profitably if they thought only of their own production in isolation from other segments of agriculture. They needed information about the context within which they were working, and its likely effect on them.

Wallace also carried out, over many years, a scientific study of weather, a subject of vital importance to the nation's farmers, applying his statistical expertise (he had taught himself higher mathematics). Initially he investigated the relationship between rainfall and crop yields, discovering from meteorological records for a twenty-nine-year period that variations in rainfall produced different results in different areas. Later he tried to test the hypothesis that the earth's weather might be related to changing positions of the moon and planets, eventually recording climatic data collected by the Des Moines Weather Bureau on eighteen thousand punch cards so that he could search for significant correlations.

Wallace's reputation as an agricultural scientist grew. He read a paper to the American Statistical Society and was invited to run a ten-week course at Iowa State College aimed at improving the accuracy with which the professors evaluated their experimental work. Out of that came the college's biometric laboratory, which Wallace would later describe as "probably one of the best if not *the* best of the biometric laboratories associated with the land-grant colleges." The respect his work was accorded is evidenced, too, by invitations to lecture in short courses at Cornell University, and to participate in an International Agricultural Economics Conference in England, at which he delivered "a very ambitious paper" on "the 'graphic' versus the 'statistical' method of computing multiple curvilinear regression lines." "I put a *lot* of time into it," Wallace said later. "And the British didn't give a damn!"[23]

As editor of *Wallaces' Farmer*, a position he assumed after his father moved to Washington in 1921 to become secretary of agriculture in Warren Harding's cabinet, Wallace became an enthusiastic proponent of hybrid corn. Even as a high school student he had become skeptical of the methods by which show judges were evaluating different types of corn. Their criteria seemed to him aesthetic rather than scientific, concentrating on uniformity of ear length and shape of kernel. Little attempt was ever made to compare the yield of corn types judged as being superior with supposedly inferior strains. In 1903, while still in high school, Wallace had made just such a comparison, and discovered that the yield from the prizewinning variety of corn was much less than for less-favored types. During his college years, he worked with the famous corn evangelist Dr. Perry G. Holden on the development of corn-yield tests, but again he was led to question the methods by which corn experts sought to improve this crop.

Although the idea of in-breeding and cross-breeding corn had been mooted some years before, specifically in a paper by George Harrison Shull in 1908, Wallace did not begin his own development of crossbred lines until 1913. He experimented first in a small plot at the rear of his Des Moines home and later at his farm outside the city. For this work, he sought out new strains of corn; in 1916, for example, he visited the Tama people, obtained some of their corn, and successfully crossed it with the Mexican June variety,[24] a predictable enough initiative since he well understood the great achievements of Native American corn breeders of the past. "The finest corn breeders who ever lived were the forerunners of the Aztecs in the highlands of southwestern Mexico," he had written in *Wallaces' Farmer*. "They caused grass to do a thing it had never done before. How these early corn breeders worked on the wild prototype of corn to make it the plant which it has been for at least ten thousand years, is a mystery which baffles the best scientists."[25]

Wallace appears, at first, not to have realized the full potential of hybrid corn, but after the development, by Dr. D. F. Jones in 1917, of double cross-hybrids, as against Shull's single-cross varieties, he became its enthusiastic proponent and from that time until he moved to Washington in 1933 did what he could to promote its use. He hired more labor and land for his own, more ambitious corn-breeding program and helped establish the Iowa State University's annual Corn Yield Test, aimed at developing better hybrid varieties. All this time he was using the pages of *Wallaces' Farmer* to spread the hybrid-corn gospel.

He concerned himself not only with the development of hybrid types but also with the production and distribution of hybrid seed on a large scale. At first, he considered the possibility of a small number of farmers within each agricultural district undertaking developmental work, but he soon saw that such tasks were too difficult, that special skills and equipment were needed. This realization and the enthusiasm and confidence he now felt led him, in 1926, to found the Hi-Bred Corn Company (later the Pioneer Hi-Bred Corn Company), with the aim of developing new and more productive hybrid strains, producing them in commercial quantities and marketing the seed.

"No seed company, farmer, or experiment station has any seed of cross or inbred seed for sale today," he had written in *Wallaces' Farmer*, as these activities got underway. "The revolution has not come yet, but I am certain that it will come within ten or fifteen years." He was nearly enough correct. In 1933, less than 1 percent of corn planted in the corn belt was hybrid. Within ten years the percentage had risen to 78; by 1965 it was nearly 100. Henry Wallace did not discover hybrid corn, but more than any other person he was responsible for extending its use in the United States, with all the resultant increases in yields and in agricultural productivity.[26]

Wallace's political ideas had been forming too. He remembered his family having strong Republican political convictions. His father, after the election of Grover Cleveland, had warned that they were in for hard times, and his grandfather had often observed that "Democrats don't read." An uncle, Newton B. Ashby, who was a Democrat, was regarded as something of a black sheep.[27] After leaving college he had read Thorstein Veblen and been deeply impressed by his insights into the deficiencies of a mature capitalist economy, though he rejected Veblen's "socialist approach" and, understandably, did not share his contempt for small businessmen. Protracted discussions with Frank Faltonson, a Norwegian farmer, whom he had first met in 1910, firmed Wallace's opposition to "reactionary capitalism" but did not persuade him to embrace Faltonson's socialist ideas. "Progressive capitalism" was Wallace's ideal, something that, as a young man, he roughly equated with the policies and personal style of Theodore Roosevelt.[28]

Yet the political process itself had little appeal to him. He was even mildly disapproving not of his father's success in this field, but of the manner in which he had achieved it. Reflecting on his father's ability, as secretary of agriculture in the early 1920s, to persuade President Warren Harding to his way of thinking, he recalled that his father had "got along very well with Harding for the simple reason that Father was a good golf player and a good bridge player. . . . He sold Harding on his approach on many things, just simply by playing Harding's own game, which was the game of being a good fellow. Father could do that— I could never have done it." His assertion, elsewhere, that "Mother made me more essentially what I am than Father. That is her fundamental attitudes are more nearly my attitudes," hints at the conflict he felt between his mother's moral strictures and his father's easy political socializing. Time and again, during his public life, Wallace would express a disdain for political maneuvering of any kind and a strong reluctance to involve himself in it. "I was never interested particularly in political parties. . . . I just can't be interested . . . it's not my method of working—that's all."[29]

In reflecting on his life before he became an important public official, Henry Wallace did not treat fully certain matters that were of great significance to him, and without an understanding of which important aspects of his political career become less intelligible. Thus, he speaks glowingly of George W. Russell, his grandfather's friend, without mentioning the theosophical beliefs he shared with him. He talks with justifiable pride of his scientific approach to agriculture and his experimental work with corn, without revealing his spiritual connection with the Native American priest and corn grower Charles Roos, whose methods were anything but scientific. He tells of his movement away from the personal and literal religion of his youth to a more realistic and rational faith, yet says nothing of the spiritual quest that, already in those pre–New Deal years, he had come to see as the major purpose of his life. The voice of the mystic, far less distinctly than the voice of the scientist, is heard fitfully in this section of Wallace's narrative, in his reference to the writings of James and Trine and in his admission to a kind of mysticism that many would similarly avow ("I'd say I was a mystic in the same sense that George Carver was, who believed that God was in everything, and therefore, that if you went to God, you could find the answers").[30] But as Wallace's private correspondence over these years plainly shows, the question of the relative strength of those voices and the degree to which they could harmonize was not so simple.

2

SPIRITUAL EXPLORATIONS

SEEKING THE RELIGIOUS KEYNOTE

OF THE NEW AGE

Wallace's solid contribution not only to practical research into plant and animal genetics but also to the methodology of such research is a matter of record. On the practical side, he developed and stabilized, out of his own research, high-yielding strains of seed corn that he marketed through the Hi-Bred Corn Company, eventually to become a multimillion-dollar business. His contributions to methodology included the development, in collaboration with Professor George W. Snedecor, who was to build an international reputation as a mathematician, of a mechanized procedure for calculating correlation coefficients, published jointly in 1925 under the title *Correlation and Machine Calculation*. In 1934 Iowa State College made him an honorary doctor of science, in recognition of his scientific achievements.[1] Nevertheless, one can trace, in Wallace's correspondence in the late 1920s and early 1930s, the gradual devolution of his scientific studies of the effect of weather on crop production into inquiries that seem alien to the orthodox scientific attitude.

Wallace with Raymond Baker, plant geneticist for the Wallaces' Hi-Bred Corn Company, founded 1926. (Courtesy of the University of Iowa Library)

ASTROLOGY, THEOSOPHY, AND NATIVE AMERICAN SPIRITUALITY

In January 1929 Wallace and John C. Evans, a weather forecaster in Lawrence, Kansas, corresponded, discussing the possibility that solstices of the planets influenced Earth's weather. Evans decried the influence of the solstices, asserting that it was the equinoxes of Mercury, Venus, and Mars that had probably had more role in creating a certain great storm at the New Year. However, he insisted on the importance of the new moon passing between the earth and the sun, citing a recent example in which the temperature in Lawrence, Kansas, had dropped thirty-three degrees in seven hours. Evans argued that when the frozen side of the moon is toward us, "it acts like a huge cake of ice and draws the warm air towards it and pulls the air out from the earth and suddenly down from above us making 33 degrees change in 7 hours, this may not be the cause, but watch it for 5 years and see."[2]

Evans's explanation may not embody very sophisticated physics, and may indeed be wrong, but it does employ a conceivable physical causal sequence. He postulated an understandable physical process (rather than some "astral influence") leaving the moon and arriving within measurable time at the earth, directly affecting its atmosphere. In his reply, Wallace showed a normal scientific concern with Evans's evidence, saying first that he had been unable to find anything about the equinoxes of Mercury and Venus in astronomical literature, while admitting that those "of the earth, Mars, Jupiter and Saturn are recognized by regular astronomers." Wallace continued: "I am unable to agree with you entirely with respect to the effect of the full moon. At any rate I have checked up the time of the full moon against actual temperatures here at Des Moines for the past fifty years and find that on the average in January and February the new moon is no colder than the average temperature or than the full moon immediately proceeding." He concluded by offering an observation of his own to the effect that "when the full moon comes at the same time that the Earth passes between Jupiter and the Sun the temperature tends to be considerably warmer than usual."[3]

In the meantime, Wallace had written to the Reverend John Jones Smith of Jackson, Tennessee, the editor of *Hicks Almanac*, asking whether he had records from 1880 to the present of the dates of all the earthquakes, severe cyclones, tropical hurricanes in or around Florida, and volcanoes that had happened in the United States, and how much he would charge for those records. Furthermore, he wondered if Smith's records indicated whether the equinoxes and solstices of Jupiter had much effect, and asked, "Are your dates as given in your 1929 publications for the solstices and equinoxes of Mercury and Venus based on recognized astronomical authority?"[4] Wallace also wrote the B. Westermann Book Company, New York City, asking whether they could obtain the second volume of *Neugebauer's Tafeln zur Astronomischen Chronologie*, published in Leipzig, and how much it cost.[5]

Wallace was still being relatively tough-minded about these matters; he regarded himself as dealing with astronomical and not astrological affairs, was not prepared to accept anyone's authority without appeal to the evidence, and despite his thriftiness was not averse to spending some money on his research provided he felt he was getting value for his dollar. He tried to get his friend O. S. Bowman, with whom he had had some business dealings in connection with building a farmhouse and with whom he was researching the weather, to put up the twenty-five dollars needed for Rev. Jones's complete list of cataclysmic weather phenomena, but apparently in the end paid for it himself. He wrote Bowman: "We have compiled a vast amount of weather data here [in Des Moines] which I am sure you will be very much interested in looking over. We now have a complete record of the exact positions of all the planets at ten day intervals for the past fifty years. We also have running five day average temperatures at Des Moines for the same period."[6]

Writing in March 1929 to another weather forecaster, Herbert J. Browne of Washington, D.C., Wallace said that in plotting Des Moines's annual temperatures against the lunar retreat he was unable to find any relationship. "The conjunctions of Saturn and Jupiter," he claimed, "explain our Des Moines temperature a little more satisfactorily than the retreat of the moon from the ecliptic." This echoed a statement he had made a couple of months earlier to Rev. Smith, adding: "I note also that when Jupiter is at parhelion and aphelion there is considerable influence on the weather for a period of several months." But Wallace's claim that the conjunctions of Saturn and Jupiter "explain" Des Moines's temperature seems unwarranted. All he had was a rather attenuated statistical correlation, but to explain that correlation properly would require the demonstration of some physical force emanating from those planets and arriving at Earth in such a way as to affect meteorological conditions—something much harder to imagine than a physical phenomenon on the moon affecting Earth. Although the intangible influence of distant planets sounds more like astrology than astronomy, Wallace's sustained and energetic inquiries arose from a practical interest, whatever their status as science. The weather and its prediction were, of course, of the greatest importance to corn growers and other farmers, and Wallace hoped to publish useful findings in *Wallaces' Farmer.*[7]

In October 1931 Wallace became acquainted with Charles and Juanita (Nita) Roos, a Native American couple who kept a studio at Taylors Falls, Minnesota. He probably met them through his astrological associates, as Roos, a prolific correspondent, seemed to be familiar with their work. The Rooses composed lyric poems and librettos, gave spiritual advice to seekers, and occasionally, when they felt it would benefit worthy recipients, interceded with the Native American gods to bring rain. A priest of the Poseyemo clan, Charles Roos was in his own eyes a medicine man whose knowledge of these gods and their powers was unrivaled.

During his first visit Wallace evidently questioned the Rooses about the bases for their beliefs to a degree Charles, accustomed to impressing people by personal force and bombast, found irritating. A long letter he wrote Wallace a few days later to exorcise this irritation gives a good impression of his general style and of how he had merged his belief in the Native American gods with Theosophical conceptions—a mixture quite in accord with the Theosophical line that there is one ancient body of wisdom underlying all particular religions.

Cherry Hill. Poseyemo. Oct. 19th. (Merc. hour). Ha—
Cornplanter:—
Noon. I am Lone Wolf. Squaw in East gathering wampum. Just a thot to start small letter to Brush Cutter. I ache with foolish burdens on shoulders raw-hided thru a thousand foothills of Karma. I assume more back-aches. Shop full of rabble. Folks of no-import. BUT the poor cobbler must not dare swift-kick one sap who comes seeking God alone knows what. I chew more tobacco and might if driven too far resort to Sir Walt's curve stem (Kinde-Pitche-Oday). And thus the pages of my poor book turn day by day. Knee deep in the leaf-mould soil of this Happy Land (Witti-Wasso-Gitche-Sebe) I have insurance of safety for I can fox-sneak (Poytakootha) into what the Halcyon Manana might hold for true Agents who come crawling into the Great Lodge Circle with their breasts and bellys [*sic*] half-mooned with scars of the long grind. Perhaps there is a Special Heaven for Finns of the T.S. who have laughed at Fear and the Seven Hundred Dugpaws who hound the trails thru the long Swamp Drag. Henry, I must remain the Finn. The Sioux Drums and the Shoshone hill-cries chill the tallow on my ribs, but always there sings in the deep of me the Song of Russia. (Devil Land). Day by day new problems arise. My great misfortune is that too many no-goods steal under my lodge flaps and annoy. They sap my creative pulse. Bums and Swamp Cats. I hope soon to deliver myself from all sand-burs and stickers and return to my shop where I am again Charles the Cobbler. "SOULS REPAIRED" (Free)

I am glad you crossed my trail. But you brot a lot of sorrow. We, the Medicine Men, stand aloof. Above annoyance. Questioning. None may question. If there is doubt, then thrash it out with your high-self. I see why the Gods sent Henry to the Cobbler's shop. After you had bussed away it all stood clear as the waters of the Indian Spring. You cleared my skirts of a lot of cobwebs and earth-litter. It was time for a bit of dry-cleaning. (Wallace Dry Cleaners, Inc.) HATE! Ah—there is a story for pop-corn and night-fires and good souls gathered together. It is written these five thousand years that of all the Peoples in the Great Meadow it is given to the Finns alone to hate without the chickens coming home to roost. In 1925 I received orders to restore in small measure the discords shrouding this earth. One Harmony can stew a million discords or Hate Thots. But the cobbler best stick to his pegs and tapper. You stand high in my estimation and I fully agree that you are the better man. There is work for you, and the Gods will call you to the colors when the trumpet calls to Hit the Hills . . .

> Will write more later
> Love and Luck
> & Sioux Blue Skies
> Poseyemo

Squaw home again. Flesh pots simmering. ah—ah—ah—ah—ah—

Of course, when Roos refers to his "Hate Thots" he means the annoyance provoked by Wallace's challenging and critical approach; medicine men should stand aloof and be above annoyance and questioning. But the annoyance dissolves in the overriding harmony. As Juanita Roos wrote Wallace about the same time, "We feel that you have an important part to play in the great Scheme of Things. . . . Whether your stops at our camp fire be long or short we shall always welcome you gladly. I think that Chas will even forgive you if you ask him more questions!"[8]

Charles's letter is sprinkled with allusions to Theosophy. "Finns of the T.S." means those Native Americans who have joined the Theosophical Society, as Roos had, and "Halcyon Manana" is an allusion to the Theosophical Temple of the People, based in Halcyon, California. That Wallace himself was already a member of a similar society is shown by a letter to him from the Reverend Irving S. Cooper, the "Regionary Bishop of the United States" for the "Liberal Catholic Church," at Ojai, California—a Theosophical church, not a Roman Catholic one. In a handwritten postscript, Cooper asks: "Are your domestic affairs the same so that it is still impossible for you to consider ordination? If so, is there any one else you can heartily recommend to head the movement in Des Moines?"[9]

Near the end of the oral history interview taped in the 1950s, Wallace, under what was obviously insistent questioning, reveals that he had joined the Theosophical Society "temporarily" six months after the death of his father, that is, in April 1925, because "Father's death made a profound impression on me and I was searching for ultimate spiritual meaning." But he had already attended "one or two" meetings of the society before this, the earliest in 1919. He says that he had once mentioned his interest in the movement to his father, telling him that "these folks in the Theosophical Society seemed to be reaching out for something." "With me," he explains to the interviewer, "it's always been a question of what best serves the interest of the greatest number in the long run. As you reach out for that, you may go in a great many different directions according to what you feel your own capacities may be at the moment and what you feel the need of humanity may be at the moment." Wallace says that he had "great interest" in the Theosophical Society for a time, but grew away from it in about 1929 or 1930 because he found its ideas too narrow. However, he continued to cherish the doctrine of karma: "Karma means that while things may not balance out in a given lifetime, they balance out in the long run in terms of justice between individuals, between man and the whole. It seems to me one of the most profound of all religious concepts. To that extent I'm everlastingly grateful to the Theosophists. Theosophy gave me a deeper appreciation of Jesus than I had had before."[10] Wallace must have been a member in good standing of the Iowa Theosophical group to be proposed for ordination. Now he was to join up also with the Halcyon group to which Charles Roos had alluded—presumably as a result of Roos's direct influence.

Wallace had been impressed by Roos, suspecting that he had "a greater knowledge of the higher type of Indian . . . music and Indian medicine than anyone now living." He invited Charles and Nita to stay with his family in Des Moines, asked a publisher to send copies of songs for which Roos had written the lyrics, and bought land at Taylors Falls for experimental corn growing. To his friend George W. Russell, or "A.E.," Wallace now confided:

The final inspiration for writing you comes, however, as a result of a visit with Mr. Charles O. Roos of Taylors Falls, Minnesota. This man has the same deep, passionate feeling about the Indian Gods that you have about the ancient Irish Gods. He seems to think that Indian egos are being reincarnated into the American race at the present time and that there is great need of some of the fundamental spirituality of the old Indian religions being introduced into our modern American attitude.

Against the background of his native habitat, he is quite an extraordinary person and I could tell you many interesting things about him if I could talk with you face to face.

And to astrologer L. Edward Johndro of California, a member of Roos's circle of contacts, Wallace now addressed a question that showed the direction his thoughts were taking:

Knowing my horoscope and that of Chars. O. Roos I wonder if you would be in a position to determine the extent to which we could be of benefit to each other and jointly to the "cause." Could we best be of benefit to each other at Taylors Falls or at some other place? Frankly I think we are both interested in our joint contact to help work out the spiritual foundations for a true creative (religious, if you please) expression for the American people. . . .

Enclosed please find $5 and would appreciate a superficial judgment.[11]

It was this creative spiritual expression that was the "cause" in question. Still fascinated by the statistical problems involved in determining the relationship between planetary movements and weather, and keen to test Johndro's hypotheses against the extended weather data he had collected, Wallace nevertheless conceded that "there are greater problems than these right now and I am wondering to what extent Charles Roos and I are destined to work together on them."[12] For, Wallace wrote Johndro two days later, "fundamentally I am neither a corn breeder nor an editor but a searcher for methods of bringing the 'Inner light' to outward manifestation and raising outward manifestation to this Inner light." Wallace acknowledged "karmic obligations" to his family but, he said, "most important I shall be seeking an opportunity to find the religious keynote of the new age. . . . Is my esoteric hookup best through Chas Roos of Taylors Falls, Dr. Wm H. Dower of Halcyon,

Calif, and L. Edward Johndro or through the Esoteric section of [the] Besant Theosophical Society of Ojai, California?"[13] Plainly, Wallace had already absorbed the fundamentals of Theosophical thinking.

The William H. Dower Wallace referred to was guardian in chief of the Temple of the People, the Theosophical group whose headquarters were in Halcyon, California. Halcyon, according to temple literature, was "under the protection and influence of the Great Ones who guide the evolution of worlds and races," and the temple was "the direct continuation of the work inaugurated by the Masters of Wisdom through their Messenger, H. P. Blavatsky." The master who particularly watched over this group was named Hilarion. In Theosophical doctrine, the masters are highly evolved beings who in the course of countless human reincarnations have progressed far beyond ordinary mortals on the path back to absolute spirituality. They have supernatural powers but may still take human form and sometimes reveal themselves to talented and dedicated seekers after the ancient wisdom, which is the origin of all particular earthly religions.

"If you would know the next step," the temple's introductory letter to Wallace said, "write now." "I would know the next step," Wallace scrawled across the bottom of the letter, and not long afterward he joined the Temple of the People and began a diligent study of its doctrines, notwithstanding that he was already acquainted with other versions of Theosophy.[14] Before long the tutelary relationship between Dower and Wallace appeared to bear spiritual fruit. "Very astounding about Hilarian connecting you," Roos wrote Wallace in November 1931. "I hesitate to confuse you with interpretation. However, it is Big Smoke. Hilarian has never contacted us personally. I rejoice he 'Made Trail' for God Cornplanter." Dower, Roos continued, is "High Spot in the World today. . . . He is Earth Master!"[15] As most of Wallace's letters to Roos are not among his private papers, no record remains of the form in which this supposed revelation from the Master Hilarion was delivered to Wallace.

By this time Wallace had concluded that both Dower and Roos were "to some extent spiritual descendants of William Q. Judge." Judge had succeeded to the leadership of the Theosophical movement, started by Madame Blavatsky in the 1870s. Blavatsky and her colleague Col. H. S. Olcott had sought to give added credence to the existence of the masters by demonstrating various spiritualistic phenomena, especially the delivery of messages from the Great Ones by means of letters apparently drifting down from chandeliers, being discovered in locked cabinets, and so on. These phenomena had been investigated and exposed as trickery a number of times, notably by the London Society for Psychical Research in 1885, and there was a felt need to purify the true doctrine of these embellishments. Both Dower and Roos, though especially Roos, Wallace felt, "laid particular emphasis on the necessity for the American religion finding its roots in our own earth," which meant that "the Indian attitude should play a more definite part." This jibed well with one of George W. Russell's beliefs. "It is interesting what you say about the mystical feeling about the American soil the Dower groups have," he wrote Wallace. "That seems to me to be the real lack in American culture. It is not at present rooted in the earth (my earth of course is a living being). Emerson, Whitman and Thoreau had that deep feeling about a living nature. Your people are restless for reverie. But all great spiritual movements must have a life springing out of mother earth."[16]

Here we see again the connection between Wallace's Theosophical beliefs and his abiding interest in promoting, by benevolent assistance to natural selection, the greatest possible richness and abundance of the earth's products, as evidenced by his lifelong experimentation with plant and animal genetics. It is part of an answer to the riddle of how a practical, Western-educated scientist like Wallace could begin to take seriously a set of beliefs that to most Western eyes seems at first and even second glance essentially unscientific. But for Wallace the scientific attitude called for an open-minded, inquiring approach to any and every assertion about the workings of the universe. In writing to the skeptical Mark Hyde on 14 July 1930, he had defended George W. Russell on the grounds of his honesty. "Some of his concepts may seem trivial but he nevertheless tries to describe what he has seen. Please do not think that I attach any spiritual validity to things of this sort. I do think, however, that there is an order of reality which can be contacted by people who have certain types of perception. . . . It is true that oftentimes these people are on the borderline toward insanity . . . [but] I have had enough experience with this kind of thing myself to believe there is something to it. . . . The essence of spirituality has nothing to do with people who fake mysticism. Just the same, I am convinced that it is a mistake for scientific and the common sense people to shut the door to some of these things which they cannot understand."[17]

When Wallace denies that there is any "spiritual validity to things of this sort" he presumably is dissociating himself from the business of spirit messages, table-rappings, levitation, and so on, but he goes on to postulate another "order of reality," which is spiritual rather than material and can be scientifically investigated by those who have "certain types of perception." The problem that more orthodox practitioners would see with this kind of science is that it puts those with this special perception in a privileged position. Those whose perception is limited to the physical world must rely on their reports of the data. Thus, toward the end of 1930 Wallace wrote Russell: "Enclosed I am sending you an economic discussion. . . . Of course, the troubles [the developing depression] find their origin in the nature of human desires, human selfishness, and the karma growing out of the action of these forces in the past. I wish I had your facility of mental movement in the spiritual world, so that I could discuss the situation adequately in terms of desires, selfishness, and karma."[18]

In his account of the Theosophical movement, Bruce F. Campbell, a former initiate, makes much of the fact that many educated, middle-class and professional people who, like Wallace, had become disenchanted with the religious establishments of the West, found in Theosophy a welcome reconciliation between their need for a more personal religion and their recognition of the validity of the scientific world view. But, as shown by Campbell's summary of basic Theosophical doctrines, the only precept that seems to have any connection with empirical science is theosophists' acceptance of the concept of evolution, and the similarity of their evolutionary theory to that of Charles Darwin is tenuous, to say the least. Theosophists reject creationism in favor of evolution, but their notion of the latter is that of "the periodic emergence of the universe from a subjective into an objective state." The true, all-pervasive reality is Absolute Spirit, which casts off a reflection of itself to form the material universe, but the latter is thought to be only a temporary illusion, spirit being the real substance: "This process can be described as one of involution and evolution. As the 'Great Breath' proceeds outward, worlds, objects, and men appear. As it recedes, all disappear into the original source."[19]

By contrast, Darwin's life-forms do not need to be sustained by a metaphysical life force; they sustain themselves, if they are able, by the exercise of their genetically determined abilities, and their genes are not emanations from the Absolute but material particles. Wallace's systematic experiments in breeding corn and chickens show that he understood the scientific conception of inheritance perfectly well, without needing to invoke the operation of an invisible spiritual force or supernatural plan behind it.

Theosophy, by contrast, places a heavy explanatory burden on unseen forces:

> Evolution is a process carried out not only on this planet alone but also on other visible celestial bodies and on invisible ones as well. Within the Absolute are innumerable universes and within each universe many solar systems. Each solar system is the expression of a mighty Being, whom we call the Logos or Solar Deity. Below the Solar Deity are the seven ministers or Planetary Spirits. And under them come vast orders of angels or devas. For each planet there is a chief celestial being, who is in control of all the evolution on that planet.
>
> Each visible planet is part of a group of seven planets, the other six of which are invisible.[20]

And so on. Compare this mode of thought with, for example, the thoroughly tough-minded, empirical attitude Wallace adopted even as a lad to the pronouncements of the corn judges as to what was the "best" corn in a show. He saw that they were basing their judgments on a kind of aesthetic intuition, and set about establishing his own criteria by down-to-earth procedures such as actually counting the grains of corn in an ear, determining by trial and error their reproductive properties, and so on. That empirical approach characterized his work in plant and animal genetics, in the economic determinants of corn and hog prices, in the relationship of rainfall to productivity and in the study of other natural phenomena.

His father's sudden and premature death, in October 1924, "made a profound impression" on Wallace: "I was searching for ultimate spiritual meaning." Perhaps that deepened his interest in Theosophy, but Louis Bean, later a statistician with the Department of Agriculture and also a Theosophist, remembered that Wallace had attended a Theosophical Society meeting in Washington in the previous year, 1923, confirming that he was already involved. This is not to say that his father's death, or the appalling record of illness and early death among his relatives, did not have a lasting effect. All seven of Uncle Henry's brothers and sisters had died young, all of tuberculosis or related illnesses. Uncle Henry's first child, a girl, survived for just three months; his youngest son died of a spinal condition. Uncle Henry himself had been forced, in

1877, to give up the ministry, having been warned that unless he did he would not live six months. Before Wallace's wife, Ilo, was four, both of her parents had died, again of tuberculosis. She herself had an episode of the disease in the first year of their marriage, and Wallace developed tuberculosis soon after (though he later disputed the doctors' opinion, preferring to believe his illness to have been undulant fever). He was to suffer a second attack in 1925. His father's health had never been robust because of a near-fatal bout with typhoid in the 1890s, and his unexpected death in 1924 was caused by complications arising from a stomach operation. According to Wallace's first biographer, Russell Lord, Wallace possessed detailed knowledge of the physical history of all his traceable relatives, a fact that might suggest an obsessive concern with his own genetic disposition. Certainly throughout his life he was eager to maintain and demonstrate his health and fitness. But apart from that legitimate self-concern, the mortality rate in this family of able and promising individuals must have prompted him to wonder what was the point of it all, and whether all that human potential had been lost forever. Perhaps, then, it was the Theosophical doctrine of reincarnation, and the notion that one's present life span is just a moment in the long, long process of spiritual development, that attracted him. Furthermore, throughout his life Wallace was bitterly opposed to the kind of orthodox religion that required its followers to feel humble, sinful, and powerless in the face of the Deity. The idea that each person's spirit is an actual part of the Absolute Spirit, sharing its nature and powers, was much more in accord with his belief in his own intellectual and moral force.

Yet there was an obvious tension between the scientific method he embraced and the Theosophical belief in a plentitude of unseen forces, all emanating from an indescribable Absolute. These were by definition not capable of empirical demonstration or refutation. They were posited solely on the basis of revelation or on the authority of incredibly ancient, secret writings known only to the adepts or masters, who occasionally revealed some of their truths to relatively highly evolved human individuals. All this directly defied the scientific requirement of demonstrable evidence. However, empirical science also demands an open-minded attitude to novel hypotheses, and Wallace felt this keenly. Faced, for example, with a long-standing folk belief that Native Americans could make rain by certain ritual procedures, a scientific agriculturist such as Wallace, to whom rainfall was vitally important, might well decide to try out those procedures for himself, if only to satisfy his own devotion to fair-mindedness, and to test every last possibility.

Charles Roos had offered to instruct Wallace in a Native American method of praying for rain — a ritual that, after all, was quite in accord with the Theosophical doctrine of the spiritual underpinning of all natural happenings. The first hint of this comes in a letter dated 10 July 1932. In a solemn warning about the dangerous forces Wallace would need to solicit, Roos wrote: "Step lightly in dealing with the Kings of the Four Winds."[21] More explicit instructions came later: "When HAW needs rain greatly for personal gain, then I allow you to quietly address the Lord of the Four Winds in the name of Ah Ning [Roos] and state and ask just when, where and amount needed. Not for Iowa, but where rain will benefit Chief Cornplanter [Wallace]." Evidently, Wallace followed these instructions, and rain fell. "You can not guess how glad I am that Rain Gods responded to HAW," Roos wrote some days later. "Tell me in detail how strong the kick-back or vibration or high-nervous-pitch was as soon as you actually contacted the Great Rain Makers."[22]

There is no recorded instance of Wallace repeating this ritual, and we are left to wonder whether he believed in the efficacy of the incantations or felt the rainfall was just a lucky coincidence. As a practical farmer, having widespread knowledge of agricultural problems through his years of work on *Wallaces' Farmer*, Wallace was intimately aware of the importance of adequate rain falling at the right time. There must have been a tremendous desire to find some way of controlling rain, and an equally strong temptation to believe that one had found it when something seemed to work. Wallace's realism could eventually triumph over his need to believe in beneficent unseen forces, but he was inclined to cling to these mystical beliefs, and to test them to their depths, to an extreme extent.

His search for Native Americans' contributions to the emergent body of belief he was seeking went further than just testing their ability to influence the physical elements. In June 1932, during a visit to Taylors Falls, Roos suggested that he visit the Onondoga nation near Syracuse in New York, a proposal Dower enthusiastically endorsed. Dower told Wallace that he himself had been a frequent visitor to the Onondoga reservation thirty years previously, attending dances and festivals. He had known Chief La Forte well and his brother Thomas La Forte, who was "deeply versed in Indian lore, having to do with reincarnation, astral bodies, Masters, etc. etc." Although these leaders had now "passed from this plane," others might remember Dower, and perhaps "the brief contact will connect up some forces in your aura."[23]

Although Roos found himself unable to accompany Wallace, as he had hoped to do, he had words of encouragement: "I do say with full Priest Authority that the old Medicine Men will walk with you and point out where the Council Fires of Long Ago threw their flickerings against the dark of the whispering forest! And I, Ah-Ning of the Blue Hills will stand at your right side. . . . The Red Gods of Far Yesterdays will walk with old HAW and this trip will renew the failing tissues of your wrinkling earth-body. Renew your outlook and insight beyond words."[24]

In preparation for his journey, Wallace wrote to Ruth Muskrat Bronson, Henry Roe Cloud, and David Owl, stating that "with both Miss Eckert and Mr Charles Roos of Taylors Falls Minnesota, I have talked concerning the spiritual, artistic and sociological contribution which the American Indian may eventually make to our American civilization," and asking whether they knew the names of the Onondoga leaders who were familiar with the ancient Indian festivals, religious customs, or names of some of the historic spots in the Hiawatha region.[25]

At his meeting with the Onondogas, apparently Wallace was told that he and Roos had known each other in previous incarnations as members of the Iroquois nation. Roos advised Wallace to report fully on his experiences to Dower. "Ask him my position and office in the Iroquois days. And your office. Do not ever forget that the Iroquois days were the Halcyon days of all our Earth-Touch thru the Long Time! That your Cousin [presumably Roos himself] walked the hills with you, or rather came to you in the Iroquois Hills is to me great and sweet Medicine. This means much to me. And to Kin Tin [Nita Roos]. And this trip you so bravely made will bring big things to you. Now you have solid ground to stand on. Before this Witti-Wasso trail-break you stood deep in the ashes of men long dead and as dead as the books they wrote." Dower, when consulted, confirmed what Roos had written: "You undoubtedly at some time lived with the Iroquois Indians as one of them, or you would not have this strong feeling of wanting to contact them."[26] Again, we have no means of knowing what Wallace thought of these suggestions.

But Wallace, who had embraced a vague pantheism in his youth, by now firmly believed in the necessarily close relationship between true religion and the earth, as Roos, Dower, and George W. Russell had insisted, an idea common to many traditional cultures, but one Western-educated people, with less cooperative attitudes toward the environment, find more difficult to understand. It was in this relationship that he found common cause with Native Americans, and it is not surprising that he wanted to feel literally at one with these ancient inhabitants of his country. We must remember, too, that at this time he had special reason to feel alienated from the modern technological civilization in which his life was cast. The agricultural community had been suffering great hardship for many years, partly from lack of unified planning, so that gross overproduction occurred and prices dropped disastrously, but also because, as farmers and their representatives with good reason believed, they were being victimized by the railroads that transported their goods to the cities, by the packers and merchandisers who bought them, and by the whole industrial complex that flourished behind high-tariff walls—walls that prevented client countries from earning enough American credit to let them buy agricultural products. By 1932 the Great Depression was reaching its nadir, and *Wallaces' Farmer*, which had fought valiantly against these inequities, had finally succumbed to it.

Back in 1929, from July to November, Wallace had been in Europe, first to attend the International Agriculture Conference in England, and then to tour the Continent. At home the stock market was booming and credit (though not for farmers) was plentiful. Against Wallace's objections, his uncle John P. Wallace made a deal to purchase a rival newspaper, the *Iowa Homestead*, which involved the Wallaces taking out a mortgage of more than $2 million. The merger was announced on 26 October 1929, three days before the stock market crashed. The Wallaces struggled on, trying to make payments on this huge debt, until 1932, when they had to go into receivership. *Wallaces' Farmer and Iowa Homestead* reverted to the previous owner of the *Homestead*, although Henry A. retained his position with the paper.[27] As he wrote on 16 May 1932 to a new friend who was to mediate momentous happenings for him, Frances R. Grant, vice president of the Master Institute of the Roerich Museum in New York, "It seems that I am to have a free hand as editor as long as I desire to remain connected with the publication. In like manner, I understand that the Roerich Museum is to have the privilege of continuing much as it has in the past." The museum too had been in financial difficulty. Wallace had first come into contact with Frances Grant in 1929, and had become deeply interested in the

Wallace at the inaugural conference of the International Association of Agricultural Economists, Devon, England, 1929. (Courtesy of the University of Iowa Library)

cultural work of the Roerich Museum, and of its founder, Nicholas Roerich, expatriate Russian painter and mystic.[28]

Wallace already felt that the Roerich enterprise was an eminently worthy one, devoted, as was *Wallaces' Farmer*, to improving the spiritual quality of life, and both had suffered grievous blows from a materialist society. In view of this, and in view of the crushing poverty of many farmers whose work he also saw as having a fundamentally spiritual aspect, it is no wonder that he was ready to give credence to doctrines asserting the overriding importance of the spiritual reality currently obscured by materialist illusions. The ancient Native American religions offered something of this, and even more attractive was the mystical force of Theosophy.

Belief in an omniscient and omnipotent personal god distinguishes Western religions from Theosophy. When a young child is presented with this concept, he or she may well confuse it with the image of his or her own father, both the stern, judgmental, punitive father as he was actually perceived and the infinitely loving father who was longed for. But if the child's relation to his or her father had not been especially close, and if the father's greater abilities had tended to inspire resentment rather than awestruck wonder, then belief of a spiritually liberating kind that, like Theosophy, specifically did not include the concept of a personal god, could prove especially attractive.

We have seen that Wallace respected his father's abilities but never felt very close to him. "The relationship of son and father is a very strange thing," he said in later life. "I question whether he [the father] ever let anyone know how deep anything really went in him." Because his father had to work hard on the family's paper, Wallace, as mentioned above, had to do a lot of arduous physical labor about the house and farmyard. His father would demonstrate how to perform these tasks and was much better at them. "He was very good with his hands— much better than I. He had much more manual dexterity than I. He could show me how to do things—zip, zip. He'd illustrate and then he was off to the office. The job was left to me." Because his father was much more competent, it was hard for the young boy to feel that his parent actually needed his help. Wallace was left to do the drudgery while his father got on with more important things, a situation unlikely to strengthen the need for a personal god. "I had a very great admiration for my father and a very great respect for his ability," Wallace said. "He was very dominant over me. His will prevailed at all times, except that in my inner being I knew I was a different kind of person."[29] Theosophy offered a welcome relief, on a metaphysical scale, from that kind of domination.

Theosophy declares that a human being is in essence "a Spark of the divine Fire."[30] The divine fire is the one Absolute Reality, from which all particular beings emanate and to which eventually they return. It is the ground and cause of everything, and thus the Theosophical version of God, but is not in personal form. One's spiritual being is a minute part of this fire, as a physical spark is a small part of a physical fire, losing its individual identity in merging with it. In the constitution of humankind, spirit became enmeshed with a human soul and incarnated in a human body. Each individual thus contains this essence of divinity, which has emanated from the Absolute and entered on an extended process of evolution that takes it progressively down through degrees of materiality and then back upward until it becomes again pure spirit, purged of the animal passions of the human body, and unites with the Infinite. Thus, every one of us possesses the same nature and powers as the divine fire. It is worth noting here that many passages in Ralph Waldo Trine's *In Tune with the Infinite*, a book Wallace says influenced him as a youth, are so similar to these theosophical ideas that one might imagine that Trine's book prepared the ground for the Theosophical seed. For instance, Trine writes that "all the prophets, seers, sages, and saviours in the world's history . . . had the powers they had [through] the conscious realization of their oneness with the Infinite Life." He also asserts that the "Spirit of Infinite Life" inspired, similarly, Christ, Buddha, Brahmin teachers, and the various sacred texts on which those who follow these teachers rely. Wallace had also made a close study of the works of Emerson, whose concept of the "Over-Soul," a unity within which each person's particular being is contained and made one with all others, seems congruent with certain Theosophical conceptions.[31]

Rationality, after all, is not the main criterion for religious belief; it is faith that is important, despite the apparent lack of empirical evidence. When Wallace came into contact with Theosophy it was not the idiosyncratic invention of some tiny inbred coterie but an established doctrine with a solid respectable following. There is, therefore, no ground for considering his confidence in it a sign of personal psychopathology, any more than in the case of competent scientists who are devout Christians. And if Wallace's calling on spiritual powers to make rain seems especially odd, we might reflect that praying for rain is not uncommon among other religious groups. Wallace's brief recourse to Native American spiritual beliefs may seem strange, but it is largely ethnocentrism that makes it so. Among those who administer great government departments, however, religious belief's influence is usually of a general moral kind, rather than a prescription for specific practical activities. For Henry Wallace, because of some special flavor of his upbringing, that was not always the case. His religious ideas sometimes penetrated his workaday activities in the most immediate, literal way; the one strand was interwoven with the other to a degree most observers find difficult to comprehend, and this in turn makes some episodes in his public career hard to understand.

It was their failure to appreciate the nature of such beliefs that often made Henry Wallace seem enigmatic to his contemporaries. Louis Bean, a Theosophist who knew Wallace in the 1920s and later worked in his department, said that Wallace dropped his association with Theosophy as an organized movement in 1933, not, Bean thought, because he had rejected its doctrines but because he felt he had learned all that it had to teach. Wallace, however, continued to reach out, to seek deeper meaning. "His interest in philosophy, in religion, in science, in the interplay between them, in things mystical, in things universal I don't think he will ever lose," Bean said. "That's part of him."[32] His contemporaries sensed this. Whether or not they had heard, as many had, of Roos (or later of Roerich), or of other vague stories of Wallace's unconventional interests and beliefs, they sensed that he was somehow detached, that he had a different, or at least an additional, agenda, that he marched, at times, to a more distant drum. Notwithstanding his accomplishments and great abilities, there was something about him they could not quite understand.

The most understandable and most open example of Wallace's spiritual conception of practical affairs was in his lifelong commitment to the improvement of agriculture. The good earth was the source of all useful and joyful things, and to cultivate it was the noblest calling of all, a sanctified life. His grandfather and father had believed this, but perhaps his mother, in her daily practice of caring for her flowers and other plants, had had the most immediate effect in his impressionable years. Her love of living things and her maternal role, giving birth to Henry and his siblings, had provided an image of procreativity that he strove to emulate all his life. This concern was one factor that led him as an adult into a sustained campaign to improve the lot of farmers, and, later, to extend the fruits of agricultural abundance to all the peoples of the world.

There was an intense moral tone to some of his utterances about the importance of the agricultural life—a moral fervor that remained strong throughout his life. Norman Markowitz comments that Spengler's *Decline of the West* "encouraged Wallace's fears that an independent rural civilization was being engulfed by cities, immigrants and 'soulless' laborers. Responding to the Spengler vogue, the young farm editor wrote in 1923 that cities were the 'lethal chambers of civiliza-tion,' the harbingers of racial suicide." On a visit to New York in "the last year of the boom," Wallace proclaimed in what Markowitz describes as a "mock-heroic" fashion: "Your standards of money and wealth are not our standards . . . you shall not have our best sons and daughters to add brilliancy to your flaming civilization." Many years later, in 1943, Wallace, then vice president, would write to an injured boy: "When the human spirit gets tired and large numbers of people drift into the cities, the soil is no longer taken care of, the families get smaller, and the population after a time decreases. In the meantime the barbarians have learned much from the nation which formerly held the torch of civili-zation. Their families are still large, their children still have the virtues which come from hard work on the soil and so the old is swept away and the new begins. Obviously our problem is to get closer to the soil again while at the same time there is a renewal of some of the fundamental virtues." It is unlikely, however, that moral convictions, so fervent and long-lasting, were initiated solely by books read as an adult. Also sug-gested here are Wallace's acceptance of what Richard Hofstadter has called "the agrarian myth," the belief found in Jeffersonian and Popu-list rhetoric that virtue belongs to "those who labor in the earth," and the conviction he had come to share with Roos and Russell that, as the latter put it, "all great spiritual movements must have a life springing out of mother earth."

AGRICULTURAL POLICIES AND THE MOVE
TOWARD PUBLIC OFFICE

The practical development of Wallace's agricultural policies in later life can best be seen against its historical background. Wallace's father, Henry Cantwell Wallace, had, in 1923, begun drafting an agricultural bill providing for a two-market plan for farm products; the govern-ment should arrange for the sale abroad of domestic surpluses at lower than domestic prices, thus maintaining the latter. This was an idea put forward by farm leaders George Peek and Hugh S. Johnson, and it eventually became the basis of the McNary-Haugen bill. From then on, McNary-Haugen, with its demand for marketing and export cor-porations, became the rallying cry of impoverished farmers, although versions of the bill were either repeatedly defeated in Congress or, if passed, vetoed, twice, by President Calvin Coolidge. After his father's death, Henry A. Wallace took up the same cause, with many editorials in *Wallaces' Farmer* and addresses to farmers, although he believed the proposals had a fundamental weakness in that they made no provision for restriction of production. In 1920 he had published his *Agricultural Prices*, urging curtailment of production, and this book established his reputation as a bona fide agricultural economist. He also became an active member of the American Farm Economists Association.

Attempts in 1924 and 1925 to get the McNary-Haugen bill into Congress failed because of opposition by the administration, especially by Secretary of Commerce Herbert Hoover. Another attempt was planned in 1926, and to promote it a group of rural leaders, the Corn Belt Committee of Twenty Two, was formed, mainly through the efforts of George Peek, who became its head, with Wallace as its next most prominent member. The committee maintained a close liaison with the farm bloc, a bipartisan congressional voting bloc of rural representatives, and helped coordinate the activities of the American Council of Agriculture and other interested organizations.[33] Wallace had gone to Washington that year to lobby for the McNary-Haugen bill. It failed again, but he talked to southern congressmen and helped to foster a strong South-Midwest voting alliance.

In 1928 a new version of the bill was pushed through Congress, but vetoed a second time by Coolidge, who was puritanical in his rigid adherence to laissez-faire and rejection of socialism. Wallace's alienation from the Republican Party was now complete, and he exhorted farmers to turn away from their traditional allegiance. He declared in an editorial: "The veto message has made it impossible for any farmer with self-respect to vote for Coolidge or for any candidate who, like Hoover, supports the Coolidge policy towards agriculture."[34] George Peek also decided to leave the GOP, and took a group of McNary-Haugenites to the 1928 Democratic National Convention. The Platform Committee welcomed them warmly and included a McNary-Haugen–type plank in the draft. Peek and his colleagues campaigned for Alfred E. Smith, the Democratic candidate, as did Wallace in his paper, but Smith, a New Yorker, was unacceptable to farmers, and Hoover duly won.

In the following year, Wallace became acquainted with a scheme developed by Harvard economist John D. Black and others for encouraging voluntary curtailment of farm produce, which became the Voluntary Domestic Allotment Plan (VDAP). This aimed to persuade farmers to restrict their production of certain staple crops in oversupply, in return for compensation paid through excise levied on food producers processing the crops. Thus prices would be kept higher and immediate hardship eased. Wallace had been arguing publicly for planned restriction of production since 1920, and the new scheme fitted well with the need he perceived to increase farm income without promoting inflation—a danger he saw developing from the Populists' "cheap money" proposals. Accordingly, through *Wallaces' Farmer* and through talks to farmers and speeches at conferences, he played a significant role in promoting support for the VDAP. Opinion within the McNary-Haugen movement was divided over the issue of production control, and its advocates, with Wallace as their most prominent member, became the leaders of the farm-protest forces.

Wallace's interest in schemes to assist the rural sector extended well beyond his support for the VDAP. From the early 1930s, he had become convinced that rising world tariff barriers had made some aspects of the McNary-Haugen scheme impracticable. To rescue the farm sector from its plight he had been calling for the removal of tariffs internationally, and a price stabilization scheme internally, which would reflate domestic prices to their 1926 levels. The latter measure, the so-called Honest Dollar plan, reflected Wallace's long-standing interest in the ideas of monetarists such as Irving Fisher. Reflation would be effected through Federal Reserve Board control of the money supply. A restoration of prices to their 1926 levels would, Wallace estimated, reduce farmer indebtedness by one-quarter or one-third, as well as stimulate production. A poll of readers of *Wallaces' Farmer* in August 1931 uncovered tremendous enthusiasm for the plan, and subsequently Wallace was able to mobilize rural editors, farm organizations, and leading monetarists in support of legislation incorporating its principles. The plan was passed by the House in April 1932, but was later defeated in the Senate, another example of Republican obstructionism.[35]

Wallace was not much more enamored of the Democrats than of the Republicans, and had earlier tentatively proposed the idea of a third party on the Progressive model, but his call to farmers to quit the GOP made him a figure whose influence the Democrats might use. In addition, his position as an influential, respected, and thoughtful figure in the agrarian movement brought him to the attention of Franklin Roosevelt, even before the latter won the Democratic presidential nomination in 1932. Their actual meeting came about through M. L. Wilson, an economics professor at Montana State College, who had also played a part in developing the VDAP. Wilson was introduced to Roosevelt by Rexford Guy Tugwell, professor of economics at Columbia University, who knew Wilson's work and favored the VDAP. The plan was explained to Roosevelt, who apparently was interested and sympathetic but made no specific commitment to it.

Being aware of Wallace's thinking along this line and of his role in mustering popular opinion in favor of the agrarian movement, Roosevelt delegated New York State Conservation Commissioner Henry Morgenthau Jr. to make contact with Wallace and form an opinion of his suitability for a position in government. Morgenthau met Wallace in July 1932, and although he retained some doubts about some of Wallace's schemes for agrarian reform, he was impressed with Wallace's general philosophy, commitment, and sense of purpose.

Now Wallace began to be drawn closer to the Roosevelt camp. After Roosevelt's victory at the Democratic convention, Louis Howe wrote Wallace asking him to contact Harold Ickes in Chicago to help form the Progressives for Roosevelt organization. The transparently political nature of the proposal made Wallace unenthusiastic: "I didn't work so awfully hard at that. . . . Howe's letter to me was a typical political kind of thing, and it sounded to me like a phony. . . . I wasn't particularly interested in working with Ickes, as a matter of fact." Then, in early August, he received a visit from M. L. Wilson, who was working on Roosevelt's farm speech, due to be delivered in Topeka, Kansas, that September, and wanted Wallace's help. Wilson was also cooperating closely with Brain Truster Rexford Tugwell, who had met Wallace some time before at a conference on agriculture at the University of Chicago, where they had discussed some of Wallace's ideas. The "M. L. Wilson–Tugwell combination," Wallace believed, was chiefly responsible for making him secretary of agriculture.[36] Shortly after this, at Henry Morgenthau's invitation, he went to Hyde Park, New York, to see Roosevelt. It was on this trip that he visited the Onondoga Indian reservation.

Wallace stayed overnight at Albany, and on the morning of the interview visited a museum to examine its collection of Indian materials. While there, he met the curator, who denounced Roosevelt as an "absolutely horrible" governor who could not be trusted. "I never heard anything more devastating against Roosevelt than what this chap said." At Hyde Park, he and Roosevelt talked for some two hours, with Henry Morgenthau also present. Roosevelt began by outlining his idea for a shelter belt to combat erosion. Wallace raised the tenancy problem, arguing that farmers who worked the land should own it and that a future government should consider issuing long-term bonds at low interest rates to enable farmers to buy their land for an annual payment no greater than present rent. He also expatiated on the VDAP, and Roosevelt listened attentively. He did not specifically commit himself to enacting it if he were elected president, but made it plain that he was sympathetic to the cause of agrarian reform. Wallace felt he had gone a long way toward enlisting Roosevelt's support. He nevertheless suspected that Roosevelt was "just a typical easterner who didn't know too much about the West or about practical affairs—that is, the way ordinary people live" and who had little understanding of the farm situation. Because of this feeling and because of what the curator had said, Wallace "had [his] fingers crossed" about the Democratic candidate. Wallace liked Roosevelt personally, however, finding him "one of the most lovable people I've come across." There was no discussion of cabinet positions, leaving Wallace to assume that he had been invited to Hyde Park to help Roosevelt win the election. The idea that he might become secretary of agriculture or hold any office in a future administration, he said later, did not occur to him at this time.[37]

Yet Wallace had already been considering a political career. "If I am freed out of the paper [*Wallaces' Farmer and Iowa Homestead*]," he had written L. Edward Johndro the previous January, "I may run for the Democratic nomination for Senator." Johndro replied that he would "see what your wheel [horoscope] looks like in Washington," and later sent horoscopes for Wallace, Roosevelt, and Hoover. To Charles Roos, Wallace wrote (it is one of the few such letters that have survived): "Fate may decide that I run against him [Brookhart, possible Democratic candidate for the United States Senate] but it will not be my decision. . . . If I was successful I fear pressure of the new situation might make my peaceful exit to the poseyemo council and Inner Life under the Golden Maple more difficult. . . . Chas, I would much rather talk with you about things of the next world than of this." But Roos was encouraging: "My medicine says you should look EAST toward Washington[;] your destiny will support you." And in mid-July, informed now of the projected meeting between Wallace and Roosevelt, Roos urged: "Yes! Poseyemo says HAW must contact Roosevelt in August and leave his totem in Big Tepee. Feel certain this is big move on your part. Go after it."[38] Wallace must try to become secretary of agriculture.

Despite the efforts of Wilson and Wallace, Roosevelt's farm speech made no specific mention of the Voluntary Domestic Allotment Plan, although principles of the scheme could be discerned in it. Nevertheless, Wallace praised the speech in his paper, claiming that Roosevelt had committed himself to the "philosophy" of the VDAP. Wallace now came out fully in favor of FDR and against Hoover, using his editorials in outspoken fashion and making a number of radio broadcasts and political speeches supporting FDR's candidacy. In December he received an invitation to call on Roosevelt at Warm Springs, Georgia, signaling that he was being considered seriously for the position of secretary of agriculture. "Of course I was interested," Wallace later said.[39]

At "the Little White House" he talked with Roosevelt and with Morgenthau and Raymond Moley. Cocktails were served before dinner, Henry Morgenthau having been deputed to obtain illicit liquor. After the meal, Roosevelt told stories all evening, including one about various attempts to recover some buried treasure on Oak Island off Nova Scotia, a project in which, Wallace deduced, the president-elect had had some financial interest. Wallace was bemused: "He [Roosevelt] spent an hour and a half elaborating the minute details of this story. . . . The idea of buried treasure has never interested me in the slightest, because I felt it wasn't a constructive effort. This particular story didn't create any particular closeness with Roosevelt, but rather a sort of open-eyed wonder at 'What kind of a man is this?'"[40]

Roosevelt did not actually make up his mind to offer Wallace the job until the following February. In a letter dated the third of that month he asked Wallace to join his official family because of his "high personal esteem" for him and confidence in his abilities. "I know that we shall have a very happy relationship." In his reply, Wallace stressed obligation rather than affection, the duties of a family member. "Your invitation can have but one reply," he wrote. "I appreciate the honor and accept the responsibility. So far as it is in me I will carry my part of the 'family' burdens."[41]

He dictated a valedictory editorial for *Wallaces' Farmer and Iowa Homestead*. He recalled how his father had left Iowa twelve years earlier to become secretary of agriculture in Harding's cabinet in an attempt "to restore the agricultural values smashed in the decline of 1920–21" and in the hope of averting the more serious disaster that would occur "unless both the Government and the city people of the United States became aware of their debt and duty to the farmer." Though the present situation was more desperate, Wallace said, "I have an advantage . . . [of] a chief who is definitely progressive, entirely sympathetic toward agriculture, and completely determined to use every means at his command to restore farm buying power. . . . I shall be working under a courageous man with a kindly heart."[42] Although Wallace had undoubtedly been impressed with Roosevelt's warmth and courage, he was claiming more than he knew. Roosevelt's attitude to agriculture was not so clear-cut and, as we have seen, Wallace's meetings with the president-elect at Hyde Park and Warm Springs had left him with reservations about the man whose official family he was about to join.

They had one more meeting before Roosevelt's inauguration, at Roosevelt's residence in New York. Wallace was introduced to some other members of the incoming administration — William Woodin, "a very gentle soul, a lovely personality," and Louis Howe, of whom Wallace would later say, "I'd never met a cynical, critical soul like Howe before. . . . He was a pure opportunist and had no interest in policy as such." Roosevelt talked mainly about his commitment to balance the budget — "how it was going to be necessary to cut, as he first said, the expenditures of the Agricultural Department by one-third. He finally said one-fourth . . . at that moment, Roosevelt was not interested in agricultural plans. He was interested in cutting the budget of the Department of Agriculture by one-fourth."

After he had talked with Roosevelt, Wallace met Arthur Mullen in the anteroom. Mullen produced a federal registry, with the names of all bureau and division chiefs in the various departments and the salaries they earned. He pointed out that these people and many of their assistants were Republicans and that "deserving Democrats" should now be found to replace them, but to Wallace the idea was repugnant:

I knew a great many of the Bureau Chiefs in the Department of Agriculture, because I had met them in 1912 when Tama Jim [Wilson] was Secretary of Agriculture, and had taken a full week visiting all the different bureaus of the Department. I knew how the Department was put together, knew the men as individuals, knew the high character of the men, knew they were genuinely serving the public. Mullen, to me, was an utterly repulsive person. He probably was a much finer man than I thought he was at the time, but I just couldn't stomach him at the moment. I didn't want *his* men running the bureaus—that's all. I knew they *couldn't* be competent—or so I thought.[43]

This was Wallace's first direct acquaintance with political patrimony, and it is plain he regarded it with contempt. He probably never managed to accept it as a normal part of the business of government, and as we shall see, there were many things in practical politicking that he "just couldn't stomach." His moral principles could win him fervent popular admiration and support, but they could be a hindrance in the Machiavellian world of professional politics.

In the pre–New Deal years, Wallace had experimented with many approaches in his search for illumination and truth, without, it seems, committing himself wholly to any. He had reached the stage, he confessed to Johndro, where he was "doubtful about allowing anyone to have occult (or other) leadership over [him]." Now, as he prepared to face the grave problems of agriculture and of the wider society—not simply "an ordinary depression," he and Johndro believed, but an event that portended "the collapse of all racial idolatry and as the cosmic compulsion to an entire revaluation of what is worth while"[44]—he was willing to cooperate with the new president, but, as Franklin Roosevelt and later Harry Truman would discover, if ever he thought the nation's leadership had faltered or lost its way, Henry Wallace could very much be his own man.

3

MATERIAL ABUNDANCE
BEYOND OUR FONDEST DREAMS

WALLACE AS SECRETARY OF

AGRICULTURE, 1933–1936

In March 1933, as Wallace took up his position as secretary of
agriculture, the nation's farmers were in a desperate plight. Corn and
oats, hogs and cattle, were bringing much less than the cost of production. Farmers were in debt, many defaulting on their mortgages and
being evicted, as credit was virtually unobtainable. There was fierce
resentment; hostile crowds intimidated judges, and there were iso-
lated instances of violent resistance to dispossession agents. From the
nation's rural areas came angry demands for radical solutions—for the
unlimited coinage of silver money and printing of notes or for a guarantee of prices that would at least cover producers' costs. Despite his
sympathy for the farmers, Wallace could see that such measures would
be financially irresponsible and administratively impracticable, and he
had to set himself in opposition to them.

Immediately he called (with FDR's approval) a national agricultural
conference to discuss the form emergency farm legislation should take.
Consisting of representatives of the major farm organizations, many
of whom had already taken part in the meetings that had helped formulate and promote the Voluntary Domestic Allotment Plan (VDAP),

the conference met on 10 March 1933. Wallace hoped that the moderate progressive group within the conference would prevail. He took no direct part in their deliberations, but with violence sputtering in the countryside and the next season's crops ready for planting, he urged haste. "Agreement will have to be immediate," he warned in a radio address on 10 March. "We can't legislate next June for a crop that was planted in April. . . . No plan can be perfect. . . . Our job will be to get a compromise."[1]

As Wallace had hoped, the meeting endorsed the basic concept of the VDAP, which in practical terms was the control of production by limiting acreage under crops, and he and half a dozen others, including Assistant Secretary of Agriculture Rexford Tugwell and George Peek, the longtime corn-belt activist, set about drawing up a legislative proposal designed to implement this general policy. The overall aim of what became the Agricultural Adjustment Act was to restore "reasonable parity" between the prices of agricultural commodities and those of manufacturing commodities, "reasonable parity" being nominated as the balance prevailing during the period from August 1909 to July 1914, when the agricultural community seemed acceptably prosperous. The legislation provided that farmers who agreed to produce less of certain basic commodities—cotton, wheat, corn, hogs, dairy products, and so on—would receive compensatory payments from the government, such payments to come not from general revenue but from a special tax on companies that processed farm products—textile manufacturers, flour millers, canners, and the like. This was the essence of the VDAP, but because of the need to obtain consensus, odds and ends of other approaches also found their way into the legislation. The federal government was given power to subsidize farm exports, to enforce marketing agreements, and even to protect consumers. Wide-ranging and ambiguous, the bill gave Wallace enormous discretion, appearing to legalize, as journalist Russell Lord pointed out, "almost anything anybody could think up."[2] Wallace saw the difficulties. "The legislation was very broad," he said later, "and the farm leaders really had it in mind that it should be that way—let's forget all conflicts. They were wishing off on the secretary and the administrator . . . the privilege of choosing any one of a great many different approaches . . . or putting them on the spot." When it came to administering the law, he observed presciently, "I knew we would be living in a veritable hell."[3]

The bill passed quickly through the House but stalled in the Senate.

John A. Simpson, leader of the nationwide Farmers Union and energetic campaigner for Roosevelt during the run-up to the election, was the first to break the consensus that had been achieved at the agricultural conference. Somehow (by trickery, he later charged) the conference had been held without him, although the Farmers Union itself was represented by Congressman W. P. Lambertson, a former director. Simpson now lobbied for an amendment to Wallace's proposal, one that would guarantee farmers received at least their cost of production. This amendment was passed by the Senate but rejected by the House. In committee Wallace opposed it on the grounds that it was not economically feasible to subsidize agriculture to such an extent, and that the necessary price-fixing could not be implemented or enforced. In the end, the president heeded Wallace's arguments rather than Simpson's, and the amendment did not appear in the final act. Further delays to the passage of the bill came from those rural representatives in Congress who believed that inflationary "cheap money" measures were the solution to the farmers' plight. Led by Senator Elmer Thomas from Oklahoma, they in fact persuaded Roosevelt to adopt modified and controlled procedures to inflate the economy, specifically, to devalue the dollar and then fix the price of gold at thirty-five dollars an ounce—measures that had little or no effect in lifting the Depression.[4]

Wallace found the pace of these early days in office frantic. "We are skating over the thin ice so fast that it doesn't break," he told his friend Dante Pierce, owner of *Wallaces' Farmer and Iowa Homestead.* "It is difficult to find time to urinate on some days." Reporters and farmers' delegations crowded into the department, demanding to know what the new legislation meant. Business and farm-organization lobbyists sought advantageous treatment under it. The "Farmers Union crowd" had just slipped another amendment into the bill, Wallace complained to Pierce. "It will give me plenty of hell. . . . The President told the Agricultural Committee that it would take 10 years off my life. Tugwell says that's the reason the Committee voted it in."[5]

Wallace also had to fend off attacks from within the administration. Proud of the Department of Agriculture's record and of the technical competence of its officers, he had already deflected party functionary Arthur Mullen's attempt to replace key personnel with suitably loyal Democrats. Now he had to turn aside Roosevelt's attempt to cut the department's budget by one-quarter. After the first meeting of the new cabinet, Roosevelt had introduced Budget Director Louis Douglas to

Henry Agard Wallace, U.S. secretary of agriculture, 1933–40. (Courtesy of the University of Iowa Library)

Wallace as "the man who's going to do the job on you." Wallace liked Douglas but decided that he knew nothing about science, a failing the president obviously shared. "Douglas thought the government had no business engaging in scientific work. He wanted to cut out practically all the scientific work in the Department of Agriculture, as well as a great many of the service activities. His was a completely impractical approach."[6] In response to this challenge, Wallace gave addresses at the Franklin Institute of Science at Philadelphia, the Massachusetts Institute of Technology, and similar venues, praising the department's scientific role. He also wrote directly to Roosevelt, reminding the president of his statement the previous July that any curtailment in the department's educational, research, or experimental activities would be little short of disastrous. Copies of Roosevelt's letter containing the statement, he warned, "are being very widely circulated and protests against the idea of reducing these services are coming in from every quarter of the land."[7] When an obviously authoritative article appeared in the *New York Times* stipulating which activities in his department should be axed, Wallace took more dramatic action: "I . . . decided I would cut out one of the activities of the department and let him [Douglas] see how he would like it. I gave the order to close up shop in the Marketing work . . . and such a political clamor arose that Mr. Douglas' economy efforts in the department ended right then and there."[8] Where threats to his department were involved, Wallace always proved himself to be a tough and politically astute fighter. It was in the matter of self-promotion that his incisiveness failed.

Russell Lord, who worked for Wallace for more than a year and whose sympathetic attitude is evident in his writings, has left a picture of the new secretary during these turbulent weeks and months. Initially he had seemed careworn and uncertain, but once the framework of the farm program had been set in place "it was striking to see him change." He grew more confident, "gave greater play to a sense of humor," and "began to enjoy his new work." Calmly, he set about ironing out disagreements, trying to achieve an act that his department could effectively administer. There were some who thought the vastly more experienced George Peek, slated to become the administrator of the new Agricultural Adjustment Act, should have been secretary, but to newcomers like Lord it seemed that Wallace, "striking off daily new patterns of candid public address and behavior . . . grew visibly, daily and weekly."[9]

Anecdotes from the period tell of Wallace's straightforwardness and lack of affection. Assistant Secretary of Agriculture Rexford Tugwell describes him as looking like "a rather untidy farm editor with a shock of unruly hair and his necktie always out of place and his suit always rumpled." Lord pictures him "negligently sprawling" at his desk, feet in the wastepaper basket, answering reporters' questions with a frankness that astonished them and brought hasty protests from his aides. He walked for an hour each morning, between his hotel and office; sometimes abandoned his government limousine to ride with friends; played tennis regularly; and, his feet becoming sore on one occasion, strolled shoeless into his office building past the saluting guards.[10]

The new secretary's knowledge and scientific expertise impressed associates. He was at home in conferences with his bureau chiefs, "putting questions about chromosome counts or multiple correlations which gave trouble to the most learned."[11] He kept abreast of new information and ideas; on a large table behind his desk lay a collection of recent publications on commodity prices, weather, and genetics, as well as works on history and philosophy. A loose-leaf folder of statistics on basic commodity price movements ("probably the most valuable volume on that subject in existence") was always at hand—Wallace had compiled it over many years and kept it up to date. On one occasion he was asked to sign a letter containing lists of such prices, but, doubting the accuracy of the statistics, he corrected them from memory. When his staff checked his figures they found them to be correct in almost every case.[12] Once Franklin Roosevelt had discovered Wallace's near-total numerical recall, he would try to catch him in a mistake. "The President called up about 6 P.M. [Wallace recorded in his diary] to say that he had almost never found me wrong on figures but he had me this time. He noticed in the evening paper that the spot price of middling cotton was 11.07 cents which was considerably different from the 10.74 figure which I had quoted the previous day. I asked him if 11.07 was not a spot price at New York and called his attention to [the fact that] the price I was quoting was the average of the 10 spot markets. He said, 'Yes,' his price was the spot price in New York and backed away and then I said, 'Well, you pretty nearly had me anyhow, Mr. President.' He then said, 'You may know about corn and hogs but I am a plantah from Gohgah.' I said 'Yessah,' and we kidded each other for a little while."[13]

Meanwhile, delays in the passing of the Agricultural Adjustment Act were beginning to produce the difficulties Wallace had foreseen. As the ideological struggles between the various factions continued, the passage of the seasons could not be delayed. Sows were farrowing and cotton fields were being planted. By the time the act finally became law in early May, disastrous unsalable surpluses were already in prospect. The new, untried secretary of agriculture was forced to some of the most unpalatable and politically perilous decisions he would ever have to make: he issued orders that ten million acres of cotton were to be plowed under and six million piglets were to be slaughtered.

The odium of these decisions hung about Wallace for the rest of his life, but in fact he had had little alternative. With stocks of cotton already huge, the new crop might push prices to the point of collapse; therefore, when officials from the Agricultural Adjustment Administration (AAA; the agency set up within his department to administer the act), Bureau of Agricultural Economics, and Extension Service recommended that one-quarter of the year's cotton crop be destroyed, he reluctantly agreed. The situation with corn and hogs was similarly intractable; both were in serious oversupply. This time Wallace rejected a major plow-up of corn in favor of planned corn and hog reductions the following year. But with prices already very low, emergency action had to be taken to reduce a surplus that threatened to glut the market and drive producers to ruin.[14]

The suggestion that the government should supervise a mass pig-killing came from a meeting of farmer representatives in Chicago and was endorsed by representatives of major farm organizations meeting in Washington as the National Corn-Hog Committee.[15] But again, the ultimate responsibility lay with Wallace. He understood that the action would cause a good deal of public incomprehension, not to say outrage, and when Chester Davis, head of the Production Division of the AAA, asked him to sign the necessary order, he hesitated. "I remember saying to him, 'What do you think Chester? Do we have to do this?' He said, 'Yes, we do,' or something to that effect. So I signed it. I knew I was in for real trouble when I did that and was very concerned."[16] As the slaughter proceeded, Wallace, AAA general counsel Jerome Frank, and federal relief administrator Harry Hopkins persuaded Roosevelt to set up the Federal Surplus Relief Corporation, with Hopkins, Harold Ickes, and Wallace as directors, to distribute the meat to the poor. However, logistical problems proved too great—only about one-tenth of the pork reached those on relief, the remainder being made into fertilizer or simply disposed of as waste.[17]

The Agricultural Adjustment Act may have helped to avert catastrophe, but it brought no dramatic improvements. Though many farmers signed AAA contracts and reduced their crops, prices remained disappointingly low. At the same time, the prices of manufactured goods, buoyed now by National Recovery Administration policies, started to rise. This situation brought demands for a degree of regimentation and compulsion that Wallace refused to accept. From the start of the emergency farm plan, he had propagandized and organized for the greatest possible voluntary participation, using the incentive of benefit payments and eventual improved prices consequent on acreage restriction, rather than the threat of negative sanctions. Acreage allotments and other details of the program were to be determined at the regional and county level with the cooperation of a network of field agents. Years later, he referred with pride to "the organization of farmer committees to enable them to plan together to meet their own problems on a township by township, county by county, state by state basis, to meet changing soil and market conditions," which the AAA had begun in 1933 and extended in succeeding years. Wallace called this "the first nation-wide example of genuine economic democracy" and counted it among his finest achievements.[18] But as a brief price rise in the summer of 1933 gave way to another slump in the autumn, discontent sharply increased and the principle of voluntarism came under strong attack.

Cotton farmers who had reduced their crops, only to see others increase theirs to take advantage of the resulting shortage, began to insist that the rebels be forced to fall into line. The governors of five northwestern states came to Washington, D.C., with more radical demands — every farm must be licensed, its output tightly controlled, and every processor forced to pay farmers prices well above those prevailing on the market. When Roosevelt, at Wallace's insistence, rejected the governors' demands, the radical Farmers' Holiday Association called a food strike, and with the farm program again under threat, Wallace had to travel to the centers of greatest unrest to denounce the violence and chide farmers and processors who refused to cooperate.

At the end of one of these speeches, in his home state of Iowa, Wallace had sounded a more optimistic, inspirational note. "Only the merest quarter-turn of the heart," he told a great crowd at Des Moines, "separates us from a material abundance beyond the fondest dream of anyone present. . . . Selfishness has ceased to become the mainspring of progress. . . . There is a new social machinery in the making."[19] Per-

Wallace defends the Agricultural Adjustment Administration's crop reduction program, August 1934. (Courtesy of the Associated Press)

haps this marked the first public expression of a philosophy that Wallace would preach for the rest of his life. He argued time and again that science and technology had made material prosperity actually and currently attainable for all the world's people. All humankind had to do was accept and willingly bring to fruition this possibility, the only technical problem being that of distribution. But to accept and promote universal abundance required a profound spiritual transformation. Competition and exploitation must be abandoned and replaced by generosity and co-operation — seemingly a simple enough option in a world where there was plenty for all, but one that was opposed by long-standing tendencies of the human spirit. In *Statesmanship and Religion*, published in 1934, Wallace wrote: "Today I am glad to say that economics, science and religion are all re-examining the facts under pressure from the common man who is appalled by the tragic nonsense of misery and want in the midst of tremendous world stocks of essential raw materials. Science has given us control over nature far beyond the wildest imaginings of our grandfathers. But, unfortunately, the religious attitude which produced such keen scientists and aggressive business men makes it impossible for us to live with the balanced abundance which is now ours as soon as we are willing to accept it with clean, understanding hearts."

The "religious attitude" Wallace referred to was specifically that of Protestantism, which he closely identified with laissez-faire economics because of its insistence on the individual's responsibility for his or her own fate. "Spencer, Darwin, Huxley, and their followers in promulgating the doctrine of natural selection and the survival of the fittest gave the whole idea an apparent foundation in nature," he wrote. "As a result Protestantism, which in its origin was highly spiritual, became in fact more and more material." One begins to see why Wallace may have preferred the theosophical doctrine of ever-increasing evolutionary spirituality to the Darwinian vision of nature red in tooth and claw. He continued: "To enter the kingdom of heaven brought to earth and expressed in terms of rich material life it will be necessary to have a reformation even greater than that of Luther and Calvin. . . . The men in the street must change their attitude concerning the nature of man and the nature of human society. They must develop the capacity to envision a co-operative objective and be willing to pay the price to attain it. They must have the intelligence and the will-power to turn down simple solutions appealing to the short-term motives of a particular class."[20]

But were not Wallace's orders to plow up ten million acres of cotton and slaughter six million piglets "simple solutions appealing to the short-term motives of a particular class"? That was certainly one criticism that was made repeatedly, if perhaps superficially, of Wallace's decisions. Hundreds of thousands of families across the United States were then in dire poverty, half-fed and poorly clad. To them it must have seemed that Wallace was simply protecting the interests of farmers, creating shortages to force up the prices of these staple commodities.

Of course the problem of rural overproduction in the nation's economy was more complicated than those oversimplified criticisms recognized. The spiritual and economic reformation of which Wallace dreamed could not take place overnight. The root cause of the current difficulties, as he saw it, was that American manufacturers were being sheltered from the competition of foreign imports by high tariff walls. This meant that foreign nations could not repay their war debts or pay for rural products imported from the United States by exporting their manufactured goods. It meant also that American industry could at will curtail production to keep its own prices high, thus throwing workers out of jobs and restricting the ability of the domestic market to consume farm products. The farmer seemed to be squeezed both ways. For the rest of his life Wallace argued against protectionism and for free trade in order to break out of this inequitable sequence and make abundance possible.

Even in the case of the pig slaughter, seemingly of sole benefit to farm interests, he contended that in fact consumers in general had benefited. Two years later, in 1935, in a radio address titled "Pigs and Pig Iron," he pointed out (somewhat misleadingly) that the slaughtered animals had not been wasted but had been turned into 100 million pounds of pork, which actually were distributed for relief: "It went to feed the hungry." With regard to the longer-term effects, he addressed himself to a typical complaint from a listener who claimed that the slaughter "has raised pork prices until to-day we poor people cannot even look at a piece of bacon." Wallace did not deny that pork prices may have been too high for some consumers, but claimed that without the reduction in the number of pigs they would have been higher still. His main point was that in 1934 there had been a severe drought (fortuitously for his argument) so that the corn crop was a billion bushels short. By the time the six million piglets had grown up, they would have eaten 75 million bushels, but because they had been slaughtered, those bushels were available to make more pork in late 1934 and early 1935 — an argument that seems to neglect the fact that there is a very large gap between 75 million and a billion, and that it was not only the hog industry that competed for corn. Nevertheless, he claimed that "it gave us more pork this year than we would have had without it." Further, Wallace argued, the fact that returns to the farmer were higher than they would otherwise have been "made it possible for farmers to buy more city products and so put more city people back to work." He certainly could have said that if the disastrously low prices had been allowed to continue and even get worse, then more hog farmers would have been forced into bankruptcy and very severe shortages would have developed in later years.

Wallace's sympathy for the rural sector appeared when in the same talk he made a sharp comparison between the pig industry and the pig-iron industry. From 1929 through 1933, according to his figures, pig production had been reduced by only 3 percent but pig-iron production had been reduced by a staggering 80 percent. "That sort of industrial reduction programme ploughed millions of workers out into the streets. It is because of that industrial reduction programme that we have to spend billions for relief to keep the ploughed-out workers from starvation. . . . People are more important than pigs."[21]

But Wallace was not normally so polemical. He could see that the depressed economic state of agriculture could not be alleviated while the economy of the whole nation was similarly depressed. Increased agricultural purchasing power was necessary for the consumption of industrial products, but by the same token, higher industrial wages were necessary to expand consumption of agricultural products. Accordingly, Wallace had been in favor of the provisions of the National Industrial Recovery Act, passed in June 1933, which brought about an increase in industrial wages, even though it meant an increase in the price index of the industrial goods that farmers had to buy. In this respect his attitude differed from that of men such as George Peek, now the first AAA administrator, and Edward O'Neal of the Farm Bureau, both of whom had developed a rigidly sectional and competitive commitment to the furtherance of agricultural interests and regarded industry as their inveterate enemy and exploiter.

In Wallace's view, by contrast, the entire country was existing on an unnecessarily restricted and impoverished scale, and here his belief in the possibility of an economics of abundance became relevant. He spoke as if, and at times believed, that all that was necessary was a communal act of will in which all the nation, and indeed all humankind, would choose to create and cooperatively share in this physically realizable abundance. Of course he knew that many of the nation's capitalists were not living an impoverished life and could continue to enjoy personal abundance indefinitely, but his notion of progressive capitalism held that they, too, would come to realize that their own interests lay in expanding markets, and that market expansion and increased prosperity would follow from a general increase in standards of living. This sounds very like an appeal to the "enlightened self-interest" of the later utilitarians, even though Wallace claimed to have turned entirely against that movement as it had developed in connection with Protestantism and social Darwinism. The issue, of course, lies in one's definition of enlightened self-interest. In his proposals as to what should actually be done in the economic field, Wallace pointed to the material gains that would accrue to various sectors, but in his more elevated, inspirational addresses it is the spiritual gains to be derived from mutual help and fellow feeling to which he commends his hearers, and the path to this was to elect to create abundance for all. Before that willed choice could be made, however, a profound spiritual revolution had to occur.

How could this sweeping moral change, in which cooperation was to replace competition and altruism to replace rugged individualism, be brought about? In his public utterances Wallace had very little to say about the means, apart from exhortation, but in private he had already developed a millennial conception, that the enlightenment would be brought about by a historical event—the appearance of a great spiritual leader, divinely inspired, coming most probably from the heart of Asia. The crystallization of this idea, already congenial to Wallace's theosophical leanings, came about through his association with a remarkable figure, an émigré Russian painter and mystic, Nicholas Roerich.

NICHOLAS ROERICH, THE ROERICH PACT,
AND THE BANNER OF PEACE

Nicholas Roerich was to play a dramatic role in Wallace's career during his first three years as secretary of agriculture. The climax of this role was prepared for in 1934 when Wallace, sidestepping orthodox administrative procedures, appointed Roerich the leader of an expedition into central Asia, ostensibly to collect specimens and seeds of drought-resistant grasses to be brought back and tested on the American plains. This was in fact one of the expedition's aims, particularly relevant in

1934 because of the extreme drought then afflicting rural areas, but Wallace had begun planning it before the drought developed. The expedition caused Wallace acute embarrassment, and the Roerich legend was afterward to hang around his neck for many years. How all this came about can only be properly understood when seen in the context of Roerich's life—otherwise his influence on Wallace will hardly seem credible.

The main facts of Roerich's life, as researched by historian Robert C. Williams, appear to be these. He was born in 1874 of an upper-class St. Petersburg family, trained as a painter at the Academy of the Arts in the 1890s, and achieved considerable success in that art in prerevolutionary Russia. He was also active in the archaeological exploration of ancient Russian burial sites, and in 1899, being only twenty-four years old, he was appointed professor of archaeology at the Imperial Institute in St. Petersburg. Before the 1917 Revolution he had been president of the Society for Encouragement of Fine Arts and the St. Petersburg World of Art Society—notable distinctions. During the revolutionary period, Maxim Gorky, who was in charge of art and culture under the new Soviet government, made Roerich chairman of the Council of Art Affairs. Roerich, however, was uneasy with the new regime and in 1919, after two months as chairman, he migrated with his family to London. Evidently he now classed himself as a White Russian, and while in London decisively distanced himself from the Soviet government by publishing, in 1919, a pamphlet entitled *Violators of Art*, in which he accused the Bolsheviks of having destroyed a great deal of art and having advanced policies that were a "thoroughly organized swindle."[22]

He came to the United States in 1920 at the invitation of art critic and promoter Christian Brinton, accompanied by his two sons, George (Yuri) and Svetoslav, leaving his wife Helena, an aristocratic Russian woman who was a considerable force in her own right, to follow later. He brought with him a large number of his paintings and was at first a striking success. Crowds attended his exhibitions in New York and Chicago, and many paintings were sold. But sales quickly fell away, and in 1921 he and Helena decided to set up an art school. They had met an exiled Russian pianist and his wife, Morris and Sina Lichtmann, and between them they established what they called the Master Institute of United Arts where all the arts were to be taught under one roof. The classes were held in rented premises, and the income barely covered costs, but in 1922 the Roerichs found a patron and backer in a wealthy foreign exchange broker, Louis L. Horch. He, and more markedly his wife Nettie, were admirers and supporters of the arts. The exact circumstances under which they met Roerich are obscure, but soon he had not only enlisted their sympathy but also established a powerful persuasive influence over them. However one evaluates Roerich in the long run, there is little doubt that he had a hypnotic personal presence and could convince people of his elevated spirituality and knowledge of higher truths. Soon Horch had paid Roerich's debts and begun advancing him substantial sums of money representing advance payments for paintings Roerich was to produce.[23]

A major source of Roerich's influence over Nettie Horch, and through her, her husband, lay in his claim to be one of those to whom the most esoteric truths of Theosophy and Buddhism had been revealed. Before the Great War, Roerich, because of his attraction to the Eastern doctrines, had planned to build a Buddhist temple in St. Petersburg and had become a member of the Russian branch of the Theosophical Society. On leaving Russia for England he had transferred his membership to the English branch and now joined the American one. Nettie Horch, too, was deeply interested in both Buddhism and Theosophy. According to Williams, Roerich now began dressing in Tibetan prayer robes and claimed that in an ancient former incarnation he had been a Chinese emperor and Horch had been his son. The fact that a hardheaded, successful New York financier could continue to be impressed by such claims is a mark of how much conviction Roerich was able to infuse into them. He established a remarkable psychological domination over the Horches and a schoolgirl friend of Nettie Horch, Frances Grant, who was to play a significant role as go-between for Wallace and the Roerichs. They saw Roerich's powers and virtues as approaching sublimity and addressed him as "Guru," "Master," and "Father," as Wallace himself was to do later. Presented as messages relayed to him from the masters, his advice and directions carried great authority.

In 1923 the Horches set up a museum, dedicated to the preservation and exhibition of Roerich's paintings and writings and to the promotion of the arts in general, the Master Institute of Arts, and a new international cultural agency, Corona Mundi Inc., all in an apartment building owned by Horch at 310 Riverside Drive, where the Roerich Museum may be found today. The museum, due almost entirely to the efforts of the Horches and Frances Grant, functioned productively as a venue for art exhibitions, lectures, and recitals by distinguished artists into the

1930s. Its work was checked out more than once by special investigators from the State Department, which had early taken an interest in Roerich because of his Russian connections, and although the museum was not Roerich's major concern, the genuineness of its activities served to allay in part the department's suspicions.

Roerich's central interest remained the ancient esoteric wisdom underlying Buddhism and Theosophy, and its fountainhead in the Orient. He conceived the idea of leading an expedition to central Asia to consult with the holy men of the Himalayas, and if possible to seek out the dwelling places of the recognized masters, supposedly living in the mountains of Tibet. During this journey he would instill the sacred ambience of the great mountains into his paintings. He put the idea to Horch in 1922, and Horch solicited contributions from wealthy art supporters and himself supplied some $300,000 in gifts, loans, and supplies.[24] In return Roerich's paintings were to be sold to Horch at one-third of the price he would nominate for the wider art public, and exhibited in the Roerich Museum. Nicholas and Helena embarked from New York in May 1923. The mission's mock-heroic character is fascinating in itself, but for the student of Henry Wallace's life, it is chiefly remarkable for its uncanny similarities to the expedition Roerich was to undertake for the Department of Agriculture some ten years later — similarities not only in geographical destination but in the dreamlike mismatch between professed intention and actual performance.

In 1924 and 1925, Roerich traveled through the Himalayan foothills of Sikkim, visiting Indian religious leaders, and the Theosophical Society headquarters at Adyar, and making religious paintings. He also made numerous attempts to return to his native Russia, and eventually, early in 1926, managed to reach Moscow, where he made every effort to demonstrate his friendliness to the Soviet regime.[25] Among other things, he told Soviet officials that his recent talks with Indian mahatmas had convinced him that an anticolonialist alliance of Leninism and Buddhism, directed principally against the British rulers of India, could come about, but the Soviets expressed skepticism. That same year saw the publication in New York of a book of reproductions of Roerich's paintings, together with celebratory essays, entitled *Himalaya*. Roerich himself contributed an essay in which he claimed that, according to "the writings of the great lamas," Christ had not been killed by the Jews. Rather, "the empire and the wealthy capitalists killed the Great Communist [Christ] who carried light to the working and poor ones."

What makes all this interesting is that four years later, when Roerich was having trouble getting a visa to reenter India and had requested aid from Washington, the State Department reviewed its files on him and had Special Agent Kinsey check on the activities of the Roerich Museum. This updated an investigation Kinsey had made in 1925, by which time the State Department, partly because of inquiries from British intelligence, had already taken Roerich under notice. Although Kinsey again reported nothing "communistic" about the museum or about Roerich himself (a judgment that reveals an ignorance of what Roerich had been doing in Moscow), there must have been quite a substantial file on him when, just a few years later, Henry Wallace appointed him to lead an expedition to Mongolia.

In the meantime the Roerich expedition, on its way back to India, had finally reached Darjeeling, and Roerich began to pursue what seems to have been his long-term plan, to settle permanently in the subcontinent. He began negotiations to purchase land at Naggar in the Kulu Valley, where he intended to set up a scientific and cultural research institution, and this eventually became a reality, the Urusvati Institute. But his plans were delayed when the government of India, acting through the government of the Punjab, intervened in the purchase. The British Foreign Office, aware by now of Roerich's visit to Moscow, suspected him of being an agent of the Comintern.

Roerich made a well-publicized return to New York in the summer of 1929, being greeted at City Hall by Mayor James Walker. His books about his travels, *Altai-Himalaya* and *Heart of Asia*, published, respectively, in 1929 and 1930, were brought out in time to capitalize on and increase this interest, and to promote his own versions of Theosophy and Buddhism. In the spring of 1930 he began to reanimate a peace movement that he had actually begun many years before. This was a proposal for the protection of artistic, scientific, and cultural institutions in time of war. Such institutions were to fly an internationally recognized flag of three red disks within a red circle on a white ground, declaring them to be neutral territory. The flag was the Roerich Banner of Peace, the visible emblem of a proposed International Covenant for the Protection of Artistic and Scientific Institutions, Missions and Collections, a draft of which he circulated to President Hoover, George V of England, and many other world leaders.

After Wallace became secretary of agriculture in 1933 he became an active and open supporter of this proposed covenant, which became known as the Roerich Pact, but, as we have seen, he had come into contact with some of the Roerich New York group earlier than that. Moreover, Roerich's name had been well known in Theosophical circles for some years before that, and it is quite likely that Wallace would have known something of him and his views through that channel. The earliest documentary evidence extant is a letter of 15 April 1929, from Wallace to Frances Grant, vice president of the Roerich Museum, thanking her for a copy of *Altai-Himalaya*, which was published that year. He says: "I have read enough to know that it is what I hoped. Both in words and in painting Roerich is an adept in the use of symbols which have a power unknown to science. And yet Roerich's mysticism has a decidedly practical aspect and eventually significance to the scientific world." He goes on: "I hope to call at the museum on August 14, 15 or 16. At any rate I am sailing from New York on August 17 for England with some Cornell professors to attend an Economics Conference in England, after which I go to Hungary to study maize growing in the European corn belt and especially the European corn borer. Sincerely, Henry A. Wallace."[26] The personal tone certainly suggests some earlier contacts, as he assumes she was interested in agricultural matters, and one might trace here the beginnings of a confluence of interests that would later give rise to the proposal for Roerich's expedition to Mongolia.

In April 1930 Roerich made ready to return to India to press the matter of purchasing the land at Naggar, but the British government, still suspecting him to be an agent of the Comintern, denied him a visa to enter the country. Horch solicited the State Department's aid, and it was at this time that their special agent's report cleared Roerich of "having the communistic taint." Partly in response to British inquiries about the Roerichs, the State Department had already sought an expert opinion from the Smithsonian Bureau of American Ethnology concerning the scientific status of the Roerich Museum, presumably in order to form an opinion about the probable worth of the proposed research station in the Kulu Valley. It had learned that there was "much unfavorable gossip in scientific circles" concerning the museum, and that with the exception of its work in Sanskrit, its scientific standing was considered dubious. Assistant Secretary of State W. R. Castle now sought the opinion of Paul J. Sailly of the Harvard Fogg Art Museum. Sailly replied that Roerich's artistic output was "of negligible importance," and that Sir Aurel Stein, a fellow of the Fogg Museum, before departing on a trip to the Far East, had warned him "in the most serious fashion to have absolutely nothing to do with Roerich." Whatever Roerich's "game" was, Stein added, it had "no scientific validity."[27] In view of all this, the State Department decided that it could make no specific commitments to the British as to the scientific standing of the Roerich Museum or to the museum's scientific activities in the Kulu Valley. The question of whether Roerich should be given a visa to return to India to negotiate the land purchase was entirely up to the British.[28]

Some time early in December the British authorities reversed their decision and allowed Roerich to enter India to rejoin his wife, and subsequently, an institute, which was named Urusvati, Himalayan Research Institute, was established at Naggar, Kulu, and continued in operation certainly until Roerich's death in 1947. A commemorative volume published on the centenary of Roerich's birth claimed that he was able to organize the exchange of scientific information with many international organizations, that his son Yuri (George) had done significant work in Asian linguistics and philology, that his other son Svetoslav, head of the Botany Department, had undertaken research into Tibetan pharmacopoeia and exchanged botanical collections with various universities, and that a "Bio-Chemistry laboratory was opened in the Institute to fight cancer."[29] It was the research in botany and into native herbal treatments for cancer and tuberculosis that first engaged Henry Wallace's interest in the scientific possibilities of those remote geographical areas and led him to see Nicholas Roerich as the possible leader of an expedition that would benefit American agriculture. The Urusvati Institute became known to him through the promotional activities of Frances Grant.

In the first surviving letter from Wallace to Frances Grant, noted above, Wallace praises Roerich's *Altai-Himalaya*. Other early letters between Wallace and the members of the Roerich Museum are brief, polite, and formal. There is one dated 25 October 1929, from Grant, addressed to Wallace at *Wallaces' Farmer*, acknowledging his "interesting letter," promising new literature on the museum's organizations, and saying that they would be happy to see him "again" whenever he was in New York. Another of 6 June 1930, from Sina Lichtmann, refers to a letter Wallace had written Professor Roerich: "You will be interested to know that he left America two months ago"—that is, on his attempt to return to Naggar. "However, as he is still in Europe I shall try to reach him and send him your letter before he leaves for India, for I know how glad he will be to receive it."[30] A few months later, on 20 January 1931, Wallace wrote Grant that he had received his copy of the first issue of the *Roerich Museum Bulletin* and had read with special interest a poem by Roerich. He continued: "If sometime you should publish a statement from Dr. Koelz [a botanist who had worked for the Roerichs in Naggar] concerning the medicinal uses of these different Himalayan plants, I would appreciate having a copy. Sometime when you are writing to Dr. Koelz, I would appreciate it, if you could ask him to send you fifteen or twenty kernels of maize as grown in Kulu."[31]

We see, then, that Wallace, the corn breeder of Iowa, was alert to the possibility of a brand new outcross of maize, but his other interests were also focusing on the Urusvati Institute. Koelz's work on medicinal plants must have touched several nerves in Wallace. Because of his family's grave history of tuberculosis, of which Wallace himself had twice been suspect, the possibility that some of these plants might be helpful in treating or preventing it would have struck home.

On 12 October 1931 Wallace wrote Grant that he expected to be in New York City on 2 November and hoped to call at the museum and talk with either Grant or someone else familiar with the development of the biochemical activities at Urusvati. By 23 November 1931 he had become sufficiently engaged by the Roerich mystique to write "AE" (George W. Russell):

> Did you happen to visit the Roerich Museum when you were in New York City? Nicholas Roerich, you know, is a great Russian painter who has traveled extensively in Tibet and the Gobi deserts. . . . [He] does not have quite the strong earth feeling for America that Dr. Dower and Charles Roos have. But he has some other things which make him exceedingly worthwhile.
>
> There are many people engaged in this work and they are in many different schools and some of them are unfortunately jealous of each other. But their paths all lead to the same destination and it seems to me it is time for them to begin to recognize this common destination more clearly.

The "common destination" referred to is of course a spiritual one; it is the wave of enlightenment that Wallace hoped would sweep over the world, fundamentally altering people's social attitudes, generated out of the stringencies of the current economic collapse. Wallace said in a letter to Grant of 22 February 1932: "The great suffering now-a-days is undoubtedly harrowing the ground for the planting of seed. But it does not yet fully appear as to just what kind of seeds will be planted. When they are planted, the tender plants may grow a little slowly at first but the soil is so rich and so well prepared and so abundantly watered by the tears of suffering that I would expect a very abundant growth unless the weeds choke out the young plants during the next ten or fifteen years."

In the same letter one can see perhaps the last flickering of Wallace's critical detachment before he subordinated, for a time, his own judgment to the superior wisdom of Roerich and Grant:

You will remember that in a former letter to you, I did not show any great appreciation of Nicholas Roerich's book "The Realm of Light." In view of that fact, it may interest you to know that I am greatly impressed and delighted with the statement by Nicholas Roerich on page 3 of the February 1932 issue of the Roerich Museum Bulletin entitled, "Souls of the Peoples." This statement seems to me to be the essence of the book, "The Realm of Light."

I am afraid the thing that I did not altogether like about "The Realm of Light" was the effort which at the time I first read the book seemed to me just the least bit strained to find something nice about every race of people. Of course, we want that and I see now that the shortcoming was quite obviously in me and not in the book. At any rate, the book prepared me to appreciate the article, "Souls of the Peoples." [32]

During 1933 Wallace became actively involved in the Roerich campaign for persuading the U.S. government to sign the Roerich Pact. He wrote explicitly to Secretary of State Cordell Hull and President Roosevelt, yet at the same time he carried on a clandestine correspondence with Roerich and more prominently with Frances Grant about precisely the same campaign, using secret code names to conceal from outside readers the identity of the persons he was discussing and referring to the Peace Pact and Banner of Peace in the most elliptical terms. Hull was against the idea, despite his personal sympathy with the principles underlying it,[33] and Roosevelt too was initially reluctant, but that seems hardly reason enough for the Roerich group and Wallace to write each other in the manner in which they did. Their correspondence began to be bruited about during the 1940 presidential campaign as the "Guru letters," in an attempt to discredit Wallace as a running mate and thus damage Roosevelt's credibility. Because the authenticity of the letters was denied at the time, disputed for years after, and seriously questioned in Norman D. Markowitz's *Rise and Fall of the People's Century*, it is necessary, before going on, to examine the questions of whether they are what they purport to be and what their content signifies.

Subsequent to the publication of Markowitz's book, the Samuel Rosenman Papers in the Franklin D. Roosevelt Library were opened to public inspection, and 117 letters apparently written by Wallace to Roerich or to Frances Grant were discovered.[34] In addition, twenty-two letters that in 1947 and 1948 formed the basis of Westbrook Pegler's attack on Wallace can be found in the Pegler Papers in the Herbert Hoover Library, West Branch, Iowa, along with evidence of the journalist's vigorous attempts to authenticate them. He had sent the letters to an examiner of questioned documents who readily identified the handwriting in some of them (others were typed) as that of Wallace, as did two other experts he consulted.[35] Furthermore, the content of the letters, when one recognizes the identity of the persons and nations referred to in them by pseudonyms, fits so readily with the established facts, as revealed in State and Agriculture Department records and in Wallace's personal papers, of the two major projects on which Wallace and Roerich joined forces, that the authenticity of the letters seems hardly disputable.

The earliest known of these "Guru letters," actually addressed to "Dear Guru," was to Nicholas Roerich, dated 12 March 1933, when Roerich had apparently recently returned to the United States to promote the Banner of Peace. It is esoteric in its manner of expression and much of its content, but is not yet conspiratorial in tone — merely adulatory:

Dear Guru,

I have been thinking of you holding the casket — the sacred most precious casket. And I have thought of the New Country going forth to meet the seven stars under the sign of the three stars. And I have thought of the admonition "Await the Stone."

We await the Stone and we welcome you again to this glorious land of destiny, clouded though it may be with strange fumbling fears. Who shall hold up the compelling vision to these who wander in darkness? In answer to this question we again welcome you. To drive out depression. To drive out fear. We think of the People of Northern Shambhalla [*sic*] and the hastening feet of the successor of Buddha and the Lightning flashes and the breaking of the New Day.

And so I await your convenience prepared to do what I am here to do.

May Peace, Joy and Fire attend you as always.

G

In the great haste of this strange maelstrom which is Washington.[36]

The initial *G* with which Wallace signs himself stands, as later correspondence shows, for Galahad, the pseudonym Helena Roerich had given him. According to some Buddha legends, the Stone is an ancient spiritual relic that, whenever it appears, heralds the dawning of a new age. The reference to the People of Northern Shambhala may well have a particular relevance to what was to come later. The Buddhist concept of Shambhala is roughly comparable to the Christian one of the Kingdom of Heaven, but as well as referring to a spiritual state in which Infinite Grace will reign supreme, it is also, in some minds, an actual geographical location, somewhere in the mountains of Tibet, where the masters might still be found in physical form.

This belief is to be found quite clearly in Nicholas Roerich's book *Shambhala*. This contains an imaginary dialogue between a seeker from the West and a Tibetan Lama. In response to a question the Lama, intent on guarding the esoteric truth, says: "Great Shambhala is far beyond the ocean. It is the mighty heavenly domain. It has nothing to do with our earth." But the questioner has already advanced far in his search for knowledge. "Lama, we know the greatness of Shambala [*sic*]. We know the reality of this indescribable realm. But we also know about the reality of the earthly Shambhala." The Lama, though with dire warnings about what may be spoken of, does in effect admit the existence of the earthly Shambhala.[37] Wallace had certainly read *Shambhala*, as shown by some of his letters to Roerich and Frances Grant. The imagery in the letter quoted above is drawn from Roerich's *Heart of Asia*, which is in two parts, the second of which is also called "Shambhala" and includes a section headed "Prophecies of Shambhala and Maitreya." (According to some Buddhist scriptures, Maitreya is a future Buddha who will come into existence when, because of an increase in evil, this age comes to an end.) The suggestion that it is to be understood as a specific geographical region appears repeatedly in Roerich's books.[38] That Wallace in turn could refer to northern Shambhala suggests that he had accepted the idea that there was a geographical destination, as well as a spiritual one, in the search for sanctity and enlightenment. But that notion had not yet begun to translate itself into an attempt to locate such a place.

What was at hand was the Banner of Peace and the attempt to get the United States government to sign the Roerich Pact. A draft of the pact had been presented to the State Department by Roerich during the previous administration, in February 1930, but had been rejected on the grounds that the Hague Convention of 1907 already directed that cultural treasures be spared in time of war, and that the present "futile, weak and unenforcable" proposal would actually hinder the development of effectual international law.[39] Similar objections would be brought again by members of the Roosevelt administration, but the spirit of the New Deal was more sympathetic to the proposal than the Hoover administration had been. Three months after the "Dear Guru" letter quoted above, on 17 June 1933, Wallace wrote a letter addressed to Professor Roerich, to be forwarded by Frances Grant (Roerich had returned to the Himalayas), in explicit formal language, expressing his interest in the endeavor to create a community of feeling among all nations concerning the arts and sciences. Also, the symbol on the Banner of Peace—three red spheres within a circle, designed by Roerich— was itself of profound interest to him. It was appropriate, Wallace felt, that there should be a meeting in Washington to consider the banner, and he was happy to offer his cooperation. In August 1933, Wallace wrote officially to President Roosevelt, and then, with Roosevelt's permission, to Secretary of State Hull giving information about the Roerich Pact and Banner of Peace, saying, "This plan has deeply interested me since 1929." On 16 September in a letter to Louis Horch he agreed to serve either as protector or honorary president of the Roerich Peace Pact Convention to be held on 17 November, "provided it is understood that in so doing, I am acting in my personal capacity and not as an official of the American Government."[40]

Throughout the remainder of 1933 there was energetic official correspondence from Wallace to Hull, relaying information obtained from Frances Grant about various international meetings supporting the Banner of Peace, and to various other politicians, national and international, on the same theme. In September he introduced Louis Horch and Frances Grant to Secretary Hull so that they could solicit him, or some other representative of the government, to take part in a meeting to be held in Washington for the purpose of furthering the Roerich Pact and Banner of Peace. Hull, however, wrote Wallace on 29 September: "I have come to the conclusion that although the proposed Pact is based on principles for which I personally have the most sympathetic leanings, this Government cannot, nor can I as Secretary of State, at this time become associated with this movement."[41]

Later that year, W. M. Phillips, acting secretary of state in Hull's absence, raised again the issue of the 1907 Hague Convention preempting and making unnecessary the Roerich Pact, and Wallace replied at length, in polite terms barely concealing some asperity, quoting various international jurists to the effect that the proposed pact was much more definite and conclusive than the earlier convention—though how this could be so, because it imposed and could impose no sanctions, is not clear. Yet while this perfectly open, official advocacy was going on, a correspondence of a different character was taking place with Frances Grant. There is, for example, an undated letter addressed "Dear M" commenting on the correspondence with Assistant Secretary of State Phillips. Most letters addressed to "M" are to Frances Grant, according to the code worked out by the staff at the Franklin D. Roosevelt Library. "M" stands for "Modra," Grant's cultic name, one that connects her with the higher levels of the Buddhist pantheon. But "Dear M" occasionally means "Dear Master"—that is, Nicholas Roerich. Wallace wrote: "In reply to my letter on the implementing of the Hague Convention of 1907 I have received a very unsatisfactory letter from the Assistant to the Sour One. I am sure that someone wrote the letter for him. I have written a reply (not yet sent) but question the wisdom of arguing with underlings. Have been trying to get in touch with Gil Borges but he has been ill. Perhaps I should wait till Rowe arrives to make the strategic call." Rowe was director general and Borges assistant director of the Pan American Union, one of the sponsors of the Third International Roerich Peace Banner Convention. The "Sour One," or sometimes "S.O." or "S," is Cordell Hull, secretary of state. That undated letter evidently closely antedated one of 17 January 1934: "No cause for alarm as expressed in the letter which I received this afternoon. An infinite number of minor irritations of no real significance. Naturally I was annoyed by the letter from the Assistant to the Sour One. . . . The Sour One will be here next Monday. When should Rowe and I make our visit to the Sour One's superior? Or would Borges be better?"[42]

Wallace's questions about what he should do are not merely rhetorical. It becomes plain that he consulted Grant about what to do and carefully followed her instructions, which were given added authority by being represented as "indications from Morya through Modra." "Indications" are messages from the masters, of whom Morya was, according to legend, one of the most senior. Years later Rex Tugwell told Harold Ickes that Grant sometimes came to Washington and held lengthy discussions with Wallace in his office, "and, as Rex put it, they could not push her out."[43] The problem at this time was just when and how would it be most propitious for Wallace to approach President Roosevelt, the "Sour One's superior," to secure his support for the Roerich Pact.

There is an earlier letter, of 29 October 1933, addressed directly to "Dear Professor Roerich," the worshipful and cabalistic tone of which is typical of the Guru letters, and shows clearly the extent to which Wallace gave himself over to the interests of the Roerich group at this time.

Dear Professor Roerich:

In these days of fiery trouble we also find opportunity for doing many things. The indications of Morya through Modra have governed under the most difficult circumstances. Surrounding the One toward whom my efforts have been addressed are many loyal to his personality but false to his ideals. This extraordinary sliminess makes even simple problems difficult at times. The One has a lovely, upward-surging spirit with a certain appreciation of what he calls "hunches." Combined with this is a charming open mindedness which makes him the prey at times of designing people—for example the tigers [the code name for the Russians]. This past week I have talked on this matter both to him and the Sour One in the most emphatic terms.

The true pleasure in times like these is to turn occasionally to the consideration of the search as conducted by such as Appolonius, Origen or Akbar. This steadfast search, this throwing of the light ahead, this preparation for World Cultural Unity will make it possible for the human spirit to explore and appreciate the most undreamed of beauty. It is the opportunity for such appreciation by the deserving ones of the multitude that we are striving to purchase with our efforts. We hope to see you not only in this country but also against the background of the snowy peaks. Work to do and Bliss to contemplate.

HAW[44]

"World Cultural Unity" refers to Roerich's vision of the time when beauty shall rule the world. In *Beauty and Wisdom*, published in 1922, he had written: "The sign of beauty will open all sacred gates. Beneath the sign of beauty we walk joyfully. With beauty we conquer. Through beauty we pray. In beauty we are united. . . . And realising the path of true reality, we greet with a happy smile the future." Again, from *Paths of Blessing*, published in 1911: "Art will unify all humanity, art is one — indivisible. . . . Art is the manifestation of the coming synthesis."[45] The adoption of the Roerich Pact and Banner of Peace was to be one part of this all-embracing confluence of interests — it was that, as well as Roerich's dedicated self-worship, that made it so important to the Roerich group. The sentence "We hope to see you not only in this country but also against the background of the snowy peaks" near the end of the letter hints at the matter already in their thoughts — the expedition to central Asia.

Early in its course, the campaign for the Banner of Peace seemed to become linked in some obscure way with the world wheat conference, and with questions of trade with and possible recognition of the Soviet government. An undated letter from Wallace to Grant reads:

Sunday

Dear F.R.G.,

On Wednesday last I had an appointment with the chief and mentioned my interest in the B. of P. and indicated the symbolism of the banner and its idealistic importance. He at once began to draw his idea of a proper symbol for World Economic Peace. I enclose a copy of it herewith. . . .

Yesterday I took two men to call on the Chief concerning World Wheat Conference. As we left I gave him a copy of the Peace Pact book with a copy of his Economic Peace diagram on the outside. He was greatly pleased with seeing the photostatic copy of his idea and then looked at the book underneath. His eyes brightened and he said, — "Oh, yes — this is what you were telling me about. I will take it with me to read on the boat." He seemed genuinely interested.

On Wednesday I had been greatly discouraged because he had indicated merely that I should take up the matter of the form of my participation [in the Third International Conference?] either with him at some future time or with Secretary Hull.

The Chief reacts in many unexpected ways but I think progress has been made although perhaps in not quite the way you would ask.

I would now suggest that you draft a letter to the chief which I would sign covering briefly the most important points. Or should we be satisfied with gradual progress. . . .

Dr. Ezekiel [Mordecai Ezekiel, economist in the Department of Agriculture] had me eat lunch with Rabinoff—no harm done. The Pres. on Friday designated Henry Morgenthau Jr. to handle any transactions with the tigers [Russians].

It is all mixed up and progress will be very slow.

HAW [46]

The proposed wheat conference was overtaken and subsumed by the World Economic Conference in July 1933. Of course, the only connection between that and the Banner of Peace may have been that they happened to be mentioned at the same meeting between Roosevelt and Wallace, but in attaching Roosevelt's economic peace symbol to the Roerich Pact book, Wallace was certainly trying to link the two things together in Roosevelt's mind as complementing one another—as being on the side of world peace.

Another letter, also undated but seemingly coming some months later, reads:

Dear F—

I think you can direct queries to D. [Dunn, an officer of the State Department] with safety. Let me know if there is difficulty in this quarter.

You might write Secy. Perkins. She has splendid cultural impulses. I will give you a letter to her if you want to call on her.

Same with Secy. Ickes.

With regard to Russia the Chief has indicated that he wants assurances that they will stop all revolutionary propaganda not only in this country but also in Cuba and Mexico. . . .

Morgenthau has charge of all Russian negotiations but actually I think the thing is being fogged up. The Russian crops are not nearly as good as they are claiming. The whole thing depends on the President.

Probably you had best refer to me as Sec. of Agriculture.

No harm to ask Mrs. Roosevelt. Perhaps great good. . . .

HAW [47]

The reference to Roosevelt's conditions for recognizing the Soviets dates this letter to about September 1933. At this time, as a preliminary to recognition, Roosevelt had appointed Henry Morgenthau Jr. to open trade negotiations with the Soviets, one main object being to dispose of surplus U.S. primary products, especially cotton, in the hope of bringing about an increase in prices. Presumably the Russians, in Wallace's view, had overstated the prospects for their own crops in order to present themselves as not in desperate need. In August Morgenthau was able to report to the president that the Soviet Union wanted to buy $75 million of raw materials, and in turn was told that through other government channels they were seeking $50 million of machine goods. Such massive purchases, however, depended on the provision of large loans to the Soviets, and the need to make this transaction respectable in the public view was an additional motive for the president to move toward recognition. Recognition was consummated in November 1933, but Morgenthau's trade negotiations ran into intractable problems because of Secretary Hull's insistence that the Soviets repay the United States for debts contracted by the pre-Soviet Russian government. This would make the Soviets unable to afford the large purchases Morgenthau was hoping for.

In the letter above, Secretaries Perkins and Ickes were mentioned presumably as possible supporters of the Roerich Pact, having such "splendid cultural impulses." But why did Wallace immediately mention the difficulties in recognizing the Soviet government? What bearing might this have on the pact? In the letter quoted he gives no indication whether he regrets or is glad that there are difficulties. Although in later years he became famous for his advocacy of peaceful, cooperative relations with the Soviet Union, at this time he was opposed to recognition of the Soviets. He had a degree of admiration for the apparent economic success of the Soviet experiment, but, with his belief in the potential productivity and enterprise of the common man, he tended to distinguish in his thoughts between what the mass of the Russian people were doing and what their Communist rulers were doing. Writing to Cordell Hull on 29 September 1933, he said that although he had no sympathy with scare talk of the "Red menace," nevertheless "the Russian leadership is so utterly without religion, in our sense of the term, and so bitter regarding certain things which we hold dear, that I don't like to place ourselves in their hands by giving them the opportunity to disorganize our markets." Some of the letters to Grant suggest that he may have been encouraged in that opposition by the Roerich group. For example, he mentioned an old friend of his "who has seen visions all his life." In one of these, he saw "the terrible frightfulness of the Jewish communists. He agrees fully with you and our Mother [Helena Roerich] about the great mistake of the President [recognition?]. In fact aside from an unusual prejudice against the Jews his visions seem to check quite well. He says Stalin is a mere figure head— that the terrible ones are others and that the greatest martyrdom of all history has been the way in which these have slaughtered the spiritual and the Christian."[48]

Writing a few months later about the progress of plans for the Mongolian expedition, Wallace says: "It seems here at times as though our friend whom you call the m——re one [that is, "mediocre one," an unflattering name for FDR] is bound to bring about the greatest eventual activity of disintegrating forces. He is lovable and charming but at times does the most appalling things in the most heartless way. As to whether it is thoughtless or the result of a carefully thought out plan I have not yet been able to decide. He is set on developing large imports and exports with the dark ones and I am inclined to think last November certain commitments were made which none of us know about."[49]

As we have seen, the recognition of the Soviet government, which took place in November 1933, was involved in "developing large imports and exports" with the Soviet Union, so the expression "the dark ones" may refer to Communist, or "Red," Russians as distinct from anti-Communist, or "White," ones. The rapprochement between the United States and the Soviet Union, Wallace feared, might "activate disintegrating forces," which would disrupt the plans for the expedition. Although Roerich may have seemed to heal his breach with the Communists in 1926, we must remember that in 1919 he had published a pamphlet accusing them of the destruction of masses of art works; thus, he may have felt that it would be a mockery to have them as signatories of his pact. But of more practical import than that delicate point of principle were the prospects for success for the forthcoming expedition, in which he would unequivocally seek the help of White Russians for purposes of his own.

CONFLICT WITHIN THE DEPARTMENT OF AGRICULTURE: PURGE OF THE LIBERALS

While these disguised machinations were proceeding, Wallace was confronting serious and growing tensions within his department. The ambiguities of the Agricultural Adjustment Act had produced the kinds

Wallace during a tour of the farm country, June 1935. (Courtesy of the Associated Press)

of difficulties he had foreseen, and before long the AAA had become a battleground for reformers and agrarians Between the two groups lay fundamental differences in outlook. City-bred, highly educated, and often visionary, the reformers saw the new act as a vehicle for ambitious social and economic reform, a chance to help the sharecroppers of the South and to control the greedy processors, who exploited consumers and farmers alike. The agrarians, by contrast, were practical men who knew the problems of agriculture firsthand, and whose years of negotiations with farm leaders on the one hand and processors on the other had taught them what was possible. The conflict between these groups would not be resolved until Wallace's highly controversial purge of several leading liberals in early 1935, but was first epitomized in the clash between Jerome Frank and George Peek.

Impressed by Rex Tugwell's argument that the new act would produce litigation of great complexity and that in an era of reform men of vision and imagination would be required, Wallace had appointed the brilliant, socially committed Jerome Frank as general counsel of the AAA. A man of "great warmth of personality and broad knowledge," as Wallace described him, Frank "belonged to that school of legal thought which believed that the full social background should be looked into before arriving at a legal conclusion." It was precisely that characteristic that made him "completely anathema" to George Peek, whom Wallace chose to head the AAA. "There was bitter and undying hatred there," noted Wallace.[50]

Wallace favored Peek, a veteran of reform campaigns of the twenties, because he was trusted by the farm leaders, whose support would be needed if AAA programs were to succeed. He knew that Peek's views differed from his own — already Peek had told a Senate committee that acreage reduction was undesirable and probably would not work — but Wallace hoped that, within the wide ambit of the act, cooperation would be possible. But Peek quickly signaled his intentions by attempting to fire Jerome Frank, explaining to Roosevelt that, as an urban lawyer and a Jew, Frank would be unacceptable to farm leaders. Roosevelt at first acceded to the request, but Wallace and Tugwell were able to change his mind and Frank was, in effect, forced on Peek.[51]

In the coming months, Peek never tried to conceal his contempt for either Frank or the bright young lawyers he hired — Alger Hiss, Lee Pressman, Abe Fortas, Adlai Stevenson, and Thurman Arnold. Such men, he complained, knew nothing of farming. They "swarmed into Washington dangling Phi Beta Kappa keys . . . enveloped in the delusion that they carried with them the tablets containing a new dispensation." They were "boys with their hair ablaze."[52] On the other hand, Peek's agrarian virtues failed to impress Frank; to him, the administrator lacked vision, played too closely with the processors, and was intellectually obtuse.

Ignoring Frank, Peek appointed Fred Lee, experienced in farm legislation, as his personal legal adviser, paying him out of his own salary. He also brought in, as coadministrator, Charles Brand, secretary of the Fertilizer Association and a McNary-Haugen enthusiast. Wallace thought Brand, who had been a friend of his father, "a fine kind of person of the old-fashioned . . . type." Frank called him "a constipated owl."[53] Peek sought to raise farm prices through marketing agreements, under which processors, in return for exemption from antitrust laws, would agree to pay farmers more. To his mounting chagrin, Frank's Legal Division held these contracts up, scrutinizing them for signs of unfairness.

Wallace occupied something of a middle position. He liked Frank immensely, instinctively responding to the lawyer's broad social views; but he also had great respect for Peek, who had expended so much time and money in the farmers' cause. For a time he and Peek were able to cooperate. "You may be interested to know," Wallace wrote Dante Pierce in mid-June 1933, "that George Peek and I are getting along fine." (Charles Brand was "a little more difficult to handle because he is a typical office martinet . . . [who] insists in turning out a few handmade Packards when we need thousands of Fords.") Wallace could sympathize with Peek, too, when the administrator tangled with the department's technocrats — "these 'blankety-blank' theoreticians," Peek called them — who were also dedicated to agrarian reform. Wallace understood the practicalities of the situation. As farm editor and seed-corn grower he had dealt extensively with businessmen; yet his own expertise in statistics, mathematics, and economics allowed him to see the force of what men like M. L. Wilson and the brilliant Mordecai Ezekiel were saying. "It's in a way a difficult position to be in," he confided later to his interviewer, "to see good points of conflicting parties. I've been in that kind of a situation, I guess, pretty nearly all my life."[54]

If, in contests between men like Tugwell, Frank, and Wallace's personal assistant Paul Appleby on the one hand, and agrarians like Peek and Brand on the other, Wallace could more often than not be found on the reformers' side, his allegiance to them was never complete. His attitude toward the veteran reformer Frederick Howe illustrates this point. Wallace had insisted that a consumers' protection clause be included in the Agricultural Adjustment Act, and had actually drafted the clause himself (though with some lack of precision, as he ruefully admitted later). For Consumers' Counsel he had chosen Howe, "an old-fashioned liberal of the rather extreme sort," as Wallace described him, and Howe had selected as his assistant Gardner Jackson, who had helped to defend the anarchists Sacco and Vanzetti. But Wallace came to feel that

Howe and his staff had taken advantage of loose legislative drafting to distort his original intention: "They thought they had a mandate under the legislation to do a number of things which I never contemplated. Marketing agreements, for example, would have to pass through their hands. They slowed things up enormously, so it seemed to me."

Wallace reached the point, he says, where his philosophy went in one direction and Peek's in another, and he was relieved when Peek resigned in December 1933. But he denied that he forced Peek out or tried publicly to humiliate him, as the press of the day charged. "I had a press conference sometime in October in which I said I didn't have much faith in marketing agreements. I remember how surprised I was when the papers came out with stories that I had done the most successful job of throat-cutting that was ever done in Washington. . . . My statement was not made with that in mind." Peek's replacement, Chester Davis, was a man of wide practical experience, with whom Wallace had lobbied in the 1920s and whom he greatly admired, and when the struggle within the AAA quickly recurred, Wallace's reservations about the reformers increased: "When Chester had the same disagreements with some of these people that George had had, I was much more inclined to take Chester's word than I had George's. I knew that Chester was not directly affiliated with any trades, and I'd always had a suspicion that George might be. . . . I knew Chester well enough so that I had very great confidence in him."[55]

The issue that finally split the AAA in February 1935 concerned the impact of agricultural policies on the poor farmers of the South. Tenant farmers had not been represented in the discussions over the act and no protection for them had been included in it. Yet it should have been obvious that the programs of acreage reduction that the bill contemplated would reduce the demand for farm labor, threatening this already vulnerable class. That general problem was ignored in committee hearings on the bill, and when Wallace was asked how government payments would be distributed between landowners and their tenants, he replied vaguely that it would be done through administrative regulation.[56]

But no sooner was the cotton program under way than complaints from tenants began to reach Wallace's office. Under AAA contracts, growers who agreed to plow up their cotton fields were instructed to divide government payments with their tenants according to each tenant's interest in the crop. Many did not do so, using the money to settle outstanding debts or simply refusing to pass it on. In some cases, with the need for labor now reduced, they evicted tenants. In choosing to work through landlords, the AAA had tried to simplify a huge administrative task; obtaining contract signatures from one million landlords was difficult enough—obtaining them from a much larger number of tenants, many of them illiterate, must have seemed all but impossible. AAA officials knew, too, that paying tenants directly might disturb traditional social relationships in the South, putting in jeopardy the cooperation of landlords on which the entire program depended.[57]

As protests increased, the AAA tried to help. It sent troubleshooters into the cotton areas to report on contract compliance and set up a series of committees, county and departmental, to deal with complaints. But none of these measures was particularly effective; county committees tended to be dominated by landlords, and within the department's Committee on Violations, representatives of the AAA's Cotton Division faced off against Jerome Frank's legal staff. The cotton contract for 1934–35 did try to give tenants more effective protection—in an attempt to halt evictions, paragraph 7 required a landlord to "insofar as possible, maintain on his farm the normal number of tenants and other employees," but paragraph 7 became subject to different interpretations and it was over these that the crisis in the AAA developed.[58]

It was precipitated when Jerome Frank discovered that the Cotton Division had taken paragraph 7 to mean that a landlord must merely retain the same number of tenants as in 1933, not the identical tenants. With Chester Davis away from Washington, Frank persuaded Davis's assistant to instruct all field agents in the Cotton Division to take no further action in relation to paragraph 7 until its meaning could be clarified—an edict that caused consternation in the cotton areas. Frank then ordered his Opinions Division to determine whether the Cotton Division's interpretation was legally binding, and when told that it was not, instructed the division to prepare a new interpretation. In early January 1935, the Opinions Division reported that paragraph 7 required landlords to keep the identical tenants.[59]

Davis returned to a deluge of complaints from landlords and county agents that the new ruling had put the cotton program in jeopardy. He confronted Wallace. Suppose the new interpretation were to be applied in Iowa, he suggested; suppose such a retroactive determination were to be made midway through a two-year corn-hog contract; what would Wallace think? "I'd say it was crazy," Davis reported Wallace as replying. "It's an utterly impossible, impractical thing." "Think how much worse it is when you project that into this explosive southern situation," Davis retorted. Davis also pointed out that, in discussions over the 1934–35 cotton contract, Frank's Legal Division had said nothing about the interpretation on which it had now insisted. Moreover, both Davis and Wallace, in official publications, had endorsed the Cotton Division's view. The AAA administrator now sought Wallace's permission to dismiss those responsible for the new interpretation—Frank, Lee Pressman, and Francis Shea among others—and Wallace told him to go ahead. Davis also invited the secretary to fire Paul Appleby, Wallace's chief assistant, who had become deeply involved in the tenant controversy, but Wallace refused.[60]

Wallace's action in purging the liberals has been seen as seriously compromising his liberalism, certainly during the first Roosevelt administration. He had lived with the tensions in the AAA from the beginning and had certainly not seemed unsympathetic to the reformers' cause. Why, his critics wanted to know, had he found it necessary now to repudiate them—men like Rex Tugwell, the reformers' acknowledged leader, now "heartsick" over the purge,[61] and Jerome Frank, whose vision of social justice he had seemed to share? Why had he effectively turned his back on the rural poor whom the farm program had failed to reach and in many cases helped to oppress?

Wallace's explanation may be read in the entries in his diary for the days leading up to the dismissals. At a secret meeting with Davis three days before the purge, he found the administrator "much disturbed," convinced of "definite intrigue" against him by Frank, Appleby, and others in the liberal group, some of whom were "socialists." Frank's reinterpretation of paragraph 7 had been designed, Davis complained, to make him, Davis, appear the mouthpiece of landlords and processors. Wallace discounted Davis's conspiratorial notions, attributing them to his overwrought state. He accepted that some of the reformers were "definitely irreligious," but felt that they were "wholeheartedly in favor of bringing about a situation where there can be a happier life in the United States." Returning to the question of motivation the following day, he wrote that the leaders of both factions were "honest and earnest," and that their "intriguing" was, on the whole, "rather unconscious" and probably inevitable in an administration whose objectives were "experimental and not clearly stated."

On the day before the purge, Wallace consulted statistician Louis

Bean, "a close friend of all of the people concerned," who hesitated to take sides but intimated that Davis would be important to the agricultural program for some time to come. Wallace concluded, after a discussion with Davis and Seth Thomas, general counsel of the department, that his press release the previous May "seems undoubtedly to show the interpretation which the department placed on Section 7 last spring" and that "this . . . is also the interpretation of common sense." Frank and the other liberals "were animated by the highest of motives," but "their lack of an agricultural background apparently exposes them to the danger of going to absurd lengths. . . . They allowed their social pre-conceptions to lead them into something which was not only indefensible from a practical agricultural point of view but also bad law." Still uncertain as to the timing of the dismissals, Wallace talked with the trusted M. L. Wilson, "usually a great conciliator [who] prefers to delay action." Wilson "hated to come to any conclusion on this particular situation because he has such high esteem for all the parties concerned, but he finally reached the conclusion that prompt action is probably wise." Wallace told Davis to go ahead.[62]

The diary entries show Wallace as sympathetic to both sides, hesitant to impugn motives, determined, as he was pushed toward a decision he hated to make, to be fair. What they do not report is the emotional storm the events provoked in him. Immediately after the purge he had agreed to see two representatives of the excluded group—Jerome Frank and Alger Hiss. Though Wallace describes Hiss as being in a highly emotional state, his account of this meeting is detached, almost matter-of-fact. Frank and Hiss "sketched out their position on Section 7 of the cotton contracts." Their case "sounded entirely reasonable and straightforward . . . just as good as that presented by Chester Davis." Wallace assured them that he had not questioned their loyalty but explained that the administrative situation had to be straightened out. But Gardner Jackson, who with the other purged liberals received a report on the same meeting, tells a different story. "We had a picture . . . of tears in Wallace's eyes, down his cheeks, saying to Jerome that he had to do it, or words to that effect. Jerome said, 'Why didn't you tell us? We might have differed, but we would have understood the necessities you felt.' Wallace said to Jerome encomiums of praise for all of us, saying what wonderful fighters we all were for a good cause, never had he worked for such fellows, and so on. He just couldn't face us." Wallace must have felt deeply guilty over the firing, as if it were an act of betrayal. His emotion shows also that he hated personal confrontation. Russell Lord reported that quarreling literally made Wallace ill, and Wallace explains in his oral history that he could not get along with Harold Ickes because Ickes "instinctively makes a fuss about things. He thinks I'm morally culpable because I don't." The significance of this attitude — which may possibly be linked to his early religious training, the feeling that anger and aggression were wrong — will become plainer as this study proceeds, but is suggested in a comment Wallace made in 1953, near the end of his interview: "I don't see the need for things like that [the breakdown in relationships leading to the 1935 purge]. . . . It's the same thing, on a big scale, between Russia and the United States now."[63]

However strong Wallace's personal feelings may have been, in the end it was his practicality that won out, just as it had in the matters of the cotton plow-in and pig slaughter, and in his pursuit of crop reduction even while invoking a vision of abundance. This was the practicality that had so impressed him in his father. He could agree with Frank and Tugwell, that Chester Davis lacked vision, but he realized that Davis "more nearly has the necessary experience and grasp of all details of the agricultural situation than anyone else who could be used at this time to run the AAA." Perhaps the goals of the liberals were higher than those of Davis, but they wanted to proceed too fast. "I knew," he said later, "that what Jerome Frank and his helpers, Alger Hiss and Lee Pressman, were urging would utterly alienate key southern Congressmen whose support we had to have to keep the program going." Had he listened to the liberals, "it would have shortened and diminished the possibility . . . of carrying on the liberal program as long as we did."[64]

There were many liberals at the time who would not have agreed with this assessment, who saw the purge as the end of their hopes for fundamental social and economic change, and the "liberal program" to which Wallace here referred as but a pale reflection of their original goals. What they could not have known was that Wallace had by then embraced objectives more visionary than any they had imagined, whose realization would have brought the fulfillment of even their most ambitious dreams.

4

FALSE PROPHET

THE ROERICH CONNECTION AND THE

EXPEDITION TO MONGOLIA

The 1934–35 expedition to Inner Mongolia was the second major project into which Wallace was to enter with the Roerichs. It is difficult to judge when and by whom the trip was first suggested. In later years, during his oral history interviews, when he had long been concerned to distance himself from the expedition and from the Roerichs in general, Wallace suggested that it was really Roosevelt's proposal. By Wallace's account, Roosevelt thought that some drought-resistant grasses in the Gobi Desert could be of use in the dry areas of the United States, and Wallace told the president that in the case of crested wheat grass this had already been proved to be correct. Then, in December 1933, Roosevelt "speculated with me about an expedition to Tibet." Both of them were acquainted with Nicholas Roerich; Wallace had met him on one occasion in August 1929, and Roosevelt "had known of him when he was governor and referred to him affectionately." Roosevelt knew of Roerich's travels in central Asia, and "we decided to ask Nicholas Roerich to head the expedition."[1]

Wallace dates the talk with Roosevelt to December 1933, but on the preceding 2 August he had written to W. H. Woodin, secretary of the treasury, reminding him of a conversation they had had about Frances

Grant and her reports of the drug plants grown in northern India and southern Tibet. Woodin had suggested that Grant prepare a statement of the plants' potential benefits, with a view to investigation either by the Public Health Service or perhaps some private foundation. Grant had now put together such a statement and Wallace wanted to know whether she could present it to Woodin at his New York home. Her intention, presumably, was to persuade the Treasury to put up funds for some as yet undefined scientific expedition. Woodin wrote asking her to send him the plan of research and material about the Himalayan Research Institute and the Roerich Museum "for joint consideration." She sent this and gave Wallace a copy. Later in August, Wallace was instrumental in getting her an appointment with Jesse Jones, chairman of the Reconstruction Finance Corporation, providing letters of introduction to Grant and Louis Horch, saying that the Roerich Museum was a "cultural institution in which I have long been interested. I do not know if there is any way that your organization can be of help to the museum, but, in any event, I would appreciate greatly the courtesy which you might extend Miss Grant. Perhaps put her in touch with the right people to handle her problem."[2]

Evidently Wallace was persuaded that the Treasury Department would provide funds for a central Asian expedition, and the Department of Agriculture began planning for it. On 3 December 1933 Wallace wrote to the president, reminding him of his suggestion that an expedition might be sent to the Gobi Desert of Mongolia to find drought-resistant grasses that might be useful on the American Great Plains. He pointed out that "the political situation in this part of the world is always rendered especially intriguing by the effect on it of ancient prophecies, traditions, and the like." The man best acquainted with such prophecies and traditions and their likely effects was Professor Nicholas Roerich, and Wallace specifically proposed him as the expedition's mentor. But officials within Wallace's own department were allowed to operate on the assumption that the expedition would be headed by two botanists of the Bureau of Plant Industry, Howard G. MacMillan and James L. Stephens, and that Knowles Ryerson, head of the bureau, would be the overall director, based in Washington.[3]

On 16 March, Wallace wrote Roerich, asking him to "lead and protect the botanical research group organized by the United States Department of Agriculture to search for drought resistant grasses in the central Asian field." Yet although this letter reads as an official invitation, it was not made known to the relevant officers of the Department of Agriculture, nor, more important, to the Department of State, which surely would have been interested in the question of who was leading an American government expedition to countries with which the United States had very delicate relations. Its function, rather, seems to have been simply to provide Roerich with a document he could present to government officials of the countries he would visit, claiming it as official accreditation from the U.S. secretary of agriculture. Roerich's letter of acceptance, 20 March 1934, has something of the same tone, as a public declaration of his credentials for the post:

Dear Mr. Secretary,

I have received your letter of March 16th, in which you invite me, on behalf of the Department of Agriculture, to act as leader and protector of the botanical expedition organized by the United States Department of Agriculture to search for drouth resistant grasses in the central Asia field.

For the past thirty-five years I had been working in the interests of the United States and during the last decade, I have been working in behalf of this country as an officer of an American institution, leading the American Expedition into Asia, and following this, as head of the Himalayan Research Institute, an American Educational corporation. Thus, your proposal coincides with my closest interests and is a natural continuation of my years of activity in this field.

It is therefore with pleasure that I accept your invitation, and I confidently anticipate that the work of this expedition will lead to new scientific benefits for America.

Very truly yours,
N. de Roerich.[4]

Of course, the "American Expedition into Asia" was in fact a quite private and self-interested enterprise, and the provision of "new scientific benefits for America" was hardly Roerich's goal, even in the most nominal way. Even in Wallace's mind, the expedition appears to have had both a declared and an undeclared aim. There is no reason to doubt that the desire and intention to procure drought-resistance grass strains, and perhaps medicinal plants useful in the treatment of cancer and other diseases, were genuine motives, but the search for new spiritual truth may have been an additional motive. At this time, it is possible that Wallace believed in the living masters' physical existence, and perhaps that they would reveal something of the coming of that Christlike figure, the Maitreya, who would transform the whole world in the ideal state of Shambhala. Perhaps Nicholas Roerich, too, actually believed in the masters and the possibility of contacting them, but he also had positive, if difficult to understand, political goals, involving both the Japanese and the White Russians of Manchuria. These in turn, as we shall see, may have been subsidiary to yet another aim, the acquisition of land or some other real property in Mongolia.

Roerich was to be accompanied by his son George, who dealt with the practical and financial arrangements with Wallace, as secretary of agriculture, before their departure, and also liaised with Ryerson concerning the general outlines of the botanical researches. Ryerson, however, thought that both Nicholas and George were simply fellow travelers, rather than that Nicholas was the appointed leader. Nicholas and George left for Japan, independently of the Bureau of Plant Industry's two botanists, early in May 1934. They still had not been given official accreditation. Wallace was intentionally bypassing the State Department, as shown by a letter of the preceding March to "Dear M," "M" in this instance almost certainly referring to Frances Grant, as the letter lacks the reverential tone of his correspondence with Roerich. It is businesslike, wheeling and dealing:

Dear M,

Talked with our R. [Ryerson] today and gave him George's pencil memorandum but not the written memorandum. He says they have always cleared in the past through the State Dpt. and the Embassy concerned and not through the Consul. I am convinced that it is wise for me to pay an informal call on Mr. S. of the Embassy in Washington. Would you care to have the Counsel [sic] write S. that I will be calling on him or shall I call on him on my own Friday or Saturday of this week?

Transportation if it is to be paid for must be on American boats. There may be a little trouble arranging the effective date of the beginning of salaries as suggested [George had wanted them to start before departure]. In fact it seems to me to be decidedly wise to delay the effective date till the arrival in M. If it were not for the stop in J. and the travel in the foreign boat the trouble would not be present.

Progress has been made but the difficulties I have to overcome are greater than you realize.

By the by the final bill is thru. All is really going very well.

Yours

G.

May the vibrancy of Maitreya Sanka stir all our hearts.[5]

One of the mysteries of this letter is the identity of the embassy and the consul in question. Because the Roerichs were planning a two-week stopover in Japan, it may have been the Japanese embassy, but such a visit would require only a visa, readily obtained. It seems as though some more important clearance were required. Wallace refers to their "arrival in M." "M" could stand for Manchuria or Manchukuo, the Japanese puppet state recently set up in Manchuria, but it seems highly unlikely that there should be any proposal of getting a clearance for Manchukuo (despite the fact that the Roerichs did go there after Japan), because it was not recognized by the United States — and of course there was no Manchukuo embassy in Washington.

The third possibility is that "M" stands for Mongolia, which was the expedition's official destination. Mongolia had become an independent Communist state, but it was heavily under the influence and protection of the Soviet government, with many Soviet troops in the country. Perhaps Wallace and the Roerichs felt it necessary to get a clearance from Russia. During the period of the nonrecognition of the Soviet government there had been no Soviet ambassador to the United States, but there was a Russian consulate general in New York to issue passports, birth certificates, and the like, and it may well have been the case that the Russian Roerichs and their friends at the museum, having had transactions with Russia arising out of Roerich's 1926 visit there, had come to know the consul. Wallace's letter presumes a certain influence over the consul on the part of its addressee, as being able to "have the Counsel [*sic*] write S. that I will be calling on him." This was "Mr. S. of the Embassy in Washington," and the fact that the consul was to write him rather than, say, telephoning, further suggests that the consul was in New York rather than in Washington. The interim Soviet chargé d'affaires in Washington was in fact a "Mr. S." — Mr. B. Shvirsky — yielding the conclusion that all this roundabout procedure was probably directed to getting the Roerichs established in Mongolia. The major point is precisely its roundaboutness, whatever the actual identity of the consul and Mr. S. may have been. Wallace could not clear through the State Department, because he must have known that Professor Roerich was a potential security risk in their eyes and that he certainly would not have been acceptable to them as the leader of a United States government expedition into politically sensitive areas.

This subterfuge, if such it was, could not long go undetected. On 7 May the American ambassador in Tokyo telegraphed the State Department in Washington that he had been apprised of the imminent arrival in Tokyo of Professor Nicholas Roerich, "presumably in connection with the cultural activities of the Roerich Museum." Should he afford Professor Roerich appropriate assistance? The State Department, having no knowledge that Roerich was connected with an official expedition for the Department of Agriculture, replied, informing the ambassador that so far as they knew, Professor Roerich was not an American citizen, that no American passport had been issued to him, and that according to their files Professor Roerich was the cause of some embarrassment in India when he made visits in 1924 and 1930.

But the following day another telegram from the State Department to the ambassador in Tokyo informed him that Professor Roerich was a personal friend of the secretary of agriculture, Mr. Wallace, and that Mr. Wallace would appreciate greatly any courtesies the ambassador might appropriately extend him. The department did not, however, expect the ambassador to take any action that might later embarrass himself or the United States, in view of Professor Roerich's previous record and citizenship status.[6]

The Roerichs duly reached Tokyo, and Arthur Garrels, American consul general there, summed up their activities in a telegram to the secretary of state. On their arrival, Nicholas and George "entered upon a field of more or less personal publicity through interviews and public addresses," but "neither Professor de Roerich nor his son in public addresses nor in conversation as far as the Consulate General knows, ever alluded to their connection with the group of the United States Department of Agriculture." The Roerichs in fact had never called at the consulate, and Garrels had learned of their activities only from reports in the press. Neither he nor anyone else in the embassy or consulate knew that they were employed by the American government. The Roerichs had made a call at the Japanese War Ministry, visited the Meiji shrine, and given interviews to the press, all the time stressing the professor's eminence as a world cultural leader.[7]

On 8 June, Garrels sent a telegram to the State Department saying that Roerich had requested the Cultural Works Bureau of the Japanese Foreign Office (their propaganda medium) to act as an intermediary for him to secure from the government of Manchukuo facilities for the expedition. To back up this request he showed them the letter from Henry Wallace requesting him "to lead and protect the botanical research group organized by the United States Department of Agriculture," and on that basis the Japanese Foreign Office gave him letters of accreditation addressed to the Manchukuo authorities. This telegram gave the Department of State its first indication that Roerich was supposed to have an official role in the Department of Agriculture's expedition, which, because of the United States' attitude toward Manchukuo, was sufficiently disturbing to Cordell Hull for him to cable the embassy in Tokyo, on 11 June, that "it now appears that Roerich is the leader of research group sent out by the Department of Agriculture which fact was not repeat not previously known to Department." He warned that the Tokyo embassy should neither trust nor give unusual assistance to the Roerichs.[8] But by this time the Roerichs were no longer in Tokyo. What their overall goal was remains obscure, but their calls on the Japanese War Ministry and Foreign Office can hardly have been arbitrary. It was as if Roerich were professing his approval of the Japanese military incursions on the mainland. If so, it was in order to advance his own interests.

Botanists MacMillan and Stephens landed at Yokohama and went on to Tokyo on 2 June, but the Roerichs had left on 24 May and by this time were in Mukden, Manchuria. MacMillan was already very skeptical of the Roerichs' intentions, and wrote ironically to Ryerson that their stay in Tokyo had been a "brilliant progression from triumph to triumph." MacMillan traveled about Tokyo for several days, contacting the consul and the embassy, trying without success to hire a Japanese botanical assistant, and arranging for Russian visas rather than Manchukuo visas to go to Manchuria. He began to get a picture of what conditions were like in Harbin, where they were bound: "There are over 70,000 white Russians in the town, and a considerable group of reds. The whole section is in the nebulous area where trouble begins to concentrate. . . . I am concerned to know that with the present set-up we can do any work of the kind we propose to do."[9]

The botanists left Tokyo late in June and went to Dairen, en route to Mukden in Manchuria. In Dairen they began to run into awkwardness and delays arising solely from the fact that the Roerichs had preceded them, seeking facilities for nominally the same expedition, but without proper authorization. The same problems arose when they reached Hsinking. On 20 July MacMillan wrote to Garrels: "There had been a growing suspicion that everything was not just right soon after Professor Roerich landed in Manchukuo. There was an organized propaganda in all the papers about him, all the Russian papers in Harbin carried long interviews in which a great deal seems to have been said. Then he came to Hsinking to make the presentation to the Emperor of the Banner of Peace and the Order of Merit. On arrival in Hsinking the Professor distributed hand-bills to all comers giving in some detail the more commonplace contributions to culture which he had made, with some inconspicuous details of his life." This last is another bit of MacMillan's heavy sarcasm. He enclosed a copy of the handbill, which described in glowing hyperbole Roerich's preeminence in archaeology, art and science, and referring to his "latest creation," the plan for the Roerich Pact with the Banner of Peace. It was emblems of this, of course, that he had presented to the Japanese puppet emperor Pu Yi, for "resplendent merits" in the field of culture, thus raising cries of protest in the American State Department. During these exploits the professor was accompanied by an escort of White Russians in Cossack uniform. Again affirming, implicitly, his support of the Japanese occupation of Manchuria, the handbill went on to say that Roerich had "constantly expressed his admiration for Japanese art and culture, . . . [and] voiced his conviction of the splendid destiny of Japan in its advance towards cultural ascendancy." MacMillan goes on to complain that, because of the Roerichs' activities, he had been held up while the Japanese authorities sought further information about him. Had he not been associated with the Roerichs, he could have begun his botanical work much earlier.[10]

After further trouble, MacMillan managed to get in touch with George Roerich in Harbin but was not able to see the professor. On 1 August 1934, both parties left for Hailar on the same train, but during a long journey had no contact with each other. On reaching Hailar, MacMillan and Stephens presented their credentials to the Japanese military commander, Saito, and were told that they were in order. However, a few hours later they got a telephone call at their hotel to go back to see the commander immediately. The Roerich party had visited him soon after MacMillan's group had left, and Professor Roerich had claimed to be the leader of the bipartite expedition and to have the authority to give MacMillan orders. He had announced that he was leaving for southern regions, but had ordered MacMillan to stay in Hailar and work on plants. The commander wanted to know what Mac-Millan had to say about that.

According to his earlier letters to Ryerson, MacMillan had always intended to stay in Hailar and work on plants, in fact had insisted to George Roerich that his group would go no further this season at least, but he was a tough-minded, independent man and the professor had annoyed him. As he reported to Ryerson: "I said that my authority did not come from Professor Roerich, that I was ordered by my Department to do certain work, such as I had outlined, and showed my Letter of Introduction. . . . The only purpose [Roerich] had so far as I was concerned was to protect the party. . . . I did not recognize any power on his part to give me orders or direct my work, or claim that he had ordered me to remain in Hailar." Both parties were summoned again to the commander's rooms the following day, whereupon Roerich produced the letter Wallace had given him. There was a long discussion between the Japanese about its genuineness, as it was quite unlike the botanists' accreditation. MacMillan said that he did not care whether the Roerichs went on or not; he just wanted to be left alone to do his work.

MacMillan described to Ryerson the departure of the Roerichs and their six Russian attendants: "They had a big automobile for the principal members of the party, and a truck for the equipment and musical comedy army. All were in Cossack uniform, which seems about as bad taste as anything under the circumstances." The letter continued, in prophetic vein: "I did not see the Professor at any time; nor have I had any word from him. . . . Under the circumstances it will be impossible to have any more contact with them, though I know there are going to be loud reports about lack of cooperation. I anticipate any amount of trouble after I get back over this affair, and of course they have the inside track in the matter. If I get fired it will be nothing more than I expect."

Despite this unpleasant prospect, MacMillan and his assistants began work promptly on the grasses in the plains around the town. His account of this has every mark of professionalism and shows why he had declared that there was no point in traveling about, stopping for a day or so and then moving on, as the Roerichs had planned to do. It was necessary to wait and see what stage the various grasses were at, when they would drop their seed, when roots could be taken, and so on.[11] Yet despite the solid work on which he could report, confirmed by the many packets of seeds and roots and information regarding them that he despatched back to the department, the trouble he anticipated was not long in coming.

On the same date, 11 August 1934, that MacMillan was reporting the trouble at Hailar to Ryerson, Ryerson was writing to MacMillan asking what he knew about the Roerichs' projected itinerary, which they had not really made clear to him, and sending a message from Wallace to MacMillan. The secretary was "very anxious that you work very closely and cooperate with the Roerichs in every way."[12] Evidently the Roerichs had begun complaining to Wallace even before the confrontation.

On 20 September Wallace sent a telegram to MacMillan and Stephens instructing them to return immediately to the United States, and another to Nicholas Roerich, saying, "Regret exceedingly insubordination MacMillan stop Am recalling him and Stephens." On 27 September he wrote George C. Hanson, consul general at Harbin, and Commander Saito at Hailar, saying that he had recalled MacMillan and Stephens "for insubordination and failure to carry out instructions on the expedition." He declared the department's good fortune in having secured Professor Roerich's cooperation as leader of the expedition, and defined the expedition as also comprising "such native personnel as Professor Roerich finds it necessary to add to his staff for the success of the work." Furthermore, "Professor Roerich's actions have my entire approval and confidence." Wallace had swung his weight entirely behind the Roerichs, and destroyed MacMillan and Stephens's credibility. In a letter to Professor Roerich of the same date, Wallace expressed his "regret and indignation at the insubordination of these two members of the expedition" and assured him of his "complete confidence and approval" in all the professor's actions in regard to the expedition.[13]

On 1 October 1934 Nicholas and George furnished "a brief report on the scientific activities of the expedition," apparently in response to Wallace's relaying a message that President Roosevelt had asked for one. A good deal of this is taken up with blaming MacMillan and Stephens for their lack of cooperation, which was supposed to have delayed the beginning of the scientific work by more than a month. As we have seen, the two botanists attributed the delay to the authorities' suspicions having been aroused by the unorthodox behavior of the Roerichs as they preceded them. Evidently the Roerichs had been provided with a copy of a long accusatory letter that MacMillan had sent to Ryerson and were setting about to undercut this by accusing him of just the same misdemeanors of which he had accused them. The charge that they were being accompanied by Cossack guards, they assured Wallace, was absurd. Wallace really had no evidence either way about the conflicting statements before him, but he had no hesitation about whom to believe.[14]

MacMillan and Stephens were dismissed. Wallace's coded letters to Grant show that he had a confrontation with Ryerson over the matter. He wrote:

> One and two carried out. Gave our friend [Ryerson] choice of signing the second. He preferred not. He proclaimed the strain of divided loyalties and nearly wept. Said trouble arose in first place because Father [Nicholas Roerich] did not remain long enough in the l of r [land of rulers — Japan] to enable the Bees [botanists — MacMillan and Stephens] to catch up with him. When the Bees were delayed so long at D [Dairen] he said G [George] should have come down and helped them. He thought Father and G at least equally to blame and felt action [presumably the sacking of MacMillan and Stephens] unfair.
>
> Used arguments to prevent but in a restrained way action One and Two. Very much wanted S [Stephens] to remain in the south and grievously disappointed at decision.
>
> Indicates his thoughts all for protecting Gal [Galahad — Wallace] and fears repercussions and publicity. Would like to relieve G [Galahad] of this and save his strength for bigger and nobler things.

It is not possible to say confidently what actions One and Two were, but the probability is that they included the recall and sacking of MacMillan and Stephens. Wallace was giving Ryerson the choice of assuming the responsibility for that in place of himself. Ryerson's "divided loyalties" were between his staff men, MacMillan and Stephens, on the one hand, and Wallace, who had sided with the Roerichs, on the other.

Ryerson's protestations that he wanted only to protect Wallace were in vain. It seems that Wallace consulted Frances Grant on what to do about Ryerson, and she advised a hard line. He wrote her in October 1934: "Cable sent read transfer or demote. Cable received transfer and demote. I assume this means transfer from present position to a lower one. If I am incorrect write me at once. This of course with regard to R.

[Ryerson]." This reads as if he had asked her whether to transfer or demote Ryerson and she had replied that he should do both. That sealed Ryerson's fate. Ryerson was demoted and transferred to the Division of Subtropical Horticulture. In Wallace's letter notifying him of this, he wrote: "You were fully aware that Professor Roerich was the leader of this expedition. I can, therefore, only regard the matter as one of serious insubordination. The rumors which you mention concerning Professor Roerich are not only ridiculous but extremely malicious, and indicate ignorance of his outstanding achievements for the last forty years."[15]

This left the Roerichs somewhere in the Inner Mongolian Autonomous Region as leaders of an American expedition untrammeled by the presence of any American officials. Only an impressionistic picture of the group's movements can be built from this point on, based on reports Nicholas Roerich occasionally sent to Wallace and on State Department reports of what various interested parties had told it. In October 1934, the Roerichs spent some time in the Khingan Mountains region gathering seeds. The following month, the professor telegraphed Wallace asking him to get War Department authority for the ordnance officer with the United States Army forces in Tientsin to provide the expedition with rifles and ammunition, and subsequently the commanding officer received such authorization. The American minister in Peiping, Nelson Trusler Johnson, gave the State Department an account of a conversation he had in early April 1935 with Mr. Pao Yueh-ch'ing, representing the Teh Wang, prominent politically in Inner Mongolia. Pao stated that "Professor Roerich had recently visited the camp of the Teh Wang accompanied by his son and four White Russian guards" and explained to the Mongols that "wealthy Americans would be glad to assist the Mongols in building up a thriving business, in this way bringing about a closer relationship between the people of America and the people of Mongolia."[16] In talking about wealthy Americans who would "be glad to assist the Mongols in building up a thriving business," Roerich may have been doing more than engaging in benevolent generalities. It seems there was a further, as yet unrevealed, purpose of the expedition.

Early in January 1935, Wallace had written to Frances Grant the following mysterious letter. In it, Roosevelt, who previously had been referred to as "the Flaming One" for his soaring, fiery spirit, has been demoted to "WO," "the Wavering One," perhaps because of his noncommittal attitude to the Roerich Pact:

How about presenting to the WO the Kansas idea, as one in which father [Roerich] is interested. Suggest that a strong Kansas might check the rulers [Japanese] and make for a balanced situation. Paint the Kansans as very picturesque and worth preserving in their own right. Get WO blessing and suggestions. Will not act till I hear from you.

Have already written air mail to the listed one. [?]

Talked with the man who represents us with the tigers [that is, Henry Morgenthau, negotiating with the Soviets] at some length. He reports that those who live to the east and south of Kansas are likely to be seriously damaged by recent monetary policies and thus will be forced into arms of rulers. Therefore he is much disturbed.[17]

It is certain that the "Kansas" referred to is not the Kansas of the United States. The "recent monetary policies" were presumably those flowing from the Pitman Silver Purchase Act passed in June 1934, which empowered the Treasury, Morgenthau's department, to buy silver at home and on world markets to push up its price, thus diminishing the bounty the American government had to pay to U.S. silver producers — paying \$1.29 when the ruling price was \$.45. The silver producers argued that the subsidy price would raise silver prices on world markets and give China, which had been accumulating silver for centuries, enough funds to purchase American goods, thus helping the economy to recover. But China had been an importer of silver, not a producer of it. Morgenthau had information that when the price of silver rose above its currency value, Chinese nationals, abetted by Japanese, smuggled it out of the country and sold it on world markets. In Morgenthau's view, this was, for Japan, a useful way of weakening China and the government of Chiang Kai-shek.

Both Hull and Morgenthau wanted to help China, but came into conflict as to how it might be done. Morgenthau favored assisting China to reorganize its currency, but Hull feared that if American currency became linked to the Chinese yuan it might be dragged down with it through the administrative difficulties of that riven country. Morgenthau attributed Hull's opposition to an excessive concern for Japan's opinion; Hull did not want to dispute Japan's claim to an interest in any developments involving China. Morgenthau believed that Japan's demands on China, unabated after its conquest of Manchuria in 1931, when it had set up the puppet state of Manchukuo, threatened the peace not only of the Orient but also of the world. If the United States did not support China, he feared that would mean abandoning the area entirely to Japan and Great Britain. Thus, we see that "those who live to the east and south of Kansas," in Wallace's letter, who were in danger of being "forced into the arms of the rulers," almost certainly meant the Chinese. That would mean that Kansas was Mongolia, which was and is embraced on the east and south by China and on the north by the Soviet Union.

Why was the Roerich group interested in Mongolia, and in getting Roosevelt to strengthen the Mongolian regime? References in their correspondence lead to the surmise that they were proposing setting up some kind of industrial enterprise, and canvasing various possible sources of the necessary capital. As early as 19 April 1934 Wallace had added a rapid afterthought to a letter to Roerich: "Rums [Mary Rumsey, sister of Averell Harriman, who financed visits by Theosophist George W. Russell to the United States in 1930 and again in 1935] thinks can find a person with money for the coop."[18] To Grant he wrote (undated): "Concerning the cooperative I need someone to whom to refer anyone who is really interested. Unfortunately the public attitude just now toward the land of the cooperative is such as to make most people feel conservative and prudent. However, Rums asked me for the name and address of a person of whom a friend of hers could get further details." An undated and unaddressed letter reads: "Our friend who is interested in Kansas showed very great interest yesterday. He has several different groups of friends who work with him on matters of this sort. . . . He wishes to know of course the nature of the security." Again, writing to "M," he comments on the need for an investigation of the scientific basis of "the project," goes on to the possibility of war in the east involving Japan, Russia, and China, and finishes by commenting on the fact that the British "are now sending capital in large quantities to India and China to start factories to be operated by cheap labor to turn out goods to compete with the cheap Japanese goods which are flooding the eastern and South American markets."[19] It seems hardly likely "M" would be interested in this if it were not relevant to "the project."

In February 1935 it seemed as if a richly promising source of funds had suddenly come into sight. Wallace wrote: "On page 4 of the H of A [Heart of Asia, one of Nicholas Roerich's books] a certain proper name appears 9 times. I met the owner of this name for the first time last week." On that page Roerich gives an account of how frequently Asians in the depths of the countryside had asked him whether a Ford car or a Ford truck would be of use in that terrain. It is the name "Ford" which appears nine times, and when Wallace says he met the owner of that name he must mean Henry Ford himself. A few days later, prompted by a letter from Grant, he followed a prescribed practice for obtaining spiritual guidance. "And then I wrote a letter to the man of the 9 times appearing name in a highly intuitional strain. I did not mention Kansas in the letter but tried to open the way so that I might if the letter took hold, follow to Kansas with the greatest speed possible. . . . This whole approach is based on the assumption that the 9 named one has a deep mystical strain. If I have miscalculated naught will come of it." [20] Evidently naught did come of it. Wallace received a polite letter from Ford's son, followed after some delay by an inquiry from Ford senior that elicited from Wallace the name of Professor Roerich. The correspondence was terminated by a rather curtly dismissive letter from Ford's secretary.

Some other businessman Wallace approached told Wallace that "the matter of Kansas had been put up to him nearly a year ago but the desire then as he roughly remembered was for somewhere between $50 and $120 instead of $11. He looked into the matter as did also one of the monkeys [British] and one from the land of the Niebelungen [Germany]. They reached the conclusion that the rulers [Japanese] were in inevitable control and so far as their particular industry was concerned it would be bucking an impossible proposition." [21] The Roerich plans perished for lack of backers.

One must take seriously the question, What is revealed about the nature of Wallace's mentality by his adopting these cabalistic ways of referring to various persons? What point could there have been in concealing Ford's identity from some imaginary spy when evidently Wallace had addressed an explicit, ordinary-language letter to him, a letter that would have been opened by one of Ford's secretaries, used Ford's name as addressee, named Professor Roerich, and was signed by Wallace himself? The development of a "cunning" private language is not only an adolescent practice but also often an elitist and authoritarian one, conjuring up the notion of exercising power in secret, outside the restraints of orthodox procedures. Such an attitude was alien to Wallace's self-concept; if he had any tendency toward it that tendency was repressed, but he was tempted in that direction by the Roerich group and succumbed temporarily because of the hypnotic force of Nicholas Roerich's dogma and messianic posture.

Just what the nature of the proposed project may have been is a matter of speculation, but the Guru letters certainly show that there was some intent behind Roerich's saying to the Mongols that wealthy Americans might help them build a thriving industry, thus strengthening them to resist oppression. During the spring of 1935 he continued his forays about the Mongolian hinterland, engaged in his confused, grandiose, and quite ineffective political machinations. Almost since he had first arrived in Manchuria he had been subject of a great deal of local publicity, both favorable and virulently unfavorable, in the Japanese-controlled White Russian newspapers. Opinions about him were divided because of the impossibility of discovering his political goals. But if any of this leaked back to Washington it was disregarded by Wallace, whose efforts to get Roosevelt's agreement that the United States should become a signatory to the Roerich Pact and Banner of Peace had finally been successful. At a ceremony in Washington on 15 April 1935, Wallace as plenipotentiary, in Roosevelt's presence, signed the pact for the United States, one of a total of twenty-one nations affirming their approval. In doing so he declared: "Today it is appropriate that we should give recognition to the genius of Nicholas Roerich in whose mind the Pact and Banner first originated." At such a time his mind was hardly open to skepticism about Roerich. In the same month he wrote Bernhard Hansen, vice president of the Nobel Peace Prize Committee: "It is my opinion that Professor Roerich would be a most worthy candidate for the Nobel Peace Prize Award," and sent copies of that letter to a dozen or so other dignitaries who might be persuaded to the same opinion.[22]

It is not until a letter of 3 July, to Louis Horch, that we find any evidence of disquiet in Wallace's mind about Roerich's activities in Mongolia. On the same day he had sent a telegram to Roerich, address Kalgan, North China, saying, "Department asks you at the earliest possible safe moment to transfer your expedition to a safe region rich in drought resistant grasses in Suiyan." To Horch he wrote that he did not know "whether there is any foundation whatsoever for the insinuations of political activity on the part of Professor Roerich in Mongolia," but that he was "exceedingly anxious . . . that he be engaged . . . in doing exactly what he is supposed to be doing." He asked Horch to bring this "tactfully and effectively" to the professor's attention. Wallace acknowledged that "these insinuations of the press in late June may be quite without foundation" but thought that caution was advisable. Roerich should move to Suiyan, an area "reputedly rich in drought resistant grasses."

The "insinuations of the press" consisted of a *New York Times* report on 24 June that Roerich's activities were embarrassing the U.S. government. The expedition had been forced by the Japanese military to leave Manchuria, because of its supposed involvement in White Russian politics. In Northern China, the Roerichs had "purchased complete equipment, including trucks, motor cars and tents with money supplied by Secretary Wallace." They had also "applied to the Fifteenth United States Infantry at Tientsin for a dozen army rifles and pistols and a considerable stock of ammunition. The army officers in charge at first declined. However, they finally complied upon receipt of instructions from the United States War Department." The expedition was now operating near the Outer Mongolian border and "although they carry credentials of the United States Department of Agriculture there has been much suspicion among Mongolian leaders, due to the presence of . . . White Russian armed Cossack guards."[23]

In view of the melodramatic charade of secrecy with which the Roerichs and Wallace had shrouded the unofficial purposes of the expedition, it is not surprising that this publicity jangled Wallace's nerves. The way in which the journalist referred to "receipt of instructions from the United States War Department," although true, made it sound as if the United States were virtually engaging in an undeclared war with the Soviet government. Naturally Wallace must have thought the Roerichs had been wildly indiscreet and were on the verge of entangling him in an international incident that could be disastrous to his political career.

Although Wallace had lent himself to some of Roerich's schemes, his motives appear to have been altruistic rather than self-interested. He had a genuine commitment to world peace, which he believed would be promoted by the revelation of the ancient wisdom; he sincerely desired that everyone in the world should partake in the abundance that advances in technology had made possible, a desire with which his efforts to promote some great industrial enterprise in Mongolia were entirely concordant. Roerich's flamboyant self-promotion and overt politicizing must by this time have seemed to Wallace a betrayal of his own endeavors to do good by stealth. His admiration turned to disgust.

His telegram of 3 July telling the Roerichs to move their operations to Suiyan was the first step in winding up the expedition. It was followed on 9 July by a letter to the professor and his son from E. N. Bressman, scientific adviser to the Department of Agriculture, saying, "The Secretary has asked me to inform you that plans should be made for drawing the Central Asian expedition to a close not later than January 1 [1936]," by which time they should submit their expense vouchers and ship the seeds and specimens they had collected. They should arrive in northern India not later than 1 February, and present their final report by 1 May 1936.[24]

Wallace was still hoping to get some useful work out of them. They did go to Suiyan and do fieldwork there, collecting seed. Wallace cabled them on 15 August asking for assurances that they were far enough south in Suiyan and that their travels "will be such as there will be no troubles for you from people interested in controversial problems." They assured Wallace by return cable that they were proceeding unhampered with their peaceful scientific research, but four days later he recommended "moving base immediately to Sining in Koko Nor Province to permit collecting early in September in that locality where many hardy grasses occur seed of which is important."[25] However, on 24 August Wallace received a letter from the Department of State that cause a rapid revision of his priorities. It referred to a telegram from the American ambassador in Moscow, saying that his military attaché had been given certain information by an "important" Soviet citizen about Professor Roerich, as follows:

Under supervision of the United States Department of Agriculture an expedition headed by Professor Nicholas Roerich and his son George is now in inner Mongolia seeking drought resisting plants and grasses.

George Roerich was formerly a Czarist officer and has recruited assistance for his expedition from among followers of the bandit Semenoff. The expedition sought armament from the commanding officer 15th infantry at Tientsin but he refused to supply the arms requested. However upon taking up the matter of armament with Czarist circles in Washington Roerich succeeded in having the Tientsin military authorities overruled and the commander of the garrison was directed to turn over rifles, revolvers and a considerable quantity of ammunition to Roerich and the Semenoff bandits.

This armed party is now making its way toward the Soviet Union ostensibly as a scientific expedition but actually to rally former White elements and discontented Mongols.

The Department of State informed Wallace that its records indicated that Professor Roerich had telegraphed him, on 30 November 1934, asking him to get authority from the War Department for the weapons to be issued — Wallace thus representing the "Czarist circles" referred to. "In this connection it occurs to me," the author of the letter, Assistant Secretary of State R. Walton Moore continued, "that you may wish to offer further comment, for possible transmission by this Department to the American Ambassador at Moscow, in regard to the information. . . . Information in regard to the future plans of the expedition with reference to visiting the Soviet Union would presumably be of particular interest to the Ambassador."[26]

Regardless of whether some details of that report could be disputed, this "please explain" from the Department of State shook Wallace even more than the *New York Times* story. The Roerichs had been complaining that they could not go immediately to Kukunor Province as Wallace had earlier directed because of bad roads and floods. They wanted to stay collecting seeds in Suiyan until the middle of September. But on 30 August, six days after the letter from the Department of State, Wallace directed F. D. Richey, Ryerson's replacement at the Bureau of Plant Industry, to cable Roerich making it "precise and definite that he is to proceed at once to Peiping and finish up work there as rapidly as possible and proceed not later than October 15 by most direct route to India and finish there not later than Feb 1," thus truncating Bressman's program for them by three months.[27]

The shutters of official secrecy began to be pulled close. A cablegram of 4 September from Wallace to George Roerich warned that publication without approval of information or comment concerning expeditions financed by the Department of Agriculture was prohibited. A letter from Wallace waiting for Nicholas and George when they arrived in Naggar stated that "precisely and definitely . . . I desire that there be no communication, direct or indirect, by letter or otherwise between the Roerichs (father, mother and sons) on the one side and myself on the other. Official business will be transacted with Frederick D. Richey, Chief, Bureau of Plant Industry." A telegram of 23 September to the Roerichs, signed by Richey, read: "We ask that there be no publicity whatever about recent expedition. There must be no quoting of correspondence or other violation of Department publicity regulations."[28]

It is easy to believe that Wallace sorely wished to cancel out of existence all his previous correspondence with them, most especially the Guru letters, but of course he could not openly mention them. He wrote officially to Louis Horch at the Roerich Museum, notifying him that he had terminated the expedition's field activities, and saying: "I ask you to notify your publicity department that no letters from myself or other members of the Department, or copies of letters to myself or other members of the Department which happened to be in your possession are to be published. . . . I trust you will be able to bring about the cooperation of all members of your organization, especially those who are likely to deal in publicity, with the spirit and letter of this communication."[29] Before many years had passed, Wallace was to find that some of those members had no intention of cooperating with either the letter or the spirit of his request.

The procedure of officially disowning the Roerichs and all their works proceeded. An Agriculture Department press release stated that the department's connections with the Roerichs had been severed and that it would never employ them again. In October 1935 Wallace wrote formally to ambassadors or ministers of some twenty-odd Latin American countries, and thirty or so European and Middle Eastern countries and the Soviet Union, saying that although he still supported the "Treaty for the Protection of Artistic and Scientific Institutions and Historic Monuments," he had lost faith in Professor Nicholas Roerich and had "decided reservations" about him. Further, his associates, Frances Grant and Mr. and Mrs. Lichtmann, shared the same opprobrium, but the Horches and the Lichtmanns' daughter Esther, who had turned against Roerich, were exempt.[30]

The rift between the Horches and the Roerichs had become overt in February 1935, when Louis Horch had commenced proceedings to divest the Roerichs of the equity in the Roerich Museum with which he had endowed them, provoking a legal battle he eventually won. He was less successful in suing Roerich for the recovery of about $200,000 advanced to him in the 1920s, because Roerich was safely out of the jurisdiction of the American courts. At the same time Roerich was being sued by the Internal Revenue Service for tax evasion and tax fraud. He had not filed tax returns for 1926 and 1927, when he had been on the Asian expedition financed by Horch and had received large sums from

Horch for the paintings he was to produce. Also he had not reported any income at all in 1934, when he was an employee of the Department of Agriculture. These investigations by the IRS must have been given further impetus by a letter from Wallace to the commissioner of Internal Revenue pointing out that in 1934 Professor Roerich had sold a painting, *Heavenly Himalayas*, in the United States for $6,500, representing income earned, and that in 1931 he seemed to have earned, according to Wallace's figures, some $6,800 in taxable income but had paid only $137.39 in income taxes. Wallace would appreciate "your early investigation in this matter."[31]

Wanting to both confirm the disgrace of the Roerich group and extend a protective hand to the Horches, Wallace wrote Governor Herbert H. Lehman of New York: "I am convinced that Professor Roerich's interests are not in the United States but are in the troubled affairs of Asia. . . . As a result of observing the actions of Professor Roerich in the East and his representatives in this country, I reached the conclusion by the summer of 1935 that the representatives in this country were worshipping Professor Roerich as a superman and were determined to stop at nothing in helping him to work out some extraordinary phantasy of Asiatic power." Mr. and Mrs. Louis Horch, however, were free from this taint and were trying to reorganize the Roerich Museum on an American basis. If they got into a legal contest with Roerich, Wallace wanted to do what he could to help them—including, presumably, writing this letter to the governor.[32] Other recipients of Wallace's confidence about his loss of confidence in Nicholas Roerich were Winthrop Aldrich, Vincent Bendix, and, poignantly enough, the "nine times named one," Henry Ford.[33]

Even President Roosevelt eventually found it necessary explicitly to disown the presumptuous professor. In 1938 it was reported to the undersecretary of state, Sumner Welles, by the British ambassador in Washington, that the Roerichs in Kulu were telling the British authorities that they were "intimate friends" of Roosevelt and that he approved of their projects. Welles promptly informed the ambassador that "the President desired the Ambassador to let the India Office know that the President had only seen Professor Roerich once in his life, and that some ten years ago, and that he had not the slightest interest in any project in which Professor Roerich was involved."[34]

Roosevelt was certainly not completely open about his connection with the Roerichs. Among the Roosevelt papers, unearthed and quoted by Torbjorn Sirevag, is a collection of eight letters to Roosevelt from Helena Roerich, some signed with her name and some with the familiar "M." There are no replies from Roosevelt in the papers, but some of her later letters indicate that he had replied to earlier ones. The first letter is dated 10 October 1934, offering Help from the Highest Source. The next, of 15 November 1934, says: "Mr. President, Your message was transmitted to me. I am happy that Your great heart has so beautifully accepted the Message and Your lightbearing mind was free from prejudice." Apparently he had asked for predictions about international affairs. There would be attempts, she said, from "the land in the East" and from "the land beyond the ocean" to involve the United States in war; he must not disarm. Subsequent letters contain similar advice and predictions about world reconstruction. In February 1935 she writes: "Your question, Mr. President, reached our heights on the eve of the departure of my Messenger, and I am happy to add to the Message the Reply given to me"—given by the masters, presumably. It was that Europe was disintegrating and attempts to change it now might be futile. In December 1935 a letter announces the betrayal by the Horch faction but says new messages could be sent by another channel. Two more brief messages end the correspondence.[35]

There is no evidence of how seriously Roosevelt intended his inquiries or how seriously he took the replies, but in the light of subsequent events the mere fact of the correspondence could have been embarrassing to him if made public. His official denial of connection with the Roerichs is inconsistent also with the impression Wallace managed to create in his oral history interview. Wallace had suggested that the inspiration for the expedition and for appointing Roerich to lead it was Roosevelt's as much as his. To his interviewer, Wallace, too, declared that he had met Roerich only once, when he was on his way to Europe in August 1929, whereas "Roosevelt had known him when he was governor and referred to him affectionately." Wallace goes on to talk about the trouble that had developed on the expedition, and how he had withdrawn Roerich from contested areas and finally terminated the expedition and Roerich's employment. "All of these actions which I took beginning in the summer of 1935 were opposed in a gentle way by Roosevelt. He asked why I couldn't be patient with the old man."[36] So, as Wallace saw the matter in retrospect after all those years, Roosevelt not only had been partly responsible for initiating the expedition but also had opposed its termination.

Wallace was reluctant to take the blame for putting Roerich in charge of the expedition and less than wholehearted in admitting to Ryerson, MacMillan, and Stephens that he had misjudged the situation and treated them harshly. On 11 October 1935, he wrote Ryerson: "I wish to say that I have given considerable study to all aspects of the situation and have reached the conclusion that your motives were of the highest. Subsequent events have in considerable measure borne out your judgment." To MacMillan, who like Ryerson had left the service, he wrote on 6 November: "In view of all developments, I can now see that your actions while on this expedition probably were guided by good motives. . . . I nevertheless feel that you did not cooperate as fully as you might have with the leader of the expedition. It appears, however, that this was due to an error in judgment as to your responsibility and obligations, rather than deliberate insubordination, as stated in my letter to you of October 23, 1934, and I am desirous of making this [a] fact of record." To Stephens he said simply that "the statement in my letter of October 23, 1934, that your actions could be regarded as deliberate insubordination was inaccurate."[37]

The dramatic denouement of the 1934–35 expedition marked a turning point for Henry Wallace. For more than two years he had accepted the esoteric leadership of Nicholas Roerich, whose special insight and visionary schemes seemed likely to hasten the general spiritual enlightenment Wallace so greatly desired. Now, the teacher whom he had revered, to whose writings he had attributed revelatory wisdom and virtue, had shown himself to be crassly self-interested and had done so in a way that exposed his disciple to political recriminations and ridicule. This produced a feeling of revulsion, a repudiation of Roerich and of the version of Theosophical doctrine he espoused, and an evident determination on Wallace's part never again to subject himself to the superior spiritual wisdom of others. Wallace's deconversion did not, however, disturb the vital core of his spiritual beliefs. As Louis Bean, statistician in the Department of Agriculture, Theosophist, and Wallace's friend later remarked, "His [Wallace's] interest in philosophy, in religion, in science, in the interplay between them, in things mystical, in things universal I don't think he will ever lose. . . . That's part of him." In particular, Wallace's convictions that all humankind fundamentally shared in the divine nature, and that a spiritual awakening could transform our physical lives here on Earth, remained firm and played a central role in his political beliefs for the remainder of his life.

5

MESSIAH FOR THE
UNDERPRIVILEGED

WALLACE AS FDR'S SUCCESSOR?

The Roerich fiasco notwithstanding, as Wallace neared the end of his first four-year term as secretary of agriculture, he was entitled to feel a sense of achievement. From a chaotic, crisis-ridden beginning he had built the essentials of the administrative machinery able to lift the agricultural community out of depression and keep it out, except under the most adverse conditions. Ironically, the severe droughts occurring in his first term had helped farmers by cutting farm surpluses and so raising commodity prices, and the New Deal's acreage-reduction programs were consolidating that position. Farm income had nearly doubled since 1932, and most farmers now supported the provisions of the Agricultural Adjustment Act.

MEETING THE SUPREME COURT'S CHALLENGE

Even the potentially disastrous Supreme Court judgment of 6 January 1936, effectively declaring the act unconstitutional, failed to halt these solid achievements, largely because Wallace, forewarned by the decision in the Schechter case, had prepared canny plans for substitute legislation. Looking back, Wallace said: "I remember thinking when the whole thing [the National Industrial Recovery Act] was invalidated,

'Well, when and if the Supreme Court invalidates the Triple-A, we're not going to be caught flat-footed the way these boys are.' They just folded."[1]

Anticipation did not prevent his indignation at and public condemnation of the Court's order that $200 million of taxes the government had already collected from processors must be returned. What angered Wallace was that the processors had already recouped this money, passing the burden of the taxes forward to consumers as higher prices or backward to producers as lower ones. In a radio address Wallace called the decision "the greatest legalized steal in history" and was generally so outspoken that Representative Allen Treadway declared on the floor of the House that the secretary of agriculture should be impeached for contempt of the Court. Undeterred, Wallace set about having legislation passed to ensure that the money was recovered by the Treasury, and in the end most of it was.[2]

Essentially Wallace's replacement for the invalidated Agricultural Adjustment Act was to reclassify many of the practical measures related to acreage restriction, compensation for land retired from use or lying fallow, and so on, as soil conservation measures, rather than as central government control of agriculture. He and his department attorneys worked up a new Soil Conservation and Domestic Allotment Bill, giving the secretary of agriculture power "to provide for the rental and withdrawal from commercial crop production . . . such land as may be necessary to promote the conservation of soil fertility and to bring about a profitable balance of domestic production with the total effective demand at profitable prices." The legality of this initiative was reasonably well assured by an existing act of 1934 authorizing the activities of the Soil Conservation Service. This was the service that, in the view of rambunctious Harold Ickes, Wallace, with the connivance of President Roosevelt, had "stolen" from Ickes's own Department of Interior while he was away from Washington on holiday in March 1935. It had seemed to Wallace a plain matter of reason (which Ickes, however, had refused to recognize) that Soil Conservation belonged in Agriculture, and in view of the Supreme Court's rejection of the Agricultural Adjustment Act it was decidedly fortunate for the welfare of the country's agriculture that he had persuaded Roosevelt to the same view.

As the processing tax that had financed adjustment payments to farmers had been declared illegal by the Supreme Court, that was deleted from the new bill, and the $500 million in revenue that had been expected from that tax now had to come through direct congressional appropriations. The president sought these additional funds by including a provision in the 1936 Revenue Act for a tax on undistributed corporate earnings. Willy-nilly, industry was required to support the agricultural program.

Because of Wallace's preplanning, the new bill was enacted into law very quickly, within two months, so that the work of his department was hardly interrupted. But the bill was not simply a device to enable the Department of Agriculture to continue to pay farmers for restricting output. Against the backdrop of the appalling dust storms of 1934, Wallace had called, in his book *New Frontiers*, for measures to stop the degradation of the soil caused by overgrazing and the cultivation of marginal land. "Human beings are ruining land," he wrote, "and bad lands are ruining human beings, especially children." In 1935 he had set economist Howard R. Tolley to work on a new farm bill, one that would place much greater emphasis on soil conservation. So, as Wallace pointed out, the idea of centering the new act on soil conservation "wasn't a phony . . . , because we had been shifting over to that very strongly in 1935 anyhow."[3]

Wallace's successful circumvention of what to others in the New Deal was a stunning setback evidently increased his confidence and his belief that in planning ability and general force of intellect he exceeded his colleagues, not excluding Franklin Roosevelt. His self-assurance was so firmly based that he felt no need to claim immediate recognition of his achievements. After the invalidation of the Agricultural Adjustment Act, Chester Davis, its administrator, was demoralized, "quite hopeless for a time," as Wallace put it. Realizing that it might be difficult for Davis to accept the soil conservation idea, Wallace had a newspaperman approach him with the suggestion. "I was close to Chester, but I figured I could have more effect if he picked the idea out of the air himself instead of having it come from me. Chester was fine about it. We all got together and pushed with all our vigor."[4]

Quietly conscious of his own ability, Wallace did not need to assert it by actively dominating other people. Authoritarianism was alien to his nature. The conscious adoption of an egalitarian, democratic mode of working — "We all got together and pushed with all our vigor" — was characteristic of him, even to the extent, as we shall see later, of handicapping him in the brawling business of politics.

DECENTRALIZATION OF THE AAA
AND ECONOMIC DEMOCRACY

A classically democratic approach to both planning and administration was embodied in another scheme Wallace and his colleagues had begun working on in 1935, which was progressively to become effective during the 1936 to 1940 term. This was the plan for the decentralization of the AAA as it then was. Wallace described it to his interviewer:

At that time, in the spring of '35, we prepared something I thought was of great significance. It was a program to get every state engaged in planning the best utilization of the land, not merely from the standpoint of the ultimate market for the products, but also from the standpoint of farm management and soil conservation.

We sent out, shortly after this, to the heads of Extension or the presidents of agricultural colleges—I've forgotten which—letters asking them to plan in these terms—farm management, soil conservation, markets and all the rest—not merely for the whole state, but to break it down to the county—break it down to the township— and have meetings with the farmers, at which the farmers themselves would engage in this planning, first by the smallest unit, next by the county unit, and then at state a meeting, with the whole thing headed up in the fall by regional meetings.

Wallace attended these regional meetings and a final meeting at Mount Weather in the Blue Ridge Mountains, at which the results for the regions were added together: "We got out there, remote from all the distractions of office, and added up the whole thing for the entire country, as to what our goals should be for the entire country with regard to land use and sound management taking into account both soil fertility and best utilization of labor. This planning went clear back to the townships and counties, state by state, and was based on an immense amount of careful scientific and economic research. It was really a good job!" When in the end Wallace looked back over his public career, he ranked these achievements in economic democracy and soil conservation as among his finest.[5]

Wallace and Tugwell had sought Roosevelt's approval for the decentralizing of the AAA, and although the president's reaction was generally favorable, the associated ideas it provoked in him met for the most part only with private incredulity from Wallace. Roosevelt wanted to guard against the possibility that each region might be treated as a one-crop region, growing nothing but corn, for example. He thought each region should be as nearly self-supporting in all regards as possible. Wallace had often heard the president expound such views, even applying them to the international context ("I've often heard him hold forth on the idea that nations should import very little and export very little and that the exports should almost exactly equal the imports"), but to him such thinking was "rather naive," revealing Roosevelt's ignorance of the concept of comparative advantage and the gains resulting from it in trade. The president's ideas were also in direct opposition to Secretary of State Cordell Hull's principle of maximizing world trade as a way of promoting world peace. When Roosevelt spoke in this fashion, Wallace said, "I used to look at him in open-eyed wonder." In discussing the decentralization proposal, Roosevelt talked of "steel being shipped from Pittsburgh to Boston—he thought that Boston would take care of its own steel needs if Pittsburgh did not ship steel in. In like manner he spoke of shoes being shipped from Boston to Pittsburgh. He thought that Pittsburgh might produce its own shoes if Boston would not ship them in." Though Wallace and Tugwell knew such notions to be "far-fetched," they listened dutifully to them, unwilling to argue at that time.

Despite Wallace's general sympathy with Roosevelt's liberal views and his genuine admiration for Roosevelt's force as an inspirational leader, he had no respect for his thinking in the field of economics, and little more for his approach to planning, which, Wallace sometimes thought, revealed more a sadistic delight in mischief making than a controlled approach to solving problems. As the president's interview with Wallace and Tugwell continued, Roosevelt found much pleasure in the suggestion that a considerable part of the Extension Service should be transferred to the AAA, not, however, because that would make for more efficient administration, but because he saw the service as a Republican machine. Wallace pressed the more substantial issue, pointing out to Roosevelt that overlapping responsibilities for rural rehabilitation, soil erosion, and land purchases between Hopkins's Works Progress Administration, Ickes's Public Works Administration, and the Department of Agriculture's Extension Service were causing great confusion, and urging the president to summon a conference of the competing agencies to sort this confusion out. But as the conversation continued, "it . . . became apparent to me that the President liked the slap-dash methods which Harry Hopkins used in setting up agricultural projects. I told him that if the projects were set up carelessly, the Department of Agriculture would have to clean up the mess. Roosevelt didn't like my saying this."[6] To speak like that was a mark of Wallace's cool independence; he knew quite well that Hopkins was a favorite of Roosevelt's.

The new administrative structure came into being pretty well as Wallace and Tugwell had proposed it. The revised farm program, of selective land use and conservation, was much more popular with farmers than the previous requirement, an automatic percentage reduction in tilled acreage irrespective of differences in the condition and profitability of individual farms, had been. By 1940 there were six million farmers taking part in unified county planning and working groups. There were nearly a thousand legally constituted county, intercounty, or watershed soil conservation districts, with district supervisors elected from among the resident farmers, directing the work of the technicians of the Soil Conservation Service. A well-functioning mixture of central planning and grassroots autonomy had been achieved by exchanging personnel in each direction — sending administration personnel out as members of the local committees and bringing farmers' representatives into central bodies. This was a prime example of open, democratic government, with channels of communication and influence open in both directions. Yet, paradoxically, it led in some quarters to the paranoid suspicion that Wallace was creating a Tammany Hall within agriculture in support of the New Deal, and building up a nationwide political machine for his personal aggrandizement.[7]

Even if such suspicions were groundless, Wallace's work in the agricultural sector was not without political entanglements. Farmers did not form a homogeneous social bloc; the division and opposition between the relatively rich and the decidedly poor was to be found here just as in the community at large. It was that division, and related differences of opinion as to whose interests should be favored, that underlay the split in the Department of Agriculture leading to the "purge" of the more radically liberal, but city-bred, officers. Wallace's training and his close acquaintance with the practical problems of the land had led him to weigh more heavily the interests of the landowners, who, although of many different degrees of wealth, were as a class clearly better off than the tenants and hired laborers. His partiality certainly did not arise from any automatic siding with the more successful; he had many times specifically rejected that part of the Protestant ethic that, allied with social Darwinism, held that the accumulation of wealth was a mark of merit and should be further encouraged. He felt, however, that it was the landowners who had to make the decisions as to what was to be done with the land, and it was they who had to be shown a way out of the desperate agricultural depression before anything could usefully be done for the hired hands or tenant farmers. And so, at whatever cost to his humanist sympathies, he had told Chester Davis to dispense with those young liberals whose interpretation of the legislation favored the rural proletariat.

RURAL POVERTY AND THE FARM SECURITY ADMINISTRATION

Toward the end of 1936, Wallace had to confront the issue of landowner versus laborer again. The previous year, Roosevelt had set up the Resettlement Administration to move the rural destitute to urban or suburban communities and to provide housing and financial assistance to enable poor farmers to acquire small holdings of their own. The new agency was independent of the Department of Agriculture and, in the view of its head, Rexford Tugwell, catered for those whom the department's Extension Service, with its close ties to the conservative Farm Bureau, had failed to reach. But in the autumn of 1936 Tugwell decided to resign, probably, as Wallace saw it, because he was finding it increasingly difficult to get funds from Congress. Yet Tugwell was convinced of the great need for the Resettlement Administration's work and hoped that Wallace could find some way of keeping a similar organization going within the Department of Agriculture.[8] That was the decision Wallace now faced. Resettlement was essentially a relief operation, not directly contributing to rural productivity, and because it threatened their supply of cheap labor, was unpopular with landowning farmers. Again pressure was on Wallace to incline one way or the other between the haves and have-nots. Tugwell and his successor-elect, Dr. Will Alexander, challenged the secretary, before he made his decision, to go to the cotton-growing South to see the work the Resettlement Administration had already accomplished and the poverty it was trying to alleviate.[9] In the fall of 1936 he went. Beginning a journey that would take them over two thousand miles, his small party traveled into Arkansas and crossed the Delta and its uplands, on both the Arkansas and Mississippi side.

Felix Belair, who covered the trip for the *New York Times*, described Wallace's reaction to the conditions they found:

We put up for the most part at little country hotels. Wallace would slip off and walk out into the country alone, stopping people, talking with them, visiting them in their homes. . . . One Sunday he slipped off and walked up into the hills and was gone all day. He said that he had gone to church with the people up there and just visited around afterwards. That was all he would say.

Along the road in the car he was watching everything, asking questions of whatever R.A. man who was with us, or just brooding, with those bushy eyebrows of his drawn down as if he was seeing more than he could bear. Just when we'd think we were going to push on and roll up a little mileage, he'd see some old people trudging along in the dust, or some kids walking from school, and "Stop for a minute," he'd say. He would get out of the car and go up and talk with these people. Nobody seemed to be shy of him or think it was strange for him to ask the questions he did. He asked the kids how much milk they drank, or how often they had oranges or green vegetables, and what they were learning in school. He asked the older people about T.B. and pellagra and malaria and crops. They all answered him with perfect dignity, black and white. What he learned didn't generally cheer him. "It's incredible," he kept saying, "incredible!"

. . . Somebody had sent him a new book by Arthur Raper, *A Preface to Peasantry*, a study of conditions among white and colored tenants in two Georgia counties. "To call these miserable people peasants," he said, "really offends the peasantry of Europe. I have been in the homes of peasants of Czecho-Slovakia and the Balkan countries and they seem now like palaces compared with what we have here in the Cotton Belt."[10]

They went on into Georgia, and Wallace was frequently told that some of the families there were so trapped in poverty that they could never be rehabilitated by the Resettlement Administration or anything else. But many of the families themselves told Wallace that they would do anything if given a chance for one of the neat cottages being built on an experimental scale by the administration. Wallace declared: "If some of these people live to become millionaires they probably never will experience anything more revolutionary than coming into possession of a mule, wagon, and a wood stove for cooking which an insignificant number have obtained through the Resettlement Administration."[11]

Wallace himself had never been one of the oppressed, one of those whose labor is exploited for their employer's benefit, and had never seen real poverty firsthand. Now he had, and his longtime policy of extending abundance to all acquired an emotional commitment over and above his abstract, principled egalitarianism. "I'd never really been inside the homes of the small Southern farmers," Wallace said later. "You have to be inside their homes to understand the thing."[12]

Not everyone recognized this deep-down change. It is interesting to contrast Belair's description of Wallace's reaction with the recollections of some of the other members of the party. Will Alexander, for example, who was to succeed Tugwell, preferred to stress Wallace's physical competitiveness. "All I remember about this trip was that when we'd get off to walk over one of these fields, Henry would try to get to the fence before you did. I didn't think he was interested in what we were trying to show him. I guess he was, though." Alexander describes one incident that seemed to show a different attitude on Wallace's part. The accompanying field director knocked at a house to show the party what the people had to eat. A woman came to the door breast-feeding her baby. The director was embarrassed and apparently said something to the woman to the effect that she should not have fed the baby in front of the secretary. But "Henry was very severe in his reprimand of Whitacre for that. That was as human a thing as I ever saw Henry do. It was all right for that woman to nurse her baby. He was very human about it." Yet overall, Alexander said, "I never felt that these people interested him. I think they did, but I think he had no capacity to show it. . . . I always felt that [the trip] hadn't made any impression on Wallace at all."[13]

In view of the practical measures that Wallace at once set in train to keep some form of resettlement going, the *New York Times* man's observations seem more perceptive than those of Wallace's colleague. It was never Wallace's way to confide in his fellows his innermost feelings, and consequently their reports of his reactions to events in his life must be treated with reserve. Years later, still thinking about the import of this tour, Wallace explained: "I had a certain amount of sympathy with what I knew Rex had been doing, but I didn't have the vivid coloring until I'd actually got into the homes of these small people who had never been served by the Extension Service and would never have

"You have to be inside their homes to understand the thing": Wallace responding to the poverty he encountered on a trip to the rural South, 1937. (Photograph by Marion Post Wolcott; courtesy of the Library of Congress)

been served by the Extension Service. I felt that Rex had made a real contribution." The Resettlement Administration, he declared, was "the most 'new deal' part of the New Deal, because it represented a specific effort to reach 'the forgotten man.'"[14]

Wallace had legislation drawn up that, as the Bankhead-Jones Farm Tenancy Act, was approved on 22 July 1937. This authorized him as secretary of agriculture to lend money to farm tenants for the purchase of farms, to make rehabilitation loans to farmers for subsistence, improvements, and other purposes, to develop a program of land use including the retirement of marginal land, and to complete projects begun by the Resettlement Administration.[15] Under this legislation the Farm Security Administration was set up within the Department of Agriculture, effectively to take over the Resettlement Administration's role.

Wallace had had to work very hard to save the Resettlement Administration, lobbying congressmen and senators and so on. It was clear to him that if it were to survive in its new form, as the Farm Security Administration, its congressional opponents would need to be appeased. He therefore simplified the construction of the administration's housing projects to reduce their cost. ("That caused great dismay among the extremists," he recalled. "They said it meant the death of the Administration — Wallace was destroying it.")[16] He also halted other activities with which he had a good deal of sympathy but that were certain to provoke congressional opposition.

A lover of music, Wallace had often attended "perfectly delightful evenings" at Rexford Tugwell's house, listening to folk songs from the South, collected by the Resettlement Administration's Special Skills Division. He could see, however, that some of these songs contained sentiments that could be considered subversive. One, entitled *I'm a Dodger*, which the division had circulated widely, ran through the list of occupations and told how those who practiced them, preachers and so on, dodged about to get their money. "That song," Wallace remarked later, "which was doubtless authentic, might have been very useful to the research worker, the psychologist, and the historian, but it was not conducive to getting appropriations from Congress."[17]

Under Wallace, the Farm Security Administration was less interested in visionary schemes for ideal communities than in solving immediate practical problems. As he explained:

> When they started out, the structure of the Farm Security Administration was rather simple. The most significant part of it had to do with the loan program, and under the loan program there was set up in each of the counties where there were underprivileged farmers a county supervisor, who typically would take care of servicing about two hundred farmers who would borrow about five hundred dollars each, with which to buy the necessary equipment and seeds in order to operate a small farm. The county supervisor was supposed to see that they were placed on a farm that wasn't too bad, see that they had the right cropping system, to help the women put up a hundred quarts of fruits and vegetables for each member in the family, and to give counsel with regard to agricultural methods. It was a busy life

for the county supervisor to take care of his two hundred clients—a very busy life. I thought the men who did that job at the county level did some of the finest human work of any men in the whole administration at any time. They solved mean little problems in a fine way.[18]

The same practicality and realism that had enabled Wallace to preserve the Resettlement Administration's best work continued to mark his administration of the department at large. He was still having to keep the more radical liberal forces in check. Frank, Pressman, and Hiss had been forced out in 1935 and now Tugwell had gone, but Appleby remained as the center of a group, which included his assistant, C. B. "Beanie" Baldwin, about whose agenda and methods Wallace often had reservations.

When Chester Davis resigned as AAA administrator in June 1936, Wallace replaced him with Howard R. Tolley, a scholarly man whom Wallace described approvingly as having "a most unusual mathematical brain with a great capacity to relate many economic facts." But Appleby disliked Tolley, just as he had disliked Davis before him; both seemed too closely connected to the processing groups. When Tolley proved not to be a good administrator, Wallace replaced him, in 1938, with R. M. "Spike" Evans, a practical, emotionally stable man who, Wallace hoped, would bring peace to the conflict-ridden agency. That proved to be the case, but again Appleby saw Evans as too reactionary, too inclined to favor the interests of relatively well off farmers. "Of course," Wallace commented later, with some impatience, "the difficulty comes in that different people have different standards which they set as to where civilization is at the moment and where it could be at the moment. Appleby tended to associate with the Tugwell group, who set very high standards as to where civilization could be. If you didn't go all out to attain the standards which they had in mind, you were falling short of the possible." As in the period before the 1935 purge, Wallace stayed somewhere between the two groups, "trying to maintain peace in the family and get something done." By and large, however, he supported Tolley and Evans, just as he had earlier supported Davis. Wallace may have become more liberal during Roosevelt's second administration, but, determined not to put his agricultural program at risk, he continued to make appointments "much further to the right than Appleby would have liked."[19]

Roosevelt had been incensed at the invalidation of the National Industrial Recovery Act (NIRA) and the AAA and, in the hope of gaining a decisive influence over the Supreme Court, he proposed to Congress, early in his second term, legislation empowering him to appoint one new justice for each existing justice aged seventy or more. The previous year, Wallace had argued in his book *Whose Constitution?* that the Supreme Court was interpreting in much too rigorous a way the Constitution's emphasis on freedom of enterprise, so that, for example, it was protecting the freedom of exploiters to devastate large tracts of agricultural land. The Constitution was designed to protect the general welfare, and the elected representatives of the people should have more power to interpret or if necessary amend it to that end. During the 1936 presidential campaign he had urged Roosevelt to put the Court issue directly before the people. If reelected, Roosevelt would then have a mandate to amend the Constitution, the procedure Wallace had recommended in his book. Roosevelt rejected this advice, deciding instead on the controversial "court-packing" plan. Out of loyalty to the president, Wallace supported him in public, but privately he found Roosevelt's tactics "a little too slick."[20]

Roosevelt's proposal was eventually defeated in the Senate. By this time the Supreme Court had altered its course, approving the National Labor Relations Act and other liberal measures, but Roosevelt was perceived as having been defeated by the Court and suffered a loss of prestige. This was exacerbated in late 1937 when certain injudicious fiscal measures that he initiated brought about a sharp recession. He had feared an inflationary boom, and being eager also to balance the budget, heavily cut government spending — the spending most economists thought had brought about the recovery. Budget balancing was a long-standing predilection of Roosevelt's, which Wallace thought misguided.

Roosevelt was also having trouble with Congress. During this second administration, legislation was passed providing for minimum wages and a maximum number of work hours per week; further, there was provision for public housing development, and the Wallace-initiated legislation aimed at alleviating rural poverty. All this, however, was opposed by conservative-minded Democrats in Congress, and the embattled Roosevelt resolved to bring about their defeat in the 1938 congressional elections. This time, Wallace's opposition was more overt.

Wallace thought the intended purge intemperate and unproductive; it would polarize the party even further and work in favor of the Republicans. He was quite willing to back his own judgment against the president's: "He asked me to go along with him in purging [Senator] Gillette of Iowa, and I just told him I wasn't going to do it. It wasn't a difference exactly. We never had any unkind words." Later, in the oral history, he said:

> I didn't feel that I should go along. I'd been urging so strongly the need for unity in view of the foreign peril—unity between business and labor—and I thought also, it was essential to have unity inside of the Democratic Party at that time in view of the foreign peril. . . . So far as Iowa was concerned, the Democrats I knew were good friends of Guy Gillette. . . . Gillette is a very fine person. He was never a supporter of the New Deal, really. He was always his own person—a completely independent man. . . .
>
> I didn't go along, because frankly I just don't like purges—that's all. It was just a question of temperament.[21]

We have already seen that Wallace did not like purges; the aggressive, confrontational aspect of the purge in his own department had been deeply distressing to him. But in addition to that, there were more specific political reasons for his not acceding to Roosevelt's wishes here: he knew that his farm program was receiving strong support from conservative southern Democrats, and the farm program, beyond almost anything else, had to be protected.[22]

Despite any irritation Roosevelt may have felt, Wallace's independence as well as his administrative ability compelled his respect. During Roosevelt's first term, their relationship was cordial rather than close, but throughout his second term and later, it became more intimate. More frequently than before Wallace stopped to talk with the president after cabinet meetings. He began sending Roosevelt supportive, not to say flattering, letters. "I am enclosing . . . herewith copy of the speech which I gave before the Young Democrats at Indianapolis," he wrote in September 1937. "Some people thought I was a little gushy at the close when I referred to the spirit of joy which I felt you had contributed to the nation. I still stand by what I said."[23]

Wallace was also more inclined to proffer advice. In November 1937, he sent Roosevelt "some ideas as to the sort of thing which I think ought to be included in the statement which I feel it so vitally important for you to make to the American people"; the president should try to get labor and capital to work together to lift the economy and allow some pump-priming expenditure. "I felt that you would be interested in having my observations as to what I believe the real objectives of this administration are and ought to be," Wallace declared in January 1938, at the end of a letter which had explained how "increased balance[d] abundance" could be achieved.[24]

As he had grown in experience and stature, Wallace had felt free to turn his attention increasingly to international affairs, and of this, too, Roosevelt was made aware. This interest had actually developed from the breadth of Wallace's conception of the role of agriculture in international trade and his realization that even the resource-rich United States could not sustain itself in isolation. Beginning in the 1920s he had propagated at countless farmers' picnics the doctrine that after World War I the United States found itself not a debtor but a creditor nation, and that it had to begin to act like one, by lowering tariffs and permitting foreign countries to earn enough from their exports to America to be able to purchase American farm products. This broad outlook had been fostered by his agricultural tours to Britain and Europe and by his attendance at conferences at which the international ramifications of agricultural policies were discussed.[25]

During Roosevelt's first administration Wallace's comments on international affairs had been sparse. He had opposed the recognition of Russia because he doubted that the claimed economic benefits would accrue (fearing that the importation of Russian wheat would depress the domestic price), because the Russian state was irreligious and therefore, he believed, untrustworthy in matters of trade, and because of the liquidation of the Kulaks — "I couldn't help having a good bit of sympathy for those people, because in Russia they represented about the same kind of farmers that I was used to dealing with in Iowa." Recalling this for his interviewer, Wallace recounted a jokingly sinister remark Roosevelt made: "President Roosevelt used to call Henry Morgenthau a Kulak, incidentally — with great glee. I think Henry Morgenthau shivered every time he heard Roosevelt use the word, because he felt he was on the point of liquidation."[26]

With the international situation becoming more threatening, Wallace tried to push Roosevelt toward a more conservative stance in domestic affairs. In late 1937 and early 1938 he was encouraging the president in letters and memoranda to issue a "call to cooperative action by all the groups to serve the General Welfare by means of Efficient Democracy. . . . I believe furthermore that with national and international affairs taking the turn which they have now taken, it is possible for you, by striking a note of this sort, to gain the allegiance of a number of business men, especially of the smaller order, who really ought to be on our side."[27] He tried to persuade the president that he was "leaning too far to the left." What Wallace meant by "Efficient Democracy," as far as can be gathered, was that the federal government should use tax incentives, shared capitalization, and other means to persuade private capital to work in the direction the administration wanted. Thus, in a letter of March 1938, he wrote:

> In my various conversations with you, I have urged again and again the desirability of making it clear to the nation that business may proceed without fear. I have no illusions with regard to the attitude which business has toward this administration. . . .
>
> Nevertheless these men control the bulk of the flow of private capital and at the present juncture it is absolutely necessary to induce that flow by making investment possibilities and by using government capital to bring on the flow of private capital along the lines I suggested to you on Tuesday. . . .
>
> After the tax bill is passed I would urge that you give out a clear-cut statement in which you reiterate your ultimate objectives that are absolutely sound and in which you reassure business men that they need have no fear of a prolonged depression. . . .
>
> The international situation is so disquieting that I believe it is vital to bring about much more harmony in the national picture than we have at the present moment. In times of international crisis the strength of the hand of the foreign minister of a nation is roughly proportionate to the harmony of purpose existing in the nation itself. To attain the necessary harmony of purpose which the United States now needs to play a strong hand on behalf of democracies in world affairs, it is necessary that there be greater confidence among business men than now exists.[28]

This tendency to favor private industry and business, however, did not mean that Wallace would abandon his deeply felt animosity to monopoly capitalism. During World War II he took determined measures to try to prevent big corporations from gaining advantages of scale, because of the country's enormous wartime needs, that would enable them to dominate industry and establish virtual monopolies when peace came.

By this time, Roosevelt was occasionally inviting Wallace to stay at the Little White House at Warm Springs, Georgia, or to join him on his yacht. "It gave me great pleasure this morning to read of your driving your car yourself," Wallace wrote to the president in March 1938. "I could so clearly call to mind the picture of your bumping over the dirt roads among the pine forests." He hoped Roosevelt would "have the utmost of pleasure in driving your car bareheaded in the Georgia sunshine and that you will come back ready to furnish that vivid, dramatic, steady leadership which we now so much need both domestically and internationally."[29] And when, the following month, Roosevelt was considering whether to send a message to Hitler and Mussolini urging moderation, he sought Wallace's opinion. "I think he came to value my judgment on foreign affairs," Wallace explained later. "I know in 1938, in April, he asked my judgment on a message he was sending Hitler, which was rather a strange thing to ask a Secretary of Agriculture about." Wallace's response was that the gesture would be ineffectual because "the two mad men respect force and force alone," and though the president went ahead anyway, Wallace saw the approach as revealing the growing depth of their relationship.[30] The significance of this increasing closeness with Roosevelt becomes greater once we understand the direction in which Wallace's thoughts were now running.

GROWING POLITICAL AMBITIONS

During his second term as secretary of agriculture, Wallace, in his own reserved way, began to develop political ambitions. Chester Davis thought these were partly inspired by some of the men in Wallace's department. "I think the boys — Baldwin, Appleby and the rest — were feeding Henry the idea that they could build up in this country, with the support of the Congress of Industrial Organization (CIO), a great political organization which would be more than a farm organization. It would work closely with the CIO movement in organized labor. They thought that the wedding of the two [the CIO and the radical Farmers Union] would make a political force that could control this country indefinitely. I think Henry was led to believe that he was the destined leader." As early as 1936, by Davis's account, Wallace was showing signs of responding to the political pressure being applied to him — "the constant work that was going on around Henry to convince him that he was the messiah for the underprivileged, and that in that way lay his political future."[31]

Davis's opinion that Appleby was one of the main movers in Wallace's turning his attention to higher office is corroborated by the oral history recollections of fellow Agriculture Department officials Oscar Stine, Samuel Bledsoe, and Spike Evans, but Appleby's own account suggests that the germ of the idea was Wallace's own and Appleby was just a willing helper:

> If I'd kept a diary I could have pointed to the day when Wallace first showed signs of desiring to be a candidate. He tried rather hard to avoid actions that would be reaching actions. . . . At the same time by about early '37, Wallace would on occasion tell me that Cordell Hull had said to him that he thought Wallace ought to be Roosevelt's successor or that Homer Cummings had said to him that he thought Wallace ought to be Roosevelt's successor. He never at the time did anything but report it. He never indicated any interest in it or any zeal for it, but the fact that he reported it, I think, would indicate that that was the time when he began to think of it.[32]

In fact, Wallace began not only to report such comments to Appleby but also to record them in his diary, when he resumed keeping it in November 1939, and the frequency with which he sets down remarks even by people not directly involved in the political scene does indeed suggest that by this time he was taking them seriously, even though, characteristically, he makes no overt comment. With the election of 1940 in mind, he would ask visitors who they thought would be likely candidates if Roosevelt did not run. Would there be support for Cordell Hull? Would there by support for Paul McNutt? It is as if he were summing up the likely competition. If he occasionally elicited the response that there would be strong support for Henry Wallace, as likely as not he would reply by speaking "in the highest terms of Jim Farley." But people began to volunteer their opinion that Wallace was the man they would like to run, if Roosevelt did not. For example, the diary entry for 4 March 1940 reads: "A. C. Horn, a paint manufacturer of New York city, ate lunch with me and Ezekiel at Ezekiel's suggestion. He . . . is head of the Anti-Defamation League of B'nai B'rith. . . . In case the President did not run, Horn was very eager for me to be in position to run. He mentioned certain wealthy friends whom he thought might promote my nomination. I told him that everything at the present time depended on the President."

Or again, in the diary entry for 25 March 1940: "Rex [Tugwell] started to talk about the 1940 situation and said that if it were left to him to maneuver events in the way most favorable to me, he could not have arranged them more favorably. . . . He was sure the President was not going to run for a third term and was equally sure that all the candidates which had been brought out had been killed off or would shortly be killed off. . . . He said the reason he was for me in 1940 was because I was the only one of the candidates who really knew anything about economics." And on 29 March 1940: "[Dan] Roper then proceeded to say that he thought the Democratic nominee should have a very strong appeal among the farmers. I have not the slightest idea whether he was holding this out as bait to me or not." On 30 April Wallace noted that Senators Herring and Birmingham (who had come in to plan the Iowa convention) "felt strongly that the delegates to the state convention should come out strongly with a resolution endorsing the President for a third term and myself in case the President were not available" and on the following day recorded Herring's opinion that "if Roosevelt made himself unavailable that the Iowa delegation should go down the line for me."

For a time Wallace thought that the chances of Roosevelt running again were evenly balanced, that if the international situation were not threatening, he might step down. But as the election drew closer, and with the war actually under way in Europe, he became convinced that Roosevelt would seek a third term. Whatever Wallace's secret wishes may have been, he was realist enough to know that if Roosevelt declared for a third term there was absolutely no point in anyone standing against him for the Democratic nomination; that in that case the most he could aspire to was the vice-presidential nomination. Even so, it must have been in his mind that the president would have a successor some day, and that that day could come even before the term was out. In the diary entry for 24 February 1940 Wallace records the opinion of columnist Raymond Tucker that "the President has been told that his health cannot stand up under another four-years term." He comments: "Frankly I question this. I think the office is the breath of life for Roosevelt and that he will live longer being President than he will outside of the President's office." But the question mark was there, and it becomes quite plain that Wallace was not ignoring any offers of help, however diffident his manner. He was positioning himself not to displace Roosevelt but to be his successor.

Wallace himself says nothing about his political ambition, so we are left to wonder about its nature. He appears to have had no reservations about his ability to play a larger role; there is never a hint in his diary or oral history that he questioned his own capacity. Since joining the Roosevelt cabinet, he had measured himself against others — Ickes, Morgenthau, Hopkins, Roosevelt himself — invariably to his own advantage. This was not just a question of intellectual superiority; quite justly, Wallace prided himself on his understanding not simply of science and agriculture but of finance, economics, and world affairs. His sympathies were broader now than they had once been. During Roosevelt's second term, he had developed a greater concern for all the people of the United States, not just for farming groups. That gave "more vivid coloring," as he expressed it, to an earlier, deeply held conviction — that one's purpose in life should be to promote what he had called "the longtime good of all mankind." Such an ideal remained, possibly inspiring him to leadership. Wallace still believed, too, that a general spiritual movement could transform the nation and even the world. Perhaps he had come to see this in much more practical terms. Perhaps he, the political, rather than Roerich, the mystical leader, might have a crucial role in bringing it about.

Of course, such things could never be spoken of. As a practical politician, Wallace had to conceal his more transcendental aims within acceptable modes of discourse. Only rarely, in public pronouncements, had he crossed the dangerous line that could betray the Theosophical origins of some of his basic beliefs, and then usually in the period before the esoteric connection with Nicholas Roerich was broken. One example, which allows us to see in more detail the ideal world he desired, may be found at the end of his book *New Frontiers*, published in 1934. For the most part this work contained a fairly hard-headed economic analysis of the nation's problems, and a vigorous defense of the policies of the New Deal. But in the final chapter (which Wallace had sent to Roerich for his perusal) he gave more definite shape to a vision he had discussed with Charles Roos, George W. Russell, and the Roerich group. He pictured a future frontier where cooperation would replace individualistic competition, where the rewards of labor would be distributed fairly, and where the worship of wealth and power would be supplanted by the worship of "beauty and justice and joy of spirit."

In this more perfect state, as Wallace and Russell had discussed and as Roos would have understood, individuals would renew their contact with the earth, drawing rich inspiration from it. "Many of the most lively, intimate expressions of spirit spring from the joyous, continuous contact of human beings with a particular locality. They feel the age-long spirit of this valley or that hill each with its trees and rocks and special tricks of weather, as the seasons unfold in their endless charm." In the new cooperative communities that would emerge "there will flower . . . not only those who attain joy in daily, productive work well done; but also those who paint and sing and tell stories with the flavor peculiar to their own valley, well-loved hill, or broad prairie." Far from being tempted to leave these little societies, children would "feel it is a privilege to learn to live with the soil and the neighbors of their fathers." The communities would become "like many colored beads on the thread of the nation and the varied strings of beads will be the glory of the world." "A great seer of the human heart who lived nineteen hundred years ago" had called this new state the Kingdom of Heaven. (It was, of course, quite in line with Theosophical doctrine to see Jesus Christ as one of those highly developed beings who carried with them the wisdom of the ages.)

Wallace had gone on to suggest that a general spiritual revolution might be at hand, arguing that the signs (the vast suffering of the unemployed and destitute, the advanced state of scientific understanding, "our mechanical inventive power," and so on) seemed auspicious. The way forward would be difficult but "the essential thing is that our spirits be continually renewed by the vision of the ageless operations that bind all humanity together." One of the "guiding principles for the future" was "a design drawn from the far past . . . appropriate because it suggests the maximum development of individual diversity within the limitations of the whole." This was the design that Nicholas Roerich had used for his Banner of Peace and the Roerich Pact for the preservation of cultural objects. Though ancient, the sign had "great depths of meaning in this infinitely more complex world of today."[33]

After the Roerich fiasco, Wallace's references to this vision of an ideal society, references that carried the implication that he might have some as yet undefined role in bringing it about, had to be more circumspect. Even in private he showed great diffidence. His diary entry for 17 February 1940 records that the anthropologist Vincinzo Patruela, who had worked with Venezuela Indian tribes, had come to see him, telling him he was greatly impressed with Wallace's writings and with those of George W. Russell. In phrases that should have struck an answering chord in Wallace, Patruela spoke of a receptiveness of country folk to the idea of a new spiritual movement, and of the indifference of those in Washington. But the anthropologist found the secretary noncommittal; religion and politics, Wallace pointed out to him, made a poor mix. In his diary, Wallace commented dryly: "Apparently he wanted me to inspire him to do some great and wonderful thing and was a little disappointed when I did not warm up to him more. I was nice to him but did not bubble." Yet as J. Samuel Walker notes, despite Wallace's "bitter experience" with Roerich, his belief in "the fundamental unity of mankind, the need to achieve a new spirit of cooperation at home and abroad, and the practicality of the Sermon on the Mount remained unshaken." For example, in an address at Louisiana State University in April 1938, speaking on the Book of Revelation text "I saw a new heaven and a new earth," he noted that the Great Depression had failed to bring about a general spiritual revolution but suggested that the menacing events then occurring in Europe might yet cause a "full awakening."[34] Perhaps these ideas, once so fervently held, made him more receptive to the suggestions of Appleby and others that he was the man to take over in the developing crisis.

According to Appleby, from about 1937 "visitors began to come who would say in Wallace's office, 'Well, you ought to be Roosevelt's successor. If there's anything I can do, call on me.' He began to say then, I think from the beginning, invariably, 'Well, talk to Paul about things like that.' That was the only indication there ever was that I was to handle political affairs. They would come and tell me."[35] It would seem from this that Appleby was rather surprised to be appointed Wallace's political organizer. But that is at variance with the opinions of Davis, Stine, and Bledsoe that Appleby out of his own interest first incited Wallace's political ambition; perhaps there was some truth on each side.

Certainly Appleby was not reluctant to manage the secretary's political affairs. There is a fascinating letter from him to R. M. "Spike" Evans of the Department of Agriculture dated 28 December 1936 that shows he had already begun organizing, though it is indeterminate as to whether he or the secretary was the prime mover:

Dear Spike,
     As I sat at home with my foot elevated during the Christmas

Holidays treating a sprained ankle, I thought a little bit about the primary essential of having an Iowa delegation in 1940, and I was impressed by the need of getting a number of Henry's friends in each Iowa county to register as Democrats. . . . it will be immensely important that we have in each county convention a handful of militant friends who will demand that the delegates chosen there be instructed to vote only for national convention delegates who are pledged to H. A. It frequently happens that half a dozen people in a county convention can determine results, but in Iowa so many of the persons who are active as Democrats are of another school that we might stub our toe on this first hurdle.

It is important enough to move in this direction that I believe you might talk to your friend Hawley so that he could begin to agitate the thing. All agitation ought to be done on the most confidential basis and it ought to appear as wholly uninspired here. . . . It is immensely important to avoid letting any word of this movement and its purpose get out, but I believe it can be done and be done quietly, almost on a sort of secret society basis. Half a dozen men who can be counted on will in turn make it a point to approach others they know can be counted on.[36]

Some of the expressions in this letter—"militant friends," "agitate," and so on—and the general air of the secret society, with men who can be counted on secretly contacting others who can be counted on, are reminiscent of the language and methods of Communists, or at least of a group that feels itself embattled and in opposition. We make this point only because the suggestion by colleagues of Wallace that in 1940 he was being run for political office by Appleby and Baldwin is very similar to the much more widespread allegations in 1948 that Wallace was being run for president by the Communist Party. But suggestions by Davis, Bledsoe, and others relating to the 1940 campaign were collected after all the publicity of the 1948 campaign, which may have colored their retrospective interpretations. The oral history contribution by Spike Evans shows how time, or perhaps prudence, can affect one's account of the past. He says:

As to the inception of the idea of Henry Wallace running for Vice President, Appleby and LeCron used to talk about it occasionally and I used to talk with them too, as would anybody else who happened to be around. . . . I might not have known anything about that until some time later, perhaps in 1937. . . .

I was in sympathy with the idea of Wallace's becoming Vice President. LeCron certainly was, too. As to Appleby, he was the forefront of the whole thing. I don't know why that was so. That had all been crystallized before I ever came to town.[37]

But the assumption in Appleby's letter that he could rely on Evans's confidential support implies that Evans was already in 1936 an active participant in promoting Wallace. Notwithstanding the conspiratorial tone employed by Appleby, the behind-the-scenes maneuverings by him and others to "run" Wallace for vice president or, eventually, for president may be seen as a normal part of politics. It is Wallace's enigmatic character and the image he consistently presented of being indifferent to political advancement that gives these comments, in retrospect, a conspiratorial cast.

Appleby worked energetically in Wallace's favor until the passage, in August 1939, of the Hatch Act, which restricted the participation of federal employees in political campaigning. "I had done everything I could do, I felt—and I had made up my mind Wallace was in position. Roosevelt was probably going to run again and I hoped he was going to run again. He was going to pick the Vice Presidential candidate, and Wallace was going to be in there where Roosevelt could pick him." Both he and Wallace felt that it would be a mistake for Wallace to push himself on Roosevelt's attention as a candidate, that Roosevelt would not look favorably on anyone who was aggressive in that way, because Roosevelt himself was not "reaching for" anything. "The things were too big and the burdens were too great," Appleby noted later. "It was going to be up to the political processes and the American people to decide this thing this time."

Appleby calculated the political support he believed Wallace could command. There were the governors of California and Arkansas and some of the delegates from Oregon, California, Minnesota, Wisconsin, and Pennsylvania. Luther Harr, state Democratic chairman of Pennsylvania, favored Wallace, as did New York's Ed Flynn. "So I knew there was going to be enough strength so that he would be in there, and Roosevelt could see that here's a man who's got a good deal of strength, but a man who'd been comporting himself appropriately. I thought things were in good shape."[38]

From Roosevelt's point of view, Wallace's credentials as a running mate were impressive. As we have seen, the two men had grown closer and Roosevelt had come to value his secretary of agriculture's advice. Wallace was reliably liberal, an "out-and-out New Dealer," as Samuel Rosenman put it, "in whose hands the program of the New Deal— domestic and international—would be safe." He would shore up support in the farm states: a Gallup poll in March 1940 showed that two out of every three farmers surveyed believed that the New Deal's farm program had helped them, and three out of four thought that Wallace had performed well in his job.[39] But Wallace had also, by 1940, won a significant following among the nation's African American population, a development of which Roosevelt was now made aware.

The impact of the AAA's acreage-reduction schemes on southern blacks had been severe, and the plight of dispossessed sharecroppers and day laborers in particular had provoked attacks on the farm program by the African American press. In 1936, Samuel Bledsoe of the AAA's Information Section had warned Wallace that "if you want to be President of the United States . . . you'll have to have the Negroes of the country. They'll have to be for you, like you, believe you are right where they are concerned." From that time, he and Wallace set out to repair the damage. They saw to it that African Americans were hired by the AAA and, a novelty in the South, were given the vote in AAA referenda. The response, according to Bledsoe, was "amazing." Then, in 1937, Wallace and Bledsoe brought African American editors to Washington to discuss their objections to AAA policies, a "revolutionary move" that conservatives in the department opposed. When the parties adjourned for lunch, the editors were refused service in the department's cafeteria and a separate dining room had to be found, whereupon, Bledsoe has recalled, "a group of us went in and ate with them. I remember old Davis [a black employee] . . . thought that was the greatest thing since Lincoln freed the slaves."

Wallace began to speak out on racial matters. In an address at Alabama's Tuskegee Institute, he announced "out of a clear sky" that "there is no scientific basis for racial superiority. That is just nonsense." The reaction, according to Bledsoe, was electric. "You could feel a wave run all through the whole audience. First thing you know, word got out among the Negroes, 'Here is a man who thinks we are people, thinks we're men.'" After some more speeches like that, and with the African American press now onside, Wallace "had them [African Americans] a hundred percent. . . . Beginning about 1938 or at least 1939, where it came to Wallace, the Negro would say, 'Ahhhhh. It's all right. That fellow I know. He's all right.' Not only that, but we had in the Department with Wallace some good policies. We opened up cafeterias for Negroes, appointed Negroes to jobs."

More was involved here than political calculation. "Wallace himself didn't have any reservations so far as race was concerned," Bledsoe asserted. "The race theory was nonsense. He didn't believe in it. He knew enough. He was a scientist."[40] In 1934, referring to the great potential of the United States, Wallace had written: "The human beings now here have been drawn from among the most intelligent and vigorous racial stocks of the old world."[41] But in early 1939, in a speech entitled "The Genetic Basis of Democracy," he decried the notion of racial superiority. "Claims to racial superiority are not new in this world. Even in such a democratic country as ours there are those who would claim that the American people are superior to all others." With the repugnant racial policies of Nazi Germany now obviously on his mind, Wallace continued: "Never before in the world's history has such a conscious and systematic effort been made to inculcate the youth of this nation with ideas of racial superiority as are being made in Germany today. We must remember that down through the ages one of the most popular political devices has been to blame economic and other troubles on some minority group."

The influence of Wallace's trip to the South in 1936, his closer identification with the poor and oppressed of all races, is suggested in the remarks that followed: "Now, it is the fashion in many quarters to sneer at those . . . who suffer from poor education and bad diet . . . live in tumble-down cabins without mattresses. And yet I wonder if any scientist would claim that 100,000 children taken at birth from these families would rank any lower in inborn ability than 100,000 children taken at birth from the wealthiest one per cent of the parents of the United States. If both groups are given the same food, housing, education, and cultural traditions, would they not turn out to have about equal mental and moral traits on the average?" He could not feel confident that America's democratic system would endure, Wallace said, "if millions of unskilled workers and their families are condemned to be reliefers all their lives, with no place in our industrial system . . . if half our people must be below the line of decent nutrition, while only one tenth succeed in reaching good nutritional standards . . . if most of our children continue to be reared in surroundings where poverty is highest and education is lowest."[42] It is not just science that is speaking here, but a deepening humanity. Democratic political advisers were quick to point out to the president the significance of Wallace's speech. Samuel Rosenman reported that it had aroused keen interest among leaders of racial minority groups, and veteran politician Ed Flynn suggested that, at a time of rising racial tension, Henry Wallace could help secure the wavering northern African American vote.[43]

Yet despite Wallace's obvious strengths, Roosevelt must have been wary. Gossip concerning the secretary's unconventional beliefs had almost certainly reached his ears. He knew something of the Roerich expedition, and, an avid reader of newspapers, would have seen reports of the embarrassing behavior of its leader and of its precipitate demise. Wallace's dealings with Roos and Roerich were known to his immediate staff, as their reminiscences show. Paul Appleby told later how Mary Huss, Wallace's personal secretary, would identify what Appleby called Wallace's "screwy letters" and bring them to him, and how he would then remonstrate with Wallace, urging him not to send them. (Interestingly, Wallace seems to have accepted these contests, even to have welcomed them. "I don't always have good judgment," he told Appleby. "I want somebody who'll fight with me.") But Appleby was not always successful: "There were some [letters] I could never get him to change . . . to do with his mystical associations." Appleby specifically mentioned, in this regard, the correspondence with Nicholas Roerich, correspondence that he "argued with him about through the years."

Department solicitor Gardner Jackson was another who recalled the Roerich expedition, how it became "a topic for gossip and discussion" at Jackson's "evening powwows" with Appleby, James LeCron, Baldwin, and their wives, and how Appleby "threw in a lot of other stuff that Wallace had been engaged in which he was able to prevent him from going all-out on in terms of its ever becoming public." Jackson was aware that "Wallace had some fellow out in New Mexico or Arizona, an Indian medicine man, whom he was corresponding with and was wont to believe as a supernatural sort of prescience in reference to prognostications on crops, weather and all that business." Entries in Secretary of Interior Harold Ickes's famous diary reveal that he knew or suspected that Wallace was "a good deal of a mystic" and was "very much interested in Indians."[44] It is difficult to believe that none of this gossip had filtered through to the president. Thus, although Wallace had much to recommend him as a running mate, persistent rumors that he was mixed up in mystical activities must have caused Roosevelt concern. It can hardly have been as anything but a kind of probe into this that the following curious incident occurred, reported in Wallace's diary for 12 April 1940, not many weeks before the Democratic National Convention was to be held.

Roosevelt, with "great gusto" as Wallace describes it, told him a story about two Englishmen who had attempted to locate the foundations of Glastonbury Abbey, a structure destroyed during the reign of Henry VIII. Failing in this, they resorted to spirit writing by means of the Ouija board, and had supposedly received a message "in monkish Latin, presumably from Anselmo," that directed them to the correct place. Their excavations there revealed the foundations. In 1917, during World War I, they again resorted to spirit writing in the hope of determining the course of future events. This time a Roman general told them that the British would suffer reverses but should not lose heart because help would arrive from across the sea, and with that help they would be victorious on the first day that snow fell. Roosevelt told Wallace he had checked meteorological records and found that the first snows of 1918 had fallen on 11 November, the very day on which peace was declared. Still later, the two Englishmen received yet another prophecy by the same means. In 1940, another world war would occur. It would be followed by a period of peace, but "a much more severe war would break out in 1960 at which time the Japs and Chinese together would sweep over Europe like a Mongol horde, and all that would be left would be England. They would also conquer all of the Western Hemisphere except the United States. There would only be left England and the United States as two islands of self-contained and puny civilization."

Wallace believed that Roosevelt was expecting him to check the authenticity of this story. Knowing that Agnes Peter, a descendant of Martha Washington, was interested in this kind of archaeological research, Wallace consulted her and she located two books in the Library of Congress by Frederick Bligh Bond, one of the Englishmen to whom the revelations had supposedly been made. The books contained the Glastonbury Abbey story but said nothing about the prophecy concerning the war. Agnes Peter's letter to Wallace concluded: "I should listen to Mr. Bond but I should not be a convert to his talk nor his reasoning. As an architect he is more convincing. He is deep in psychical research and too much of it is not always a balanced diet." Wallace reported this skeptical assessment to Roosevelt, who was apparently satisfied with his endorsement of it, but the "mysticism" stigma was to reappear at a critical time for the election.

At this stage Roosevelt had not yet declared himself a candidate for a third term and of course had not picked Wallace for a running mate. Just two weeks earlier Wallace had had a visit from Senator Gillette of Iowa, the man whom he had supported against Roosevelt's attempted purge. Gillette said "he thought the best way to straighten out the Democratic party situation in Iowa was to have the party get enthusiastically behind me *as the Presidential nominee* [emphasis added]. If the Iowa Democratic Convention got behind me vigorously, and stayed behind me in the National Convention, this would demonstrate to the farmers of the Middlewest that the Democratic party really was interested in agriculture." Wallace took this quite seriously. "I told Senator Gillette that if any active work were to be done for me in the precincts and counties of Iowa between now and May 11, I felt I should tell the President about it as soon as he got back from Warm Springs. I mentioned that several months ago the President had told Ed Birmingham that he wanted the Iowa delegation to go instructed for me. . . . I have always been disposed to take this statement of the President with a grain of salt." [45]

On 6 May Gillette showed Wallace a telegram signed by seventy Iowa Democrats proposing that he seek FDR's "approval of an instructed Iowa delegation for Wallace." Wallace felt that "there was sufficient possibility of embarrassment in this telegram so that I should let the President know about it." He had already telephoned the president about Gillette's earlier proposal, saying that he did not want this movement to embarrass either FDR or himself. Now he wrote, repeating that wish, but saying: "The names on the telegram are representative of the leadership of the Party in Iowa and collectively are of such strength as to require the most serious consideration by the Iowa Congressional delegation." [46] This letter was calculated to make Roosevelt feel that here was a man and a movement of substance, yet a man who at the same time, by notifying him, was demonstrating his loyalty. Wallace was reaping the benefit of his support of Gillette against Roosevelt in 1938, yet using his frankness about it to cancel out any demerit he may have incurred for disloyalty.

In his diary for 24 May 1940, Wallace reported a view expressed by

James Farley that whoever won the vice-presidential nomination that year "would probably be the strongest single force in the Democratic Party by 1944." Farley had gone on to speculate that, if elected, Roosevelt would not live out his term, but Wallace downplayed this suggestion, believing that the president's relish for the office maintained his vitality.[47] On 10 July, the month in which the Democratic National Convention was to be held and the candidates nominated, Wallace went to see the president at the White House and found him in a deep study. He told Roosevelt he had never seen him like this before, and then handed him a memorandum "which assumed that he would be running, suggesting that he stay on a high plane and deal continually with the theme of national defense—not as a candidate but as President." Roosevelt told Wallace that he had hoped to avoid running for a third term, but that Ed Kelly had insisted that it was his duty to do so, even though the job might kill him within a few months. It now seemed as though he would have to take up this unwanted burden. It is typical of Wallace that one cannot tell from his words whether he felt sympathy for Roosevelt or not. "I said in that case I hoped he would conduct the campaign from the high pinnacle of a President dealing with the problems of national unity and national defense."[48]

The issue of the vice-presidential nomination remained open until the last moment. Looking back, Wallace endorsed a comment made in James Farley's book to the effect that, at the start of the convention, only Speaker Bankhead, Paul McNutt, and Wallace himself remained in the vice-presidential race and that Wallace had a mere handful of personal votes. "There was no organized effort whatever to get me votes. The nominee literally was to be whomever Roosevelt chose—definitely."[49] But although there may have been no organized effort, Wallace had helpers at the convention, namely, Paul Appleby and Claude Wickard, undersecretary of agriculture.

Appleby had decided not to go to Chicago because, still being assistant to the secretary, he was restricted by the Hatch Act. But two days before the convention opened his telephone began to ring with calls from Chicago. Wickard was already there but feeling inadequate, not sure how to consult the relevant people. Luther Harr called to tell Appleby about support for Wallace for president from the Pennsylvania and Connecticut delegations. "Then, I think, along about two o'clock Harr called again and said, 'Paul, I'm just leaving the room to go down and rent rooms for a Wallace headquarters. We've got just now delivered so many thousand balloons, so many thousand of these folder match books, and so on[,] all "Wallace for President." We're going to get banners painted.'"

Evidently Appleby was alarmed, knowing this aggressive promotion would alienate Roosevelt. "I said, 'Hold your horses. Don't rent any rooms, don't let out a balloon, and don't hand out a match. I'll be there in the morning.'" He telephoned his secretary, dictated his resignation, and two hours later boarded the Capital Limited for Chicago. The lobby of the Stevens Hotel was crowded with people he knew; no one seemed surprised to see him. Senator Joe Guffey was with Harr in his room, and they had more to tell Appleby about support coming in from all sides. Appleby warned them about being overaggressive, but told them to send reports of Wallace's growing support to Hopkins, so that he could relay them to the White House. He asked Guffey to contact the White House directly, urging that Wallace be nominated, and to have others do the same. But no one must give the impression that Wallace himself was "on the make for this."[50]

Appleby goes on to say how rapidly he got involved, as word spread that he was there and had taken a room. Thinking about the support of organized labor he recalls that long ago he had had Wallace and John L. Lewis meet at his house for dinner; now he went and lunched with Phil Murray of the CIO and some of his people. "In the course of that lunch, they committed their handful of votes that they had at that time scattered around — some in West Virginia, one labor delegate at large from Ohio, I believe, and one labor delegate in Michigan."[51] So, despite Wallace's carefully noncommittal air, there was plenty of politicking going on — but of course not all of it in Wallace's favor.

FDR'S RUNNING MATE

On 17 July, two days after the convention began, the delegates overwhelmingly endorsed Roosevelt as the party's presidential candidate, and on the same day Roosevelt let it be known that he wanted Wallace as his running mate. His decision was immediately contested by close political advisers. From the convention, Harry Hopkins warned that it would provoke "a hell of a lot of opposition" — at least ten candidates had greater support. Roosevelt brushed the objection aside: "All the conservatives in America are going to bring pressure on the convention to beat Henry," he declared. "The fellow they want is either

Jesse [Jones] or Bankhead. I'm going to tell them that I won't run with either of those men or with any other reactionary."[52]

Next, Democratic National Committee chairman Jim Farley tried to change Roosevelt's mind, arguing that a more conservative running mate would balance the ticket. Again, Roosevelt stood firm. "I think Henry is perfect," he told Farley. "I like him. He's the kind of fellow I want around. He's honest. He thinks right. He's a digger." Farley then protested that Wallace would hurt the ticket because "the people look on him as a mystic." "He's not a mystic," Roosevelt snapped. "He's a philosopher. He's got ideas. He thinks right. He'll help people think." In what Farley saw as an unconscionable move, Roosevelt then telephoned Wallace at the convention and told him what Farley had said. A "very much disturbed" Wallace called on Farley in his office in the Congress Hotel, seeking an explanation. "He said he thought I was a friend of his," Farley recalled, "and I told him I was, but that didn't mean that I would like to see him President of the United States. And he was very much distressed about it."[53] Eight years later, in the 1948 campaign, Wallace would again show a degree of emotional hurt unusual for him and again because someone he thought an ally, Henry Morgenthau Jr., publicly described him as having a mystical bent. It was the reaction of someone whose cherished yet vulnerable convictions had been given a debased and unsympathetic representation — beliefs that precisely because of their vulnerability should have been treated respectfully by a friend.

Further humiliation was to follow. Angered by Roosevelt's attempt to dictate to the convention, the delegates and crowds in galleries made Wallace the focus of their resentment. They shouted down speakers supporting his nomination, booed and hissed every mention of his name. Seated with his wife on the platform, Wallace appeared shocked, numbed by the ferocity of the crowd's reaction. Frances Perkins remembered him "stooped . . . forward, listening," with a "way off" look in his eyes, his face registering "utter, blank suffering." Ilo Wallace's "brain was reeling. . . . The antagonism was crushing. I remember seeing Mrs. Roosevelt take her hand." L. Taber, master of the National Grange, another eyewitness, felt "as sorry for Mrs. Wallace and for Henry as I was for anyone in my life. . . . I'll never forget the tears I saw in Mrs. Wallace's eyes at the treatment that Henry received."[54]

When Wallace did badly in the early balloting, the president, listening to the proceedings from Washington, drafted a message to the convention. At stake, he declared, was the issue of whether the Democratic Party would continue to be "the champion of progressive and liberal policies and principle." Conservative and reactionary influences were disrupting the convention. Unless the party took a clear stand for liberalism (that is, by choosing Henry Wallace), he, Roosevelt, would decline its nomination.[55] In the final count, Wallace narrowly defeated his remaining rival, Speaker William Bankhead of Alabama, but so great was the antagonism toward him that he was unable to deliver his acceptance speech.

In his own acceptance speech, Roosevelt made a slip of the tongue that was quickly and perhaps correctly seized on as revealing one current of his thinking—he expressed gratification that Wallace had been chosen as Democratic candidate for "the high office of President of the United States," thus lending plausibility to the belief that Wallace was really being run for president. In the House of Representatives, Representative Andersen of Minnesota asserted that if Roosevelt were elected he would turn the presidency over to Wallace in a year or two. But toward November 1940, Roosevelt told the press that "God willing" he would serve the full term.[56]

When Wallace resigned as secretary of agriculture a month later, he did so without regret, believing that his work was done. In general the agricultural community was comparatively prosperous in relation to its state in 1933. Farm income, which had slumped from $79 billion in 1929 to $39 billion in 1933, had reached $66 billion by 1939.[57] The problem of overproduction seemed to be under control because the Ever-Normal Granary, which Wallace had been advocating publicly since early in the New Deal, and which he had been able to put into legislative form in 1938, was working well, storing agricultural surpluses in times of plenty and releasing them in times of drought. He was proud of his achievements—in planning the restoration of soil and the prevention of soil erosion, in the organization of local farmer committees ("the first nationwide example of genuine economic democracy we've ever had"), and in the strong impetus he had given to scientific work in agriculture.[58]

He must have been gratified by the tributes paid to him, on his departure, by those with whom he had closely worked. After the "indecision and unwillingness to face facts" he had encountered in the Federal Farm Board, economist and statistician Mordecai Ezekiel declared, it had been a "tremendous thrill" to see how Wallace "faced issues squarely, tried to see what the real facts were," and then "took action positively and fearlessly." In this manner the New Deal farm program had been developed. Wallace was intellectually honest and "the opposite of egocentric and selfish." He had run the affairs of government with "intelligence and statesmanship instead of by hunch, misinformation, and prejudice."

Scientists in the department spoke of their leader's "keen understanding" of genetics, mathematics, and economics, of his "remarkable knowledge of plants and animals." "To an extent almost beyond belief," said one, he had interested himself in their work. Dillon S. Myer, assistant chief of the Soil Conservation Service, recalled how Wallace, on a trip through the West, had spent several hours quizzing a staff member about the vegetative species they saw. Myer was then surprised to hear Wallace, in subsequent conversations with field officers, referring to these vegetative species by their correct scientific names and displaying an understanding of their economic importance. At Wallace's conferences with departmental personnel, Myer added, it was essential to remain alert: the secretary might suddenly seek confirmation of a statistic, request detailed information relating to one's field of expertise, or ask searching questions about some aspect of the department's work.

The "curious, probing, vigorous quality" of Wallace's mind was also stressed by Gove Hambidge, editor of the Agriculture Department's *Yearbook*. There was "no escaping H. A. when he set out to ask disconcerting questions, attack accepted fundamentals, formulate a bold new hypothesis, and suggest a campaign to turn up badly needed scientific facts." Then there was his "democratic approachableness": "I have never seen H. A. put on the slightest bit of dog or assume the slightest air of self-importance." Wallace's search for meaning and truth had never ceased, Hambidge declared; the secretary had a "profound" interest in spiritual questions. " 'What,' he will ask, 'do we have to replace the values given to men and women by the old-time faith that has been weakened and destroyed by modern science? . . . What will give us a sense of dedication and purpose that religion used to give us so powerfully?' " [59] Such questions continued to exercise Henry Wallace, and he continued to seek answers to them.

Wallace began his formal campaign in late August, and before it was over he had covered a grueling twenty-five thousand miles. On one three-day tour of Iowa, Nebraska, and Michigan in late October, he made twenty-nine appearances. As might have been expected, he contrasted the Democrats' record on agriculture, labor, and social security with that of their opponents, and portrayed the Republican challenger Wendell Willkie as the captive of party reactionaries and "predatory financial manipulators." After years of Republican obduracy and inaction, the New Deal had established a national farm program. The Ever-Normal Granary held ample reserves, and commodity loans had stabilized farmers' incomes. Soil fertility had risen and the balance between agriculture and industry had been restored. Given the chance, the Republicans would destroy all this. Pledges to the contrary by their candidate meant nothing, as congressional Republicans had already made their party's real intentions clear by voting against the first and second farm acts and opposing parity payments in 1939 and 1940. "The Republican platform pledging aid to agriculture," Wallace told one rally, "was nullified four days after the national convention when Republican representatives in Congress voted 106 to 39 against loans on corn, wheat, cotton and other commodities, while Democrats voted 100 per cent for them."

The New Deal's National Labor Relations Act, wages and hours legislation, and provision of old-age pensions had given labor "new hope and new security," but these measures, too, the Republicans had tried to block. Again, Willkie's good intentions counted for little, given the attitudes of leading Republican supporters. Had not a subsidiary of Commonwealth and Southern, the holding company of which Willkie himself had been president, recently been ordered by a U.S. Circuit Court of Appeals to stop intimidating workers? Had not other Republican backers hired labor spies? [60]

The nature of Wallace's forays into international affairs, however, come as something of a surprise. In his own nomination acceptance speech, delivered on 29 August in his hometown of Des Moines, he caused an outcry over the introduction of party politics into foreign policy, which ideally was supposed to be bipartisan, by referring to the Republicans as "the party of appeasement, whether it knows it or not." He claimed that there were many in the United States who wanted the United Kingdom to give up the struggle and the United States to engage in "economic appeasement" with a German-controlled Europe. "That way," he said, "lies slavery." He sought to associate the Republican leadership with the spirit of Nazism, telling his audience that Roosevelt's efforts to build international goodwill through expanded international trade had been made more difficult "by the opposition of Hitler abroad" and "by a continuous and bitter partisan opposition at home." The identity of those who had inspired this "bitter partisan opposition" was easily deduced from Wallace's succeeding remarks. "The dominant leadership of this Republican opposition has never understood . . . what the rise of Hitler meant to farmers, workers and business men in the United States. . . . When Roosevelt tried to adjust the internal affairs of the United States to a sick world they fought him at home as Hitler fought him abroad." Like their leaders, Republican supporters, even if inadvertently, were also in danger of aiding the Nazi cause: "Every evidence of opposition to Roosevelt within the United States has been reason for rejoicing in Berlin." He did not mean to imply, Wallace added disingenuously, that Republican leaders were "wilfully or consciously giving aid and comfort to Hitler"; but "I do want to emphasise that replacement of Roosevelt, even if it were by the most patriotic leadership that could be found, would cause Hitler to rejoice. I do not believe that the American people will turn their back on the man Hitler wants to see defeated." [61]

Not surprisingly, this series of egregious smears provoked some sharp criticism. On Wallace's resignation as secretary of agriculture, the *New York Times* had declared that opposition to New Deal farm policies had always been accompanied by "respect and esteem" for Wallace the man, and that the secretary's "integrity, sincerity, disinterestedness and good will are manifest to all." Now, the *Times* called Wallace's claim that, in effect, "a vote for Mr. Willkie is a vote for Hitler," "unjust," "irresponsible," and "reckless." By describing the Republican candidate as a man whose victory Hitler would applaud, Wallace had tried "to arrogate patriotism for the Democratic party." He and the Democrats "will be advised to cut this line of attack, and forget that they began it." [62]

But Wallace was not to be deflected. He went on to charge that labor leader John L. Lewis, who had declared for Willkie, had aligned himself with "the totalitarian elements in big business"—which was why a recent Lewis speech "sounds so much like Herr Goebbels"—and that Nazi agents in the United States were working to defeat the president and elect his opponent. When Willkie objected that events in Europe should not be dragged into a domestic campaign, Wallace professed amazement. Surely the Republican candidate "does not mean to say that the fact of his Nazi support should be hushed up until he is elected and the bells start ringing in Berlin." [63]

There are plenty of grounds for believing that Wallace set high moral standards for himself and others and tried always to follow them rigorously, never consciously allowing his actions to be motivated by mere self-interest. He claimed always to feel nothing but distaste for the grubby daily business of low-level politics, the business of trading favors with potential allies and cynically vilifying one's opponents. But was he not now indulging in just that kind of vilification? Could he really have believed that elements in the Republican Party and in big business had a totalitarian mentality and were in active sympathy with Nazism?

Perhaps he was sincere in these protestations, even though they went beyond any evidence he could have collected. There are some surprisingly vehement denunciations scattered through his oral history of the mutual admiration and fellow feeling that he believed existed between the powerful and wealthy elite of all nations, those who regarded themselves as of a superior breed to the common people, and were intent on holding onto and increasing their privilege and power. He felt he could intuitively identify that kind of authoritarian ideology in business moguls and their conservative political allies; for him they were in spirit all bearers of the seeds of Nazism, even if they had no actual link with the German movement. In important moral matters Wallace thought in stern, puritanical dichotomies, in terms of good versus evil, and it may have been through some such rationalization that he felt justified in making these sweeping accusations. Yet he had come as close as he could to accusing Republican leaders of being Nazis in fact, not just in some moral aspects, without actually saying it—an accusation he could not have sustained.

Questioned later about the nature of these attacks on the Republicans, Wallace admitted that some of his opponents had thought he was "hitting below the belt" when he referred to them as "appeasers," but explained that he had felt compelled to make the international situation and the need for preparedness into the dominant issues in the campaign. That decision might have been politically costly, Wallace said, because he came from the strongly isolationist Midwest, but the national interest had demanded that he take this course. "The only thing that may be said about the whole period at the end of 1940," he said, "was that I was wholeheartedly on the side of every possible effort for maximum preparedness."[64] Later, during World War II and the Korean War, Wallace was to show that the preservation of the United States was his overriding concern, and if he felt the country was put at risk by the Republicans' policies, the most vigorous political tactics were justified.

Roosevelt had selected Wallace as his running mate against weighty advice, and before the campaign had run its course he must have questioned the wisdom of his choice. The termination of the 1934–35 expedition to Mongolia may have seen the end of Nicholas Roerich's influence over Wallace, but the Guru letters still existed and now reappeared to plague him. If Wallace had felt vindictive against Roerich over the debacle of the expedition, then even more vindictive were Roerich's followers against Wallace after his defection. The collection of worshipful, fantastical, and conspiratorial letters he had written to the professor and to Frances Grant became their main weapon. They had first tried to use these in the hearings in 1935–36 before George Frankenthaler, a Supreme Court–appointed referee, concerning the disputed title to the apartment house at 310 Riverside Drive, the original home of the Roerich Museum. According to the story given by Grant to the *New York Journal American* in March 1948, Roerich's followers demanded that the case be heard in open court, but Horch managed to have the public and press excluded. Maurice and Sina Lichtmann and Frances Grant tried repeatedly to inject Wallace's name into the proceedings, only to be overruled by the referee. Grant had produced letters she claimed were written by Wallace to Professor Roerich, but the court had ruled them inadmissible. Wallace's name was never once mentioned in the two thousand pages of testimony.[65]

As the campaign of 1940 got under way, some people whose identity remains shadowy but who almost certainly included Grant thought they had another chance to damage Wallace with the letters. Democratic Party functionaries began to hear rumors about "some letters of a very disturbing nature" written by Wallace to "a Professor Roehrich [*sic*] and to certain officials of the Roehrich Museum." According to this gossip, the letters had been bought by the Republican National Committee, which intended to publish them. Presidential assistant Samuel Rosenman became very worried. "I could not help thinking back to that day in the White House when Farley had phoned the president to remonstrate about the nomination of Wallace and had referred to him as a 'mystic.'"

One evening during the campaign, Rosenman received a call from Harry Hopkins to come to his room in the White House. When he arrived he found Hopkins "sitting at a bridge table with some photostatic copies of letters spread out before him. He was poring over them with a very worried expression." Hopkins passed the letters to Rosenman and, according to a memorandum Rosenman made later, "as I read quickly through the letters I felt a sinking sensation in the stomach. This could be dynamite in the campaign if it were established that our candidate had written them." As well as referring to various cabinet members (readily identified by the context) as "the sour one," "the wavering one," and so on, "the general tenor of the letters indicated a kind of mysticism which to a hard-headed American voter might well appear quite ludicrous."

How could they discover whether Wallace was the author? It was impossible to ask him directly because he was out of town, so Paul Appleby was summoned. Hopkins and Rosenman showed him the letters, and "to our dismay, he did not seem shocked to read them. Obviously, it was not the first time that he had seen some of them." Appleby confirmed that some of the letters had been written by Wallace, though he could not vouch for all of those that had no more than a typewritten signature. He told Rosenman and Hopkins that the secretary had "been an associate and friend of Roehrich [sic] for some time, that they had had many conferences and talks together, that he had been helpful to the Roehrich Museum and that from time to time he had written letters similar to those which he held in his hand." After Appleby had departed, Hopkins and Rosenman "looked at each other — shocked and dumbfounded." Hopkins asked whether there was any way they could get Wallace's name off the presidential ticket, but a check of the statutes showed that there was no legal way he could withdraw.

Next morning Hopkins and Rosenman went to see Roosevelt and told him about the letters. According to Rosenman, "his face clouded over. It was a terrible blow." Perhaps the possibility of his own letters to Mme. Roerich being made public added to Roosevelt's dismay. Fearful that Wallace would make some ill-considered remark about the letters, Roosevelt asked Appleby to go to Chicago and, in Rosenman's words, "not to leave Wallace's side for the rest of the campaign." Appleby would later describe this assignment as "the meanest . . . that a person could have." He had to tell Wallace that all statements Wallace might make would have to be cleared with either Roosevelt or himself. "The President called Wallace on the phone and told him he was sending me out for that purpose."

Apparently, Appleby was not the only one despatched to Chicago. In April 1946, Steve Early, press secretary to FDR, told a group on Truman's yacht that, at the time of the 1940 convention, the White House discovered that a newspaper had a collection of Wallace's letters in its possession and had sent a reporter to Chicago to interrogate Wallace as to their significance. At Early's suggestion, Morris Ernst, the New York lawyer, flew to Chicago, joined Wallace's train, which had been halted in the Chicago yards awaiting his arrival, and, when the train pulled into the station, threatened the reporter with a libel suit if the story were published. It was not published.

At one point in the campaign a reporter asked Wallace directly whether he had written the letters in question. According to Rosenman, Appleby had coached Wallace in what to say, to this effect: "The documents in question have been hawked around for many years, at times to private individuals, at other times to publishers. . . . Your publisher must know the story of the disgruntled discharged employee — a tax evader, who dare not re-enter this land — from which all this stems." Early in 1950, Rosenman sent Paul Appleby a copy of his summary of events for Appleby's comments. Appleby agreed: "I was responsible for that reply, and it is a sore point on my conscience because it was as nearly a dishonest thing as I remember ever having been party to. I felt that the higher good of the success of the administration justified me. But feeling unhappy over the recollection, as I should, I am itchy about the language. . . . In view of all this, I should prefer some such language as this: 'Wallace gave in reply a somewhat vague statement which seemed to imply that some of the letters in question at least were forgeries, and that their use consequently might be expected to lead to action for libel.'" [66]

In his oral history, Wallace dismissed this whole matter as of no significance.

> After I ended the expedition a few of [Roerich's] fanatical followers began to undermine me. They got their first opportunity in 1940. . . . Certain material was being peddled around concerning Willkie's private life and some of the fanatical Nicholas Roerich followers peddled around certain material which I was alleged to have written to Nicholas Roerich. . . . I never saw the material I was alleged to have written to Nicholas Roerich until quite a while after the campaign when Roosevelt laughingly showed me some photographs of the material which had been offered for sale. The material was composed for the most part of unsigned, undated notes, which I knew I had never sent to Nicholas Roerich, but there were a few letters addressed to Nicholas Roerich signed by me and dated which were

written in rather high-flown language. None of the material seemed to cause FDR the slightest concern.[67]

That last sentence is hardly convincing. The phone call from Roosevelt telling him of Farley's objections to his candidacy, the sudden appearance of Appleby during his campaign—these were signs of presidential concern that Wallace can hardly have failed to read. If, as he claims, Roosevelt later "laughingly" showed him the letters, that was in order to warn Wallace that he knew of his indiscretions and that he must not stray into such politically perilous areas in the future.

By the end of the second New Deal administration, the relationship between Wallace and Roosevelt had grown complex. Looking back, Wallace could identify only two areas of disagreement between them in the period before he became vice president, one arising from his refusal to cooperate in the 1938 purge, the other from Roosevelt's irritation over the protracted dispute between Wallace and Ickes over the Forest Service, but that was not the whole story.[68] Wallace had greatly admired Roosevelt's stirring leadership in the early perilous days of the New Deal and continued to believe in his ability to inspire the people, but privately, as his letters and diary show, he could be quite critical of the president's actions. He could hardly respect Roosevelt's knowledge of economics and finance, or approve his predilection for setting cabinet officers against one another, knowing the confusion and discord this caused. He may not wholly have agreed with Jim Farley, that Roosevelt encouraged such personal rivalries because of a sadistic streak, but his own explanation was hardly less damaging. After Roosevelt had attempted, on one occasion, to have fun at his expense by proving him ignorant of an obscure aspect of his department's activities, Wallace wrote in his diary: "He [Roosevelt] then went on to embroider his story, assuming I had demonstrated my ignorance as to Nematology at the Cabinet Meeting. . . . It was obvious to me, from looking at him, that he knew he was not telling the truth. . . . I would say that Jim Farley was incorrect in calling the President a sadist, although there is a certain amount of that element in his nature. The predominant element, however, is the desire to be the dominating figure, to demonstrate on all occasions his superiority. He changes his standards of superiority many times during the day. But having set for himself a particular standard for the moment, he then glories in being the dominating figure along that particular line. In that way he fills out his artistic sense of the fitness of things."[69] Roosevelt seemed to Wallace to lack intellectual depth, to be too greatly influenced by the last person to speak to him or the most recent speech he had made. "He is," Wallace wrote in his diary on 13 February 1940, "a continuous and vivid mirror of that which has been happening in the immediate past." The words of encouragement Wallace sent to the president—that he "must furnish that firm and confident leadership which made you such a joy to the nation in March of 1933,"[70] that it was vitally important that he should make such and such a statement (which Wallace formulated for him) to the American people—had a double-edged quality, carrying the implication that Roosevelt was somehow failing in his task.

There were more general criticisms. Looking back at the period between 1933 and 1937, Wallace would later declare that "the administration did not have, in any sense, a coordinated policy on anything." It had moved from emergency to emergency in a haphazard way. "The domestic policy was not coordinated with the foreign policy. There was no real planning."[71] These rather sour comments were made at a time when Wallace felt he had reason to be bitter against Roosevelt, but even in those New Deal years, to one so dedicated to planning, Roosevelt's preference for competitive, slapdash administration must often have seemed unfortunate. Though Wallace liked and admired Roosevelt, he was never emotionally dependent on him. There was always, in his attitude, a critical detachment, an independence of mind.

For his part, Roosevelt evidently recognized the vigor and depth of Wallace's intellect, his administrative ability, and his steadfast commitment to liberal goals. Yet he, too, must have had reservations. Those strange letters Wallace had once been prepared to write would have left disturbing questions in his mind. Perhaps, as the matters they referred to had occurred several years before, and as Wallace had shown no tendencies in that direction since that time, he could entrust his vice president with great responsibilities in the coming critical times. Whether, if he were in a position to prevent it, Henry Wallace ought ever to be left in a position where he could become president of the United States was a question he might one day have to decide.

6

A VISION FOR THE

POSTWAR WORLD

AN INTERNATIONAL NEW DEAL AND

THE "CENTURY OF THE COMMON MAN"

The origins of Henry Wallace's liberalism, of that commitment to humane and farsighted goals that had perhaps most persuaded Franklin Roosevelt that his secretary of agriculture could best preserve the New Deal's achievements, lay far back in the vice president–elect's past. His early religious instruction and study of devotional literature had led him to serious and thoughtful conclusions as to what the purpose of his life should be. Rather than living for himself, he would do what he could to promote the long-term good of all humankind. The expansiveness that characterized his thinking came in part from writers such as Emerson and Trine, but more from ideas Wallace developed through his study of Theosophy and his relationship with fellow devotee George W. Russell. In particular, Wallace's millennial notion of a profound spiritual transformation that would usher in an era of abundance and harmony seems to have owed more to Theosophy than to the New Testament idea of the establishment of the Kingdom of Heaven on Earth.

To say that theosophically derived conceptions underpinned Wallace's liberalism is not to impugn the latter. Though in the hands of a Nicholas Roerich it might be distorted, Theosophy was not a pernicious doctrine. In some of its various forms it was capable of being embraced by intelligent and eminent people, who obviously found its notions of progressive illumination and ultimate merging in the divine spirit more satisfying than belief systems that required submission before the Divinity and threatened ultimate judgment. Wallace was in the difficult position of never being able to refer to this most important source of his political ideas, but the lavish praise he would accord Louis Bean, in the last stages of his oral history, may be seen as both an oblique acknowledgment of what he saw as Theosophy's benign influence and a subliminal defense of himself. After noting that Bean was probably still a member of the Theosophical movement, he added: "He's one of the sweetest, finest persons I know. He's a lovely person. I put him at the top when it comes to spiritual quality. . . . If the Theosophists can produce people of that kind, they've done some good work."[1] Wallace made similar comments about George W. Russell, but, to our knowledge, about no one else. Of course, the tragic paradox for Wallace was that the religious beliefs that made him a liberal visionary in both domestic and international spheres were effectively exploited by political opponents who sought to destroy him.

Other strands to Wallace's liberalism were slower in forming. His early, unselfconscious friendship with George Washington Carver may have helped save him from racial prejudice, though it does not appear to have sympathetically aligned him, at an early stage, with the nation's African American population. By and large Wallace does not discuss the racial question, in either private correspondence or in the reminiscences he has left, until near the end of Roosevelt's second term; it appears, over this period, not to have been an issue with him. But under the promptings of Samuel Bledsoe, and with the dreadful example of Nazi racism increasingly before him, Wallace did take a strong and unequivocal stand. Similarly, before his journey through the Cotton Belt in 1936, he had no real understanding of the plight of the Depression's worst victims or of those whom the enormous economic and industrial advances of the nation had left behind, but his meeting with families living on the edge of subsistence opened his eyes to their plight and strengthened his commitment to "the common man," a phrase he would soon make famous. Henceforth, Wallace would see himself as a champion not merely of farmers forced to bear the brunt of shortsighted government actions, or of other sectional groups, but of the disadvantaged and the oppressed. This was a perception that Wallace's close associates appear to have encouraged; recall Chester Davis's observation that from 1936 onward Paul Appleby and others sought to convince Wallace that he was "the messiah for the underprivileged, and that in that way lay his political future."[2] It was also a perception that firsthand experience with the ordinary people of Latin America would soon significantly strengthen.

TRIP TO LATIN AMERICA

While still secretary of agriculture, Wallace had recognized the importance of Latin America to the United States' security. He saw the nations to the south as America's "Achilles' heel," and believed that grave problems would come unless the United States could win the confidence of their people rather than merely that of "the man who might be dictator at the moment and who could readily be supplanted by another dictator just a little later on."[3] Should the Axis powers triumph in Europe, the Western Hemisphere would come under direct threat. Thus, the United States' economic, military, and even cultural ties with the region needed to be strengthened.

But Wallace also felt a spontaneous sympathy for the agricultural and laboring masses of Latin America, just as he had for those in the southern United States. Perhaps also his view of the social and economic influence of the Catholic church, predominant in the region, heightened his feeling for the poor. He had always appreciated the "devotion and manner of worship" of the Roman Catholic church but was "repelled by the fact that in all countries dominated by the Catholic faith there is great misery and poverty in the midst of great riches." Not only that, but his ingrained revulsion against the imposition of authority, and even his patriotism, alienated him from Catholicism to a certain degree: "I have resented it that an American should give allegiance in matters of faith and dogma to a particular person in a foreign land. I have rejected as unworthy of humanity and humanity's religion the extreme emphasis on fear, guilt and a sense of sorrow and inferiority. 'Mea culpa, Mea culpa, Mea maxima culpa.'"[4]

Thus, it had long seemed to Wallace that not only national interest but also a general humanitarianism might be served by gaining the confidence of the ordinary people of Latin America and trying to improve their material conditions. In preparation for that task he had begun to study Spanish in 1938, taking lessons at the Berlitz School and arranging weekly luncheons at which conversations were to be conducted only in Spanish. Now, with the 1940 election over, he broached with President Roosevelt the possibility of his making a short visit to some Latin American nations, not only to improve his knowledge of the language but also, through his position as vice president–elect, to foster goodwill. Roosevelt took up the latter idea straight away and consulted the undersecretary of state for Latin America, Sumner Welles, as to the possible implications of such a visit.[5]

Welles's reaction changed the nature of the proposed trip. He was gravely concerned about the situation in Mexico, where the recent election of the pro-American Manuel Avila Camacho was being contested by the conservative Juan Andreu Almazán, thought to have Nazi sympathies. Welles suggested that Wallace's attendance as official U.S. representative at Camacho's inauguration might strengthen the Mexican leader's position as well as bolstering U.S. defenses, as Camacho was willing to negotiate the establishment of eight U.S. naval and air bases. The visit was therefore approved, and in late November 1940, Wallace, bearing now the title of Ambassador Extraordinary and Plenipotentiary, set off on what had become an important diplomatic mission.[6]

After attending the inauguration, Wallace held productive talks with Camacho — "a square shooter striving to do the constructive, fine thing" — and then embarked, with Mexican secretary of agriculture–elect Marte Gomes, on a tour of the countryside to meet the people and to study farming and grain-storage methods. Because he had been the target of a Nazi-inspired demonstration, he and Gomes were accompanied by Mexican secret service men, but "everything was marvelous in every way. The Mexicans are marvelous hosts and the Mexican people are a lovable people, so I thoroughly enjoyed myself." At many of the towns he and Gomes visited they were greeted by large crowds, with children waving flags and throwing confetti. To the crowds' delight, Wallace addressed them in Spanish, talking frankly of the difficulties they faced. "Your democratic simplicity," Camacho would later tell him, "and the interest which . . . you showed in the modest problems of rural life . . . , have given rise to the most cordial comments on the part of the people."[7]

Wallace quickly appreciated the great scope for increasing the yields of Mexican corn, so vital for improving the conditions of the poor.

Wallace with Félix Ireta, governor of the state of Michoacan (on Wallace's right), and President Manuel Avila Camacho during his trip to Mexico in 1940. Wallace is holding a volcanic rock on which there is an imprint of corn. (Courtesy of the University of Iowa Library)

He therefore encouraged Gomes to begin a concerted program of corn breeding and soil enrichment, and on his return to the United States was able to secure the assistance of the Rockefeller Foundation for this and other Mexican agricultural schemes. The gratitude of his hosts found an echo during the presidential election campaign of 1948. Protesting that the former vice president and now Progressive Party candidate was being subjected to a "campaign of antipathy," a correspondent for the Mexican weekly *Revista de Revistas* reminded his readers that "to Wallace is due personally . . . the initiation of the intensive cultivation of the hybrid corn system which will mean beginning next year, the total recovery of the Mexican farms in production of said seed."[8] Wallace's first trip to Latin America had done much to promote Roosevelt's "Good Neighbor" objectives; it had also given Wallace direct acquaintance with the problems of these neighboring countries, including the conditions under which the poor lived.

After Roosevelt's inauguration, Wallace settled easily into his new official role, quickly mastering the complex procedures of the Senate and presiding over its deliberations with courtesy and impartiality. Two months into his term, *New York Times* correspondent Harold Hinton reported that the vice president was meeting his constitutional duties "faithfully and with apparent zeal" (on one occasion, during the protracted debates on the Lend-Lease Bill, he had remained in the chair for seven hours straight), was working harmoniously with Senate majority and minority leaders, and had taken care to make the acquaintance of every member of that body.

Unlike former vice president Garner, Wallace was uninterested in the political maneuvering that went on behind the scenes. He was, however, concerned to improve the senators' health. "My motto," he soon announced, "is an inch off the waistline of every Senator whose girth is above 40 and whose age is below 60."[9] He abolished Garner's liquor cabinet, known to members as "the bureau of education," and, a physical-fitness devotee himself (Wallace played tennis, sometimes walked up the 898 steps of the Washington Monument, and threw boomerangs in the Ellipse), he began, when he could find a sparring partner, to box in the Senate gymnasium. When the senators declined to take up paddleball (they "were hopeless from the standpoint of using the gymnasium except for taking hot baths and getting a rubdown"), he moved to the House gymnasium, where "almost steadily through the time I was Vice President I would play paddle ball with the House boys." It was, Wallace said later, "my equivalent of Garner's bar."[10]

Wallace's passion for physical fitness never flagged: that July, a Washington columnist told how, on a recent vacation in Atlantic City, Wallace had played squash with professional players all morning, tennis during the afternoon, and table tennis in the evening, before taking a five-mile walk to ensure a good night's sleep. A year after he took office, the *Washington Evening Star* noted that it was Wallace's regular practice to play tennis with his brother-in-law each morning at his residential hotel before walking five miles to his office.[11]

Wallace was unusual, too, in the breadth of his intellectual and practical interests. On the shelves of his Senate office Frank Ryhlick of the *New York Daily Worker* saw Department of Agriculture reports, as well as books on other nations, on economics, and on military strategy.

Katharine Lumpkin's *South in Progress* was there, as were many works on current U.S. problems. One staffer told Ryhlick that the vice president "likes to read everytime he gets a chance," and that "he reads fast and just about everything."[12]

For a time after he took office, Wallace continued to pursue Good Neighbor objectives. During his visit to Mexico the previous year, the government had requested planes and instructors for its pilots. Because of domestic shortages, Wallace could obtain neither, but he was able to arrange with the State Department for Mexican pilots to train in the United States. He energetically pursued his study of Spanish, inviting a tutor to his apartment at eight o'clock each morning to give the family lessons over breakfast, holding "Spanish luncheons" in his Senate office each Friday, and adding to his staff a young Mexican-born American who talked to him only in Spanish and took dictation in that language. Wallace also became closely associated with a CBS program to popularize the Spanish language and culture through music, and announced publicly that he hoped the president would send him on another goodwill mission to Latin American once Congress had adjourned.[13] It soon became clear, however, that Roosevelt was prepared to entrust Wallace with important wartime responsibilities.

WALLACE AND THE BOARD OF ECONOMIC WARFARE VERSUS JESSE JONES

In July 1941, following Hitler's invasion of Russia, Roosevelt set up the Economic Defense Board (EDB), consisting of eight cabinet members, and appointed Wallace as chairman. After Pearl Harbor, the EDB evolved into the much more powerful Board of Economic Warfare (BEW), whose immediate function was to develop sources for the supply of essential war materials, such as rubber and quinine, previously obtained from areas now in Japanese hands.[14]

Wallace characteristically took a farsighted view of his new role. He recognized not one but two vitally important aspects of the agency's work, aspects that could be made compatible only by constant vigilance. Not only must the BEW do everything possible to ensure victory in the war, it must also prepare for a humane and durable peace. If the nation lacked confidence in the nature of the peace, it might not have the courage to defeat the enemy. A sustainable peace would require adjustments in both international and domestic spheres. In the international sphere, Wallace wrote, "the most careful delineation of national boundaries is not in itself enough. . . . Nor can war be prevented simply by the establishment of an international league. We know now that the modern world must be recognized for what it is—an economic unit—and that wise arrangements must be made so that trade will be encouraged."[15] The measures he proposed to bring this situation of free trade and international harmony about formed a familiar litany of his long-term views—the removal of tariffs, the breaking of monopolies, and so on. But this postwar goal of a liberal world order also had a particular connection with the work of the BEW, because that work consisted preeminently of the most aggressive attempts to corner, and thus debar from the enemy nations, the world's supplies of the commodities necessary for the prosecution of a war of enormous scale, and, in every way available to the board, to inflict what damage it could on the enemy's economic welfare. The United States must stand ready, Wallace felt, to try to reverse this damage when hostilities had ended, allowing the defeated nations to regain economic viability—always provided that they met stringent arms limitations—otherwise their economic desperation and the hatred engendered would make further wars inevitable in another quarter century or so.

The domestic goals Wallace thought worth fighting for included a condition of economic democracy, ensured primarily by guarding against any plans of big business to form cartels or monopolistic agreements under the cloak of meeting the exigencies of war. A situation in which the central government had to invest vast sums of money to increase industrial production as rapidly as possible, at almost any price, was very favorable to companies already of sufficient size to take advantage of massive war orders. Such companies might emerge from the war with unchallengeable dominance over particular industries.

Under the tension of wartime conditions, therefore, a sharper edge appeared in Wallace's liberalism. He had never been actively hostile to business (he had been a businessman himself), but certain of his experiences in agrarian reform movements and some of the writings with which he was familiar had made him somewhat distrustful of its possible influence. In his twenties, he had read Thorstein Veblen's *Theory of the Leisure Class* and *Imperial Germany and the Industrial Revolution*, and Veblen's championing of productive activities against pecuniary ones—the making of goods as against the making of money—and his postulation that the instinct of workmanship was stronger than that for profit had appealed strongly to Wallace's farmerlike interests. In 1940, with the war beginning in Europe, Wallace had reread *Imperial Germany and the Industrial Revolution* and found it so relevant to the present events that he published a paper on it in *Political Science Quarterly*.[16] He had wanted to sound a warning that if Veblen's analysis were correct, the German military-industrial machine must be very strong because their social structure had not yet evolved out of dynasticism, but he also discussed Veblen's criticisms of business, commenting that they were probably justified for the immigrant Scandinavian farmers of the Northwest (Veblen's background) at the time Veblen was writing—they may well have been cheated by small-town businessmen. "Moreover, during the time Veblen was on the farm, prices were continually going down and most of his neighbors doubtless felt the trouble was largely due to manipulation in the cities." Further, "as a Norwegian farm boy attending college with the sons and daughters of the local business men, he was oftentimes ill at ease because of his farmer-like clothes. Out of this psychological situation no doubt came his ever-recurring phrase, 'wasteful conspicuous consumption.'" There is a touch of irony in the fact that much of what Wallace says to explain Veblen's prejudice against business interests could also have been said about Wallace as a farm boy (recall his own embarrassment at school when told that his clothes were smelly from farmwork), and of course he had been strongly inclined to the same view of the manipulations of food processors, of the railroads, and so on. But writing in 1940, Wallace wanted to exempt the American businessman from some of Veblen's criticisms, possibly because he really felt that American business in general had adopted fairer, more socially conscious practices. As the war progressed, however, and he came to grips with particular monopolistic interests, his general benignity toward business waned.

He became more combative in both personal and broader political terms. A large-minded man with broad vision, Wallace had hitherto been disdainful of politicking and had had no relish for the bitter personality conflicts that often broke out around him. A tough enough fighter where the interests of his department were concerned, he had avoided scandalmongering and personal vilification. In those sections of the diary and oral history relating to Roosevelt's first two terms, he is almost fastidious in his refusal to comment disparagingly on the actions or motives of others, despite manifold opportunities, and even provocations, to do so. After his assumption of wartime responsibilities, however, his liberalism became more sharply defined by the enemies he believed he faced, not only greedy monopolists, but also Tories, certain elements in the Catholic church, and, most dramatically, those within the cabinet who seemed to represent such forces, to be enmeshed in the same elitist, power-loving social stratum, and to be hindering the conduct of the war or jeopardizing the eventual peace. Of no cabinet officer would this seem more true than of commerce secretary and Reconstruction Finance Corporation head Jesse Jones.

It was not long before serious friction developed between Wallace's BEW and Jones's Reconstruction Finance Corporation (RFC). In creating the BEW, Roosevelt assigned to its chairman certain powers to determine policy on international trade, powers that had traditionally been within the province of the RFC, which disbursed the necessary funds. Jesse Jones was extremely sensitive to this infringement on the almost unlimited power he had enjoyed in controlling the administration's lending agencies. Further, he personally detested Milo Perkins, formerly of the Department of Agriculture, whom Wallace had appointed executive director of the BEW, and it was Perkins and his staff who carried out the immediate interactions with RFC staff.

Roosevelt had told Wallace that he wished him to be protected from the strain of the daily executive work of the BEW; he was just to oversee policy. The same qualification applied to another position Wallace acquired at almost the same time, the chairmanship of the Supply Priorities and Allocation Board (SPAB), later the War Production Board, a body Roosevelt set up in August 1941 to handle some aspects of the domestic defense program. As with the BEW, Wallace's job in the SPAB was to oversee policy and iron out conflicts. But, as he would later ruefully remark: "I suppose I ought to have had more sense than to get into that. . . . It was the idea that just by power or position you could straighten out things without getting into the hard, intimate, daily work. It's a very nice thought, but you don't really accomplish things by sitting on high." [17]

When Wallace took up these two positions, Budget Director Harold Smith warned him that he would need much delegated power if the organizations were to succeed, but although Roosevelt had given him the responsibility for their functioning he had not given him the direct authority to secure the funds necessary for those functions, and this aggravated the BEW's problems with the RFC.

Wallace had put former Sears Roebuck chief Donald Nelson in administrative charge of the SPAB, and Nelson was having trouble with key members Sidney Hillman, the labor leader, over proposals for the disposition of labor forces, and William Knudsen, General Motors head, over production priorities. Knudsen, in particular, was refusing to accept that virtually a total commitment to the war effort was required and wanted specifically to maintain a sizable flow of automobile production for the domestic market alongside war production. Just after Pearl Harbor and under intense lobbying from Lord Beaverbrook, Wallace and Nelson had increased the production of tanks to such a degree that what Wallace subsequently saw as a "tremendous over-production" of tanks had occurred. "We produced more tanks than we ever had men to run them."[18] But despite this initial error of judgment, caused by the urgency of the situation, Wallace and Nelson agreed with Beaverbrook's general view that more of everything in the way of war production was needed, and, with Wallace's backing, Nelson overruled both Knudsen and Hillman.

Jones and the RFC also lacked Perkins's and Wallace's perception of the urgency and scale of the war's demands. Jones believed that the war would only be a short one and therefore, as the BEW saw it, seriously underestimated the need to build up stores of war-related materials. As Wallace later observed: "Milo felt that Jesse Jones and [Assistant Secretary of Commerce] Will Clayton were interfering with accumulating the supplies that were going to be necessary to win the war . . . not showing sufficient keenness. . . . Undoubtedly Jesse Jones believed in winning the war but there was a difference in assessment of the situation." Perkins and Wallace were not alone in their judgment. Wallace reports that Eugene Meyer, owner of the *Washington Post*, and the great financier Bernard Baruch agreed with Perkins and conferred with him about the problem. All were agreed that Jones was "dragging his feet" in the matter of building up sufficient quantities of vital strategic materials.[19]

Wallace's retrospective estimate of the basis of the dispute was just that it was a straight clash of values. In his view, Jones and his colleagues had had all their lives an ingrained sense that the careful husbandry of money was the prime moral priority in the business of government and could not change that priority in a situation in which, as Perkins and Wallace saw it, the value of money could not compete with the value of defeating Axis aggression as quickly and decisively as possible, without squandering unnecessarily the life of even one American serviceman. (Perkins's personal commitment would later be brought to fever pitch by the death of his second and last surviving son, George, in May 1943, who crashed while training as a marine pilot.)[20] Consequently, Perkins was prepared to pay well over normal prices for strategic materials rather than delay their acquisition or risk the successful competition of enemy purchasers.

Jones's contempt for such unbusinesslike practices was only increased by the element of a pragmatic kind of humanism that both Perkins and Wallace insisted on adding into many BEW contracts. Wallace already knew something of the desperate poverty and exploitation of agricultural and mine workers in Latin America, especially, and apart from humanitarian considerations he believed that if the workers were better fed and in better health they would be much more productive, which in turn would increase the chances of the United States obtaining adequate war supplies. Thus BEW contracts contained the proviso that Latin American governments or enterprises should ensure that their workers had adequate shelter and water, should take active measures to improve their health, and should consult with the BEW on whether the wages paid to them were such as to maximize their productivity.[21] Jones and Clayton simply held that workers' conditions were a purely domestic matter and should be left to market forces to decide.

Wallace had even more ambitious liberal goals. He hoped to use BEW contracts not just to improve the lives of the masses but also to weaken the reactionary regimes that oppressed them. Only then could Latin American peoples resist the economic exploitation to which they had long been subject and achieve sustained economic and social gains. With no less determination, Jones opposed what he saw as the wild schemes of the BEW's "socialist-minded uplifters and uppity underlings." Loose talk of extending Tennessee Valley Authority and Rural Electrification Administration–type organizations throughout the hemisphere simply enraged him.[22]

Secretary of State Cordell Hull also opposed Wallace's wider aims. Like Jones, he resented the BEW's intrusion into areas that had traditionally been his department's responsibility. Moreover, the inclusion of special humanitarian conditions in BEW contracts amounted, Hull believed, to interference in the domestic affairs of other states and therefore violated State Department policy. Because Hull had been invoking precisely that policy to block economic sanctions against the pro-Axis government of Argentina, sanctions for which Army Intelligence and the Treasury Department had repeatedly called, the doctrine of noninterference was for him a matter of great sensitivity. He therefore insisted on his department's right to oversee BEW negotiations in foreign lands and in this way was often able to thwart Wallace's plans. For his part, Jones was able to frustrate the work of the BEW by having his lending agencies hold up money for that agency's procurement contracts, and by opposing every effort the board made to obtain alternative funds.[23]

Exasperated by the obstructiveness of both the RFC and the State Department, and by the general insecurity of being given responsibility without power, Wallace wrote Roosevelt on 18 March 1942, not directly criticizing Jones or Hull but pointing out the potentially disastrous administrative entanglements between not only the State Department and the lending agencies but also the Office of Production Management and the Department of Agriculture. These had caused "frustration and confusion" and were hindering war preparations. What was required, Wallace said, was one action agency with centralized power on the foreign economic front. That agency must be given "clear-cut authority to do a job for which you can hold it strictly accountable" and "its own money to carry out its own policies." "Centralized authority under aggressive leadership," he declared, "is imperative."[24] If Roosevelt's predilection for slapdash administrative arrangements was regrettable in times of peace, in war it could be ruinous.

In a letter of 3 April 1942 Roosevelt rejected Wallace's conclusion about the need to concentrate action authority in the BEW, saying he thought it best "to leave the actual financing the way it is but to have the BEW determine the policy which should govern our foreign purchases,"[25] but on 13 April he did make an executive order removing decision making about important purchases from the RFC and giving it to the BEW. However, as Wallace clearly saw, the question of financing was the crux of the whole problem. Jones and his colleagues could not now dispute Wallace's and Perkins's policies or refuse outright their requisitions for funds, but the money still had to be fed through the RFC, and it could still be delayed by all the legalistic obfuscations known to bureaucracy. As Wallace would later remark: "We never did get the real authority over Jesse Jones. . . . The crux of the matter — the responsibility for split authority and so on — was never resolved. This played its part in my growing distrust of FDR. . . . It is this situation which probably was in the background of what came on later in 1944."[26] But Wallace's dark speculations here were the result of some years of perhaps rather morose brooding over his having been in effect forsaken by Roosevelt at the Democratic National Convention of 1944. That crucial event, as we shall see, was enmeshed in a web of intrigue, guesswork, and deception, and the reasons behind it even now remain unclear.

Looking back, Wallace claimed that the letter from Roosevelt quoted above had been drafted either by the State Department or by the RFC. Rightly or wrongly, he saw Jesse Jones and Secretary of State Hull as linked by their common origins. Both were from Tennessee, both belonged to the conservative wing of the Democratic Party and were subject to the influence of the same business interests. Almost predictably, therefore, both had made common cause against the BEW, preventing it from effectively procuring the raw materials essential to the successful prosecution of the war.[27] At times, he was prepared to believe that the State Department held things up not from malice or any concealed motive but simply because its machinery was very slow and cumbersome and its officers wanted to know all the details of anything that passed through their hands. But without making any direct charges, he seems to have felt that Jones's delays sprang from his manifold involvements in the world of big business. "Jesse Jones had contact with many business men who operated in the foreign field. . . . These businessmen wanted to see the commercial work going ahead in the customary fashion." Vested interests, then, were inimical to the desire of Wallace and Perkins to see working people in foreign countries getting more pay, reflecting in some degree the higher prices the Board of Economic Warfare was prepared to pay for the commodities they produced. Evidently harking back to events in the Department of Agriculture, Wallace said: "It was an old, old dispute, you might say, between the point of view of folks who had grown up in the art of exploiting the people of the South and those who believed it was good business to see that the poorer people of the South got a larger share of the money paid by the consumer."[28]

An incident that occurred just at this time gives an index of the bitter feeling between the Commerce Department and the BEW. In a public letter to Wallace in late March, Congressman Martin Dies, head of the House Un-American Activities Committee, charged that the Board of Economic Warfare had in its employ a number of people affiliated with Communist, or Communist-dominated, organizations as well as a prominent nudist. Dies described the man in question, Maurice

Parmelee, as "a prolific writer," whose "revolutionary" works included *Nudism in Modern Life*, "a book of 300 pages with thirty-five photographs taken in nudist camps, all of which are obscene." On 27 March Wallace replied in a press release blasting Dies for "stirring up discord among patriotic Americans"—a statement well received by liberals. A few days later he heard through a BEW employee that Dies's statement had been instigated by Jesse Jones.[29] True or not, such rumors did not augur well for cooperation.

Wallace knew that Jones and Hull had been greatly angered by the executive order increasing the BEW's authority. At a meeting with them and the president on 23 April 1942, the first under the new order, Wallace "made it very clear that I was tired of having State and Commerce go around my back to the President—without [my] having any opportunity to be there at the same time." This brought the sharp response from Jones that "he did not like to have an Executive Order formulated and signed without his knowing anything about it."[30] Not only did Jones continue to hold up BEW requests for finance, but he set about rallying congressional support to negate Roosevelt's executive order. Hull, too, worked to get a modification of the order, using tactics that aroused Wallace's ire; it seems, Wallace noted in his diary on 2 May 1952, that the State Department "has passed out the word to cut my throat whenever possible." To help solve the impasse, it was proposed that a memorandum of understanding, signed by Hull, Roosevelt, and Wallace, be released, but to Wallace the document "makes it clear that BEW has been given another spanking." Finally, Milo Perkins suggested that they should accept the modifications Hull wanted, and Wallace reluctantly agreed. But he sent a message to Roosevelt that, though submissive, barely concealed his contempt for the president's role in the affair. "I told Milo to tell [Budget Director] Harold Smith that he could tell the President that any time it would help lighten the President's load and promote the general welfare he (the President) could hang Milo's ass and my ass on the Lincoln Memorial Bridge and paddle them every morning." Wallace's disposition had not improved when, immediately after this, he and Undersecretary of State Sumner Welles addressed a radio audience. Welles, Wallace admitted, had spoken "with great dignity," and had sounded "very impressive." "Nevertheless, I had the feeling in looking at him that behind this rather impressive exterior, there was inside a soul of a rather badly frightened small boy."[31]

By this time, the need to ensure sufficient supplies of rubber for the enormous demands of the armed services as well as for the domestic market had become the focus of Wallace's concerns. It also became the focus of his impatience with the complacency of Jesse Jones, and of his suspicion of the oil industry. The connection between rubber and oil was that, by a complicated series of chemical processes, butadiene, an essential component of synthetic rubber, could be made from oil, and BEW calculations showed that domestically produced synthetic rubber would be necessary to make up the shortfall in natural rubber caused by the cessation of supplies from Malaya. But Wallace also knew that synthetic rubber would be uneconomic in peace time, and, seeing that the United States would be a very large creditor nation after the war, he wanted it then to be possible for other countries to sell their natural rubber to it. They would not be able to do so if Congress were to impose a tariff to protect a synthetic U.S. rubber industry that wartime conditions had called into being.

THE CENTURY OF THE COMMON MAN

It was just about this time, on 8 May 1942, that Wallace delivered the speech that was to become famous as his "Century of the Common Man" speech, one of the things of which he was most proud as he looked back over his career. The speech showed his breadth of liberalism and his firm commitment to internationalism even when the United States was locked into a desperate war. Even his views as to the proper functioning of the BEW, and his antipathy to Jones's plans, can be seen to form a consistent, integral part of his global thinking.

Norman Markowitz questions the practical content of Wallace's liberalism, arguing that "the contradictions within twentieth-century social liberalism were most dramatically expressed in the crisis years between Pearl Harbor and the inauguration of the Marshall Plan." Markowitz continues: "Henry Agard Wallace, scientist, devout Christian, and progressive capitalist, acted as the leading liberal philosopher and politician of the time. Summing up liberal hopes through the vision of a people's century, Wallace, during the war, also delineated liberal false consciousness by defining that vision in capitalist terms, muddling conceptions of an international people's revolution and a world mixed economy with images of reformed capitalists bringing prosperity to America and the world through expanded trade and nonimperialist investments." He sees Wallace as not attempting "a serious examination of what the division of society into functional groups, i.e., business, agriculture, and labor, meant for both individual freedom and popular democracy."[32] But a consideration of the policies Wallace fought for as secretary of agriculture—for reduction of the tariffs protecting manufacturing industry, for full employment in order to increase consumption of agricultural products, for farmers to organize for self-advancement just as industry did—and of his recognition that individual freedom and popular democracy depended on adequate living standards for the masses, provides a broader context for evaluating Wallace's larger aims. As was the case when he was secretary, if one attended only to Wallace's more rhetorical public addresses there would seem to be some basis for Markowitz's comment on Wallace's "dubious and ultimately self-defeating assumption that an expanding capitalist economy would produce an essentially non-capitalist cooperative commonwealth." However, Wallace's strenuous efforts during the war to protect the public interest against opportunist monopolistic manufacturers provide clear evidence, as we shall show, that he had a thoroughly realistic understanding that government regulations were necessary to control certain exploitative trends intrinsic to capitalism.

In the "Century of the Common Man" speech, Wallace repeated his warning that after the war America would be a creditor nation and must not again make the mistake of maintaining tariff barriers against debtor nations, preventing their recovery from the burden of debt. He then directed attention to the larger ethical and historical background of the conflict, of "this fight to the death between the free world and the slave world." He spelled out in practical terms something of what freedom would mean. Freedom will reign, he declared, "when the farmers have an opportunity to buy land at reasonable prices and to sell the produce of their land through their own organizations, when workers have the opportunity to form unions and bargain through them collectively, and when the children of all the people have an opportunity to attend schools which teach them the truths of the real world in which they live." But where general education and self-government are new and unstable, "it is easy for demagogues to arise and prostitute the mind of the common man for their own ends." It was wealthy industrialists who provided backing for such demagogues, in order to safeguard their wealth by having the common people suppressed into a helpless workforce—"into slavery of the most degraded kind." Wallace continued: "Through the leaders of the Nazi revolution, Satan is now trying to lead the common man of the whole world back into slavery and darkness. For the stark truth is that the violence preached by the Nazis is the devil's own religion of darkness. So also is the doctrine that one race or one class is by heredity superior and that all other races or classes are supposed to be slaves."

Despite Wallace's obvious commitment to the principles of "progressive capitalism" rather than centralized socialism, he did not hesitate to list the Russian Revolution, along with, among others, the French and American Revolutions, as one of the great strides toward freedom of the common man. He warned against an excess of nationalism on the part of the victors in the current war: "The peace must mean a better standard of living for the common man, not merely in the United States and England but also in India, Russia, China, and Latin America—not merely in the United Nations but also in Germany and Italy and Japan." There had been talk, he said, of the "American Century," but "I say that the century on which we are entering—the century which will come out of this war—can be and must be the century of the common man." Those who designed the peace would need to think in terms of the whole world. "There can be no privileged peoples. We ourselves in the United States are no more a master race than the Nazis. And we cannot perpetuate economic warfare without planting the seeds of military warfare."

Wallace looked ahead once more to the power of modern science to bring a world of abundance, but warned that "modern science must be released from German slavery." "International cartels that serve American greed and the German will to power must go. Cartels in the peace to come must be subjected to international control for the common man, as well as being under adequate control by the respective home governments."[33] The reference to American-German cartels reflects a simmering unrest in Wallace's mind about actual international agreements within the oil and rubber industries. He would soon speak out about these, and his feeling that Jesse Jones was, whether intentionally or not, promoting the interests of the American companies involved was one of the powerful forces leading to a clash between the two.

By late May 1942, the conflict of interests over sources of rubber had come into the open. Wallace recorded in his diary that at a meeting of the War Production Board, Jones had announced that after the war factories producing synthetic rubber would continue to operate "in a big way." Wallace pointed out that they could only do so with the aid of a substantial tariff because the United States would be able, once hostilities ceased, to obtain plantation rubber from Latin America at much lower prices. He advised Jones to discuss this with the technicians, but Jones merely replied that "he did not care what the technicians said, he knew they were wrong." He was aware, he said, that "the President wanted the government to take over the synthetic plants after the war was over—but he thought that Congress would have something to say about the matter." Wallace wrote in his diary that it was now becoming clear that "the oil and alcohol people between them, with agricultural support sucked in from the alcohol end, are going to form a bloc to gouge the American consumer on the plea that in order for us to be safe in time of war, we shall have to produce all the rubber we can consume in the United States, right here in the United States." Jones's argument, he said, "is that of the isolationists and his slant is purely political."[34] Whatever Wallace meant by saying that Jones's policy on rubber was "purely political," it was clearly a policy that would benefit the oil industry. That may not have been Jones's intention, and Wallace was at some pains to deny that he was attributing sinister motives to his cabinet colleague, but Jones's policies would inevitably have had that result.

As the war progressed, Wallace's determination to oppose the encroachments of big business on government became still keener. Late in 1942, when Roosevelt motioned him to sit with him after Thanksgiving service, Wallace confided to him that many liberals were becoming concerned at the drift of events. They had heard suggestions that the military would attempt to direct national affairs for the next decade or so, or, alternatively, that "business men in [the Department of] Commerce, and their kindred spirits in the State Department, were increasingly getting the idea that big corporations were going to run the country." The president agreed about the threat coming from the military, but made no response to what had become Wallace's major concern. When Wallace reported this conversation to Milo Perkins the following day, Perkins said that the stage was being set for "monopolizing the nation in the most extraordinary way that the world has ever seen." He believed that throughout the administration liberals were on the run, and that Wallace, their greatest standard-bearer, was the only one who could change the situation.[35]

Just previous to this conversation with Perkins, Wallace had told Roosevelt that he was "exceedingly interested in the post-war peace problem and preparatory for that I would very much like to travel, with a minimum of publicity, to the various spots of the world so as to get acquainted with the leading people." With these objectives in mind, he suggested to Roosevelt that he might go once more to Latin America, and Roosevelt readily agreed. Wallace's concern about what might happen to the BEW in his absence now came to the fore. The BEW would need to be protected while he was away, he told the president, because "the State Department was making it very difficult for Milo Perkins in small and mean ways," and "Jesse Jones was very restive under Milo's direction in the import field." Wallace also complained that the State Department was altering telegrams sent by or to Perkins and himself, so as to misrepresent instructions they were sending to BEW employees abroad.

Wallace did not record any response the president made to his statement about wanting protection for the BEW, but as he was soon to discover, the board's fate was already hanging in the balance. In another conversation with Roosevelt, on 26 November, Wallace said that he understood there was an executive order drawn up that would put an end to the BEW's independent existence. He took the position that ideally the board's functions should be divided between the State and Commerce Departments, but argued that, given the situation in those two departments, such a move "would be exceedingly unfortunate from the liberal point of view." Roosevelt indicated agreement with this sentiment, but the issue remained undecided.[36]

At the end of 1942 Jones went to the Senate for extra funds for the RFC. At a hearing before the Committee on Banking and Currency on 2 December, called to consider increasing the borrowing authority of the RFC by $5 billion, the implication was conveyed that the need for more money was due to the vast and uncontrolled expenditures of the BEW and the virtually unbridled power of Milo Perkins, its chief executive officer. As the hearing proceeded, Jones talked about the quantities of synthetic rubber beginning to be produced, whereupon Senator Tobey asked this prepared, tendentious question:

What is your thought, Mr. Jones, on the future, as to these tremendous operations we are doing in building up a synthetic-rubber industry in this country, in the post-war period? And I ask the question because — without casting any aspersions at all — I refer here this morning, and cannot agree with it, to the thesis of Henry Wallace, whom we all respect very much, in the New York Times Sunday

Magazine of about three months ago, wherein he annunciated [*sic*] the idea that we should not build up a synthetic-rubber industry in this Nation beyond our immediate war needs; that thereby we would build up a vested interest as a result of which we will find ourselves in the position that when the war is over we would not come back in the post-war period and resume trading with the Dutch and England in the Orient again. What do you say as to that policy?

Wallace's article had elaborated on the arguments he used against Jesse Jones at the War Production Board meeting referred to above. If the immediate question was how to get rubber quickly, the question "just over the hill" was, "Will the rubber policies we adopt now lead to World War No. 3 later on?" America's reversion to isolationism after World War I had "led up to the present war"; the same tragic mistake must not be repeated.[37] Tobey's adverse opinion on the article, and his patently insincere reference to Wallace as someone "whom we all respect very much," gave Jones the opportunity to argue that the United States should make itself self-sufficient in rubber forever, thus defending the expenditure on refineries that evidently he had encouraged against Wallace's advice. But oddly enough he went so far in his reply as to boast, in effect, that the U.S. agencies were building so many synthetic-rubber plants that after the war not all of them would be needed, even if the United States did not import any natural rubber at all.[38] What becomes relevant here is Jones's earlier comment that the president wanted the government to take over the synthetic-rubber plants after the war was over—that is, to "socialize" them—but that in Jones's opinion Congress would have "something to say about the matter." What Wallace feared, whether or not this was in Jones's mind, was that the big oil companies, rather than the government, would take over the plants on very favorable terms—plants that had been built with great infusions of government funds and could easily be converted to make aviation and other special grades of gasoline. That could result in these powerful companies establishing near monopolies through cartel formation, a danger against which Wallace had repeatedly warned.

Evidently Jones was using this hearing, and his declared need for more funds, as part of a move to have the executive order of 13 April 1942, which had given Wallace authority to determine foreign purchases, rescinded. The Senate hearing had been on 2 December. Two days later Wallace noted in his diary that Senator Robert Wagner, chairman of the Senate Banking and Currency Committee, had told him that Jones appeared to have done intensive lobbying among members of the committee, particularly those who were Republicans. "He said he had the feeling that Jones was slipping something over."[39]

The following day Wallace met Senators Barkley and Brown to review Jones's testimony and to urge that the BEW be given a right of reply before an amendment effectively transferring the BEW's power to the RFC was put to the vote.[40] He was successful in asking to be heard, and when the committee reconvened on 8 December he took the stand to defend his position. He began by reminding the committee that the president had issued the new executive order so that the BEW could do its job of preclusive buying and getting in stocks. Roosevelt's order had made it possible for the BEW to give directives to the RFC and thus to get on with its vital work. Before that, he said, the BEW's work was "so purely advisory that in fact we had no effect," and he repeated this for emphasis. To forestall any RFC allegations about BEW aggressiveness, he went on: "For the most part, our relationship with the RFC has proceeded in a very orderly and a very fine way. I feel, however, that to go back to the situation existing before April 13 would carry with it a very real peril for the war effort. And I would want it to be made very clear, if it does go back, as to where that responsibility lies. I would want the Senate to know what it is doing when it attempts to do that." Nor did Perkins charge ahead regardless of others' opinions, which was the impression that both Jones and Tobey had been establishing. In fact, he and his staff spent extraordinary, and even unjustifiable, amounts of time trying to reach agreement with other agencies.

Next, Milo Perkins gave evidence, and detailed some of the apparent failures of the RFC, prior to the executive order, to get necessary materials, even when asked for them by the Office of Production Management. These failings were due to administrative delay rather than direct refusal. Out of hundreds of cases there had been only three in which the RFC had disputed the propriety of BEW initiatives. Two of those had had to do with natural rubber, and in each case the BEW had issued a directive over the protest of Jones. One concerned the planting of cryptostegia, a vine that, though inferior to the rubber tree, could be used as a source of natural rubber in Haiti. The other proposed a trial program in Africa of "slaughter tapping"—the accelerated tapping of young rubber trees long before normal maturity, which resulted in the destruction of the trees. Jones had contended that the war would be too short for either of these programs to come into useful production, and that after the war the United States would have to accept the rubber, which would be more expensive than traditionally produced natural rubber.[41] It is worth remembering, however, that in the case of synthetic rubber Jones had brushed aside the long-standing evidence that it would be more expensive than natural rubber and had concurred in the building of more synthetic rubber plants than the country could use. Wallace's suspicions about Jones attempting to have the 13 April executive order rescinded were to be proved correct a few months later, and certain experiences of his own in the meantime made even firmer his determination to defend the BEW's authority at whatever cost.

Wallace's struggle with Jesse Jones was to become even more bitter before the vice president went on his South American journey. Wallace had been angered by Jones's testimony at the December hearings before the Senate Committee on Banking and Currency, by his charges that Milo Perkins had virtually complete control of the BEW, that BEW board meetings were infrequent and its methods unbusinesslike, and so on.[42] To add further gall, Jones succeeded shortly after this in having the Rubber Reserve Company, which exclusively handled the procurement of that commodity, incorporated within the RFC. Wallace had already been critical of Rubber Reserve's "record of caution and unexplained delays," which, he informed its director, William M. Jeffers, "constitute[s] one of the sorriest chapters in our whole economic history and now presents us with one of the gravest threats to our current war effort." Now the Rubber Reserve would be under Jones's close control. In a conversation with the head of the Office of War Mobilization, James Byrnes, on 10 February 1943, Wallace said that "there was only one alternative as far as I was concerned and that was to return to the situation which existed prior to last December, and give us back the rubber, and have assurance from Jesse Jones that there would be full cooperation and not the frozen situation which existed since the fight before the Senate Banking and Currency Committee, a fight which had been started by Jesse Jones himself by the way in which he answered questions before the Committee."[43]

The following day Perkins told Wallace that Jeffers had been in to see him, saying that "he intended to shut BEW completely out of the foreign rubber picture." Then we read in the diary entry for 12 February that "Atherton Lee, who is in the employ of Jeffers, came in to say that he . . . was so seriously disturbed about the war effort that he wanted me to know Jeffers was doing a very bad job; that . . . there seems to be an actual prejudice against natural rubber; that they are actually failing to get 37,000 tons of natural rubber from Ceylon which they could get if they tried. He thinks the chemists in the organization are so interested in setting up a tariff-protected rubber industry in the United States that they want to have all the rubber we can possibly consume produced synthetically." This of course reinforced Wallace's darkest suspicions. Relations with Jesse Jones were still tense when, a month later, he started his trip to Latin America.

LATIN AMERICA ONCE MORE

Wallace's Latin American trip was another triumph, as local press coverage and FBI reports show. (The agency's close monitoring of Wallace's visit was based on direct observation by its personnel and on information gleaned from FBI-intercepted private mail.) The vice president was widely seen as an upholder of human rights and a champion of the common people. Reactions to him in Chile were typical. He "delighted" its people because he addressed them in Spanish, "didn't want a special train or dances or anything unusual," and was "very simpatico." His knowledge of the language, expertise in agriculture, and long-standing interest in the region had made him "second only to Roosevelt in popularity in the South American countries."

He took Bolivia "practically . . . by storm." "I think the one thing that has endeared him most to the Bolivians," one letter writer surmised, "was the two sets of tennis he played on the afternoon of the day he arrived in La Paz—at 12,000 feet altitude." At the Plaza de Armas, in Lima, Peru, the vice president was welcomed by "an unprecedented throng" and "showered with thousands of flowers." A resident of the city wrote that he had "captured everyone's sympathy, by his pleasant manner and democratic behavior."

Some of these demonstrations were stage-managed by governments that probably hoped for more United States aid. For Wallace's official welcome in San José, Costa Rica, free trains were laid on to bring people from all over the country. Before his arrival in Santiago, beggars were taken from the streets and locked up. In Quito, Ecuador, a government edict directed all workers to join the welcoming parade. In Peru, opponents of the regime were jailed. But such measures did not invariably succeed in hiding hostile feelings toward the ruling elites. At the

Wallace, with Colombian president Alfonso López, visiting a grocery store during Wallace's trip to Latin America, 1943. (Courtesy of the University of Iowa Library)

Plaza de Armas, Wallace's address was wildly applauded, but, although opposition Aprista party members had been arrested as they attempted to enter the square, as soon as President Prado began to speak the people turned their backs and whistled, drowning him out and calling for meat, bread, and potatoes.[44] It is unlikely that the warmth with which ordinary people greeted Wallace was counterfeited. After he had returned to Washington, columnist Drew Pearson quoted Latin American diplomats as saying that press accounts "were inadequate to convey a popular enthusiasm not equalled since New York welcomed Charles Lindbergh in 1927."[45] Wallace's sense of identification with the common people, outside the United States as well as within, must have deepened as a result of these experiences.

Wallace had been determined, on his tour, to discover what actual conditions were like. FBI agents reported that during his stay in Lima he had made "an early morning visit . . . to several of Lima's large markets where, hatless and with rumpled hair, the Vice-President conducted a one-man inquiry as to how the common people . . . live." Wallace told later how he had been contacted by a liberal-minded individual, a former Peruvian secretary of state named Salomon, who had agreed to take him among the workers. They left the presidential palace early in the morning and went to the workers' district, where they found "the kind of thing you find up on the high hillsides in the south of France or in the outskirts of an industrial city in Italy, only worse if anything. They had very primitive sewage, plumbing and all that. It was really very pathetic." When the people discovered Wallace's identity, they asked him to address them and "I said that what we were interested in after this war was to make sure we'd get liberty, bread and peace." Then the women took him to a rice store and showed him the long queues and the inadequate amounts of rice being handed out. "It was true," he said, "that they did have a rice shortage. . . . I mention this because later on, it came back again and again that I was busy in Latin America stirring up revolution." [46]

The nature of the power structure in many of these countries disturbed him. It seemed to him that three giant tin companies—the Patino, the Aremayo, and the Hochschild—controlled the Brazilian economy and no government could prevail against them. Noting that the tin companies had links with American businesses, he pointed out that "it was on this tin front . . . that we had some disagreements with Jesse Jones and Will Clayton [that is, concerning workers' pay stipulations]. I visited some of the tin miners' homes. They live under very primitive conditions indeed." [47]

His comment here about American affiliation with Bolivian tin companies is just one expression of his sensitivity about American economic imperialism and the way that big business seemed able to co-opt certain elements in government to help further their exploitation of client economies. Although he never made outright accusations, there is little doubt that in Wallace's mind Jesse Jones was suspect of involvement in this kind of collaboration, even if unwittingly. Some months before, on 14 November 1942, he had noted in his diary: "Chairman Fly, of the Federal Communications System, wanted to let me know that the man whom Jesse Jones had put in charge of the communications problem in Latin America was a Wall Street man, and that as soon as he had been put in charge the value of the stock of I.T. & T. had gone from about two to about six. Fly had a lot of details to indicate there was a scandal brewing. Fly said that the State Department was almost as much to blame for the situation as Jesse Jones." [48]

In each of the Latin American countries he went to, Wallace spent time visiting enterprises started by the BEW for the production of commodities useful to the war effort — rubber, quinine, tin, quartz crystals, mica, and so on. He tried to assess whether the labor conditions clauses in BEW contracts had improved the conditions of the workers and concluded that they had, but not to any great extent. Looking back, he said that his main objective on this trip had been to convince the common people that the war was being fought to secure "liberty and a square deal" for them. "I felt this was essential," he explained, "because many Latin Americans felt that the United States was representing merely Yankee imperialism and was cooperating with the most reactionary elements in their particular country. I thought it would be helpful to take the curse off of that." [49]

But whether Wallace's Latin American trip had taken "the curse off of Yankee imperialism" is another question. His government was in fact "cooperating with the most reactionary elements" and could hardly do otherwise, because those elements included the big proprietors and their allies in government. Wallace's own attempts to get a better deal for the workers were brave but forlorn; there was no way to ensure that the money paid for BEW purchases filtered down to its intended recipients. He explained later that it was because he had "go[ne] out on such a limb" on this trip, and also in his Century of the Common Man speech, that he would feel so strongly after the war about peace and the cause of liberty having been betrayed. "I think it is being betrayed especially in Latin America by the various types of reactionary individuals who have risen to seize power. We have been much less concerned about these iniquities than we have about iniquities in other parts of the world." [50]

Returning to Washington in April 1943, Wallace warned Roosevelt that Axis agitators in South America were spreading the word that the poverty of the workers was due to Yankee economic imperialism. He had seen much evidence of economic warfare, both overt and covert, during his travels, and wanted therefore to press on with the BEW's procurement programs even more urgently. But during his absence Jesse Jones had been mustering forces for an assault on the BEW's privileged position. On 4 June 1943, reportedly at Jones's instigation, Senator Kenneth McKellar, a member of the Appropriations Committee, attacked the BEW on the floor of the Senate, asserting that it had spent immense sums, that it was run by Milo Perkins alone, and that all Perkins had to do to obtain money was to ask Jesse Jones, whereupon Jones had to provide it. No appropriations for the BEW had ever been made by Congress, he said. The aim of this attack was to get the Senate to restore the secretary of commerce's right to "pass" on and, if he thought proper, to defer the BEW's expenditures, and the tactic was to discredit Milo Perkins's management. "That's what really started the whole thing in a big way," Wallace claimed in retrospect, as he reviewed the sequence of events that were to have such a profound effect on his career. "The Tennessee-Texas group, in effect representing Jesse Jones and Cordell Hull, were certainly out to get Milo. It was probably directed at both of us but more particularly at Milo, I think." In Wallace's view, it would "be fair to say" that "Jones brought it on himself through McKellar."[51]

Wallace and Perkins had drawn up a twenty-eight-page statement detailing many failings of the RFC to build adequate stockpiles of strategic materials that it had been directed by Congress to do well before the attack on Pearl Harbor.[52] Wallace had been holding this statement back because it seemed too provocative an attack on Jones, and because Roosevelt had decreed, the previous August, that differences between department heads had to be negotiated and resolved out of the public gaze. Quarrels in the media were forbidden, considered as distractions from a concerted war effort. But attacks on the BEW in the House continued through June 1943, and on the twenty-ninth of that month Wallace, unable any longer to choke down his resentment, released the prepared statement. Soon the press was highlighting sensational charges, such as that Jones was obstructing the BEW's efforts to obtain quinine, notwithstanding General MacArthur's pleas for greater supplies, and was thereby causing American deaths in the Pacific. A furious Jones immediately issued a counterblast: "The release given out by Mr. Wallace today is filled with malice and mis-statements. . . . I will answer the statement in detail and be glad to have a committee of Congress fully investigate the facts.' "[53]

The following day James Byrnes, director of the Office of War Mobilization, called Wallace and Jones to a conference in his office in the White House. By Wallace's account, "Jesse Jones came in, glowering and glum, saying that Henry Wallace had called him a traitor. I said to Jesse, 'I see by the New York News, which has a circulation of 2,000,000, that they think you are going to hit me the next time you see me.' I said, 'Is that true, Jesse? Are you going to hit me?'" We must assume that this was a joke, if only because Jones was older and less physically robust than Wallace, the fitness devotee, but if it was a joke it was a very edgy one. Wallace continues: "Jesse came back to the refrain of his song, 'Henry Wallace called me a traitor.' Then he got out a paper on which he had picked out all the different things I had called him — bureaucrat, back-door complainer, etc, etc. Jimmie then said, 'You don't think Jesse is a traitor, do you?' I said, 'No, I haven't called him a traitor and I don't think he is.' Jimmie said, 'Will you make a statement to that effect?' I replied, 'I am sure there is no statement which I could make that would be satisfactory to Jesse.'"[54]

Byrnes tried to move toward getting a statement of reconciliation drawn up. Wallace said that the important thing was to achieve some constructive solution for the future. He suggested that the BEW be given authority to go directly to Congress for funds, rather than to Jones. If this were to be done, the BEW should also get an assurance that RFC men would not continue to speak privately against Wallace and the BEW on the Hill — saying, for example, that Wallace gave preference to foreigners rather than to Americans. Jones simply denied that such things had ever happened.

Finally the two of them, with Byrnes mediating, agreed on a statement to be released, saying that "the Board of Economic Warfare will initiate steps through the Budget Bureau which will result in a proposal to the Congress that there be made available to BEW the necessary program funds for the procurement and development of all imported strategic war materials under public purchase so that BEW may be completely independent of RFC. Mr. Jones did not object to this policy decision." Wallace added that he had had no intention of reflecting on Jesse Jones's patriotism in his press release, but said "the delays in RFC in acting upon projects had delayed the war effort."

Although Jones had apparently signified his assent to this statement, it is plain Wallace had got more of what he wanted into it than had Jones, and that evening Jones put out a release of his own, calling Wallace's assertion that RFC delays had hindered the war effort a "dastardly charge," denying that Wallace had authority to speak for him, and declaring his determination to have a congressional investigation of the entire matter.[55]

Five days later, on 5 July 1943, Jones issued a thirty-page press release replying in detail to Wallace's release of 29 June. Wallace was out of town that day, but Milo Perkins at once replied, in a single-page document on which Wallace later congratulated him, saying: "If Mr. Jones would publish a simple statement indicating the imported war materials actually warehoused in government stockpiles as of either December 7, 1941 or April 13, 1942, it would become apparent to everyone that he failed dismally to build the government stockpiles authorized and directed by the Congress some eighteen months before Pearl Harbor."[56]

This public acrimony had gone too far. The following day, 6 July 1943, Byrnes wrote Wallace insisting that no further statements be issued unless in relation to a congressional inquiry. Not to be outdone by Jones, Wallace also demanded a congressional investigation, but Roosevelt said very emphatically that this was not to be. A resolution had already been introduced in the House providing for an investigation of charges made by both sides, but on the same day, 6 July, Roosevelt asked Wallace to talk to Speaker Sam Rayburn, to see about getting this resolution defeated.[57] That was done, but now scandalous allegations concerning Jones came to Wallace's attention.

He received a letter from Irving Brant of the *Chicago Sun*, saying:

Some weeks ago I was told by a close friend of J. J. that he has a letter from FDR holding him back on building up rubber stockpiles, the story being that Winston Churchill (another friend of J. J. told me it was Lord Lothian) assured FDR that there was no chance of the British losing Malaya.

This was being cited a few months ago in Texas circles as evidence (1) of Jesse's great devotion to the President, he had taken a cruel public beating in order to shield his boss, and (2) as proof that if FDR knew what was good for him he wouldn't tangle with Jesse on the stockpile issue.

This seemed to Wallace too good to keep to himself. On 12 July he wrote to the president, asking anew for a congressional inquiry, and referring to Brant's letter, thus: "I should like to call your attention to the enclosed letter from Irving Brant. We have heard similar stories from many quarters; the sum and substance of them is that Mr. Jones has been very careful to get your initials on all questionable programs so that he can escape personal responsibility if any serious investigation of RFC activities is ever undertaken by Congress. This emphasizes the importance of continuing your policy of gradually stripping the RFC of its vast powers."[58]

If Wallace's diary entries are to be believed, it was common gossip in the administration that Jones would take Roosevelt a pile of papers to be approved and initialed at a time when Roosevelt could not possibly read them all, tacitly assuring him that they were quite routine and acceptable, and indeed getting his initials on them. Wallace had alerted Roosevelt to the potential threat from Jones, but the nature of the threat made it very unlikely that a request for a congressional inquiry would succeed. It could easily produce evidence embarrassing to the president.

At this critical juncture, with the fate of the BEW hanging in the balance, Wallace's enemies revived the question of his mysticism. On 15 July an article headed "Milo the Messiah of Mystic Washington" appeared in the anti–New Deal *Washington Times-Herald.* In it the writer, Georgiana Preston, related an imaginary conversation between herself and a messenger who had brought her news of another attack by Wallace on Jesse Jones. Preston told this imaginary messenger that Jones was at a disadvantage in this contest because, although he was "a hard, worldly man, . . . the mysteries of the ancient East [were] closed to him." Wallace, by contrast, had a guide in such matters, a former "high priest of his own mystic cult," one Milo Perkins. Perkins, she revealed, had at one time been a bishop of a branch of the Liberal Catholic church (which she correctly identified as "an offshoot of the esoteric cult of theosophy," and of which, as we saw in chapter 2, Henry Wallace had also at one time been a bishop), which met in his Houston residence. Devotees had attended services in Perkins's attic, which they reached by means of a retractable ladder. She also revealed the contents of an inspirational letter Perkins had written to Wallace, seeking employment with the federal government, which told of his desire to uplift humankind. The supposed mystical link between the two men was made more graphically in a large cartoon under the article's title. It showed Jesse Jones sternly looking up into an attic where Wallace, in a witch's hat, stirred a bubbling cauldron and gazed into a crystal ball. Scattered around him lay books entitled *Incantations, Exorcism, Magic,* and *Shibboleths.* A boomerang was at his feet. From within the cloud issuing from the cauldron, Milo Perkins, dressed in strange regalia, transmitted thoughts into the vice president's head.

Also on 15 July Roosevelt, urged on, Wallace later concluded, by Harry Hopkins, Sam Rosenman, James Byrnes, and probably Cordell Hull, issued an executive order abolishing the BEW.[59] The order also took away from the RFC all those of its subsidiaries that were engaged in financing foreign contracts, but this evenhandedness was only apparent, because those RFC subsidiaries were regrouped under a Jones henchman, Leo T. Crowley, in the new Office of Economic Warfare. Jones saw the president's action as a triumph for himself, an assessment shared by the press. Moreover, the vice president's dismissal from the only position from which he could demonstrate effective wartime leadership looked like a serious, perhaps even fatal, setback to his political career. Yet according to Russell Lord, Wallace himself "seemed more relaxed and tranquil than he had been for years." Prompted years later by his oral history interviewer, he said: "If I were asked whether I felt scuttled by the President at this time, I would say, 'No, not at all—not in the least.' While Milo was exceedingly bitter, I was not."[60]

Wallace's ability to achieve this serene acceptance of defeat allows further insight into his motivation in getting into public confrontation with Jesse Jones in the first place. He knew that Roosevelt had forbidden such public disputes; that was the reason Wallace had initially held back the catalogue of the RFC's sins of omission. Neither side could expect anything but overt disciplinary action from the president, and the likelihood of covert action favoring him over Jones was equivocal. Why then did he change his mind and release his thunderbolt? A practical point was his fear that an amendment sponsored by Senator McKellar restoring the RFC's veto power over the BEW might soon succeed.[61] Jones's lieutenants had kept up their sniping against him on the Hill, both on the floor of the Senate and behind the scenes, and Wallace thought that kind of backstabbing action was contemptible, as well as extremely irritating. Besides, being convinced that Jones and his colleagues were delaying the war effort, it became for him not only a duty but also a hot-blooded pleasure to speak out. His action was also in the nature of a test of Roosevelt's character. Earlier Wallace had had doubts about the president's firmness. He would give Roosevelt a chance to stand up for the right, whatever Jones's power might be.

Underlying all this was Wallace's ingrained antipathy to the elitist, power-loving social stratum in which he saw Jones as enmeshed. This harked back to the beginning of his thinking about social processes, and carried not only moral authority but biblical authority as well. Was not the abundance of the earth intended for all humankind, not just the powerful? Meditating later on his social philosophy, he said: "The privileged classes of the world, in their last ditch fight to have and to hold the ill-gotten advantages filched by them and their forebearers [*sic*] from the common man, are openly or covertly banded together in bonds of brotherly interest if not of love, regardless of nationality."[62] The bearing of this on his beliefs about hidden dealings undermining procurements for the war — the war he insisted should not be for power and possessions, but for the rights of "the common man" — is clear.

Despite Wallace's apparent equanimity, being sacked from the BEW was a severe blow. Having been granted responsibility greater than any previous vice president, he had now had that responsibility humiliatingly removed. He had also lost the agency through which he had hoped to help shape the postwar world. From the outset, Wallace had tried to persuade Roosevelt that the BEW, rather than the State Department, should have the major responsibility in this critically important area. Roosevelt had initially rejected this appeal, but in February 1942 Wallace had tried again, telling Roosevelt that "we are writing the post war world as we go along." Evidently, his persistence was rewarded; a few months later he noted in his diary that "the President told Milo and me that it was all right to work on post war plans . . . provided that the State Department did not catch us doing it." Now the organization through which those plans could have been pursued had been abolished.[63]

Through all his bitter contest with Jones, Wallace had believed that these great liberal issues were at stake. But Roosevelt had not seen the controversy in that light, and for his rashness, it now seemed, Wallace must pay a high political price. Though many liberals, shocked by the president's action, quickly rallied to his cause, it appeared to most observers that Wallace's political career had been decisively set back, and that if Roosevelt should decide to again seek office in 1944 it would not be with Henry Wallace as his running mate.[64]

7

LIBERALISM, INTERNATIONALISM,

AND THE NEW WORLD ORDER

Wallace reacted to his sacking from the BEW, and all that that action portended for the character of the Roosevelt administration, in an aggressive manner. In a major address in Chicago on 11 September 1943, he cast the recent conflict between the BEW and Jesse Jones in a yet more serious light, charging that, to a significant extent, the United States' international relations had been determined by "a small group seeking to parcel out the resources and markets of the world so as to control production, prices, distribution and the very lifeblood of world industry." The "cliques" that ran this huge system had "their own international government by which they arrive at private quotas. Their emissaries are found in the foreign offices of many of the important nations of the world. They create their own system of tariffs and determine who will be given permission to produce, to buy and to sell."

Taking rubber as his main example, Wallace pointed out that well before the United States entered the present war the government (including his own Department of Agriculture) had tried to build up a stockpile of this strategically vital material, encouraging natural production in the hemisphere and synthetic production domestically. These efforts had continued during the conflict and, as a member of the War Production Board, Wallace had been involved in them. But what neither he nor the American people had realized was that "synthetic rubber was the subject of a private treaty between a giant American oil company and I. G. Farben, the German chemical colossus," by which the German firm obtained a monopoly on the production of synthetic rubber and the American firm obtained a monopoly on the production of synthetic gasoline. In accordance with this "secret agreement," the American oil company, even while assuring the U.S. government that it was doing all it could to provide all the synthetic rubber that was needed, had actually restricted other U.S. firms from supplying that commodity, even though a U.S. company had invented the process by which synthetic rubber was made.[1]

What evidence did Wallace have for these charges of international conspiracy and domestic economic sabotage? The basic fact of the alliance between I. G. Farben and "the American oil company," which can be identified as Standard Oil of New Jersey, was not really a secret and in its beginnings was not controversial with regard to war production, as it dated back to about 1930. Wallace's statements about the current effect of this alliance on war materials may have been based largely on hearings before the Senate Committee on Patents held during July and August 1942, or on the accumulation of information that gave rise to those hearings. His assertions about the intentions of the companies were, as far as we know, interpretations he placed on such evidence, plausible perhaps, but hardly established as objective fact.

The hearings were not directed to revealing unpatriotic, self-interested motives on the part of the oil companies, but rather to demonstrate by example that patent and licensing restrictions did as a matter of fact work in such a way as to hamper the production of necessary war materials. This evidence had been used to argue in support of a proposed new bill directed at changing the law on patents so as to obviate such handicaps. However, in presenting the case for the bill, Assistant Attorney General Thurman Arnold, acting for the Department of Justice, did not hesitate to use the term "abuses," though it seems that he had only the German company in mind. "I appear before this committee," he said, "to present a bill to correct those pressing patent abuses which have so disastrously affected our war effort. Through these abuses a vital segment of American economy has been strait-jacketed into a foreign cartel system, and the free flow of strategic materials vital for war and for internal security has been impeded and delayed."

Arnold went on to talk about the restrictions embodied in the licenses given by patent holders. "I. G. Farbenindustrie, the largest corporation in Europe, and Standard Oil of New Jersey, the largest industrial corporation in the world, have divided between them world production of synthetic petroleum products and chemicals. It was through this cartel that the Hitler movement was able to impede the development of synthetic rubber, acetic acid, methane steam, and other vital chemical products in this country."

The complicated interchange of licensing rights between I. G. Farben and Standard Oil of New Jersey meant that Standard Oil gave I. G. Farben licensing rights to certain techniques in return for licensing rights for processes requisite for the production of synthetic rubber. Standard Oil of New Jersey and its partners could then refuse other American companies licenses and information for the synthetic-rubber processes except on terms acceptable to the group.[2]

Standard Oil was not on trial in these proceedings; it was the state of patent law that was being put to the test, as to what kind of business dealings it licensed. The oil companies undoubtedly believed they were operating under laws that protected business interests they regarded as legitimate. What exercised Henry Wallace and like-minded liberals was the tremendous power that international cartels could acquire under the law, whether in times of war or times of peace. For him, as we have seen, such coalitions were a case of the privileged classes of the world banding together across national divisions to protect their privileges.[3] The fact that he made his Chicago speech about the deals between I. G. Farben and the "greatest American oil company" so soon after losing his battle with Jesse Jones (which must have stung, however he managed to rationalize it to himself) strongly suggests that he saw RFC policies as creating favorable conditions for unscrupulous, unpatriotic, and monopolistic big business, whether Jesse Jones and the RFC executives knew it or not. In view of the postwar history of some sections of the oil industry, one can sympathize with Wallace's suspicions.

FIGHTING FOR LIBERALISM AT HOME AND ABROAD

Wallace's Chicago address of 11 September was only one of a number of combative speeches he made in the wake of his sacking from the BEW. In Detroit, he warned that powerful, moneyed groups — "some call them isolationists, some reactionaries and others American Fascists" — were opposing Roosevelt because he had "stopped Washington from being a way station on the way to Wall Street." At Des Moines, he predicted a coming confrontation between, on the one hand, the administration, labor, and agriculture, and, on the other, corporations who wished to maintain a "capitalism of scarcity." "I welcome this fight," he declared. "The sooner it comes and the hotter it gets, the better." Mixed in with these bellicose statements, however, were the familiar references to abundance and harmony, which, he declared, could soon be within reach: "God . . . gave all of us a world rich in soil and minerals. . . . In the world of modern technology the possibilities of abundant production are so great that it is only a question of time until we can bring the blessing of freedom from want to everyone."[4]

This vigorous speechmaking led to public speculation over his motives. *New York Times* correspondent Arthur Krock wrote that the vice president appeared to have put himself at the head of those in Washington who, at a time when Roosevelt seemed to be making "a wartime detour," wished to see the objectives and spirit of the New Deal maintained. Even in the face of presidential displeasure, this liberal group was determined "to guard the New Deal from the ravages of war and to keep the way open for Mr. Roosevelt to return to his own creation." Not only was Wallace maintaining a busy speaking schedule, Krock pointed out, but he was also giving exclusive interviews to selected journalists, who then broadcast his views. Others saw the speeches as an attempt by a man whom most political experts had written off to establish himself firmly as "the only man high in government who's in there fighting for the 'little fellers,' labor, minority groups."[5]

An incident occurring at this time indicates how open Wallace was to opportunities to publicize his views about the importance of economic liberalism not merely in the present conflict but also in the postwar world, a subject to which his thoughts were increasingly turning. In his diary for 15 December 1942, he records that at a dinner party given that month by Charles E. Marsh, a Texas newspaper proprietor, he had joined in a discussion between Erich Maria Remarque, author of the antiwar novel *All Quiet on the Western Front*, and Gabriel Pascal, the Hungarian-born film producer and director, about a proposed film that Wallace describes as "a more or less allegorical movie of the fight between the children of light and the children of darkness through the ages." Wallace was immediately interested. The film, he noted, would illustrate "the principle of liberty and unity down thru the ages"—that is, the unity of all humankind as equally valuable individuals, and their consequent equal right to liberty. "I gave them a great many suggestions but I don't know whether they will take any of them or not."

At home after the party, Wallace recorded in his diary further thoughts about the film, which was to contain not merely a report of the war but a set of proposals for the subsequent peace:

What I personally hope for is to put through the eye of the Common Man throughout the world, the story of his way of life for the future—only incidentally why he is fighting now. The road from Buenos Aires to Moscow—education, food, and the development of the so-called backward peoples toward a world in unity, would be in it. Since every picture must have its devil for contrast, I would have the Bolivian highland in tin in it—the robbed Peon and the man who robbed him. In it I also would have the Russian march through the East with flashes of Siberian industrialization. I would have America at work, following the war, building the machines for the development of Brazil. There would be an immediate flash of American food ships feeding Southern Europe.

The proposed film was discussed as a serious project for some time. Pieces by Thomas M. Pryor, "A Song of the Soil," and Andrew R. Kelly, "Wallace Ideals Planned as Motion Picture Story," appeared in the press, and there was a three-way correspondence between Wallace, Pascal, and Marsh, their host at the party. Each of them was addressed by a pseudonym smacking of concern with nature and the spiritual life—Pascal, who had cattle interests, as "Cowkeeper," Wallace as "Beekeeper," and Marsh as "Puritan."

Wallace wrote Pascal on 9 January 1943: "I hope that the pain caused by the Four Horsemen of the present apocalypse will finally bring forth the birth of a new world-nation, or the new democracy, or the new freedom, or whatever you want to call it. In any event the heart of the new era for which the common man longs is 'work in peace' and now the common man would like to see this peaceful labor contribute not merely to satisfying his own needs but toward enhancing the greater welfare." In the last sentence is an echo of the optimistic eighteenth-century utilitarian version of liberalism, the belief that the "enlightened self-interest" of the individual would bring about the good of all, but Wallace had a much more realistic apprehension of what was required to ameliorate the lot of the common man. Pascal replied a few days later, saying: "I am certain that after this (let's hope so) cavalcade of the Four Horsemen there will be no other way of continuation but the miraculous rebirth of a world-nation as you call it, in which the common man will be both member and leader and no privileged caste will be permitted to rule."

As the months went by, Wallace seemed to draw back from Pascal's rather mystical imaginings and to introduce a practical, realistic note, stressing the importance of understanding and working with the soil and its products. "I think I agree with you with regard to the luciferic element. It can release certain energies which the righteous would not otherwise have at their disposal. Discord, like manure, may be the source of abundance." He hoped that Pascal's farm would be fruitful, and said that the next time Pascal was in Washington he would show him "some animals produced by crossing Jerseys with Danish red cattle." Across the bottom of the letter is handwritten: "Our acquaintance is on an agricultural basis" — as if to say, let's not get any fanciful ideas. Pascal, however, replied that although he was indeed happy that their acquaintance was on an agricultural basis, nevertheless it was "as old as the soil since the eternal flames let it begin to cool and human beings found out how to plant seeds to reap the harvest with which nature blesses us: our acquaintance is as old as the fight between Lucifer and God, because we both descend from that period of the struggle of the spirits." To claim such a degree of intimacy would hardly have appealed to the self-contained Wallace.

Pascal was a flamboyant, extravagant person — extremely extravagant with the money provided by J. Arthur Rank, for whom he had made *Pygmalion* and *Major Barbara* and would soon make the disastrously expensive *Caesar and Cleopatra*, a failure despite the presence of Vivien Leigh. He had overwhelmed George Bernard Shaw with his effusiveness to such good effect that Shaw gave him the film rights to these plays almost for nothing. Such intrusive and manipulative behavior was precisely the thing to send Wallace back into his shell.

In a later letter Pascal refers to his feeling that "somehow the secret mystical forces down below in the soil, burning like the latent passion of our own striving hearts are working and shaping everything, as it organically stretches towards the light, and forming a new rhythm, a new faith, a new hope for this strange animal called homo sapiens." Wallace's reply was that he was sending an autographed copy of his latest book and two packets of sweet corn. The nature-mysticism of his early Theosophical period had burned itself out, leaving a worldly determination to get on with practical social programs. The Theosophical belief that each individual has a spark of the divine fire had evolved into the basic liberal conviction of the importance of human individuality, and that the individual must be liberated from complete submergence in the group—freed from the selfish interests of powerful sectors.[6] In view of the differences between his idea of progress and that of Pascal, it is perhaps not surprising that the proposed film was never made.

Wallace had outlined the major parameters of his own, more practical postwar plans to Roosevelt in a letter of 25 April 1940. These included the continuation of the reciprocal trade program to enable free international exchanges of goods and services, a world ever-normal granary to stabilize prices and encourage consumption, and an extension of credit to war-torn countries to enable reconstruction and allow them to repay their debts. These proposals, which he argued for time and time again, typify his realistic approach to the business of promoting "the greater good of all mankind," as distinct from relying merely on the hoped-for emergence of a great spiritual leader and the consequent enlightenment of the world. Yet the continuity of his practical proposals with his religious vision is seen, for example, in a *New York Times* article of March 1943, in which he urged that the United States should deal "honestly and fairly with Russia" and recognize that "all men are brothers, and that God is their father."[7] That belief, that all human beings have an equal share in divinity, underlay his claim that each had an equal right to life, liberty, and the fulfillment of their personal goals. He could see, however, that those freedoms would never be granted simply by right, and that the weak needed to be aided in resisting the depradations of the strong and unscrupulous.

It is plain that by late 1943 Wallace had become concerned at the growing conservatism of administration policies, a development that his own dismissal as head of the BEW had dramatically signaled. Early in November he was shown a letter from a Democratic Party sympathizer complaining that liberals "feel that they have been let down by Roosevelt," and that the party had failed "to give an inspiring lead to the people and to crystalize [progressive] potential." Prominent Democrats, the writer said, must "begin coming out with statements and speeches in which they do more than parrot F.D.R., but, as Wallace has done, take a position far in advance of him." Not long after this Wallace was told by pro–New Deal columnist Jay Franklin that the only hope he saw for the Democratic Party was for it to become genuinely liberal.[8]

In another of the exclusive press interviews, to which *New York Times* correspondent Arthur Krock had earlier referred, Wallace responded to questions from Associated Press reporter Jack Bell concerning the political significance of his recent speeches. Wallace made a record of their conversation:

> I told him there were certain views which I had long held, which I thought were of importance to the general welfare . . . and that as Vice President I was continuing to talk [about them]. . . . He wanted to know if I thought the President was running for a Fourth Term. I said I didn't know any more than he did but that I assumed the President would be nominated for a Fourth Term. He wanted to know, point blank, if I was running for Vice President. I told him what I was interested in was getting my ideas over. He said, "Well, you could get your ideas over much better if you were Vice President than you could if you were out of public life." He continued, "I suppose you know that some of the men around the White House are against your being nominated again." I said I didn't know that, but that I understood from general conversation that some of the men around the White House had been quite active in the Jesse Jones affair.

Bell's subsequent account of this interview indicates either that he had ignored Wallace's circumlocution or that the vice president had been a good deal more forthcoming than the above account suggests. Wallace, he wrote, was convinced that Roosevelt would try for a fourth term and was therefore conducting a campaign to win the vice-presidential nomination. In defiance of those "insiders" who wished him removed from the ticket, he was determined to show Roosevelt that "he represents labor and liberal elements in the Democratic Party that must be reckoned with at the next national convention." The views he had been expressing—about the common man, about the threat from American Fascists and international cartels, about the need for government planning for the postwar world—were long-standing ones. They reflected his determination to mobilize public opinion behind liberal policies. The vice presidency provided Wallace with the best forum for propagating these ideas, which was why he wished to retain it.[9]

In his Jackson Day Dinner address of January 1944, Wallace came close to openly challenging the president. Roosevelt had recently announced an at least temporary end to reform; "Dr. New Deal" must make way for "Dr. Win-the-War." As if in direct contradiction, Wallace told his audience that the New Deal was not dead; had it been so, the Democratic Party would also have been dead "and well dead." He then denied (disingenuously, as his retrospective comments show) that Roosevelt had ever abandoned the New Deal's principles, and (as if to strengthen his wavering leader's resolve) declared that "God willing [Roosevelt] will in the future give the New Deal a firmer foundation than it ever had before." As Wallace later wryly observed, his remarks were not appreciated by people who had been informed of the New Deal's demise and had paid one hundred dollars a ticket to have that diagnosis confirmed. He knew that he had displeased the president's wife—"Roosevelt . . . had tried to bury the New Deal and Mrs. Roosevelt, I think, thought that I should have thrown on a few extra shovelsfull"—and speculated that she, like her husband, probably believed that it was time to bring the party together, to conciliate the southern Democrats.

Wallace explained later that he had made the speech because Roosevelt had begun to cultivate many of those who formerly had opposed him, signaling his change in direction. Wallace, on the other hand, was "looking ahead toward the 1944 convention and what type of thought would control the Democratic party." Unless "a real fight" were made, "reactionaries" would gain control of the party. A Washington columnist commented that Wallace's speech had been a "doughty" one, but that it might turn out to be his "political swan song."[10]

In major addresses on the West Coast that February, Wallace continued on his politically injudicious course. His claims that American Fascists (carelessly defined as "those who believe that Wall Street comes first and the country second") were working to control the coming political conventions can hardly have impressed a president now eager to cooperate more closely with the business sector; nor, in the light of Roosevelt's wish to concentrate on winning the war, could his vice president's assertion that postwar planning must begin immediately. Convinced by now that the Allies would be victorious, Wallace believed, as he explained later, that "it was high time we began thinking about full employment, full production, and fair distribution in time of peace. Knowing the political politician slant of hushing everything up and leaving well enough alone, I figured I was the only one who would be likely to come out and battle for adequate post war planning—so I did it, that's all."[11]

When, in 1942, he had proposed to Roosevelt the idea of his visiting Latin America, Wallace had said that he wanted to go to the various areas of the world where important postwar developments might be expected, to establish personal contact with important leaders and try to get some feeling from direct contact what the conditions were. He had long been interested in Asia, and now that the United States and the Soviet Union were allies in a tremendous conflict, and an indigenous popular Communist movement was stirring in China with unpredictable consequences for that country's relations with the Soviet Union and the United States, he began to make plans for a visit to those countries as well. It is plain that the idea was originally his, but Roosevelt went along with it willingly.

In his diary entry for 6 March 1943, Wallace tells how he showed the president a map with a route for the proposed trip marked on it. "He put his finger on the 3300 mile hop from Australia to Ceylon and said that that was too much risk to take. He thought sixteen hours in the air was too much. He suggested I leave on the trip in early June and get back . . . about the time the National Democratic Convention begins, say about July 17."[12] The reference to the date of the Democratic convention may have had a subliminal pointedness. When news of Wallace's journey became more widely known, heads began to nod wisely or shake gravely. The 1944 convention was not too distant, and several intriguing and interlocking questions were in people's minds: Would Roosevelt run for a fourth term? If he did, would he again call for Wallace as his running mate? If he did not, would he nominate Wallace as heir apparent? These questions would not be formally resolved until the actual convention, but obviously there would be tremendous politicking over them while Wallace was out of the country. Was Roosevelt seizing this opportunity to effectively put Wallace out of contention? In his oral history interview, Wallace said that at the time he did not think the president wanted him out of the way, but that later he was not so sure. Roosevelt's rather unusual degree of solicitude in not wanting him to make the long flight from Australia to Ceylon may have been an attempt to assuage his own feelings of guilt about selling Wallace down the river. Or it may have meant quite the opposite.

That Wallace's itinerary was still undecided suggests that he had not been entrusted with the negotiation of any major affairs of state. On

13 March he recorded that he had discussed a possible agenda for the trip with Cordell Hull, Secretary of War Stimson, and General George Marshall and had found Roosevelt "much stronger" for the trip than he earlier had been. "I told the President that . . . I did not want to go on the trip unless I could do some real good. The President said, 'Oh, you must go. I think you ought to see a lot of Siberia.'"[13] Could this have been a stroke of the president's mordant sense of humor? Was Wallace, perhaps, being "sent to Siberia" metaphorically as well as literally? But if, as many suspected, Roosevelt was taking this opportunity to remove Wallace from the domestic scene, it was an opportunity that Wallace himself had presented. It had been he who had suggested the trip, and the interesting question is why he should have done so.

Wallace was probably convinced, as he had been in 1940, that active campaigning would only alienate the president. "If you ask why I didn't follow suggestions to get delegates," he said later, "I would say that I felt in 1944, as I did in 1940, that a man who went out to get delegates would inevitably get his throat cut. . . . Roosevelt wouldn't tolerate that kind of thing." His deep-rooted hatred of political scheming and organization may also have played a part. Illustrations of this occur frequently in the records Wallace has left. For example, after his controversial Chicago speech of 11 September 1943, Barney Hodes, whom Wallace describes as a "very practical politician," had warned him to stop upsetting the Democratic organization and concentrate his efforts on winning the vice-presidential nomination, by lining up delegates and even cooperating with Hodes to set up a supposedly nonpartisan but actually pro–Henry Wallace campaign organization. But "I told Hodes that practical politics of this kind simply did not appeal to me." Beyond all this, there was Wallace's sincere belief in the importance of his mission. Though apparently politically unwise, his decision to go to Siberia and the Far East was consistent with his expressed desire to visit areas where important postwar developments were expected. It was probably with such a trip in mind that he had begun to study the Russian language in late 1942. Brawling for political advantage, always so distasteful to Wallace, ought not to be allowed to stand in the way of these longer-term and vastly more important goals.[14]

As he prepared to depart for the Far East, it must have been difficult for Wallace to gauge his chances of retaining the vice-presidential nomination. He knew that powerful southern Democrats, business interests, and many Democratic bosses opposed him. So also, he had repeatedly heard, did the "palace guard"—Hopkins, Rosenman, Byrnes. Early in January 1944, Gene Casey of the White House staff had given him "specific details as to how Hopkins had tried to cut my throat at various times." Wallace had replied, characteristically, that he knew that Hopkins had "wholeheartedly" opposed him, but that he also believed Hopkins "had been wholeheartedly for winning the war" and had worked very effectively with Roosevelt to that end. Casey was less charitable. "Gene came back and said, 'You are a Christian and I love you for it. But you are wrong about your attitude toward Harry. He is selfish and a no-good and I am going to get him.'" But Wallace had also received strong indications of support—from members of the administration, from public opinion surveys, from analyses of mail received after his speeches—all carefully noted in his diary. In early March, for instance, he had seen the results of a Gallup poll, which placed him far ahead of other possible vice-presidential candidates. Forty-six percent of Democratic Party voters were for him, as against 21 percent for Hull, 13 percent for Farley, and 12 percent for Rayburn. Every section of the nation had preferred him, including, rather surprisingly, the South. "Although a number of Southern political leaders have been highly critical of Wallace," Gallup's report read, "their revolt against him has apparently not extended to the rank and file."[15] None of this would matter, however, if the president decided to replace him.

Though at times Roosevelt had conveyed the impression that he wanted Wallace to stay at his post, the signals had generally been confusing. In October 1943, Wallace had been "amazed" when Eleanor Roosevelt remarked to him at a White House dinner that if he were nominated he could win the presidency. The difficulty, she said, would lie in getting him nominated. Both she and the president looked on him as the logical person to carry on Roosevelt's liberal policies, but southerners were bound to oppose him. It was hardly an unambiguous endorsement. Shortly after this, Wallace heard that Democratic boss Ed Flynn had been told by the White House to boost House Speaker Sam Rayburn for the vice presidency. "The game was . . . to give Sam every possible newspaper break and to play him up as a great progressive, the father of TVA, FSA, etc." The source of Wallace's information, Washington lobbyist Ted Hayes, had remonstrated with Flynn, saying, "Aren't you a friend of Henry Wallace?" Flynn agreed that he was, but added that the order had come "from the top."[16]

Wallace had had his successes as vice president, particularly in the

Latin American sphere, and, at least in his own opinion, in mobilizing resources for the war. Perhaps these factors, his unquenchable liberalism, and the inspirational power of his ideas would stand him in good stead with the president. But there were other things to weigh in the balance. However much he tried to rationalize it, his sacking as head of the BEW hardly boded well for his political future. And although his recent defiant speechmaking had probably helped to shore up liberal support, it might easily have irritated the president, whose leadership he had implicitly challenged. Moreover, as Wallace well knew, just before the 1940 election, Roosevelt had seen the Roerich correspondence, with its damaging revelations of his earlier secret life. Could he realistically expect that factor to play no part in the president's deliberations?

Any hopes that Wallace may have had that Roosevelt would forget his earlier indiscretions must have been dashed by an incident that occurred just a few weeks before he departed for the Far East. On 30 April the *New York Herald Tribune* carried a review of the recently published autobiography of Charles Michelson, associate publicity director of the Democratic National Committee. The reviewer made much of the fact that, in discussing the 1940 presidential campaign, Michelson had "air[ed] for the first time some long-circulated under-cover gossip about letters 'supposed' to have been written by Vice-President Henry A. Wallace." Michelson's "enigmatic" remarks on this matter, the reviewer pointed out, had left every politician in Washington asking what was in the letters, why Michelson had decided to reveal their existence at this time, and whether his revelations were part of a Democratic National Committee plot to remove Wallace from the ticket. Michelson claimed that in 1940 the Republicans had tried to have the anti–New Deal press publicize the letters in order to "provoke an unfavorable curiosity" and damage Wallace's candidacy. Was not Michelson, now, attempting to achieve the same result? Whatever the truth of these speculations, the controversy provoked by Michelson's revelations must have reminded Roosevelt of Wallace's political vulnerability. If the documents in question had at one time been widely circulated, they might appear again.

Initially, Roosevelt seems to have believed that the Asian expedition could have mainly propaganda value in enlightening people as to the huge potential trade with that region. Immediately on his return, the president suggested, Wallace should make a speech on the West Coast "telling about the marvels of China and, especially, Siberia."[17] But Wallace saw the trip as taking place within a grimmer international context. From State Department expert Lauchlin Currie he learned that Great Britain had been holding back on the deployment of her forces and letting the United States and the Soviet Union do the fighting. The Soviets had already become suspicious of the intentions of both Britain and the United States and in consequence was likely to "play a lone hand" after the war and to seek new strategic boundaries. The British were determined to hang on to their empire, and the United States seemed to be willing to assist them rather than pressing for the institution of a new world system based on the ideals of the Atlantic Charter, the Four Freedoms, and the Century of the Common Man.[18]

Currie's analysis reinforced some of Wallace's most fundamental fears. From early in the war he had been suspicious of the concealed aims in British foreign policy, or certainly of the Tory element in it, anticipating that Britain was prepared to neither give up her empire nor reach peaceful accommodation with the Soviet Union. He was concerned that the United States may have been "picked for the specific purpose of pulling chestnuts out of the fire for the British Empire." He also deplored the idea of racial superiority on which British imperialism seemed to rest. This had already led him to clash angrily with Winston Churchill. At an embassy luncheon, the British prime minister suggested that Britishers and Americans should enjoy joint citizenship after the war and more or less run the world. Wallace immediately queried whether Churchill's implicit assumption of Anglo-Saxon superiority might not be offensive to other nations and to many in the United States, but Churchill said dismissively that there was no need to be apologetic about the matter because "we were superior." Wallace then proposed that joint citizenship be extended to Latin Americans as well, but Churchill disliked the idea: "If we took all the colors on the painter's palette and mix them up together, we get just a smudgy grayish brown." Did this therefore mean, the vice president asked, that Churchill "believe[d] in the pure Anglo-Saxon race or Anglo-Saxondom-uber alles"?[19]

Wallace was concerned, too, that developments within the United States were making war with Russia more likely. He worried that the State Department, too greatly influenced by conservative forces within the Catholic church, might come to see the Soviet Union rather than Nazi Germany as the ultimate enemy. In January 1943, for instance, he noted gloomily in his diary that certain elements in the Catholic church seemed to fear communism even more than Nazism and that the State

Department "believes that its patriotic duty is to save American boys' lives by handing the world over to the Catholic church and thus saving it from Communism. They are willing to run the risk that in so doing they may also be handing the world over to Nazism. Both the Catholic Church and the State Department are treading a very thin and narrow line."[20]

To Wallace, by contrast, cooperation between America and the Soviet Union was essential, and not simply to preserve peace. In an address to the Soviet-American Friendship Congress in November 1942, he had argued that these two great nations could together promote the long-term happiness of the common people. They could build a new type of democracy, which would bring greater economic security to the United States and greater political freedom to the Soviet Union. Of course, he conceded, the Soviet regime had committed grievous crimes, brutally purging its opponents and signing the nefarious pact with the Nazi dictator; but unlike the Fascist powers, it had neither preached racial superiority nor sought to dominate the world. In a *Survey Graphic* article published in February 1944, Wallace argued that Americans, conquerors of their own vast frontier, could "appreciate the spirit in which the Russians are developing Siberia." Some years before, he now revealed, he and Soviet foreign minister Molotov had envisioned a great highway and airway stretching from Chicago through Canada, Alaska, and Siberia to Moscow, a project that, if realized, promised future friendship and peace. Of course the United States must cooperate with the West and with Latin America, but it must never be forced into a position of antagonism toward Russia. "I have every reason to believe that Russia is the natural friend of the Americas in the years ahead."[21] Whatever expectations Roosevelt may have had of his vice president's journey to the Far East, Wallace, as usual, had his own more ambitious and visionary agenda.

Wallace landed in Siberia on 23 May, and in twenty-five days visited eighteen different centers, mainly inspecting mines, munitions factories, farms, and so on, and trying in his speeches, as he wrote, to bring about "world security on the basis of broader understanding." According to a despatch from United States ambassador Harriman to the president and the secretary of state, Soviet agriculturalists and officials treated him with great respect, impressed by his exceptional knowledge of agricultural matters, and also by that fact that, at Tashkent, he had delivered a speech in Russian.[22]

Wallace, too, was impressed by what he saw. The book *Soviet Asia Mission*, in which he reported to the American public on his expedition, gives, with few qualifications, a very complimentary, not to say idealized, account of the tremendous developments taking place in Siberia, and of the apparently unanimously patriotic and optimistic spirit of the masses of "volunteers" who had flocked there to realize the region's great potential. He wrote, for example, that "Komsomolsk was founded in 1932 by *Komsomols*, members of the Communist Youth Organization, who came east from European Russia in a great volunteer movement to settle the wilderness. The first settlers were enthusiastic young men, who were soon joined by equally high-spirited young women from all over the Soviet Union." The town had become a major center of heavy industry. Wallace knew something of the coercive nature of Stalin's resettlement schemes, but though he was not entirely blinkered (noting, for instance, that "the young city of Komsomolsk looked dishevelled and run down, and the people seemed overworked"), he seemed prepared at this moment to accept the official version of the town's beginnings. Of a visit to an anti-aircraft factory at Kranoyarsk, he wrote: "The spirit at this plant was splendid. . . . The war-bond drive had been well organized, for [the captain in charge] said that purchases by employees averaged 12 per cent of their earnings. Often, patriotic individuals turn in all their savings, saying to the government, 'Use it to buy a warplane or a tank.'"

On its travels through Siberia, Wallace wrote, his party was "accompanied by 'old soldiers' with blue tops on their caps. Everybody treated them with great respect. They are members of the NKVD, which means the People's Commissariat of Internal Affairs. I became very fond of their leader, Major Mikhail Cheremisenov." But as Cheremisenov, Wallace also relates, was a "major of the Soviet secret service," it is little wonder his men were treated "with great respect." At Balkhash Wallace was told again of the willing nature of the migrants. "'Founded by volunteers,' the city's remarkable mayor [a woman] told us. 'They came from Kiev, from Kharkov, from Moscow and Leningrad—180 people 15 years ago. Now we have 70,000.'"

Perhaps Wallace was finding it hard to choke all this down, because three pages later we find him rationalizing that even though Americans might think the human cost of forced collectivization too great, that policy had produced the agricultural surplus necessary to create these new industrial towns. Yet it is hard to understand the naïveté of com-

Wallace and Russian general Ilya S. Semeonov during the vice president's trip to the Soviet Union, 1943. (Courtesy of the University of Iowa Library)

ments such as the following: "The Kolyma gold miners are big, husky young men, who came out to the Far East from European Russia. I spoke with some of them. They were keen about winning the war. 'We wrote to Stalin asking to be sent to the front,' their spokesman said, 'but Stalin replied that we were needed more right here.' Stalin had made gold mining a preferred war industry, we learned, and had frozen the men in it." [23]

Subsequent "defector" testimony has shown that the workers of Kolyma were not volunteers but prisoners, part of a vast system of forced labor on which Russian industry depended. They had hoped that Wallace's visit might improve their conditions, but instead saw him deceived by bogus displays of relative comfort and prosperity. Watch towers had been taken down by the authorities, starving prisoners removed, office workers disguised as farmhands, and stores temporarily stocked with goods. [24] Such revelations, however, came to light much later, and it is difficult to assess just what Wallace might have been expected to know in 1944. Certainly the "show trials" of the 1930s were public knowledge, as they were intended to be; so were the disappropriation and liquidation of the kulaks. The purging of many thousands of army officers and political functionaries had been reported and was being exposed by Leon Trotsky in Mexico. But the larger picture, now generally accepted by the West, of, as Robert Conquest expresses it, "terror rag[ing] . . . throughout the country," "massive executions," and "a vast system of slave labour camps in the Arctic and desert areas of the country" depended in significant degree on firsthand accounts by former inmates of the camps, which did not begin to appear until the late 1940s. Among the earliest were Victor Kravchenko, *I Chose Freedom*, published in London in 1947, and D. J. Dallin and B. I. Nicolaevsky, *Forced Labour in the Soviet Union*, published in London in 1948. Several of the major sources, including Elinor Lipper's *Eleven Years in Soviet Prison Camps*, appeared in 1951, and Lipper is the only source of information about the Kolyma mine fields quoted by either Robert Conquest or William L. O'Neill, whose researches highlight Wallace's apparent naïveté.[25] Wallace's book may have put as good a face as reasonably possible on conditions in the Soviet Union, but he did not deliberately ignore or falsify matters that were open to direct inspection or about which he might reasonably have been expected to know. There were also obvious pressures on an eminent government figure reporting in time of war on a major ally.

If Wallace's tour of Siberia was intended mainly as a goodwill mission, in China the president had given him more specific and serious goals. The major issue here was whether Chiang Kai-shek and the Nationalists could be persuaded to come to some kind of accommodation with the Chinese Communists, before the latter fell into welcoming Soviet arms and before Manchuria was in effect taken over by the Soviet Union. In the event of civil war, Roosevelt certainly did not want the United States to be put in a position of backing the Nationalists against Moscow. Wallace was to tell the generalissimo that the president was prepared to mediate between Chiang's government and the Communists, but also to warn him that if accommodation were not reached, Roosevelt might not be able to hold the Russians to their promise not to intervene. The president had also outlined various suggestions Wallace could make to the generalissimo about the runaway inflation of the Chinese currency, which had caused the black-market exchange rate with the American dollar to become many times the official one. The generalissimo should be urged to issue a new currency and enforce fixed prices.[26]

On 18 June Wallace crossed from Siberia to China, where he visited Tikwa, Sinkiang, Chungking, and Lanchow, and then Ulan Bator in Outer Mongolia. In Chungking he conferred with Chiang Kai-shek. About one of the main reasons for his visit, the attempt to control inflation, he could do nothing, because the Chinese government's head of treasury happened not to be in the country at the time. He did, however, succeed in obtaining from the generalissimo permission to have the U.S. Army enter areas held by the Communists in order to rescue American B-29 pilots and crew shot down on bombing missions to Japan. The Chinese leader had been adamantly against this, but while Wallace was there, Roosevelt sent Chiang Kai-shek a cable urging very vigorously that permission be granted, and in the end it was.

But on the question of accommodation between the Nationalists and the Chinese Communists, Wallace found the generalissimo closed-minded, and in any case found it difficult, in this instance, to convince himself of the justice of the Communist cause. In his reminiscences he attributes this attitude to his being exposed only to opinions favoring cooperation with the Nationalists. He was not able to see General Stilwell, who was critical of Chiang, and writes: "I had completely the point of view as expressed by the Generalissimo, by [Joseph] Alsop and by [General Claire] Chennault."[27] He had no contact with the Communist leadership.

After their conference in Chungking, Wallace and Chiang issued a joint statement announcing a three-point program for the preservation of peace in the Pacific. Points one and two called for the demilitarization of Japan, and cooperation in the region between China, the Soviet Union, the United States, and Britain, point three for "recognition of the fundamental right of presently dependent Asiatic peoples to self-government, and the early adoption of measures in the political, economic and social field to prepare those dependent peoples for self-government within a specified practical time limit." Wallace claimed that "this joint statement was in line with Roosevelt's global strategy. It helped clear the road for August, 1945, when Russia not only entered the war against Japan but did so at a time when the Chinese Foreign Minister, T. V. Soong, was in Moscow engaged in Sino-Soviet talks that resulted in the new thirty-year treaty of friendship."[28] Whatever we may now think of the thirty-year treaty of friendship, the joint declaration probably did for a time assist Roosevelt's aim of keeping the Soviet Union onside with America, not in conflict with either segment of China, and against Japan. But not all the Allies were happy with the joint statement. As we shall see, the British were very sensitive about point three, referring to the rights of colonial peoples to self-government.

Wallace's visit gave him a fairly clear idea of what would happen in the future. The graft and corruption he saw, the actual conditions in the countryside, and his conversations with college professors convinced him that the Kuomintang would eventually be overthrown, and he made this clear to Roosevelt in his report. But he also concluded that, for the time being, America should continue to support Chiang Kai-shek.[29] Looking back, he felt that his trip to China "broadened out on a world basis what I had learned from [my] trip to the South." Like that visit to the South and his journeys to Latin America, it "furnished illustrations for what had been a philosophy with me in a general way for a long time—an intellectual philosophy. I'd had, what you might call, the broad strokes, but it was a question of putting in color."[30]

BETRAYAL

He received no news on the political situation at home until he reached Fairbanks, Alaska, and telephoned Joseph Guffey. This was on 5 July, two weeks before the Democratic National Convention was to commence. Guffey, a good friend, told him: "Things are not going well. Some of the people around the White House are saying, 'We need a new face!'" Then, portentously, Samuel Rosenman telephoned him at Fairbanks and said that he and Harold Ickes would like to see Wallace at the earliest convenient moment, if possible at lunch on Monday, 10 July.

Of course, the major political issue now in Wallace's mind was whether he would be renominated as his party's candidate for vice president. As the president had earlier proposed, he made a major speech, reporting on his mission, in Seattle on 9 July. He got to Washington on the morning of the tenth after a rough all-night flight and called the president, only to be told he was bathing. Some time later presidential assistant General Watson called him back and told him that the president wanted him to see Ickes and Rosenman before coming to the White House at 4:30 P.M. for an on-the-record conference.

So Ickes and Rosenman came to lunch. After half an hour of polite generalities, Ickes broached the subject of Wallace's political future. He flattered Wallace about being one of the last of the true liberals, but pointed out that he had made many enemies, would be likely to divide the convention, and therefore should not contest the vice presidency. Rosenman had just previously hinted that although Roosevelt wanted Wallace as his running mate, he did not think he could win the nomination. Wallace had had a bad night and was not feeling tolerant. "I terminated the conversation very promptly by saying, 'I am seeing the President at four-thirty. I have a report to make on a mission to China. I do not want to talk politics.' They beat a hasty retreat."[31] In fact, Ickes and Rosenman were among those who had been telling the president for months that he could not win with Wallace, and the fact that Roosevelt wanted Wallace to talk with them before coming to the White House shows how seriously he had taken their views.

For two hours that afternoon Wallace talked with the president about China. Then, Wallace reports, Roosevelt said: "'I am now talking to the ceiling about political matters.' He said I was his choice as a running mate, that he was willing to make a statement to that effect. I asked him if he would be willing to say, 'If I were a delegate to the convention I would vote for Henry Wallace.' He said, 'Yes, I would.'" In view of what the president had just said, this was a very moderate request on Wallace's part. A statement from Roosevelt that he would vote for Wallace if he were a delegate — which he was not — would hardly be as strong as a declaration that he wanted his vice president to remain at his post. Perhaps Wallace's moderation came from a realistic estimate of how far he could push the president, although as the conversation went on he seemed totally impervious to manifold hints that the president was regretfully going to dump him — as if he could not believe it. For example: "[Roosevelt] then went on to say that a great many people had been in to see him, saying that I could not be nominated unless the President did what he did in 1940." Wallace replied that if he had known in advance about Roosevelt's insisting on him in 1940 he would not have advised him to do it. "I said I did not want to be pushed down anybody's throat, but that I did want to know definitely whether or not he really wanted me and was willing to say so. He was very ready with his assurance. Then the President returned to the theme of his visitors who had told him that I would cost the ticket from one to three million votes. I said at once, 'Mr. President, if you can find anyone who will add more strength to the ticket than I, by all means take him.' The President did not say that he believed those who thought I would cost the ticket from one to three million votes." (That the president did not actually say—yet did not deny—that he believed them was surely a slender straw to grasp at.) "He then said he could not bear the thought of my name being put before the convention and rejected. I said I had been used to hard situations."[32] Wallace's need to believe in the president's affection and respect, and his need to believe in his own destiny, would not let him see that Roosevelt was trying to let him down gently.

That evening Joseph Guffey came to see Wallace and handed him a draft he had drawn up for a statement to be made by the president that he said would assure Wallace nomination on the first ballot. It read: "It appears the convention will name me [Roosevelt]. I trust the name with me will be Henry A. Wallace. He is equipped for the future. We have made a team which pulls together, thinks alike and plans alike." At lunch the next day, Wallace gave this statement to the president, who said that he had worked out an alternative wording but wished to keep Wallace's. Roosevelt then remarked that many people regarded Wallace as a Communist or as something worse.[33] Thus the game continued.

At lunch again with Roosevelt on Thursday, 13 July, the intimations of Wallace's political mortality went on unheeded. The president told him that he was going to send a letter about the vice-presidential nomination to Senator Jackson, the permanent chairman of the convention, the next day, Friday the fourteenth. "In the letter he would say that he had known me a long time, that he thought a lot of me, and that if he were a delegate to the convention he would vote for me. He would also go on to say that he did not wish in any way to dictate to the convention." There was no sign here of Joseph Guffey's draft. Roosevelt then mentioned that powerful Democratic leaders—national party chairman Robert Hannegan, Edward Flynn, Edwin Pauley, Edward Kelly, and others—had told him the previous Tuesday that Wallace would hurt the ticket. Wallace again offered to withdraw, but Roosevelt merely repeated that he had no means of judging whether the opinion of these advisers was correct; it was "mighty sweet of me to make the offer but he could not think of accepting it." The president did say, however, that the professional politicians believed that Truman could strengthen the ticket. Wallace then wanted to know whether Roosevelt would do as Hannegan wished and suggest an alternative candidate. That, Roosevelt protested, would amount to dictation. But, as Wallace was to find out much too late, on the next day, the fourteenth, after Roosevelt had written for Senator Jackson his lukewarm endorsement of Wallace, he also wrote Hannegan mentioning two alternative names:[34]

Dear Bob:

You have written me about Harry Truman and Bill Douglas. I should, of course, be very glad to run with either of them and believe that either one of them would bring real strength to the ticket.

Always sincerely,

Franklin D. Roosevelt.

Later on in that fateful lunch of 13 July, the president told Wallace: "Even though they do beat you out at Chicago, we will have a job for you in world economic affairs." At parting, he drew Wallace close, pulled him down, and whispered: "I hope it'll be the same old team."

His letter to Jackson, which was at once labeled by everyone "the kiss of death," read:

The easiest way of putting it is this: I have been associated with Henry Wallace during his past four years as Vice President, for eight years earlier while he was Secretary of Agriculture, and well before that. I like him and I respect him, and he is my personal friend. For these reasons, I personally would vote for his renomination if I were a delegate to the Convention.

At the same time, I do not wish to appear in any way as dictating to the Convention. Obviously the Convention must do the deciding.[35]

That second paragraph may as well have read: "Please don't take any notice of what I just told you," and was so understood.

In 1951 Wallace was still struggling with his feelings and doubts about whether Roosevelt had deliberately deceived him. He could no longer deny the inconsistency of Roosevelt's behavior, but tried to explain it by saying that the president was a sick man. "When I say that the President's mind was a sick mind, I say it advisedly, because a well *man* could not have handled the situation when I was with him on Thursday the way he did. I mean he would have told me clean and straight." It was not, Wallace believed, that the president had been too tired and enfeebled to keep up with events, but that there may have been an inadequate supply of blood to his brain. "It's conceivable, for example, that at one time the blood would reach one part of his brain and at another time another part of his brain. There's no accounting for the way in which he vacillated back and forth during that period. I account for it to some extent because he had a very great affection for me and I had a very great affection for him."[36]

Wallace thought that while he had been away in Siberia and China the pressure of the political bosses had swung Roosevelt against him, but when he returned and their close relationship reasserted itself, Roosevelt swung back in his favor. But reading the passages quoted above, one can only feel that Roosevelt's intention to replace Wallace as vice president remained quite firm and consistent; the only inconsistency was between his intention and his overt behavior. When faced with the demand for a forthright and brutal declaration, Roosevelt, because he had affection and something like a protective attitude toward Wallace, could not administer the blow, muffling it instead with soft words. Certainly Wallace's desire to find that it was affection for him that was working in the president's mind had more plausibility than his hypothesis about the blood flowing now to one part and now to another of the president's brain.

He continued to speculate about what might have been happening in the background prior to that 13 July meeting—about how likely it was that Roosevelt had been subject to pressure from Hannegan, speaking, Wallace felt, for big business and the political bosses. He thought that if Hannegan had said to Roosevelt directly, "Look what your commitments are here to so and so and so and so. . . . Look what you've said—are you going to come through or not?" the president would have yielded. "When a man who meant business, as Hannegan meant business, was talking that way to the President, the feminine side of the President would succumb to the dominant Hannegan and say, 'All right.' "[37]

As the convention got under way, Iowa state Democratic chairman Jake More wrote to Wallace urging him to come to Chicago as soon as he could. There were many candidates for the vice-presidential nomination, More warned, and much confusion. Wallace's ideas were coming under attack and he was being criticized for stirring up revolution in Latin America.[38] Wallace arrived on Wednesday, 19 July, and on entering the assembly hall was accorded a friendly reception. A Gallup poll of rank-and-file Democratic voters, published that day, showed that he had overwhelming support—65 percent, to Senator Alben Barkley's 17 percent, Sam Rayburn's 5 percent, and Byrnes's 3 percent. Harry Truman scored just 2 percent of the vote. Wallace must have known, however, that popularity, whether with the voters or the delegates, would not decide the issue.[39]

After the formality of Roosevelt's nomination on the evening of

20 July, Wallace went to the platform to make a speech seconding it. At his appearance, the week's most enthusiastic demonstration broke out, as the galleries and the delegates on the convention floor paid him tribute. His wife, so humiliated four years earlier, was heard to say: "I won't mind if he loses, now. Four years ago there was so much unfriendliness and booing that Henry couldn't go onto the platform. And just look at this ovation that he's getting now."[40] As well as sincerely praising Roosevelt as a great liberal and "the only person in the United States who can meet on even terms the other great leaders in discussions of war and peace," Wallace went on, on his own initiative, to make commitments about the future course of Democratic policies:

> The future belongs to those who go down the line unswervingly for the liberal principles of both political democracy and economic democracy regardless of race, color, or religion. In a political, educational, and economic sense there must be no inferior races. The poll tax must go. Equal educational opportunities must come. The future must bring equal wages for equal work regardless of sex or race.
>
> Roosevelt stands for all this. That is why certain people hate him so.[41]

If Wallace's displacement from the ticket had not already been decided, Roosevelt might have found some of these brave commitments embarrassing. The threat of the abolition of the poll tax, for instance, would have alarmed many southern senators, whose support he continued to need. Wallace himself later admitted that this section of his address may not have been good politics, and that it probably lost him the Texas delegation, but "I said it because I believed it, I guess, though it was a bit of a luxury to say it at that time."[42]

At the conclusion of Wallace's speech, a tremendous and long-sustained demonstration for him built up, with wild acclamation from the galleries. As it reached a climax, Senator Claude Pepper, a liberal ally, tried to place Wallace's name in nomination so that the issue of the vice-presidential nomination could be decided that night. Wallace saw Pepper desperately trying to catch the attention of the convention chairman, Senator Jackson, and Jackson just as determinedly ignoring him. Instead, an adjournment motion was put. Depending on the observer's political stance, it was either a close vote or the "Noes" had it by a wide margin, but Jackson, under Hannegan's orders, at once declared the motion carried on the voices and adjourned the meeting.[43]

Wallace appended in his diary page after page of quotes from newspapers and from friends saying that if the vote had been taken that night he would have won, that this was obvious to everyone, including the machine politicians, and that that was why they had brought on the adjournment—to give themselves time to work on the delegates. But this was disputed by an experienced and clear-eyed observer, Benham Baldwin, who had been working as hard as he could for Wallace. In his report on proceedings, he noted that the enthusiasm shown for Wallace would never have been reflected in delegates' votes, because many of them were obliged to follow the orders of the political bosses.[44] Baldwin had been sounding out delegates and casting up votes and knew that Wallace did not have enough.

Whether or not Wallace would have won on the evening of twentieth, it is plain that a great deal of intense politicking went on before the convention resumed the following day. A few hours after Roosevelt's broadcast acceptance speech, Hannegan had released the second letter, in which Roosevelt named Truman and Douglas. Even more dramatically, Hannegan carried in his pocket, or so it is alleged, a third note, written in pencil in Roosevelt's own hand, saying, "Bob, I think Truman is the right man. FDR." According to the story, Hannegan showed this, on the morning of the twenty-first, to Truman, who appeared taken aback, or completely dismayed, and said, "I don't want the darned thing," or some such words.[45]

The intriguing aspect of Truman's reaction is that up to then he had been going about at the convention soliciting support for James Byrnes, who very much wanted the nomination. But Wallace came to believe that the move for Byrnes, in which Hannegan had also had a hand, was only a feint, as Hannegan knew that Byrnes, because of his antilabor voting record, was quite unacceptable to the labor movement. If some votes were secured for Byrnes, this might constitute a sufficient threat to the labor leaders to persuade them to support Truman, Hannegan's real choice. Wallace claims in his oral history record that "Hannegan said to Sidney Hillman on the evening of Monday, July 17, that 'We will withdraw Byrnes, if you will withdraw Wallace.' That was reported to me by Phil Murray."[46] According to Baldwin's report, Truman had been told by Sidney Hillman before the convention that he would be acceptable to the CIO—by implication, as a substitute for Wallace, who had strong support in the labor movement but had been damned by Roosevelt's faint praise. If there is a basis of truth in all that, it would be remarkable if Truman did not know that Hannegan was thinking of him as a possible nominee, and if he did, then his canvasing of votes for Byrnes may have been a surreptitious way of getting votes for himself.

The crucial vote was taken on the twenty-first. Wallace was ahead after the first ballot, but the second ballot gave the nomination to Truman, who was the choice of the South and the city machines and whom, it turned out, Roosevelt had been persuaded by Flynn, Hannegan, former postmaster general Walker, and others to support as long ago as 11 July.[47]

Evidently feeling insecure, Truman came to see Wallace on the morning of 3 August. He stated that the last week had been the most miserable of his life and that he had not been involved in any machinations aimed at securing his own nomination. Wallace was "exceedingly happy" during their conversation, Truman "very doleful." "He asked for the continuation of my friendship. I said, 'Harry, we are both Masons' and smiled at him very sweetly and said I would do everything I could to make the election come out right. . . . He said he was not a deep thinker like I was and he needed my help on policy matters during the campaign. I made no comment whatever that I would help him, neither did I say I would not." Wallace's description of himself as "exceedingly happy" during this interview sounds true. He had claimed to his friends that he felt much freer now that he "had not been hired again," and Truman's coming as an apologetic supplicant to beg his help only served to reinforce Wallace's patronizing, even contemptuous, attitude toward him. He had not been defeated by Truman but by the machine. After Truman's deep protestations of friendship, he refrained from mentioning that before the convention Truman had declared for Rayburn and during the early part of it had worked for Byrnes. Yet three months earlier he had told Wallace on the floor of the Senate that he hoped Wallace would retain the vice presidency and that all he himself wished to do was to remain in the Senate. "This kind of action," Wallace wrote in his diary, "convinces me beyond doubt that he is a small[,] opportunistic man, a man of good instinct, but, therefore, probably all the more dangerous. As he moves out more in the public eye, he will get caught in the webs of his own making."[48]

Wallace still wanted to know who or what had brought about his downfall. His perennial suspicion of the self-seeking motives of the Tory British and of elements in the Catholic church was brought to bear on this issue. He recalled that a preliminary drive against him had been started by Thomas Corcoran, a drive probably originating with these two groups, both of which, Wallace believed, had influence with Democratic power brokers. He had reason to think the Tories were specifically motivated to get rid of him at this juncture. His pamphlet, *Our Job in the Pacific*, dealing with the United States' postwar aims, had not long been published. In it he had drawn a distinction between "free Asia" and "subject Asia," the latter consisting of "countries whose present rulers have not yet permitted themselves to name definite dates for the emancipation of their colonial subjects" — India, Burma, Malaya, Indo-China, the Dutch East Indies, and the like. The United States, Wallace had announced, looked forward to the institution of an orderly process by which subject areas of Asia would become free.[49]

These comments had elaborated point three of the statement released after his discussions with Chiang Kai-shek, a statement that itself had been reinforced by a speech Wallace made in Chungking on 21 June 1944, at a dinner given by the generalissimo. After saying that territories forcibly taken from China by Japan would be restored, he went on: "In Asia there are other political and racial entities, now in a state of colonial dependency, whose aspirations to self-government should receive prompt and positive attention after victory." Many of the areas to which he tacitly referred had been under British rule, and at this stage the British did not have any intention of relinquishing their empire. They were enraged, according to British Secret Service commander Robert Dahl, who in conversation said that "Churchill is likely to ask the President to get a new Vice President."[50]

Shortly after the convention, Wallace learned firsthand of Britain's anger over his anti-imperialistic statements. On 5 October 1944, at Ambassador Halifax's party for the Chinese delegates to the Dumbarton Oaks conference, Halifax started talking to him about the joint statement and the Chungking speech. He said that the Foreign Office was deeply disturbed and had asked him to make representations to Wallace. In his diary entry referring to that day, Wallace comments: "I had no doubt that Halifax was representing very accurately what he and Churchill, and the other British Tories feel. Also I had no doubt that my presentation represented the way in which ninety-nine out of one hundred Americans feel. The British certainly have lots of nerve when it comes to doing everything possible to maintain their hold on subject peoples. I can see now why the British should take so much interest in pulling the strings to see that American politics come out the right way."[51]

The extent of Wallace's rumination over the origins of Roosevelt's decision not to support him surely shows that he felt hurt and let down; however, there was some psychological benefit in the situation too. Looking back, he said, "I did begin to look on myself as much more my own man after I began to realize what Roosevelt had done in July 1944. I'd begun to feel that way after the Jesse Jones affair, but I'd still taken what you might call an extreme Christian attitude with regard to the President up through the convention."[52] That all-understanding, all-forgiving attitude served for Wallace the function of blanking out any hurt that he felt from being betrayed, and helped him in his own mind to rise morally superior to the offender, in effect turning defeat into a kind of victory. Perhaps, too, his new status would allow him greater freedom. Departing Washington soon after the convention, for a holiday in Des Moines, Wallace told a reporter: "I really think that I can do more for the cause of liberalism this way."[53]

As the time for the campaign approached, Wallace told Philip Murray that although he had gone straight down the line for the president thus far, he would make no speeches for "the ticket" unless he received personal assurances from Roosevelt that he would pursue liberal policies after the election. Almost precisely the same sentiments appear in an article by James Reston in the *New York Times* of 10 August. Reston quoted friends of Wallace to the effect that Wallace intended to have a "completely frank" talk with Roosevelt in order to discover whether he was committed to the goals of collective security, full employment, and improved living standards. The vice president was "not talking for publication," but "it is known that he has received several suggestions about how he might carry on his fight for the adoption of 'liberal' policies outside the Government." Whatever Roosevelt's response, Wallace would support his reelection, but "the extent of his support and the place he accepts in any fourth Roosevelt Administration . . . will depend on the answers he gets." The words Reston used suggest that the source of this story may have been Wallace himself, or possibly persons acting at his behest. In either event, the president had been publicly warned.[54]

Late in August 1944 Wallace was called to lunch with Roosevelt, who praised him for the work he had been doing, and then attempted to justify his failure to nominate him for vice president. In his diary Wallace wrote: "He then started to skate over the thin ice at once as fast as he could, saying that I was four or six years ahead of my time, that I had stood for what would inevitably come. I told him I was very happy about what had been demonstrated at the convention and following the convention because I now knew that the people were for me." There is almost an implied threat here: his strength with the people would serve him well in any future struggle. Roosevelt told him his difficulty at the convention was that he did not have reserve political strength to throw in, and he compared Wallace's position in 1944 with his own in 1932, when he had had to make a deal with Garner (who had William Randolph Hearst's backing). Wallace, proud of his own purity and lonely independence, said: "Mr. President, I could have made a deal too, but I did not care to do it." Wallace then declared that he was perfectly well aware of what had gone on at the convention but had decided to back Roosevelt "because his name was a symbol of liberalism." These coals of fire heaped on Roosevelt's head had their effect. He warmly thanked Wallace for his support at the convention and offered him any cabinet post he desired, except that of secretary of state. He also said that he would replace certain members of the cabinet and that the first to go would be "Jesus H. Jones." Emboldened by Roosevelt's talking as if the two of them were equals in running the administration, Wallace said, "Well, if you are going to get rid of Jesse, why not let me have Secretary of Commerce with RFC and FEA [the Foreign Economic Administration] thrown in? There would be poetic justice in that." Roosevelt agreed with the "poetic justice" sentiment.[55]

Wallace gave as his reason for taking secretary of commerce that it was the only position that would not mean his unseating some old friend, but of course there were other considerations as well. He had believed and publicly argued for many years that agriculture and industry needed each other as market and supplier of necessary goods, that neither could be in good health if the other were ill. He also saw commerce secretary as a position from which he could encourage the growth of small business, as a counter to the increasing monopolization of industry the war had brought about. He felt that, like agricultural and unskilled workers, small business was not properly represented in economic decision making and therefore needed government aid. Most important, Wallace believed he could use this powerful cabinet office, and his control over lending agencies, to achieve a new liberal goal to which he had by now become strongly committed, the full employment of the nation's labor force.[56]

Even though by the end of the 1944 convention Wallace's "extreme Christian attitude" toward Roosevelt may have been wearing thin, nevertheless like a good soldier he played his part in the campaign for those closing months of his vice presidency, traveling widely under spartan wartime conditions to speak in support of Democratic policies and of the president himself. An incident that occurred on one of these speaking tours casts an revealing light on his attitudes toward race and social justice at that time. He had taken a Pullman car from Albany to Chicago and then on into Iowa. There were six bedrooms in the car, all occupied by the vice president's party, and a lounge in which the African American porter slept when and as best he could. As the porter, Mr. L. R. Richie, later told the story, Wallace came into the lounge on the second night and sat down opposite him. After a while, he asked Richie what time he went to bed:

> I said "I don't go to bed." He said, "You don't go to bed?" I said, "No." He said, "Well, how do you sleep?" I said, "Well, I sit here and sleep. . . ." So he said, "Oh, you must have a bed to sleep in, porter." I said, "No, they didn't make room for me on here, only to be on here to work." He said, "Well, listen, we don't know how long we're going to keep the car, maybe a month. How are you going to sleep?" I said, "Just sitting up where you see me now." He said, "Oh, no."
>
> The next morning he told the waiters, the reporters. He said, "Now, you will all have to find another place to sleep, because when we leave here, we catch a train. You'll have to sleep in the train, because the porter is going to use that room." . . . So they did that.

The party traveled through Iowa for twenty-one days, but as they neared the end of the journey Richie became apprehensive. Because he had not been supposed to sleep the Pullman Company would "take the sleep away" by reducing his pay. Wallace said he would take care of that. He gave Richie his vice-presidential card and told him to present it to his superior, to whom Wallace would also write. Should Richie not receive his pay, he was to contact Wallace personally.[57]

A week after the election, when Wallace was in the White House for a cabinet meeting, Eleanor Roosevelt told him that liberals were looking to him for leadership. She said that she would soon be attending the CIO convention and asked whether he would agree to lead the CIO's expanded Political Action Committee, but he declined saying that liberalism was best expressed nationally through the Democratic Party. He regarded these friendly approaches with some skepticism, wondering whether the president might not be "up to his usual maneuvering tricks." In his diary he noted sourly that the cabinet meeting had proceeded "in the customary futile way." Roosevelt seemed to have aged considerably; though he had "lots of vitality left in his system . . . I would judge from the character and quality of his remarks that his intellect but not his prejudices will now begin to fade pretty rapidly. He will have to take awfully good care of himself to last out the four years in a state of competent leadership." [58]

Late in December Wallace took Roosevelt a comprehensive statement of the functions of the Department of Commerce as he saw them, with which Roosevelt, after reading it, indicated general agreement. Echoes of Wallace's bitter disputes with Cordell Hull may be heard throughout the document: communications from Commerce Department staff working abroad must come direct to the department, rather than being routed through Department of State; while overseas, such employees should not be subordinate to diplomatic personnel; the secretary of commerce must enjoy ready access to the president and have his full support. Still smarting from his experiences in the BEW, he also delivered an oblique but unmistakable rebuke: "I told him it was my observation that one of the most fatal things around Washington was to have responsibility without having adequate authority or power to carry out the responsibility."

Wallace looked ahead, telling the president, in effect, that his slipshod administrative methods would not do in the future: "I told the President that several years after the war was over, I thought there was going to be the most extraordinary kind of a back lick which was going to bring serious trouble on us and it would be necessary to act with very great comprehension and imagination in planning to avoid this trouble. I said after World War No. 1 Hoover had very big plans for [a] large export trade but these plans as a result of our high tariff policy eventually came to naught. I said we would have to have a very comprehensive and well thought out long-time plan if we were to avoid the same pitfalls which overtook the Republicans in 1930." Roosevelt indicated his agreement with these ideas, but Wallace felt that he did not really understand them: "His thinking is completely in other fields. . . . It was obvious to me that the President's mind roams as far afield as ever, that he still talks endlessly about everything under the sun but that he is losing considerable of his old power of focus. His mind isn't very clear any more. His hand trembles a great deal more than it used to."

Wallace tried to shift the discussion to the the the full-employment bill, shortly to come before Congress. He talked of Simon Kuznets's theory of capital formation, of the way the tax system might be modified to encourage capital investment, and of how Wall Street's high-interest method of financing was restricting the flow of capital—weighty and important matters. Rather than engaging any of these subjects, Roosevelt discussed the political machinations of Jesse Jones, the fact that friends of U.S. Steel could travel around the world on the corporation's nonpassenger boats by signing up as members of the crew, the way in which Africa's peanut growers were being exploited, and how it had been shown that South Pacific natives who wore clothes were susceptible to tuberculosis. The point of this lengthy diary entry is then made clear: "I mention these matters merely to indicate a few of the many subjects which the President and I thought had a point when he started telling them but which point he promptly forgot as he went further afield. His whole habit of mind is that of a man who is continually traveling, seeing fresh pictures. His extraordinary discursiveness may have served a very useful purpose as President but as he gets older, it makes him less and less capable as an administrator and more and more irritating to administrators."[59] The contrast between ailing leader and vigorous, imaginative subordinate can hardly be missed.

For the time being, however, Wallace had no obvious status, a situation brought home to him on the night of Truman's vice-presidential inauguration. When the festivities were over, Samuel Rosenman and his wife went to see him. It was, Rosenman has said, a "touching experience": "We were struck by the fact that he was sitting there all alone. No person had been there even to say 'hello' to him now that he wasn't Vice-President. He was sitting there with his phonograph playing some Russian records, Russian language records, trying to learn the language."[60]

SECRETARY OF COMMERCE

With his fourth administration about to begin, Roosevelt took pleasure in promptly keeping his promise to unseat Jones and put Wallace in his place. On the day of his inauguration he wrote Jones, conventionally acknowledging the value of his past services, but saying that

Wallace, who had worked magnificently during the campaign, deserved whatever job he felt he could best perform. Because Wallace believed he could do the most good in the Department of Commerce, he should have this position in the new administration.[61]

The impact of this unceremonious dismissal was exacerbated by the president's going on to suggest in an offhand manner that possibly the State Department might be able to find Jones an ambassadorship somewhere. One can imagine the sense of outrage the self-satisfied Jones, still smug over his defeat of Wallace on the BEW, must have felt at having his major post usurped by his old enemy. True to form, Jones did not just write to the president but released an immediate public reply declining the diplomatic post, praising his own contribution, and saying that Wallace's inexperience in business and finance would make his appointment difficult to understand.[62]

Wallace's confirmation as commerce secretary was anything but a foregone conclusion. Truman said later that "when Roosevelt told me he was going to make Henry Secretary of Commerce, I said, 'Jesus Christ!' FDR called me to help and I told him I'd see every Senator I could."[63] Truman did his best to gather support for Wallace but soon concluded that unless the RFC was separated from the Department of Commerce, the nomination would fail. Conservative senators did not want Wallace to control federal lending agencies. Senator Walter F. George of Georgia introduced a bill to effect this separation, and it and Wallace's proposed appointment were referred jointly to the Commerce Committee on 24 and 25 January 1945.

It was of crucial importance that the George bill be considered first, but Senator Alben Barkley, who was to call it up, had fallen asleep and Senator Robert Taft jumped to his feet to introduce the nomination. Truman ignored Taft and recognized the newly awakened Barkley, thus saving the Wallace nomination. Truman would later claim, with some justification, that Wallace had forgotten everything that he, Truman, had done for him.[64]

The first day of the confirmation hearings was given over to Jones and his supporters setting out Jones's own massive qualifications for the office and belittling Wallace's. Jones listened complacently as friendly counsel read out the imposing list of his financial posts and summarized the tremendous scope of the operations of the Department of Commerce under his command. At the end of the day Senator Claude Pepper, Wallace's fellow liberal, wanting to secure for Wallace both the post of commerce secretary and the loan powers George's bill was threatening to separate from the department, asked Jones: "Out of your experience, Mr. Jones, is it not your opinion that these two offices can be administered by one man, assuming the competence of that man?" Jones replied: "If you are trying to ask me if Henry Wallace is qualified for both jobs, I will say, 'No.'"[65]

On the following day it was Wallace's turn to testify, and by friendly questioning he was led to recount with justifiable pride how, entirely on the basis of his own research and through the application of his own organizational ability and financial common sense, he had established and built up his crossbred corn and chicken business from nothing into a $4 million enterprise. "I know the problems of the small businessman because I have lived with them," he told the Senate committee. "I have been on the note for more money than I could possibly pay. I depended on whether or not the corn was sold. I know what that experience is. I have been up against that more than many men who claim that they are hard-headed, realistic business men and I am not."[66] In addition he could point to the outstanding successes of his eight years as secretary of agriculture.

In the end he was confirmed as secretary of commerce, but without the loan powers Jones had enjoyed.[67] This, of course, restricted Wallace's freedom of action; it meant that he could not, with a stroke of the pen as had Jones, disburse funds directly for projects he regarded as worthy, but had to have loans approved by other government agencies. It also limited his ability to use Keynesian-type measures to promote his desired goal of full employment.

He had hardly time to affect the working of the Department of Commerce before the event he had expected and feared came about. On 12 April 1945, Franklin Roosevelt died, his health broken by the accumulated strain of a dozen years as president, culminating in the burden of leading his country in the world's most destructive war. Harry S. Truman was immediately sworn in as president. Wallace undoubtedly realized that, but for underhanded political scheming, he would now have been the nation's leader.

His disbelief in Truman's ability or will to maintain a liberal course in government manifested itself even on the train returning from Roosevelt's interment. As he and Harold Ickes passed through Truman's car, they noticed that Democratic machine politicians George Allen and Edwin Pauley were there. Ickes "spoke very disparagingly

Wallace appearing before the Senate Commerce Committee in January 1945 to argue against the stripping of lending functions from the Department of Commerce. (Courtesy of the Associated Press)

about them, particularly Pauley," and Wallace, too, was full of forebodings. "Having worked with a man who in his prime had genuine spiritual lifting power," he wrote in his diary, "I was overcome with sadness as I thought of what the Pauleys would do to a man like Truman." To Henry Wallace, it now seemed, the "era of experimental liberalism," with all the hopes for national and international betterment that he had invested in it, was at an end.[68]

8

ONE SINGLE HUMAN COMMUNITY

COOPERATION WITH THE SOVIET

UNION AS THE PATH TO PEACE

Initially, Wallace was surprised by the new president's apparent eagerness to accede to his wishes. Two weeks after Roosevelt's death he had an interview with Truman, which he used to explain how closely he had been allied with the late president's social and economic goals, and in effect to lay down as a condition of his cooperation that Truman should continue in the same tradition. With a tinge of irony he enumerated in his diary Truman's declarations of agreement. Wallace said that he had been very surprised at the outcome of his struggle with Jesse Jones, and Truman said he had been surprised too, and had been on Wallace's side through the long dispute. They agreed that Milo Perkins was a man of integrity (an important litmus test, as we have seen). Wallace said that although he had the best possible relations with Roosevelt, there had been people close to the former president who had worked to undermine him. He told Truman that he was "prepared to serve him as loyally as I had Roosevelt, provided he wanted me to do so" (and Truman was "very emphatic in saying that he did"), but that he was no longer prepared to put up with a situation in which some of those close to the president connived against him. Truman "spoke very vigorously about connivers, saying that he was against them and that he was going to get rid of them as soon as he could." The president, Wallace wrote in his diary, seemed "exceedingly eager to agree with everything I said," and "to make decisions of every kind with the greatest promptness. . . . It almost seemed that he was eager to decide in advance of thinking."[1]

It should have been clear to Wallace that these too-ready assurances were not a reliable guide to eventual action, but apparently he gave them a good deal of credence at the time. He said later that at this interview Truman had declared his intention of perpetuating Roosevelt's liberal policies, and that he "continued to seem very clear-cut in it at all times when I talked to him clear up to September 16, 1946" (the date Truman sacked Wallace). Even after it became apparent that Truman was taking a different political line, "he always agreed with everything I said—he never disagreed once in any iota."[2] It was a procedure of which Wallace might one day take advantage.

Wallace settled into his work as secretary of commerce, intent on doing what he could to keep alive a Rooseveltian liberalism and to achieve full employment as a basis for future prosperity and peace.[3] He threw his weight behind the Murray bill, then before Congress, which set down full employment as a specific goal and required the government to estimate each year the level of total expenditure necessary to achieve it. To mobilize public support, he published *Sixty Million Jobs* in late 1945. Since election day, he told his readers, he had spent more than half his time studying the labor problem and now believed the goal of a fully employed workforce attainable. A unified national full-employment budget, rather than the present "horse-and-buggy" affair, could ensure the provision of sixty million jobs by 1950. That would mean a doubling of living standards for the poor, and secure incomes for the rest of the population, so that "all would have the satisfaction of living in a broadly based democracy for the first time." High wartime employment had promoted cooperation between labor and capital and helped eliminate religious, racial, and sexual inequalities. Peacetime full employment would do the same, as well as easing rural poverty, especially in the South, and providing jobs for service veterans.

To some, Wallace's proposals looked like a recipe for central economic planning, and he was sensitive to that charge. He was an enthusiastic advocate of planning, not, as he had explained in a *Reader's Digest* article in May 1945, in the sense that "all economic decisions would be made by a small group at a central spot," but planning "to keep our American economic system free." Concentration of economic power in the hands of a minority of corporate leaders, he pointed out, could lead to "a private Planned Economy just as tyrannical as any public Planned Economy." There must be a diffusion of economic decision making, an outcome the federal government could promote by assisting small business through the elimination of barriers to competition, easier access to credit, and the like. Wallace proposed that the Department of Commerce expand its research services and make them available to businesses, just as the Department of Agriculture, through its Extension Service, had done. "Such, in this field," he declared, "are my proposals as an unabashed governmental *planner*." He added that no government could avoid its responsibility to "plan" fiscal, tariff, and monetary policy.[4]

In *Sixty Million Jobs* Wallace again stressed that the planning he favored was democratic rather than centralist, originating from the grass roots rather than from the top. It was the kind of planning he had instigated as secretary of agriculture and was exemplified in the Tennessee Valley Authority, which he praised as "a model for decentralized liberty, for true economic democracy, with the people actively and directly participating in the decisions that affect their daily bread." Similar initiatives, Wallace claimed, were now being taken in cities across the land — the beginnings of voluntary cooperative planning for prosperity and peace.[5] But the relationship between all this and and a centrally directed fiscal plan for the economy was not spelled out.

THE SOVIET UNION AND THE DEBATE OVER NUCLEAR POLICY

Gradually, as the months went by, the split between Wallace and almost the entire administration on attitudes toward the Soviet Union became clearer and sharper — Wallace with his belief in the need for economic cooperation as a necessary precursor to the development of less warlike international relations, and the remainder convinced that Russia was irredeemably aggressive and untrustworthy, and that helping it would only make it a more formidable enemy.

Conflict over nuclear policy reflected that developing situation. At a cabinet meeting on 21 September 1945, Secretary of War Henry Stimson, quoting the opinion of War Department scientists that the United States could not for long retain the secrets of the atomic bomb, proposed a free exchange of scientific information with other members of the United Nations, including the Soviet Union. Stimson also reported the scientists as warning that future nuclear war might conceivably destroy the world. Some of those present—Dean Acheson, representing Secretary of State James Byrnes, Postmaster General Robert Hannegan, and Wallace among them—supported Stimson's ideas; others, most notably Secretary of the Navy Forrestal and Secretary of Agriculture Anderson, strongly opposed them.[6]

When it was Wallace's turn to speak, he asked the president to clarify the subject being discussed. Truman said that the issue was whether scientific knowledge on nuclear energy should be internationalized, not whether the secrets of making the bomb should be released. Since early in the war, Wallace had been kept informed about nuclear research by physicist Vannevar Bush, head of the Office of Scientific Research and Development, who regarded the vice president as the only cabinet member capable of understanding such matters. Now, for his cabinet colleagues' benefit, Wallace sketched in some scientific and historical background, explaining how "the whole approach had originated in Europe and that it was impossible to bottle the thing up no matter how much we tried." He went on to argue for "the interchange of scientific information but not the interchange of techniques or 'Know Hows.'" As a quid pro quo for the former, American scientists should be able to work in the Soviet Union. The following day, several newspapers carried the story that Henry Wallace had advocated in cabinet giving the secrets of the atomic bomb to the Russians.

The distinction that Wallace sought to draw between nuclear energy information and nuclear weapons technology may have been a fine one (Stimson himself had failed to maintain it), but in the version leaked from cabinet to the press it disappeared altogether, and Wallace became the target of a good deal of intemperate press criticism. "Of course," editorialized the *New York Daily Mirror*, "this preposterous proposal came from Russia's No. 1 Special Pleader in our Government, Secretary of Commerce Henry A. Wallace, pet of the pinks, officially stripped of great power by our Senate." Had Wallace won the vice-presidential nomination in 1944, the *Mirror* pointed out, "he would be in a position today to deliver us hand and foot, atomic bomb and everything, to Stalin's imperialistic, thieving slave state." But even *New York Times* correspondent Felix Belair accepted the leaked version of cabinet discussions—that Wallace had suggested that the Soviet Union be given the secrets of nuclear weapons construction.[7]

In a letter to Truman a few days later, Wallace himself abandoned the knowledge/technology distinction, arguing that the United States could not prevent other nations getting the bomb within five years or so, and that if in the meantime it "played dog in the manger," the world would divide into two hostile camps, Anglo-Saxon and non-Anglo-Saxon. Only if America moved quickly to share its scientific information could international agreements aimed at using nuclear energy for peaceful purposes be reached.[8] At a cabinet meeting in early October, however, Truman rejected the Stimson proposal.

Wallace tried again to change Truman's mind. He showed the president a paper he had prepared entitled "The Significance of the Atomic Age," in which he argued that "the first effect of the atomic bomb had been to make the United States appear to the world as the greatest potential aggressor nation" and advocated setting up a world body to pool nuclear knowledge and use it constructively. If the latter were done, the world could solve the age-old problems of scarcity and want. Able to believe for the moment that his longed-for era of prosperity and peace may have been at hand, Wallace had written: "We can enter in the near future into the golden age of abundance. It is as if God were saying to us, 'Enter now into the land of abundance and enjoy all its fruits.'" In this millennial state, "isms" would "lose their old meaning." The old order would resist the new, but could not prevail against it. "Too many nations know the secret. . . . God has given us, through this tremendous discovery of atomic energy, the unique opportunity to build one single human community on the highest spiritual level, accompanied by unlimited material facilities."[9] Wallace was not the only one to make such optimistic forecasts about atomic energy. One scientist announced that "universal and perpetual peace" could now be anticipated because "there will no longer be any reason to fight for oil or coal," and because seabed mining, using atomic power, would yield a superabundance of raw materials. Some scientists involved in the Manhattan Project also spoke in expansive terms of the immense social and industrial gains that could now be expected.[10]

Truman read the statement through and, predictably, indicated his agreement with it. He foreshadowed a conference with the Soviets at which the matters Wallace had raised would be considered. By Wallace's account, he also endorsed Wallace's view that the British must never be permitted to create an unbridgeable gulf between the United States and Russia. But though Wallace was heartened by the president's sympathetic response, he could not for long retain his optimism.

Later that month, nuclear scientist Robert Oppenheimer came to see him in an agitated state, warning of future catastrophe, and specifically attacking the attitude of Secretary of State James Byrnes. "It seems," Wallace wrote in his diary, "that Secretary Byrnes has felt that we could use the bomb as a pistol to get what we wanted in international diplomacy." From Anatole B. Gromov, first secretary of the Soviet embassy, he learned of Russian resentment at U.S. nuclear policy and at its willingness to give generous loans to Great Britain but not to the Soviet Union. Gromov wondered why Byrnes was "play[ing] England's game so exclusively," and why the United States was insisting on the democratization of the Balkan states while tolerating the excesses of the Argentine regime.[11]

Wallace did what he could to heal the developing breach between the United States and the Soviet Union. In talking to Truman on 18 July 1946, he sought Truman's collusion in a tactic to set funds aside, ready to be made available to the Soviets, without arousing the opposition of Congress. Congress should be asked to vote extra finance for the Export-Import Bank, but not in sufficient amount to arouse suspicion that a loan to Russia might be in prospect. "I indicated that there might come a time sometime during the next five or six months when it would be very important to world peace and world trade to be in position to loan Russia some money. I indicated that the National Advisory Council was now loaning—not on a country basis but on a project basis, and therefore it seemed possible to me to keep the Russian discussion out of the request for additional funds." Truman found this an occasion to say, "We don't have any aggression whatever in our plans against Russia," but Wallace contended that Russia nevertheless suspected America of belligerent intent, because of its exclusive possession of the atom bomb, its ring of air bases around most of the world, and other aspects of its foreign policy. He told the president that he would soon be sending him a letter regarding the whole Russian situation.[12]

He delivered this important letter on 23 July 1946, remarking to Truman that it would not be approved by those who believed war with Russia to be inevitable, stressing that U.S. relations with Russia were as important as those with England, and urging that the United States should resist British attempts to make it take sides. With these statements the president "agreed wholeheartedly." In the letter Wallace argued that the United States' actions since the war—its atomic bomb tests, increased military spending, setting up of air bases throughout the world, and so on — "must make it look to the rest of the world as if we were only paying lip service to peace at the conference table." How would the United States react "if Russia had the atomic bomb and we did not, if Russia had 10,000-mile bombers and air bases within a thousand miles of our coast lines and we did not?"

Wallace claimed that there was a school of military thought in the United States that, recognizing that if each side had atomic bombs a mutually destructive war would result, advocated a preventive war against the Soviets before they developed any such weapons. Wallace argued that this would be not only immoral but also stupid, because Soviet ground troops would at once occupy all of continental Europe, where atomic bombs could not be used. He went on to criticize the plan for international control of atomic energy recently presented to the United Nations Atomic Energy Commission by Bernard Baruch, though without mentioning his name. This plan had a "fatal defect":

> That defect is the scheme, as it is generally understood, of arriving at international agreements by "easy stages," of requiring other nations to enter into binding commitments not to conduct research into the military uses of atomic energy and to disclose their uranium and thorium resources while the United States retains the right to withhold its technical knowledge of atomic energy until the international control and inspection system is working to our satisfaction. . . .
>
> Realistically, Russia has two cards which she can use in negotiating with us: (1) our lack of information on the state of her scientific and technical progress on atomic energy and (2) our ignorance of her uranium and thorium resources. These cards are nothing like as powerful as our cards — a stockpile of bombs, manufacturing plants in actual production, B-29s and B-36s, and our bases covering half the globe. Yet we are in effect asking her to reveal her only two cards immediately — telling her that after we have seen her cards we will decide whether we want to continue to play the game. . . .
>
> We must be prepared to reach an agreement which will commit us to disclosing information and destroying our bombs at a specified time or in terms of specified actions by other countries, rather than at our unfettered discretion.[13]

Truman said that he would read the letter carefully and discuss it with Wallace later, but apparently did not do so. He did, however, acknowledge it a few days later, after deciding, as he expressed it in his diary, "that '*my friend*' Henry was making a record '*for himself.*' " Wallace's letter, Truman noted dryly, "covered everything from Genesis to Revelation."[14]

In a press release in late July, Wallace alluded again to the great spiritual movement that he still hoped would save and then transform the world and that was now a matter of practical necessity. "To prevent atomic energy from destroying mankind," he declared, "it is essential that there be a psychic revolution, a profound change in the moral values and thinking habits of people the world over. . . . I say that Christian morality, not as practiced during the last nineteen hundred years, but as Jesus himself taught it, has finally become the most practical thing in the world." Were such an "international moral code" to emerge, he speculated, atomic energy could "unlock for us one door after another to abundance and joyous living."[15] But such optimistic imaginings only served to measure the distance between his desperately hoped-for ideal and an ever more threatening reality. Since Roosevelt's death, Wallace's dissatisfaction with the Truman administration's conduct of world affairs had never been far from the surface. Now, as that policy hardened and as the international situation seemed more threatening than ever, it broke spectacularly through.

CHALLENGE TO U.S. FOREIGN POLICY

Wallace's dramatically provocative speech on American foreign policy, given at Madison Square Garden on 12 September 1946, had had a long gestation. Insofar as its theme was the reconciliation of national differences by negotiation, and friendly cooperation for one world of abundance and peace, it embodied Wallace's position from at least the time he was appointed secretary of agriculture in 1933. And insofar as it expressed his urgent belief in the need for friendly relations and extended trade with Russia, it reflected the conviction, explicit in his diary, that since 1944 or earlier, before World War II had even ended, powerful forces in the munitions industry, in the army and navy, in the Catholic church and elsewhere, actively desired and were planning for war with the Soviet Union.[16]

Wallace had already made a number of speeches on these general themes without provoking any overtly hostile reaction from others in the administration, but this one was more plainly directed against specific points in the official foreign policy. In making it, Wallace could

hardly have hoped to modify the policy Byrnes was engaged in imposing on the Paris Conference. The experience of a dozen years in cabinet
must have told him that such sudden public reversals were virtually impossible to bring about. In his oral history, he claims that the immediate objective of the speech, delivered at a rally organized by the CIO's
Political Action Committee (CIO-PAC), the National Citizens Political
Action Committee (NC-PAC), and the Independent Citizens Committee of the Arts, Sciences and Professions (ICCASP), "was a very clear
one — to win the 1946 Congressional election." Wallace recognized, he
said, that left-wing groups in New York were concerned about the possibility of conflict between the United States and the Soviet Union, and
he thought that if he delivered an address on this subject to the rally,
the voting turnout in New York might be greater, thus saving the seats
of several congressmen.[17]

But was there a further purpose? In late August *Philadelphia Inquirer* political correspondent John O'Brien reported that the activities of Wallace and Pepper were causing concern among members of
the Democratic machine working for Truman's renomination in 1948.
Wallace and Pepper had openly allied themselves with various liberal
and left-wing groups in an attempt to ensure that the next Congress
would be more progressive. Both would soon address a rally at Madison
Square Garden, sponsored by some of these groups. In a recent speech,
Wallace had told the Confederated Union of America that labor would
need to "fight like hell to make the Democratic Party the continuing
party of progress." O'Brien stated that "old guard Democrats" did not
believe that Wallace and Pepper were attempting to start a third-party
movement; they did suspect, however, that they might be attempting to
build a sufficiently strong personal following among labor and liberal
and left-wing Democrats to secure the vice-presidential nomination for
one or other of them at the coming national convention.[18]

An odd circumstance about the delivery of Wallace's Madison Square
Garden speech was the rather unusual concern he showed, if his account
is correct, in getting Truman's approval of it. It was routine for cabinet
members to clear their speeches with the president, but this was often
a very cursory matter. Yet in his diary for 10 September 1946, Wallace
claims that he sat with Truman and went over with him page by page
and sometimes even sentence by sentence the draft of the speech to be
given at the Garden two days later. "Again and again he said, 'That's
right'; 'Yes, that is what I believe.' He didn't have a single change to sug-

gest. He twice said how deeply he appreciated my courtesy in showing him my speech before I gave it." Wallace did not believe that Truman was simply adopting the kind of tactic FDR had often used, of appearing to agree with people to their faces in order to keep them onside while privately reserving the right to do something quite different. So unqualified and apparently sincere was Truman's agreement that Wallace successfully pressed him for permission to include in the text of the speech itself the assertion that President Truman had explicitly endorsed its content.

Truman's account of this 10 September meeting, as recorded in his diary entry for the seventeenth, after the storm caused by the speech had broken, is significantly different. Wallace, he wrote, had stayed only fifteen minutes. They had talked of Wallace's Mexican trip, Truman's vacation in Bermuda, the political situation, and various other matters. When Wallace produced the speech he intended to deliver that night at Madison Square Garden, only three of the fifteen minutes were left. "I tried to skim through the speech—supposing always that Henry was cooperating in all phases of the administration—including foreign policy. One paragraph caught my eye. It said that we held no special friendship for Russia, Britain or any other country, that we wanted to see all the world at peace on an equal basis. I said that this is, of course, what we want." [19]

The important point about Wallace's claim to have got Truman's approval was the inconsistency between Wallace's line and that of Byrnes and the State Department. Truman himself, during this conversation with Wallace, referred to a Byrnes speech given four days earlier, saying that it had been cleared with him over the telephone. "The President apparently saw no inconsistency between my speech and what Byrnes was doing;—if he did he didn't indicate it in any way"—so Wallace recorded in his diary. He backed this up in his oral history interview five years later. "He gave every indication of adopting my complete attitude and was so eager that it be known as his complete attitude that he wanted a statement to that effect included in the speech. When Truman mentioned that Secretary Byrnes' September 6th speech had been cleared with him I wondered if he had given sufficient consideration as to whether or not there was a difference in what Byrnes was doing and I was doing. I believed there was a difference but he saw no ultimate inconsistency. I don't remember whether I pointed that out to him but I assume that I did from the way the note reads." [20]

What the diary note says is: "The President *apparently* saw no incon-sistency . . . if he did he didn't indicate it in any way" (emphasis added), which surely suggests that Wallace had not directly raised the matter.

If we ignore the developing right-left split in cabinet that led up to the delivery of the speech and just look at its content, it is possible to have some sympathy with Truman in his failing to understand its import. Afterward Wallace himself was concerned lest people should think he had departed from the one-world stance with which he had been identified since coming into public life and had turned in favor of dividing the greater part of the world between the United States and the Soviet Union. He insisted that that was not so, but that the politi-cal realities of the international situation demanded the recognition of separate "spheres of influence" for the Soviet Union and the United States. In his oral history, he says that he did not actually use the ex-pression "sphere of influence," but as we shall see, that was a lapse of memory arising, presumably, from the need to deny that he was advo-cating "two worlds" rather than one.[21]

Referring implicitly to the ongoing conference in Paris, he said, in part:

> The real peace treaty we need now is between the United States and Russia. On our part, we should recognize that we have no more business in the political affairs of Eastern Europe than Russia has in the political affairs of Latin America, Western Europe and the United States. We may not like what Russia does in Eastern Europe. Her type of land reform, industrial expropriation, and suppression of basic liberties offends the great majority of people in the United States. But whether we like it or not the Russians will try to socialize their sphere of influence just as we try to democratize our sphere of influence. This applies also to Germany and Japan. We are trying to democratize Japan and our area of control in Germany, while Russia strives to socialize eastern Germany.
>
> As for Germany, we must all recognize that an equitable settle-ment, based on a unified German nation, is absolutely essential to any lasting European settlement. This means that Russia must be assured that never again can German industry be converted into military might to be used against her — and Britain, Western Europe and the United States must be certain that Russia's German policy will not become a tool of Russian design against Western Europe.

. . . We know what Russia is up to in Eastern Europe, for example, and Russia knows what we are up to. We cannot permit the door to be closed against our trade in Eastern Europe any more than we can in China. But at the same time we have to recognize that the Balkans are closer to Russia than to us — and that Russia cannot permit either England or the United States to dominate the politics of that area.[22]

He argued that there need be no general restriction on trade between the two "spheres of influence," apart from trade in armaments, and that the division was neither absolute nor permanent. Communism and "progressive" capitalism could coexist, engaging in "peaceful competition" to demonstrate which of the two could "deliver the most satisfaction to the common man in their respective areas of political dominance."

It was not a pro-Soviet speech but an evenhanded one, making critical comments about the actions of each side. But, of course, the official U.S. view was that the Soviet Union's attitude toward other countries was aggressive and imperialistic, whereas U.S. policies aimed to achieve peace and freedom. Thus, in his *Speaking Freely*, published the following year, Byrnes wrote: "Wisdom and justice will prevent the United States from ever acceding to the Soviet demands either on the Ruhr or on reparations. . . . The first step already had been taken. At Paris, on July 11, 1946, I announced that action which we had determined to take only as a last resort — the merger of the zones of occupation, with or without the Soviet Union."[23] As Wallace saw it, there was direct competition between the Western allies and the Soviet Union for control over the potential industrial might of the Ruhr, a contest the West was winning. Although Byrnes referred to "the merger of the zones of occupation, with or without the Soviet Union," what was actually going to happen was that the Western allies would merge their zones of western Germany, leaving the remainder to the Soviet Union, thus making impossible the "unified German nation" Wallace saw as "absolutely essential in any lasting European settlement." He could see no reason why the Soviets would trust the West to control the Ruhr with "wisdom and justice." On the other hand, it was true that Russia wanted reparations from Germany on a scale so massive that it would be beyond Germany's power to pay for many years, delaying its recovery disastrously. Yet in view of the depradations inflicted on the Soviets by Germany, it beggars imagination to say what demands would be "unjust," as distinct from economically impracticable.

Again, in *Speaking Freely*, Byrnes says that if the Soviets "do go to the point of holding Eastern Germany and vetoing a Security Council directive to withdraw occupation forces, we must be prepared to assume the obligations that then clearly will be ours." Those obligations extended to taking "these measures of last resort if, for the peace of the world, we are forced to do so."[24] With regard to Byrnes's comment on Russia's keeping "occupation forces" in eastern Germany, we should note that at the Paris Conference he had said that the Western allies would maintain "security forces" in western Germany for forty years if necessary — but that was in the service of "peace and justice" rather than economic exploitation.

Wallace had similarly debunked U.S. claims to virtue earlier in his speech when he said: "We most earnestly want peace with Russia, but we want to be met half way. We want cooperation and I believe we can get that cooperation once Russia understands that our primary objective is neither saving the British Empire nor purchasing oil in the Near East with the lives of American soldiers. We must not allow national oil rivalries to force us into war." He felt that the economic motive of securing Iranian oil supplies underlay not only the presence of Soviet troops in that country but also the West's smokescreen of righteous indignation about that presence.

The other major difference between Wallace's advocacy and the established foreign policy was with regard to Rumania, Bulgaria, and Hungary. According to the compacts entered into at Yalta and Potsdam, the United States would not recognize those three countries until they had democratically elected governments — rather than puppet governments under Soviet control. That was the specific issue that prompted Wallace to say that the United States should recognize Russia's sphere of influence in the countries adjoining its European boundaries, and he seemed later to feel some compunction about it:

I didn't realize it at the time but this was in effect saying, "Well, Russia you can go ahead and violate the Yalta Agreement with regard to democratic elections," if we were saying "hands off" there.

A little later on that year I made speeches and I rationalized it by saying that even if the Yalta Agreement did provide for democratic elections in the countries adjoining Russia on the west, in view of the fact that we had no way of insuring the elections, it's a part of wisdom on our part to stay out of such countries as Bulgaria and Rumania and so on.[25]

Thus the intention of the Madison Square Garden speech was in direct conflict with the major objectives Byrnes was pursuing. Small wonder then that it provoked immediate press comment and questioning as to whether it meant a change in official policy from "tough" to "soft" on the Soviet Union. Even before the speech was delivered, reporters at the 4:00 P.M. White House press conference wanted to know from Truman whether he had expressed approval of the speech, as Wallace claimed in the text. Truman said that was so, and in response to a further question, added that his approval covered the entire speech, not just one paragraph. He was asked whether he thought the speech in conflict with the foreign policy as advanced by the secretary of state and said the two were exactly in line. But he was virtually alone in holding that opinion.

In a special article in the *New York Times*, James Reston wrote that even though Washington observers accepted Truman's statement that Byrnes and Wallace were agreed as to the ends they were pursuing, they saw the means advocated by the two cabinet officers as contradictory. "But," Reston continued, "few observers, even though they concede that the spheres of influence have been created, believe that Mr. Wallace outlined a feasible plan for achieving this objective [peace between the Soviet Union and the United States] and Mr. Truman seems to be the only person in the Capital who thinks that Mr. Wallace's proposals are 'in line' with Mr. Truman's or Mr. Byrnes'." The main issue was not the soundness of Wallace's proposals, but whether he was reflecting official policy. Reporters had initially seen Wallace's speech as a political utterance, an attempt to appeal to the liberal groups he was addressing, but when Truman had endorsed the entire speech "it was widely cabled abroad that the United States policy was veering from a parallel policy with Britain to a 'softer' policy with the Soviet Union." It was more likely, Reston speculated, that an overburdened president, having read the speech in a cursory manner, had failed to appreciate its deeper implications.[26]

Reproducing this article in his oral history record, Wallace described its author, James Reston, as "the spiritual godfather of the reformed Senator Vandenberg," who was assisting Byrnes in Paris.[27] It appeared to Wallace that Reston, acting for the State Department, was trying to devalue Wallace's proposals and rescue Truman from the embarrassment of having seemed to agree with them.

In his *Memoirs*, published in 1955, Truman repeated the claim he had made in his diary that on the critical day he had only a fifteen-minute appointment with Wallace, and that Wallace had only mentioned the speech just before he left. "There was, of course," Truman wrote, "no time for me to read the speech, even in part."[28] When he told reporters he had approved the entire speech, he really meant only that he had approved Wallace's right to give a speech expressing his views on foreign policy. At least, that was the nature of his explanation to a special White House press conference convened for the purpose on 14 September. His statement concluded by saying that the established foreign policy of the administration had not changed and would not do so unless there was extensive consultation between the president, the secretary of state, and the leaders of Congress.

Faced with this direct contradiction between Truman and Wallace as to whether Truman read the forthcoming speech, how shall we decide whom to believe? The fact that Wallace's diary note, saying that Truman had read the speech carefully, was made before the trouble blew up adds to its plausibility — however, it remains possible, if perhaps not very likely, that he falsified his account in anticipation of the controversy that was bound to arise. It is quite plain that Wallace himself was aware of the (intentional) discrepancy between his views and Byrnes's — it was precisely for that reason that he either sought Truman's approval or, for the benefit of future readers of his diary, claimed to have sought it.

Could Wallace seriously have believed that he could persuade Truman to agree with the content of the speech? Byrnes's policy in Paris had in fact been outlined and insisted on by Truman. Immediately on Byrnes's return from the preceding Moscow conference, Truman, according to his memoirs, had told him he was convinced that the Soviet Union would invade Turkey and seize the Black Sea Straits and that in order to avert war it must be "faced with an iron fist and strong language." Compromise was no longer possible. The United States must, among other things, refuse to recognize Rumania and Bulgaria unless they were democratized, retain control of Japan and the Pacific, and insist that the Soviets repay their Lend-Lease debts. Truman declared himself to be "tired of babying the Soviets."[29]

It is possible that Wallace was in ignorance of this exchange, despite the prevalence of leaks between departments. But he certainly had evidence of Truman's inclination toward a hard-line policy in the latter's having shared the platform in Fulton, Missouri, with Winston Churchill, when Churchill made his notorious "Iron Curtain" speech accusing the Soviet Union of presenting "a growing challenge and peril to Christian civilization" and calling for "a fraternal association of the English-speaking peoples." And, more recently, there was Truman's failure to respond in any substantial way to Wallace's letter of 23 July to him concerning U.S. relations with the Soviets and international control of atomic energy, especially its military use.

In view of all this, Wallace could hardly have realistically hoped to guide Truman toward a more moderate, conciliatory approach to the Soviet Union. If, then, we believe Wallace's statement that he got Truman to go through the speech thoroughly, with his help, what did he hope to gain? It may be relevant that Wallace well knew that Truman seemed capable of agreeing with contrary statements at the same time. In his diary entry for 24 July 1946, he points out that at a cabinet meeting Truman had spoken vigorously about the need to cut down the budgetary requests of the army and navy but had declared a short time later that the United States had reduced its naval strength too rapidly after World War I and must take care, now, to maintain appropriations to its armed forces. Wallace commented: "I was utterly amazed that he could go two different directions within the hour. It reminded me of Tuesday [23 July, the day of the above letter] when within the hour he spoke of being patient with Russia to me and then at the Cabinet luncheon agreed completely with Jimmie Byrnes in a number of cracks he took against Russia. . . . He feels completely sincere and earnest at all times and is not disturbed in the slightest by the different directions in which his mind can go almost simultaneously." Consequently, we cannot dismiss the possibility that if Wallace did get Truman to go through the speech carefully, he was trading on Truman's failure of discrimination in order to get his explicit approval of a foreign policy that was at variance with that of his secretary of state.

If so, it is very difficult to decide what Wallace's motive was. Perhaps he thought that if he could trap Truman into publicly endorsing his views, Truman would be compelled to modify his foreign policy accordingly in order not to seem inconsistent. Perhaps also Wallace would not have been averse to embarrassing one or both of Truman and Byrnes.

He had some ground for believing that Byrnes had conspired to prevent his endorsement as vice-presidential candidate in 1944, and if there was little such evidence concerning Truman, nevertheless Truman had been the successful candidate and had therefore succeeded to the presidency that might have been Wallace's. Wallace would not have been human if he had not felt some envy, some rivalry toward him, particularly as he regarded Truman as very limited and lacking in vision. Wallace was eminently capable of keeping his own counsel and concealing his likes and dislikes at least from the future readers of his diary, and in view of the common reaction to him as being "cold" or "withdrawn," it is plain he did not open up to his associates either. But he was far from stupid or simpleminded, and it is a good guessing game to speculate as to his real attitudes on any occasion. Although in his diary he insists that he always got on well with Truman and there was never a cross word between them, this blandness is belied, as we shall see, by a couple of vicious but quickly suppressed outbursts during the 1948 presidential campaign.

If on the other hand we were to believe Truman's statement in his *Memoirs* that he had not read the speech "even in part," then of course many further levels of conscious deception on Wallace's side open up. Also, it would require that we reconstrue Truman's statement to the press that he had approved the whole speech, and conclude that he had been hustled into that foolish statement by clever press probing and by his desire to be seen as being in control, not having his secretary of commerce run wild. The balance of probabilities favors Wallace's story. Either way, whether he had read the speech or not, Truman's judgment was seriously at fault in saying that he agreed with its content, and the embarrassing consequences were soon brought home to him.

It was the press outcry on 14 September that caused Truman to retract his blanket approval. On Monday morning, 16 September, Wallace telephoned him and told him: "I thought he had done the only thing he could have done on Saturday." In his oral history Wallace says: "It was obvious from his statement he'd been lying but I guess I got used to that kind of thing. Roosevelt had done that kind of thing, why shouldn't Truman?"[30] But because Wallace had incorporated Truman's alleged statement of approval in his speech, not only was Truman lying but he was in effect calling Wallace a liar.

Another person might have challenged Truman outright, but such aggressive, face-to-face confrontations were completely distasteful to Wallace. What he did was much more typical of him. He offered the president a face-saving and morally respectable way out that would also be to Wallace's own benefit. He said that he thought "the President had given him a good out—that he [the president] stood up for his [Wallace's] right to say what he wanted to say, which was a good out for him [Wallace]." This was a polite way of putting pressure on the president in case he was intending to muzzle Wallace. Truman, according to Wallace, proposed they should have a private session to see "what we can do without cutting the ground out from under Byrnes. . . . I don't want to hurt anyone—either you or Byrnes." Naturally, Wallace agreed, but the same day put out the following statement: "I stand upon my New York speech. It was interesting to find that both the extreme right and the extreme left disagreed with the views I expressed. Feeling as I do however that most Americans are concerned about, and willing to work for, peace, I intend to continue my efforts for a just and lasting peace and I shall, within the near future, speak on this subject again." [31]

This was, of course, an honest and courageous statement by a man determined to stand by his principles. It was also a deliberately provocative one—Wallace himself later called it "defiant." [32] In effect, it declared to Truman that whatever patching up he managed to do, it would not include Wallace's changing his stance or keeping quiet about it. Also, it implied that if Truman sided with the State Department (as he was obviously going to do), he would be labeled as one of the "extreme right," something unwelcome to Truman, who would soon need the support and votes of the moderate left, the liberals. The challenge to the president could scarcely have been more direct.

In Paris, Byrnes was incensed by Wallace's Madison Square Garden speech and the ferment of speculation it raised in embassies around the world. He already had found some of Wallace's public comments disruptive to his diplomatic endeavors. Wallace had made a public statement on 12 March 1946 that American troops should be withdrawn from Iceland, just as Russian troops had been withdrawn from the islands of Bornholm in the Baltic; otherwise the Soviet Union would see the American bases in Iceland as aimed at them—surely not an unreasonable conclusion. At a cabinet meeting not attended by Wallace, Byrnes had complained bitterly that his efforts to get leases on air bases in Iceland "had been aborted to a considerable extent by the statements and speeches of Secretary Wallace and Senator Pepper"— so navy secretary James Forrestal recorded in his diary. In *Speaking Frankly*, Byrnes wrote that "Wallace's statement was effectively used by the Communists in Iceland and it had obstructed the efforts of the State Department to secure an agreement important to the defense of this hemisphere."[33]

Now came the impact of Wallace's speech. Byrnes heard that even after Wallace's interview with the president on 16 September, the commerce secretary had told reporters that he and Truman had agreed that Wallace would make no further speeches until the peace conference had concluded. To Byrnes and other members of the United States delegation, this implied that Truman had raised no objection to future attacks by Wallace on official foreign policy. Consequently, on the eighteenth Byrnes sent this message to Truman: "If it is not possible for you, for any reason, to keep Mr. Wallace, as a member of your Cabinet, from speaking out on foreign affairs, it would be a grave mistake from every point of view for me to continue in office, even temporarily. Therefore, if it is not completely clear in your own mind that Mr. Wallace should be asked to refrain from criticizing the foreign policy of the United States *while he is a member of your Cabinet*, I must ask you to accept my resignation immediately" (emphasis added).[34] Plainly the italicized phrase meant that Byrnes was making an ultimatum: either sack Wallace or Byrnes would quit.

Truman asked Wallace to come and see him on 18 September, the day of Byrnes's message. The situation was exacerbated by the appearance the same day, in papers across the country, of Wallace's 23 July letter to Truman, a letter demonstrating that he had made Truman aware of his views on relations with the Soviets long before his Madison Square Garden speech. A reporter from the *Baltimore Sun* had heard that columnist Drew Pearson was going to run the letter and wanted a copy for himself. Pearson had apparently got a copy from someone in the State Department. Wallace checked with White House press secretary Charles Ross as to whether to release copies of the letter to the press, in order to prevent Pearson from obtaining a scoop, and records in his diary: "Charles Ross called up to tell me to go ahead and release the Russian letter. I called in the boys and got them to work at once. A little later on he called up to say not to release it. It was too late; the letter was out."[35]

Again, Truman's diary account is different. By 17 September, he says, he had realized that Wallace's letter of 23 July was "a political document and not intended for my information." Charles Ross had learned that columnist Drew Pearson had a copy of the letter and intended to use it as the basis for one of his political commentaries. Ross, Wallace, and others discussed the situation and decided that the letter should now be given general release, but Ross and Truman subsequently demurred, and Wallace was telephoned and asked to await Truman's final decision. He agreed to do so. However, shortly after this, when Ross informed Wallace that the president had decided against releasing the letter, Wallace replied that the New York newspaper *PM* had a copy and that "another copy had gotten away." "All this," Truman wrote, "after he'd told Charlie that it wouldn't be turned loose without my approval." The diary entry concluded: "Well, I'm sure it was an arranged proceeding. N.Y. speech, based on memo to me, rushing me to read speech, release of memo and misstatement to Ross that it would be held."[36]

Wallace's account of his meeting with Truman the following day, 18 September, is fascinating. When he came in, Truman told him he had had "more sleepless nights than at any time since the Chicago convention"—the convention at which he had been selected as vice-presidential candidate over Wallace. Byrnes had been "giving him hell," and he had had wires on the unfavorable reaction in Brazil and Bulgaria to Wallace's speech.

Wallace had come prepared with statistics about public comment on the speech. Of the first 1,150 communications received at the Commerce Department, 950 were favorable, he reported, and this indicated that the risk of war with the Soviet Union would be a big issue in the congressional campaign. "You yourself," he said, "as Harry Truman really believed in my speech." Truman rejoined: "But Jimmie Byrnes says I am pulling the rug out from under him. I must ask you not make any more speeches touching on foreign policy. We must present a united front abroad."[37]

Wallace said that he would therefore have a specific problem about a speech scheduled at Providence, Rhode Island, for 24 September, in which he wanted to talk again about foreign policy. Should he issue a disclaimer, saying that he was not representing the official policy of the administration? Then he read a prepared statement he had brought with him, framed as if intended for the press. It affirmed the right of the American people to be fully informed about the nation's foreign policy, whose success or failure "will mean the difference between life and death for our children and grandchildren," and declared the nation fortunate to have a leader who had "enough faith in the workings of democracy not to fear the consequences of free, open, and honest discussion." This flattering reference to the openness of a president who was obviously intent on curtailing the freedom of its author to engage in an open and honest discussion was followed by an indignant condemnation of the unnamed parties who were trying to impose exactly the same constraint. The statement insisted on its author's right to "express my views and to encourage other people to think the issues through." It went on to attribute the present bipartisan foreign policy to the "warmongering" Republican Party, called on the Democratic Party to free itself from the "entangling Republican alliance," and concluded with a ringing question: "How can we learn to live in one world?" [38]

Not surprisingly, he found that "Truman would have none of it. I must quit talking on foreign affairs." There was a good deal of conversation then on the role of foreign affairs in the congressional election and how various Democratic candidates had told Wallace that they and their constituents were for his approach. Truman said "he had always liked Stalin and that Stalin liked him," and denied there was a "get-tough-with-Russia" policy. He was not an imperialist and did not want war with Russia. As soon as the peace treaties were signed, he would go to Congress and try to get a loan for Russia. Wallace was very skeptical as to the reception of such a proposal. He kept assuring the president that he knew that "in his heart" he agreed with Wallace's views and warned him against elements in his government that were "beating the tom-toms against Russia."

It is piquant to recall that not only Wallace's enemies but also his friends agreed that as a political practitioner he was hopeless. He may well have been hopeless at the sort of politicking that consists of the sub rosa trading of political and material favors and altering one's views to fit the electorate, but the subtlety with which he pushed Truman into a morally indefensible position, making him resort finally to an outright, undefended fiat, shows that at a higher level he could be a very skillful politician indeed. He was certainly not just a naive, woolly-minded idealist.

Finally Wallace asked what he should say to the press who were waiting outside. Truman called in his press secretary, Charles Ross, and he and Wallace debated for forty minutes the form of the brief statement to be given to the press. Finally, it read: "The President and the Secretary of Commerce had a most detailed and friendly discussion after which the Secretary reached the conclusion that he would make no public statements or speeches until the Foreign Ministers Conference in Paris is concluded." [39] That he was to make no speeches at all was Wallace's own decision. Both Truman and Ross wanted him to speak on the Democratic Party's domestic policies to help in the congressional campaign, but "I said I had become a Democrat after World War I on the basis of foreign issues and it would be impossible to campaign without getting into foreign issues." Ross wanted to know what would happen when the conference ended, but Truman said they could take that up later. "Ross evidently favored muzzling me after the Peace Conference was over. The President was willing to wait and take a chance."[40]

In his original diary note on this meeting, Wallace wrote: "In the early part of the conversation the threat of forcing a resignation in case I refused to stop talking was definitely in the background of his conversation." That observation was omitted from his oral history account (though Wallace normally had the diary in front of him as he reviewed these matters with his interviewer), when he wanted to argue that the sacking was quite unexpected. But the questions are whether he had not deliberately provoked it, and if so why.

If Truman was prepared to "wait and take a chance" on what Wallace would do and say after the conference, Byrnes was not. In a teletype exchange on 19 September, the day after the foregoing interview, he told Truman: "The world today is in doubt not only as to American foreign policy but as to your foreign policy." The American delegates could not make a useful contribution in Paris if the other delegations believed that once the conference had ended contrary views would again be expressed by the U.S. secretary of state and secretary of commerce. He went on to impugn Wallace's sincerity and hint that he was a Communist sympathizer, suggesting that "if Wallace is influenced by any ill feeling toward me it is possible that if you accept my resignation he might be willing to support your foreign policies or at least refrain from attacking such policies," and also that "if Mr. Molotov believed that on October 23 there would be a re-examination of the question of permitting Wallace to again attack your policy he would derive great comfort."

Then came the ultimatum again, preceded by a disclaimer that he was giving it. "I do not want you to do anything that would force Mr. Wallace out of the Cabinet. However, I do not think that any man who professes any loyalty to you would so seriously impair your prestige and the prestige of the government with the nations of the world. . . . You and I spent 15 months building a bipartisan policy. We did a fine job convincing the world that it was a permanent policy upon which the world could rely. Wallace destroyed it in a day."[41]

Faced with the threat of a disastrous split with his secretary of state over an issue on which the attention of the world was focused, Truman had little option. He wrote Wallace a letter, demanding his resignation, which Wallace describes as being "of a low level—not actually abusive in a vulgar way, but of a low level." In his diary entry for that day the president noted angrily that "in purposely putting it over on me with his Madison Square Garden speech," Wallace had adopted "the 'Commie'-'Jesuit' theory that the end justified the means." Wallace was a "pacifist 100%," who wanted America to "disband our armed forces, give Russia our atomic secrets and trust a bunch of adventurers in the Kremlin Politburo who have no morals, personal or public." He was like "the 'parlor pinks' and the soprano-voiced men" of the Art Club, who thought of themselves as leftists, but who constituted "a sabotage front for . . . Stalin."[42]

True to his creed, Wallace heaped metaphorical coals of fire on Truman's head by telephoning him on the morning of 20 September and saying, "You don't want this thing [Truman's letter, demanding his resignation] out." Truman agreed and immediately sent a man over to retrieve the letter. The conversation with Truman was "very amicable because he realized that he'd been very hot-headed." Wallace wrote a three-line note tendering his resignation and saying: "I shall continue to fight for peace. I am sure that you approve and will join me in that great endeavor"—an interesting reversal of roles. The same day the president announced to a press conference that he had asked for Mr. Wallace's resignation because of a "fundamental conflict" between his views on foreign policy and those of the administration. "I deeply regret the breaking of a long and pleasant official association," he said, "but I am sure Mr. Wallace will be happier in the exercise of his right to present his views as a private citizen." It may have been acceptable for private citizens to make public their views on such matters but certainly not for members of the government. "No member of the Executive branch of the Government will make any public statement as to foreign policy which is in conflict with our established foreign policy."[43] He ended by expressing complete confidence in Byrnes.

By boldly challenging the administration's foreign policy, Wallace had brought about something that he must have known would happen. He had been reckless before—in secretly backing Nicholas Roerich's private schemes, in publicly attacking Jesse Jones—but on this occasion an element of cool political calculation may have been involved.

Truman seemed likely to win the Democratic nomination in 1948, but after that, it was commonly believed, faced almost certain defeat. In that event, the liberals' next chance would come not in 1948 but four years later. If Wallace desired to take advantage of that situation, to be in a position to turn the nation away from policies he saw as disastrous, there must have seemed little point in his remaining in an administration with which liberals had already become disenchanted. These arguments had been put to him by Undersecretary of Commerce Alfred Schindler just a few weeks before the Madison Square Garden speech. Schindler, Wallace recorded in his diary, "says the liberals are without a leader but that I can't be a leader with the liberals and remain indefinitely in the position of Secretary of Commerce. He thinks I should get ready to run in 1952."[44]

Wallace said later that he had wanted his resignation to bring about greater understanding between the United States and the Soviet Union, and to "dramatize" the issue of peace.[45] It might also have been in his mind that his action could put him in a position to lead the nation's liberal forces to victory in six years' time.

9

WALLACE AND THE
PROGRESSIVE PARTY CRUSADE

In a brief, dignified radio address on the evening of the day he was sacked, Wallace reiterated his conviction that the peace of the world was the major problem facing Americans at that moment, and stressed that the reference in his Madison Square Garden speech to "spheres of influence" did not mean that he had departed from his dedication to one world. He was grateful, he said, that he was no longer under any obligation to be silent about the administration's foreign policy, a policy that, he now openly charged, "does not recognize the basic realities which led to two world wars and . . . threatens another war—this time an atomic war."[1]

The congressional campaign speeches for which he had been booked that fall were canceled by Representative John J. Sparkman, the director of the speakers' bureau for the Democratic National Committee, so that Wallace now had no official connection with the party. But he did not turn against it, beginning instead to develop the line that it had been losing electoral support because it had moved away from the liberal policies of Franklin Roosevelt. Should the Democrats lose control of Congress in the coming midterm elections, he told an audience at the Olympic Auditorium in Los Angeles on 24 October 1946, there was but one way in which they could get it back, and that was to become more progressive. He himself remained a Democrat, was more progressive than ever, and would do what he could to ensure the election of as many progressive Democrats to Congress as possible.

Wallace had seemed in this speech to soften his opposition to the administration's foreign policy. He was "very happy," he said, "that the prospect for a peaceful world [had] brightened greatly during the last month," a reference to the moderate tone of Secretary of State Byrnes's report of 18 October on the Paris Conference, during which Byrnes had said that "the development of sympathetic understanding between the Soviet Union and the United States is the paramount task of statesmanship" and that the United States "must guard against the belief that delays or setbacks in achieving our objective make armed conflict inevitable."[2] Later that month Wallace again gave Byrnes oblique support when he charged that the secretary of state was being "needled" into war by Republican senator Arthur Vandenberg, the War and Navy Departments, and a "mischief-making" Winston Churchill. Wallace could hardly believe, he said, that Byrnes had authorized Admiral Halsey to announce that the United States Navy "would go wherever it damned pleased," or that he had urged an American takeover of the Ryukyu Islands, thereby threatening Russia's use of its only warm-water port on the Pacific.[3] But if Wallace hoped, by such comments, to move the administration's foreign policy in more pacific directions, he would soon be disappointed; before long Byrnes retired, and subsequent events showed that the "iron-fist" policy toward the Soviet Union remained unchanged.

By now Wallace was certainly aware of a growing wave of public disenchantment with both major parties, and he must have known that there was talk of starting a third party, a progressive party, but for the remainder of 1946 and much of 1947 he spoke against this idea, arguing that a third-party movement would merely split the liberal vote and weaken the cause of reform. When the Democrats lost control of Congress that November, he urged "progressives" not to be discouraged but to continue the fight for liberal goals. With Republicans now in control of Congress, the economic situation was bound to grow worse, and those "who fundamentally are always progressive" would look for liberal leadership again. As for the Democratic Party, it would "either become more progressive or it will die." Though Wallace added that he did not expect the Democratic Party to die, his words carried the implied threat that should it fail to change course, it might need to be replaced by a new political grouping.[4]

That grouping had already begun to take shape. In Chicago on 28 and 29 September a "Conference of Progressives" was held. It had been called by leaders of the National Citizens Political Action Committee (NC-PAC), the Independent Citizens Committee for the Arts, Sciences and Professions (ICCASP), the Congress of Industrial Organization Political Action Committee (CIO-PAC), the National Farmers Union, and the National Association for the Advancement of Colored People even before Wallace had made his Madison Square Garden speech. For some reason of principle he declined to attend, but the conference passed a number of liberal resolutions having to do with civil liberties and economic justice that he would certainly have approved. However, a warning of future ideological discrimination appeared when CIO president Philip Murray passionately declared that organized labor "wants no damn Communists meddling in our affairs."[5] Here, then, was the opposition between those who thought in terms of a popular front composed of all anti-Fascist elements, including the Communists if they wanted to cooperate, and those who were convinced that participation by Communists in any political movement would inevitably be cynical, deviously Moscow-directed, and anti-American. This ideological confrontation would eventually prove fatal for the new party, because the greater part of the trade-union movement joined or was led into the anti-Communist camp, and without labor support a progressive party could not succeed. Already in May 1946, Murray had persuaded the convention of the United Steelworkers to adopt a resolution including the statement: "This union will not tolerate efforts by outsiders—individuals, organizations or groups—whether they be Communist, Socialist or any other group to infiltrate, dictate or meddle in our affairs." He got a similar resolution passed at the CIO convention in November 1946.[6]

In December 1946, three hundred delegates from twenty-one states, meeting in Washington, D.C., voted to merge ten liberal organizations, including the ICCASP and the NC-PAC, into the Progressive Citizens of America (PCA), which was immediately recognized as a potential base for a third political party. Speaking at the end of the two-day convention, Wallace, conscious of the threat of ideological division and of the charges of disloyalty that the new group might easily attract, attempted to enunciate the movement's fundamental aims. Though Progressives had the potential to win widespread support, they must "have no allegiance outside this country of any sort—except to One World, peaceful and prosperous." He went on to argue that "the fundamental progressive faith," which he defined as "the belief in the goal of peace, prosperity and freedom in one world," was so broad that disagreements over minor matters could be accommodated within it. Progressives should refuse either to engage in Red-baiting or to give their main allegiance to a foreign power.[7]

A few weeks after the Conference of Progressives was held, a comparable event on the opposing side of the intellectual progressive movement occurred. In January 1947, in Washington, D.C., there was an invitational meeting of some 150 persons called by the Union for Democratic Action. These were persons who regarded themselves as politically liberal; many had been prominent in the New Deal. The meeting declared its support for the United Nations Organization, endorsed "the American plan" for the international control of atomic energy, and resolved that "within the general framework of present American foreign policy, steps must be taken to raise standards of living and support civil and political freedoms everywhere." The delegates resolved further to "reject any association with the Communists or sympathizers with communism in the United States as completely as we reject any association with Fascists or their sympathizers."[8] Out of this conference came the organization called Americans for Democratic Action (ADA).

More clearly than had the founding meeting of the PCA, this ADA conference heralded the bitter division of allegiances between the progressive forces that was to bedevil and frustrate the campaign of the third party when it finally emerged. More radical progressives viewed the resolutions of the ADA meeting with some disquiet. The call for "civil and political freedoms everywhere" would naturally elicit automatic assent, but just for that reason, the radicals felt, it could be used by military and industrial forces to disguise their economic and geopolitical rivalry with the emerging power of the Soviet Union, with its more overt restrictions on civil and political freedoms. The ADA's Washington resolutions also challenged Wallace's position on certain key issues. The reference to "the American plan" for international atomic energy control recalled his 23 July letter to Truman and an acrimonious public dispute that flared up between Wallace and Bernard Baruch after the publication of the letter on 18 September. Baruch, the main author of the American plan, had loudly insisted that Wallace had misrepresented it. He had claimed that the various conditions that had to be met by other nations before the United States released details of its atomic expertise had been set out in one clear package, rather than being determined successively and arbitrarily, as Wallace had argued. Challenged, Wallace had been prepared to admit that he might have been guilty of some minor misunderstanding, but Baruch had demanded a general public retraction, which Wallace had refused to give. Thus, the force of the ADA-sponsored meeting's statement was to align itself against Wallace, and that of course was made much more explicit when it went on to talk about operating "within the general framework of present American foreign policy." It was already becoming plain, then, at the beginning of 1947, that any future Wallace-led third party was likely to find a much more restricted power base than once might optimistically have been expected.

Writing in the *New Republic*, of which he had become editor in October 1946, Wallace again appealed for unity among Progressives, criticizing those who were depicting an Eleanor Roosevelt–led ADA as opposed to a Henry Wallace–led PCA. He was not, he said, an officer of the PCA, and Mrs. Roosevelt, he claimed (incorrectly), did not hold a position with the ADA.[9] But further divisions between the two fledgling liberal groups appeared with Truman's promulgation, on 23 March 1947, of Executive Order 9835, instituting a loyalty investigation of federal employees. According to this order, a government department or agency could exercise its own discretion as to how much an employee should be informed of disloyalty charges against him or her, and could refuse to disclose the names of confidential informants. On 31 March, at another Madison Square Garden meeting, Wallace charged that the president's loyalty program would set Americans against one another, breed intolerance and suspicion, and destroy the integrity of public officials. "The President's executive order creates a master index of public servants," he warned. "From the janitor in the village post office to the Cabinet member, they are to be sifted and tested and watched and appraised. Their past and present, the tattle and prattle of their neighbours, are all to be recorded." In the *New Republic* two weeks later, Wallace struck again at the basis of the program, scathingly dismissing FBI director J. Edgar Hoover's recent estimate that one person in every 1,184 in the United States was a Communist.[10] The PCA joined Wallace in protesting strongly against the loyalty investigations, but, true to its founding principle, the ADA endorsed what it saw as a legitimate attempt "to exclude from Government employment people who adhere to foreign governments or totalitarian philosophies in any case where such adherence may endanger the best interests of the United States."[11]

Much the same situation arose in relation to the administration's foreign policy. Earlier in March the policy of containment of Russia had become clarified in the Truman Doctrine. Truman asked Congress immediately to appropriate $40 million for military and economic aid to Greece and Turkey, including the sending of civilian and military personnel to those countries. The undeclared aim was to guard against Communist disruption from within and pressure from the neighboring Soviet Union from without. Again, the ADA welcomed this development and the PCA deplored it.

Wallace's support for the latter position was unequivocal. In a series of speeches, he attacked Truman's policy toward Greece and Turkey, predicting that because of it America would "eventually . . . bleed from every pore." Should Russia move into Turkey, the United States would have to resist, but by first moving into Greece the administration had provoked the Soviets into a possible dangerous retaliation.[12] In his regular column in the *New Republic*, Wallace made a forecast that now seems chillingly accurate: "Once American loans are given to the undemocratic governments of Greece and Turkey, every reactionary government and every strutting dictator will be able to hoist the anti-Communist skull and bones, and demand that the American people rush to his aid. Today we are asked to support Greece and Turkey. Tomorrow Peron and Chiang Kai-Shek may take their turn at the head of the line. American dollars will be the first demand, then American army officers and technicians, then American GIs."[13]

EUROPEAN TOUR

The Truman Doctrine was to provide Wallace with a focus for his criticism of American foreign policy during the speaking tour of Britain and several European countries on which he embarked the following month, initially at the invitation of Kingsley Martin, editor of the English Socialist journal, *New Statesman and Nation*. Wallace's speeches and his personal doings attracted tremendous attention wherever he went on this tour. They made front-page news in every English newspaper during his ten days in that country, from 8 to 17 April 1947. His opposition to the Truman Doctrine, and by extension to Truman himself, was pointed and outspoken. At the Central Hall, Westminster, on 11 April, he attacked the withdrawal of United States financial support for the United Nations Relief and Rehabilitation Administration (UNRRA), charging that that organization had perished not because of its failure but because of its success: "U.N.R.R.A. aid was administered most efficiently in the Ukraine, White Russia, Poland, Yugoslavia and Czechoslovakia. It was because these countries were due for continued assistance from U.N.R.R.A. that U.N.R.R.A. was destroyed."

In his view, the Truman Doctrine was an extension of a campaign of attrition against the Soviet Union that was already in train. He described it as a policy of "unconditional aid to anti-Soviet governments":

A very small part of the Greek loan will supply the needs of the Greek people—the remainder will provide better weapons for the Greek army and a better transportation system to help the army to get around. The Greek government may be encouraged, but never told, to reform a corrupt civil service, a vicious taxation system, an unjust economy which permits the worst extremes of wealth and poverty, and a system of police brutality and political persecution that makes a mockery of Greek democracy.

In Turkey, where there are no free trade unions, no true political representation, no real civil liberties, no conditions are attached to a loan given to maintain an oversized army against an unmentioned foe.

These loans presumably are the first of many.[14]

Wallace, who had always wanted to promote an effective role for the United Nations Organization, now claimed that the United States was sabotaging such a role because of its own discriminatory treatment of the Soviet Union. He contended that the reason the Greek and Turkish loans had been made direct to those governments was that they could not be made by medium of the UN because "the Charter of the United Nations says nothing about stopping Communism. . . . [It] speaks of maintaining world peace." He wanted American wealth to be directed towards a kind of program that was at once altruistic and self-benefiting, and his descriptions of such schemes strongly recall one of his ulterior, though hardly blameworthy, motives for promoting the Roerich Asian expedition—that is, that it could seek out a desirable venue in Mongolia for Henry Ford to establish a manufacturing plant:

American fertiliser plants and farm machinery can help make a new life for millions of impoverished peasants and farmers who are today still living economically in the Middle Ages. American machine tools and equipment for factories, plants and railways can help establish industrialization programs and raise living standards. . . . None of these ends are served by maintaining swollen armies on Russian borders by the use of American funds.

[Truman's] program is both demoralizing and inadequate. . . . The limits to the program will be set by the utterly unproductive nature of loans for military purposes. America may be a wealthy country, but even America is not wealthy enough to pour indefinite millions to support large armies when none of these funds yield a return in increased production and trade.[15]

Wallace's pacifism was far from "woolly idealism." It was a thoroughly practical-sounding application of his general utilitarian thinking — "the greatest good of the greatest number" — an example of "enlightened self-interest." For many years he had argued that the basic economic causes of World War II lay in America's refusal after the first World War to act responsibly as the creditor nation it had become. Nations in its debt could not possibly pay unless America first made it possible for them to embark on productive enterprises. Even nations that as yet relied only on agricultural exports could be benefited by the United States lowering its tariff barriers so that debtor countries could export to it competitively, and thus earn funds to purchase American industrial machinery — an economic gain on both sides. To him the administration's two-world program, supposedly designed to stop communism, would instead lead to further Communist revolutions, as poverty-stricken people lost faith in democratic methods of improving their lot: "Communism is an idea for ending poverty and exploitation. It cannot be destroyed by tanks and guns. It can only be made superfluous by a better idea; it can only be ended when poverty and exploitation are no longer a part of democracy. I believe that by democratic planning we can end poverty and exploitation. Communism can never satisfy all the needs of mankind; Democracy can, if we give to it our full devotion."[16]

In the light of passages such as the foregoing, it is a sign of the rigidly dichotomized thinking on the part of his opponents that he was stigmatized at home as serving the cause of communism by these very speeches. Wallace was aware of the prevalence of that kind of prejudice, and its lamentable impact on civil liberties. He pointed out that the administration's foreign-policy program "has been sold entirely on the basis of halting the menace of Communism," and that to gain popular support for that policy the government had had to persuade the people that communism was an immediate threat. This was why Truman's program had been "coupled with a domestic witch hunt in which innocent people are victimized and men of the highest integrity are besmirched and driven from public life."[17] Surely as he said those last words he must have thought also of his own dismissal not so many months before. In a speech at Manchester on the following day, there was a hint of the direction he might be prepared to go as he fought back against what he regarded as that unjust action, however provocative he may have been. Twenty-five million former Roosevelt voters still existed, he declared, and though many had fallen away from the Democratic Party, they had not yet joined the Republicans. Those people were "waiting for leadership today."[18]

Because Britain's foreign policy was still based on fear of Soviet expansion, despite Churchill's government having been replaced by a Labor administration, Wallace's views were publicly criticized by a number of British political leaders, but this was mild by comparison with the outcry in the United States. "Capitalizing on the high honors once accorded him by his country," the *Washington Evening Star* cried indignantly, the former vice president "has been grossly misrepresenting the motives of our government" and "painting a lurid picture abroad of the United States officially bent on a course of ruthless imperialism." In Congress, too, outrage was expressed by members of both parties over an American citizen making speeches in foreign countries denigrating his own nation's foreign policy. Republican senator Arthur Vandenberg called Wallace an "itinerant saboteur," Congressman John Rankin demanded his imprisonment under the Logan Act of 1799, and Representative Herbert A. Meyer of Kansas, describing Wallace as a "red stooge" and a type of quisling, wondered "how much longer the American people had to tolerate his false preachments which incite human emotions toward riot and insurrection." Senator Walter F. George, a Democrat from Georgia, deplored the fact that the State Department's Office of International Information and Cultural Affairs, through its Voice of America program, had recently broadcast a review not of anything Wallace himself had written, but of Russell Lord's recently published book about him, *The Wallaces of Iowa*. The senator asked angrily "whether the right hand of our State Department knows what its left hand is doing" and submitted that "no more untimely broadcast could have been made by our State Department . . . at a time when Mr. Wallace in Europe was seeking to divide at least the sympathies of the British and the French people from our own people." On board the presidential yacht *Williamsburg*, Stephen Early, former press secretary to FDR, remarked that "this would be the time to have published the letters Wallace wrote to his 'mystic mistress.'"[19]

But Wallace's ideas were also eliciting a measure of support. A PCA-sponsored speaking tour across America, which he undertook soon after returning from abroad, proved highly successful. According to Northwestern University journalism professor and PCA member Curtis Mac-Dougall (who was to become the historian of the Progressive Party campaign and one of its senatorial candidates), professional politicians and the press were dumbfounded by the size of the crowds Wallace drew and by the willingness of his audiences to contribute financially to the cause. At one rally in Chicago on 14 May, twenty-two thousand people packed the stadium and five to ten thousand more listened to Wallace's address on loudspeakers outside.[20]

At meeting after meeting Wallace met with tumultuous, rapturous applause as he attacked the administration's policies abroad and the rise of political repression at home. At Gilmore Stadium, Los Angeles, on 19 May, he accused the major powers, including the Soviets, of allowing the world to drift toward war and called for a replacement of the Truman Doctrine with a fifteen-year program to provide $10 billion in UN-administered relief for devastated areas of the world. Then, responding to the now frequently heard charge that he had not repudiated Communist support, Wallace declared: "If I fail to cry out that I am anti-Communist, it is not because I am friendly to Communism, but because at this time of growing intolerance I refuse to join even the outer circle of that band of men who stir the steaming cauldron of hate and fear." In another speech he denounced the government's loyalty program as "a $25,000,000 witch hunt." PCA and pro-Communist unions may have urged their supporters to attend Wallace's meetings, but most of those present—middle-class liberals, workers, the idealistic young, African Americans—were non-Communist opponents of current American foreign policy. There could be no doubt, acting national chairman of the Democratic Party Gael Sullivan admitted, that "Wallace has captured the imagination of a large segment of the population."[21]

In regular despatches to the *New Republic*, Wallace spoke optimistically of "a new spirit . . . stirring in America which before long will be felt in Washington and throughout the world." Should the major parties fail to respond to "this new and vibrant mood," significant political realignments would undoubtedly follow. "Watch the West!" he wrote a week later, after touring California, Washington, and Oregon. "I am certain that the next progressive movement in America is coming from this region."[22] Perhaps he had begun to hope that his dream of a transforming spiritual revival might even now be realized.

In succeeding months Wallace kept up his attack on internal repression and foreign adventurism. He had long been critical of the FBI, noting in his diary entry for 19 December 1944 that J. Edgar Hoover, then evidently gathering information on public figures, "is apparently on his way toward become a kind of American Himmler." Now he charged that that agency's "campaign of terror" against liberal government employees was "reminiscent of the early days of Adolf Hitler." FBI agents were "awakening . . . employees in the middle of the night and interrogating them at great length." The nation was drifting toward a police state with the threat of communism being used "merely as a weapon for political purposes." In November, at an unsegregated meeting at the Wheat Street (African American) Baptist Church in Atlanta, Wallace accused the government and big business of using smear tactics to silence their liberal critics, called for an end to racial discrimination, and charged that the administration's foreign policy and its proposed introduction of universal military training were pushing the nation toward war.[23]

Heard amid the applause of his supporters was the cry of "Wallace in '48," and of course the possibility of a third party had been considered by professional politicians for a considerable time. Yet still Wallace hung back. He occasionally hinted at the possibility of a new party, "on an 'either/or' basis," as he later put it—"either the Democratic party becomes a real peace party/or"—but he claimed later that until just before he announced his candidacy in December 1947 he had had no intention of calling the Democrats' bluff.[24] One realistic problem was the shortness of time. He had a good idea of the legal difficulties in getting a third-party slate onto the electoral rolls, and probably realized in an abstract way that it took time to build the necessary street-level organization. On the other hand, given the dangers facing the United States and the world, he could hardly afford to take the long-term view and think seriously of developing a party organization for 1952. Caught in this dilemma, he let too much time slip by, and when, right at the end of 1947, he seized the nettle and announced his decision to run, it was either too late or too early. The tide of affairs had swung against him.

As the months had gone by, many convergent factors had begun to eat away his support. A good deal of early Progressive sentiment had come from liberals and sections of the labor movement, alienated by the policies of the president. On 6 September 1945 Truman had submitted to Congress a legislative program much of which was prolabor. But although both houses of Congress were Democratic, they did not enact this program, and Truman failed to follow it up, giving rise to suspicion as to the strength of his liberal attitudes. Then, when the coal miners went on strike on 21 May 1946, Truman took over the coal mines, and four days later, to a joint session of Congress, made a violent antilabor speech, asking Congress to enact emergency powers to break strikes in any industry he nominated and providing for the drafting of recalcitrant strikers into the armed forces. Labor leaders who refused to cooperate in ending a strike would be liable to fines or even imprisonment. These extreme measures were passed by the representatives; the Senate refused the measures but passed the Case Bill, directed to much the same end. Within a few days the president had regained his balance and in fact vetoed the Case Bill. Nevertheless, labor leaders and many liberals had come to regard Truman as being unreliable in the face of pressure from reactionary industrialists.[25]

Oddly enough, the Republican victory in the 1946 congressional elections had given Truman many opportunities to win back the sympathies of former allies, especially on domestic issues, without needing actually to change the course of events; he could always blame the lack of achievement on the recalcitrant "do-nothing" Republican Congress. He was now in a position to veto the repressively antilabor Taft-Hartley Act passed by the Republican Congress, and although his veto was in turn overruled by Congress, so that it had little more than gestural value, it caused many labor leaders to turn back in his favor. Similarly, he proposed measures to control inflation and to protect civil rights, and although these were only marginally effective, they contributed to an image more appealing to labor and liberals.

In the area of foreign relations, Truman had always had a stronger position than Wallace as far as the mass of the population was concerned. The apparent threat from a foreign power would call out their traditional patriotism and conservatism, and anti-Communist feeling had for years been the dominant attitude in most trade unions. Further, after the obviously partisan Truman Doctrine, which had been the cause of moral concern for many liberals, was overtaken by Secretary of State George Marshall's proposals for a European recovery program, intended to cover the Soviet bloc as well as Western Europe, the conscience of liberals had been salved. Wallace himself had given qualified support to the Marshall Plan as long as it made for one world rather than a divided one, but in July 1947 the Soviet Union withdrew from participation and the Soviet bloc refused to attend a Paris conference called to draw up lists of needs so that the recovery program could begin. Now Wallace's arguments began to sound strained. To most Americans the Soviet withdrawal seemed evidence of hostility toward a generous offer, but Wallace began to present it as a legitimate reaction to a concealed threat. In an interview in New York with the official Yugoslav news agency, he stated that the Marshall Plan would be deplorable "if it divided the world in two parts and if the primary aim is to revive Germany for the purpose of waging a struggle against Russia." [26] This kind of special pleading, of justifying apparently aggressive or oppressive Soviet actions as rational responses to concealed threatening machinations from the West, became increasingly frequent in Wallace's pronouncements on foreign affairs.

Perhaps Wallace's profound revulsion against aggression together with his hopes that the Soviet Union, in cooperation with the United States, could show the way to a new type of economic democracy, prompted this form of argument. He wanted to believe that the Soviet Union, despite the hideous excesses of, for example, the collectivization program, was essentially peaceful and concerned only to promote economic justice and welfare among its peoples — a goal Wallace had always felt should be universal. Consequently, any of its actions that seemed aggressive must be rationalized as legitimate self-defense against wanton threats from the other side. But such arguments provided ready material for political opponents who were only too eager to smear him as a "Communist," "Communist sympathizer," or "Communist dupe." Already in 1947 there was a steadily rising chorus of such charges, and they would become full-throated and orchestrated during the actual 1948 campaign.

In Wallace's Labor Day editorial in the *New Republic* on 1 September 1947, he tried to point out the cynicism of this smearing, and to appeal to rank-and-file workers and liberals to join him, despite the "opportunism" of many of their leaders. "It is a never-ceasing wonder to me," he wrote, "that some experienced leaders of labor remain vulnerable to adjectives hurled by the opposition — 'idealistic,' 'impractical,' 'communistic,' and the dozens of others used by reactionaries." But in the rising tide of Red-baiting, such pleas tended to be lost. On the very day Wallace made this appeal the *New York Times* reported that school authorities in Rochester, New York, had "impounded" the book *Twenty Famous Americans*, formerly a social studies text, because recent events had made the chapter on Henry Wallace "rather controversial." This action had been thought necessary, Superintendent of Schools James M. Spinning explained, even though some of the other biographical studies were very good, especially the one on J. Edgar Hoover.[27]

If, as Curtis MacDougall believed, Wallace still felt at this time that he had a real chance of becoming president, that could only have come about had he run as Democratic Party candidate, rather than as the leader of a third party. Many of Wallace's 1947 speeches can be read as leaving open the possibility that he would accept the former role. For example, on 11 September 1947, the day before the anniversary of his crucial Madison Square Garden speech, he spoke again in the Garden to an audience of some nineteen thousand inside and six thousand listening to loudspeakers in the street. After attacking the bipartisan foreign policy of the president and the "war-with-Russia" hysteria, he announced that as long as there was hope of change he would continue to work with liberals within the Democratic Party in an attempt to save it. But, he went on, if "the Democratic party is a war party, if *my party* continues to attack civil liberties, if both parties stand for high prices and depression, then the people must have a new party of liberty and peace" (emphasis added).[28] Was he, then, holding himself ready to lead the Democrats back to the principles of Roosevelt, if he were asked? If that were the case, it would help to explain his delay in declaring himself a third-party candidate, at a time when others — Benham Baldwin and Frank Kingdon — were urging him to do so.[29]

In view of the trend of liberal thinking, Wallace's was not, perhaps, an irrational hope if only he would divest himself of Communist support. The ADA, for all its anticommunism and espousal of the policy of containment, had in its founding policy statement notably declined to endorse Truman as its choice in 1948. It would, however, it declared, continue to work for a liberal Progressive front without Communists and to do so through the Democratic Party "with all its faults" and without "any illusions about a third party."[30] If Wallace had disowned the American Communist Party and rejected Communist support he may well have been an acceptable candidate in the ADA's eyes, and in those of the labor movement as well. The latter was massively against any third-party proposal, realistically preferring to work with the administration in power. But given Wallace's principles, anticommunism was not an available option. Having attacked Red-baiting as an offense against civil liberties, he could hardly indulge in it himself.

Yet Wallace persistently and truthfully declared himself a non-Communist—on the grounds that he believed in God and in progressive capitalism—and stated that if there was a real threat of Soviet expansionism he was as much against that as he was against an aggressive United States policy. For example, at a press conference in October 1947 he said: "I don't hold either with the reactionary capitalists who want world government in their name or with the Communists who want world government in their name," and this statement was repeated in a number of his speeches.[31]

During the remainder of September and the first two weeks of October, Wallace gave a series of speeches along the East Coast, again to packed houses and an enthusiastic reception. The tour must have been "devastating" for Truman, *Boston Herald* journalist W. E. Mullins observed, for Wallace's audience included not only manual workers, ethnic minority groups, and college students, but also "professors, well-dressed men and women of cultured and refined backgrounds and persons obviously in the professional fields. If they [the Progressives] continue they surely will destroy Truman and they make no secret of their intention to accomplish this objective."[32]

In the middle of November, sponsored by the Southern Conference for Human Welfare, Wallace carried his campaign to the South, speaking on foreign policy, universal military training, and civil rights issues. Before his departure it was announced that all his meetings were to be unsegregated, and because of this some half-dozen of them had to be abandoned because the towns and cities in question had no public places where such meetings could be held. Some organizers received ominous warnings from the Ku Klux Klan, but the police presence was adequate and no violence occurred.

Despite the headway he appeared to be making, there had been, during 1947, a steady drift of potential Wallace supporters back to Democratic Party orthodoxy. In June 1947 Senator Claude Pepper, who had spoken out as vehemently as Wallace against the Truman Doctrine, backed up Wallace's demand that the Democratic Party must become the liberal party, but publicly insisted that he would never follow Wallace or anybody else into a third party. He praised Truman and endorsed him for reelection.

From different though obscure motives, yet felt even more keenly as a betrayal, came Henry Morgenthau's disclosure of politically embarrassing episodes in Wallace's early New Deal days. This was contained in the third installment of "The Morgenthau Diaries," which appeared in the 11 October issue of *Collier's*. Writing about Roosevelt's diplomatic recognition of the Soviet Union in 1933, Morgenthau noted that "opposition came also, strangely enough, from Henry Wallace who called on the President late in October in order to express his fears about the 'religious effect' recognition would have on the country. That conversation left the President thoroughly puzzled. Wallace, he told me later the same day, 'is a kind of mystic.' " Wallace read this installment of his former cabinet colleague's diaries just after a speaking engagement in Pittsfield, Massachusetts, and, according to Curtis MacDougall, who was traveling with him at the time, he "sat dejectedly on the edge of his bed, obviously grieved at what his former New Deal partner had written about him."[33] Not only had Morgenthau made Wallace out to be inconsistent, but in doing so he had reported an unkind remark that Roosevelt had made about him behind his back. This must have been hurtful to Wallace, who believed himself to be carrying on Roosevelt's ideals. The former treasury secretary had also, at a politically inopportune time, revived the issue of Wallace's mysticism.

At a subsequent press conference, Wallace explained his earlier opposition to Soviet recognition by saying that he had been shocked by the brutality employed in the Soviet collectivization program. Then, in an attempt to account for his apparent change of heart, he resorted to an argument whose moral basis he himself would normally have rejected—one that implied that the end justifies the means. "But," he told the reporters, "looking back on the whole situation, if Russia had not done it, the United States would probably be a German dependency today."[34] Presumably he wanted to claim that Russia's struggle against fascism had rehabilitated that country.

Wallace must have known by now that any remaining hope of being drafted as Democratic Party presidential nominee was vain, and on 29 December 1947, after strong persuasion by associates in the PCA, he announced that he would run as candidate for a third party. He left open the possibility of a reconciliation with the Democrats before the election, if they would abandon their proposal for universal military training and get rid of the "Wall Street–Military appointees" whom he saw as working for a war with the Soviet Union, but he could hardly have expected such an appeal to succeed.[35]

What did he hope to achieve? The most obvious prediction was that he would divide the liberal movement, drawing votes away from Truman and the Democrats and ensuring the election of a Republican president. At times Wallace seemed to regard that as a desirable outcome, believing that a few years of Republican rule would cause such a swing in public opinion as to bring about a Democratic victory in 1952. Either way, he hoped that his Progressive Party would win enough votes and perhaps gain enough seats to establish itself as a significant political force, and so be able to compel the Democratic Party to abandon what he saw as its prowar drive and adopt his own policies of worldwide peace and prosperity. He claimed later that, despite many promises of support from many liberals and labor groups, he had had no illusions about winning. He had believed, however, that if the party could gain three million votes, his candidacy would help the cause of peace.[36] Perhaps, too, he saw in the Progressive movement a last chance to involve himself in a crusade of spiritual renewal, to which he had so often alluded.

There was also a lesser and more personal motive contributing to his decision. MacDougall reported a conversation between Wallace and Pittsburgh businessman Leon Mohill, after a December 1947 meeting with a PCA delegation from Massachusetts: "Mohill asked Wallace bluntly why he wanted to run. At first the answers were in the form of the usual arguments related to the political issues of the moment. When Mohill persisted, however, Wallace finally blurted out: 'Harry Truman is a son-of-a-bitch.'"[37]

Even before the official declaration, contemptuous articles had begun appearing in the press, charging that Wallace had been picked and groomed for the job, even if without his knowledge, by the Communist Party, and that the anticipated third-party move was a Communist maneuver. The immediate cause of this outcry at this time, although there had been similar murmurings for months, was a meeting organized by Benham Baldwin on 18 December with some forty-five union leaders, aimed at reassuring Wallace that he would have labor on his side. One of the leaders was Irving Potash, a member of the National Committee of the Communist Party, who pledged not only the backing of his union, the New York Furriers, but also a contribution of $100,000 (which in point of fact was never given). This minority Communist support was seized on by a number of leading figures in the PCA — Frank Kingdon, Bartley Crum, J. Raymond Walsh, Albert Deutsch, A. J. Liebling, and others — as grounds for their immediate resignation. Their defections enabled columnist Stewart Alsop to declare that the Progressive movement "has been indecently exposed for what it is: an instrument of Soviet foreign policy. Since the PCA invited him [Wallace] to head a third party, the whole movement has been stripped bare. The bones revealed are communistic bones."[38] Statements from Alex Rose, vice chairman of the American Labor Party, and Walter Reuther, president of the United Automobile Workers, followed, to the effect that since Wallace was being used by the Communist Party, the labor movement must oppose him.

On the day Wallace announced his candidacy he told a press conference in Chicago that he "supposed" Communists would vote for him because he was "sincerely in favor of peace," just as he expected support from Quakers and some Methodists who also desired peace. Of course he was "eager to have the support of all those who want peace," but hoped that "if the Communists in this country vote for me they don't come out and say so in a formal resolution."[39] The last sentence indicates what Wallace would say explicitly later on, that he always knew that overt Communist support would cost him many more votes than it gained. But openly to reject such support ran contrary to his concept of civil liberty. It was still not illegal to be a Communist, and to put members of that party beyond the pale because of their political views was to detract from their right of free speech and assembly, as he saw it. But to assume, as Wallace had done at his Chicago press conference, that the reason Communists would vote for him was that, like himself, they were "sincerely in favor of peace," shows a faith many regarded as naive and misplaced.

The same charge of naïveté would be leveled against Wallace because of his failure to dissociate himself from Communist influences within the Progressive Party itself and because of his benign reading of Soviet intentions. Admitted Communists did play significant roles in its founding and subsequent operation, and some of them anticipated that their participation would expose Wallace to "guilt by association." John Abt, for example, who had been associated with the New Deal as a lawyer for the Works Progress Association and then the AAA, became, at Baldwin's suggestion, the new party's general counsel. Before he accepted the position, Abt raised with Baldwin and Wallace the question of whether his presence might embarrass Wallace. His wife edited the magazine *Soviet Russia Today*, his sister worked for the Communist Party, he himself was involved in a federal grand jury investigation of subversion in New York. Wallace did not inquire of Abt whether he was a Communist, but turned to Baldwin and declared: "I guess we can carry that load," adding some strong remarks to the effect that it was necessary to meet "this sort of thing head on." "In those days," he said later, "I always pooh-poohed the idea of guilt by association."[40] In relation to the Soviet regime, Wallace's continuing resistance to the bipartisan U.S. policy of containment, and his determination to reconstrue what others saw as Soviet expansionism as a legitimate response to right-wing aggression, seemed to many critics to be little more than a gullible swallowing of the Communist "party line."

Earlier in 1948, events in Europe and Wallace's response to them had prepared the scene for the chorus of vilification of him as a Communist sympathizer. First there was the Communist coup in Czechoslovakia in February. There had been strain between the Communist and non-Communist members of the Czech cabinet for some time, and on 17 February the non-Communists walked out and tendered their resignations to President Eduard Benes, in protest over the reorganization of the security police. Apparently under pressure from the Soviet Union, Benes after a few days accepted their resignations and permitted Communist premier Clement Gottwald to form a new government, putting the entire country under Communist control. On 10 March, Jan Masaryk, the Czech foreign minister and a leading advocate of democracy, either leaped or was pushed to his death from the third-floor window of his apartment in the Foreign Ministry, to the horror of Western liberals.

Five days later Wallace alleged in a press interview that it had been an intended rightist coup in Czechoslovakia that had provoked the Communist takeover. According to Wallace, the U.S. ambassador to

Czechoslovakia, Laurence S. Steinhardt, had issued a statement a few days before the coup that aided the rightists and thus helped precipitate the crisis. If there was any factual basis for this allegation, it was that on 20 February Steinhardt had told Czech newspapermen that it was still possible for Czechoslovakia to obtain some indirect benefits from the Marshall Plan, and that he hoped the Czech government might still involve themselves in it. Because the Soviet Union had compelled the Eastern bloc countries to withdraw from the Marshall Plan in July of the previous year, this could have been interpreted as an attempt to woo Czechoslovakia away from Soviet influence. Yet it was also true that the non-Communist resignations had been given three days earlier, as Steinhardt pointed out. On 17 March Wallace replied that Steinhardt "knew and the Communist leadership knew that our policy of aid had been proclaimed as aid for governments that exclude Communists." He went on: "Coming at this crucial moment it was a clearly provocative statement and a contributing factor to the Czech crisis. There can be no doubt that Mr. Steinhardt hoped for the same result in Czechoslovakia as in France and Italy where the pressures of our State Department forced Communists from the government."[41] Whatever the truth of these charges, to make them in the midst of grave public concern over the Soviet coup was, politically, extremely bad timing.

On the same day Wallace made his accusations, President Truman called on Congress for a rapid enactment of the European Recovery Program, the institution of universal military training, and the revival of selective service, or the draft. He based these demands on his view of the Soviet Union's policies — to disturb the peace and obstruct by repeated vetoes the work of the United Nations. Since the war's end, Truman argued, the Soviets and their agents had ruthlessly destroyed democracy in several Eastern and Central European nations; such actions, and the Kremlin's obvious desire to dominate the rest of free Europe, had produced the present crisis. "The tragic death of the republic of Czechoslovakia has sent a shock throughout the civilized world," the president declared. "Now pressure is being brought to bear on Finland, to the hazard of the entire Scandinavian Peninsula." Truman justified universal military training and the draft by saying that "until the free nations of Europe have regained their strength, the United States must remain strong enough to support those countries of Europe which are threatened with Communist control and police state rule."[42]

In a public address on the evening of the same day, 17 March, Truman said:

> I do not want and will not accept the political support of Henry Wallace and his Communists. If joining them or permitting them to join me is the price of victory, I recommend defeat.
>
> These are days of high prices for everything. But any price for Wallace and his Communists is too high for me to pay. I'm not buying now.[43]

Truman's reference to the possibility of joining forces with Wallace reflects the Democrats' concern over his winning away from them the votes of disillusioned liberals. For most of 1948 they, and practically everybody else, believed that Truman had virtually no chance of winning the presidential race against Thomas Dewey. If Wallace succeeded in splitting the liberal vote that would be the deathblow. But Truman's total repudiation of Wallace "and his Communists" proved to be a most effective counterstroke.

It followed a strategy for Truman's campaign provided by presidential adviser Clark Clifford, in a memo on 19 November 1947. Anticipating Wallace's candidacy, Clifford had advised Truman to move to the left on domestic issues so as to undercut Wallace in that area, and to make all major pronouncements on international affairs from the White House rather than through the State Department. Most specifically, he should allow leading Democrat supporters to attack the third-party movement as Communist-infiltrated whenever a suitable occasion presented itself. Plainly, Truman thought the coup in Czechoslovakia and Wallace's response to it to be most opportune, and delivered the thrust himself. Not only would his linking of Wallace with the Communists discredit the Progressive Party, but it would forestall and deflect the "Red smearing" of the Democrats that was to be expected from the Republicans. With evident satisfaction, Truman wrote in his diary for that day that he was intentionally "reading Henry Wallace out of the Democratic party."[44]

There had already been suggestive generalizations in the press concerning Communist machinations in the new party, but now that the innuendoes had been given official factual status by the president, the press was soon in full voice and continued so throughout the campaign. It was this that ate away the party's already slender support. During

May 1948 a number of prominent political columnists released "exposés" of collaboration between Communist leaders and left-wing union officials in planning for a third party to be headed by Henry Wallace. The publicists included columnist Dorothy Thompson in a radio forum, Philip Murray, and Louis Hollander, chairman of the New York state CIO, speaking after Murray at the biennial convention of the Amalgamated Clothing Workers of America on 10 May 1948. Hollander said that the impetus for the third-party movement had come "from the 'international political cartel,' from the 'brain trust' of those who think for these page boys all over the world. The page boys were ordered: 'You must obstruct CIO now. You must not permit CIO to carry out its European program. It is dangerous because Russia refused to participate in it.'"[45] By the CIO's "European program," he meant its support of the Marshall Plan; the Communists' fell aim, according to Hollander, was to vitiate this plan by creating a breakaway party originating within the CIO.

On 11 May an exchange of diplomatic notes between U.S. ambassador Brigadier General Bedell Smith and Soviet foreign minister Molotov was made public. The basic purpose of the U.S. note was to impress on the Soviet Union that Henry Wallace's foreign-policy ideas would never be adopted by the Truman administration, which intended to maintain its firm stance in relation to Soviet demands. It said, however, that "the door is always open for full discussion." Moscow apparently chose to take this assurance seriously, replying that the Soviet Union "views favorably the desire of the government of the United States to improve these relations as expressed in said statement, and agrees to the proposal to proceed with this end in view, to a discussion and settlement of the differences existing between us." President Truman and Secretary of State Marshall, however, had never intended the diplomatic cliché about the "open door" to be a proposal to confer, and consequently did not proceed with it.[46]

OPEN LETTER TO STALIN

On the same day, in a speech at Madison Square Garden, Wallace made public his open letter to Stalin, which by contrast did make specific proposals. He prefaced it by saying that even though the U.S. and Soviet notes had been "characterized by the same self-righteousness which has led to the international crisis," both "represent[ed] great hopes to those of us who have consistently maintained that peace is possible." A meeting between the two sides must now follow, Wallace urged, and "with the prospect of such a meeting, I present my thoughts on the steps necessary to achieve the Century of Peace."

He called for a general reduction in armaments and an end to the international arms trade. Free trade, free movement of citizens, and free exchange of scientific ideas between the Soviet Union and the United States should be permitted, and the UNRRA should be re-established or a similar United Nations agency set up. Wallace further specified that peace treaties should be concluded with Germany and Japan, that both American and Russian troops should be withdrawn from Korea, that atomic energy should come under the control of the UN, and that neither the United States nor the Soviet Union should interfere in the internal affairs of China. Concerning the contrasting ideologies of the two great powers he wrote: "The ideological competition between communism and capitalism is a different matter from the misunderstanding between the USSR and the USA. The latter can be resolved in a way which will preserve peace. But the competition between the capitalist and communist systems is never ending. It is the concern of both nations to see that this competition remains constructive and that it never degenerates into the status of such a religious war as the Thirty Years War which so devastated Europe at the beginning of the 17th century."[47] We note in this the evenhandedness that characterized Wallace's foreign-policy pronouncements. Neither nation was regarded as the repository of all virtues; neither was free from fault. His major points required that each side renounce some of its autonomy and some of its jealously guarded advantages, and his peroration shows that he certainly did not believe that capitalism — or at least the state-regulated capitalism he favored — would ever collapse into communism.

On 17 May 1948, Moscow Radio broadcast Stalin's reply. Its tone was serious and moderate, calling Wallace's letter a most important document. Although Wallace's proposals were not perfect, "the main thing is that Mr. Wallace in his letter makes an open and honest attempt to give a concrete plan for a peaceful settlement." Stalin stated that he did not know whether the United States government approved of Wallace's proposals, but that they could serve as a "good and fruitful basis" for agreement between the two governments — which is to say that he was not using the letter to undercut the existing administration.[48] But the Truman administration's argument was that all these proposals had been talked about before in the United Nations, to no avail.

A fascinating hint of Wallace's conception of the nature of his action in writing the letter is that he was working very privately on it — so MacDougall's investigations led him to believe — as early as 14 April, that it was not prepared just in time for the 11 May speech. A week before that speech Wallace had given two of his associates an envelope that they were told contained the open letter, asking them to deliver it to a Dr. Vladimir Hondek, Czechoslovakian delegate to the United Nations. They had subsequently handed the letter to Hondek in the lobby of a New York hotel. According to MacDougall, "The Wallace aides were of the opinion that the purpose was to expedite delivery of the letter to Premier Stalin."[49]

Here one might suspect a temporary revival of the cloak-and-dagger attitude of the Roerich period, of the business of finding secret and unofficial channels for the passing of messages. On the other hand, there may have been realism in Wallace's procedure; he could hardly expect the State Department to transmit his letter to Stalin, and he could hardly just drop it in a mailbox and expect the premier to receive and read it. Yet it would have been reasonable to think that the Soviet Foreign Office would monitor his speech at Madison Square Garden and that that would be as effective a way as any of bringing the letter to Stalin's attention. Wallace apparently aspired to a more direct person-to-person contact, and indeed he reiterated in his speeches that he was willing to meet with Premier Stalin if such a meeting would "advance the cause of peace." Later on he seemed to manifest a touchy conscience about his procedure. In answer to a question from MacDougall he wrote, on 21 August 1952: "I had no assurances from anyone and made no effort to get assurances that Stalin would reply to my open letter which was released in May of 1948 *but which was never sent to Stalin*" (emphasis added). MacDougall's account of the affair continues: "That was almost a year before I learned of the Hondek incident. During my last interview with Wallace, on Aug. 17, 1953, I started to ask him about it. His response was what is commonly called 'blowing your top.' That is, he flared up and snapped, in a loud voice, 'I've told you all about that that I'm going to tell you!'; which, up to that time, had really been nothing."[50]

If Wallace had in fact been impelled to seek his own roundabout means of communication, we must remember that the work of the Progressives in trying to set up the new party was already subject to continual harassment and snide interference not only by a largely hostile press but also by public officials and by activists incited by Democratic Party leaders. Hotel accommodation was denied them, their meetings were picketed and interfered with by hecklers, and there were instances of physical intimidation and actual violence. Academics who openly supported the third party were threatened with the loss of their jobs and often did indeed lose them; schoolteachers were especially vulnerable.

One week after Wallace released his open letter, Glen Taylor, soon to be Wallace's running mate on the Progressive Party ticket, gave the Senate details of the intimidation to which he and other Progressives were being subjected. He informed the senators that he had just returned from Birmingham, Alabama, where he had gone to address a meeting of the Southern Negro Youth Conference. Organizers of the meeting had been ordered by a man called "Bull" Connor to segregate it, but Taylor had nevertheless tried to enter by the front door, instead of the side door reserved for whites. For this he had been assaulted by police, arrested, and put in a bull pen. When he was eventually able to return to his hotel room he found that his wife had received numerous phone calls from friends begging her to get him out of town while this was still possible.

These events had occurred in the South, but, Taylor complained, "this Fascist technique, according to which anybody opposing the status quo is a [sic] labeled red, a subversive of some kind, is permeating all America. Henry Wallace is running into it, I am running into it." He went on to tell of ministers who had agreed to open Progressives' meetings with prayer being dissuaded from doing so by the press and their own congregations, of the party's petition circulators in West Virginia being intimidated or bribed. He told how in one West Virginia county "the constable and two aides, all armed, illegally took away the credentials of a petition circulator, confiscated his petitions, [and] visited the homes of those who had signed his petitions and intimidated them into removing their names." The campaign worker in question had then been offered $150 "if he would beat up any Wallace circulators." In Pittsburgh, sections of the press had regularly published the names of those who signed petitions for the new party, drawing special attention to teachers, labor leaders, and other prominent persons.[51]

Federal agencies, too, had been involved. In a *New Republic* article of 8 March, Wallace accused the FBI and the Immigration and Naturalization Service (INS) of spreading "subtle terrorism." Announcing the formation of the Freedom League, with headquarters at the offices of the *New Republic*, he invited anyone with evidence of government or business attempts to stifle freedom to send such information to the league. They should state the names of those who had exerted such improper pressure and provide details about the form their investigations had taken. "Did the investigator ask whether you read the 'New Republic,' the 'Nation,' 'PM' or 'Reader's Scope'? Did he ask if you knew Henry Wallace or . . . Albert Einstein? What other questions were asked designed to make you feel like a criminal if you entertained a progressive idea or knew a progressive American?" Wallace referred to instances of persons being dismissed for wearing a Wallace button, of businessmen having to keep donations to his campaign anonymous, of INS officers asking a man seeking citizenship whether he was acquainted with the third-party candidate.[52] All this had begun before the new party had its founding convention, while its workers were collecting the thousands of signatures necessary in each state to get the party on the ballot. The harassment was to continue right through the presidential campaign.

WALLACE AND THE FBI

Wallace's anger at political repression would have been greater had he realized the extent of FBI surveillance of the new party's activities and, indeed, of himself. At least since his trip to Latin America in 1943, the FBI had been watching him, concerned over Communists' and other dissident groups' efforts to enlist his support. One heavily censored document in the FBI's files (some documents in Wallace's file have been removed altogether; others have very large sections blacked out) refers to evidence that Wallace was being influenced by Bolivian Communists, information FBI director J. Edgar Hoover passed on to Attorney General Francis Biddle.[53]

The surveillance continued after Wallace returned to the United States. The FBI reported on a reception in Wallace's honor at the Shrine Auditorium in Los Angeles in February 1944, noting that although the vice president had acknowledged sponsorship of the meeting by the CIO, the American Federation of Labor, and Railroad Brotherhoods, he had made no mention of the United Citizens Committee, a suspect organization. Actor Edward G. Robinson ("a well known follower of the Communist line") had chaired the meeting, and one of the skits that had been performed had satirized opponents of Communist-supported projects such as the campaign to outlaw the poll tax. Wallace's speech, on labor matters and his vision for the postwar world, had been "very well received."[54]

Just before Wallace departed on his Asian trip in May 1944, the agency monitored a conversation between him and Ambassador Andrei Gromyko in which Gromyko told Wallace that the Soviet government was willing to issue visas to anyone whom he wished to take, and Wallace had informed Gromyko that John Vincent Carter, Owen Lattimore, and John Hazzard would be accompanying him. FBI files on Carter, Lattimore, and Hazzard were sent to Hoover for his perusal.[55]

The FBI kept records of Communist support for Wallace's retention of the vice presidency and for his confirmation as secretary of commerce. After the latter had occurred, it assembled a ten-page memorandum entitled "Possible Communist or pro-Soviet Connections upon the Part of Mr. Wallace." Among other things, the compilers noted that Wallace had had contacts with African Americans associated with "communistic controlled organizations," that while vice president he had "frequently appeared as a speaker before pro-Soviet and allegedly Communist organizations," that his secretary had attempted to contact a union with Communist ties, and that Whittaker Chambers had stated that Lawrence Duggan, a State Department employee who accompanied Wallace to South America, was connected to the Soviet Intelligence Service.[56]

A short while later agents compiled an even longer report revealing, inter alia, that Wallace had been associated with the League of American Writers and the American Youth Congress, both thought to be Communist-inspired; that he had sent greetings to Paul Robeson on the occasion of Robeson's forty-sixth birthday; that he had been approached to try to prevent Communist union leader Harry Bridges's deportation; and that he had visited the offices of *People's Voice* in New York and held discussions there with Adam Clayton Powell Jr. about employment prospects in Harlem after the war. Wallace had also been placed second on a Negro honor roll for 1943, published by the *Chicago Defender* ("a Negro publication subject to considerable Communist influence"), excerpts from his Century of the Common Man speech had "received considerable publicity throughout the Communist-controlled press," and Communist newspapers in Argentina invariably referred to him in favorable terms.[57]

In August 1947 the FBI received a request from the State Department, acting on instructions from the White House, to open an envelope addressed to Wallace, copy the contents, and return the resealed envelope. The correspondence that had aroused suspicion had come from a former textile manufacturer from Vienna, who had developed some ideas as to how spiritual forces might be harnessed to solve world economic problems, and who hoped Wallace might publish these insights in the *New Republic*.[58]

As the Progressive Party campaign got under way, Hoover received regular reports on Wallace's speeches, some of which he passed on to the attorney general. He was kept informed, too, of Wallace's attacks on the loyalty program and the FBI. Hoover also had the activities of Progressive organizations closely monitored, and on occasion passed on political intelligence to the White House. In June 1947, for example, he directed that a close watch be kept on the Young Progressive Citizens of America ("a new front organization which is propagating the Communists' political aims for 1948"), and later that month sent word to the president, via Truman's military aide, that Wallace had told a PCA-sponsored meeting at Norwalk, Connecticut, that "he prefers to run on a liberal Democratic ticket and he has hopes that such a ticket will materialize," but that "if the Democratic Party fails to develop a liberal ticket, he would head a third party of independent voters." He also reported that Wallace had said: "Let's not worry about Communism, let's make democracy work; and you can do that by practicing Christianity. The life of Christ is strangely parallel to the doctrines of Communism."[59]

In April 1948 FBI agents in Chicago sent reports to Washington on two very important meetings held in that city to organize support for Wallace's third-party candidacy — that of the National Wallace-for-President Committee, which had met to organize the national convention in Philadelphia, and that of the Illinois branch of the Progressive Party, which had made plans to mobilize support in that state. Among the resolutions passed by the former group was one condemning selective service and universal military training and another dissociating the party from the U.S. government's threat to halt food aid to Italy should results in forthcoming elections there displease it. "The whole program," FBI agents concluded, "was a virtual adoption of moves to further the foreign policy of the Soviet Union." At the second meeting, Progressive candidates for governor and lieutenant governor of Illinois and U.S. senator were nominated. With regard to senatorial candidate Curtis MacDougall, the compilers noted that, although "there is no specific evidence that Professor MacDougall is a member of the Communist party," he was "looked upon by the Communists as one of their dupes in that he is easily influenced to follow the Communist Party line."[60] The FBI also investigated Wallace's open letter to Stalin of May 1948, concerned among other things to discover whether Soviet sources had given Wallace advance information of the proposed exchange of notes between the United States and Soviet governments, and arranged with him to issue his own letter at the same time.[61]

Wallace himself was never accused by any serious political commentator of being a Communist, but the tone of many of his statements about American foreign policy could easily be misinterpreted as "Communistic," anticapitalist thinking. Moreover, his thorough debunking of the supposed moral rightness of that foreign policy must have been further alienating to the average patriotic citizen. For example, on 21 May he said: "If we recognize the fundamental fact that American foreign policy today is based on serving private corporations and international big business, rather than on serving great masses of people — when we recognize this fact we can understand their unwillingness to reach agreement with Russia. Conflict with Russia is the excuse, it is the alibi for using the resources of our country to back up the same kind of cartels which contributed so greatly to the start of World War II."[62] We know that Wallace was a lifelong supporter of "progressive" capitalism; it was unregulated, monopolistic capitalism he opposed, yet passages such as that above could easily be read as orthodox Marxism. Further, because he still retained the view that the Soviet Union was basically nonaggressive, he could not find similarly stringent denunciations of its motives.

What finally ensured public rejection of his approach to foreign policy, and the defection from the Progressives of large numbers of liberals, was the Berlin blockade beginning in June 1948 — yet this again could easily have been represented as a response to hostile Western moves. In early June the Western powers had announced plans for a West German government, to be brought about through the amalgamation of the Allies' zones. In response the Soviets blockaded all road, rail, and barge traffic to Berlin. This action came after some months of increasing friction between the two sides. On 26 June President Truman ordered the beginning of a massive airlift of supplies into Berlin, then ordered the movement of two groups of B-29 aircraft, potential atom bomb carriers, to Germany. The airlift continued around the clock week after week, and in the eyes of the American public and the West in general it was a heroic, nonviolent reply to Soviet bullying. At the height of the crisis, consultations between the State Department and John Foster Dulles, the Republicans' foreign-policy expert, led to Dewey's committing himself to the bipartisan foreign policy; that policy was not to be an issue between Republican and Democratic candidates in the presidential campaign. In consequence, Wallace began to sound more and more idiosyncratic and unreasonable.

THE PROGRESSIVE PARTY FORMED

The founding convention of the new party — at which by unanimous consent it was named the Progressive Party — began on Friday evening, 23 July 1948. It was attended by 3,240 delegates and alternates, some 1,000 observers, and up to 8,000 visitors, and from the beginning it became obvious what kind of treatment the convention was to get from the press.

The main business of the first session was the report of the rules committee, which was presented by Vito Marcantonio, the American Labor Party senator from New York, who had long been identified by sections of the press as a fellow traveler if not an outright Communist. Mimeographed copies of the rules were distributed to the delegates and the reporters. One of these — article 3, section 4, concerning the conduct of committees — specified the quorum requirement: "Fifty per cent of the members of the national committee present in person or by proxy shall constitute a quorum for the transaction of business" — exactly the same quorum provision as that adopted by both the Democratic and the Republican parties. Without a quorum those present could proceed with deliberations and the forming of proposals, but these could not be implemented until all the absent members had been notified of them in writing and majority approval had been obtained. Yet *Time* magazine, for example, said: "One rule permitted a 'simple majority of those present' of the party's national committee to carry on the party's business. Where two or three were gathered together, that would be enough.

That was a hoary Communist device to give the Leftists solid control of the party." *Newsweek* added that the Progressive Party rules studiously omitted any quorum provision for meetings of the national committee, and the ADA newssheet chimed in with the same patently false accusation. This was just one sample of the extraordinarily biased reporting that was to continue throughout.[63]

On 24 July, the first full day of the conference, Wallace held a press interview for some four hundred reporters at the Bellevue-Stratford Hotel, the convention headquarters. In the midst of it a most unwelcome specter from the past reappeared, and indeed it was a portent of doom for Wallace's credibility as a presidential candidate. As MacDougall recounts it, an unidentified reporter asked: "Mr. Wallace, do you repudiate the 'Guru letters'?" Wallace replied ("his face frozen"): "I never comment on Westbrook Pegler." Two or three more asked the same question and got the same answer. Next conservative columnist Westbrook Pegler rose, and after reminding Wallace that he had requested the press to search out and report all the facts, asked "whether you did nor did not write certain letters to Nicholas Roerich, addressing him as 'Dear Guru' and to his wife as 'Modra.'" Wallace replied: "I never engage in any discussions with Westbrook Pegler."

Two other reporters rose in turn and repeated Pegler's question. To each Wallace said coldly that he would not engage in any discussion with any stooge of Westbrook Pegler. To H. L. Mencken, who asked why he would not answer the question, Wallace said, "Because it is not important," and to Doris Fleeson that he would answer in his own way in his own time. Then the subject was changed. According to MacDougall, Wallace's more sober associates were stunned. "They realized that, as far as the working press was concerned, it was all over. Wallace had had his chance. Granted that it was only a slight chance at best, he had nevertheless blown it completely." MacDougall quotes a typical extract from a *Chicago Daily News* editorial of 27 July: "If only Wallace, the Master Guru, becomes President, we shall get in tune with the Infinite, vibrate in the correct plane, outstare the Evil Eye, reform the witches, overcome all malicious spells and ascend the high road to health and happiness."[64]

Wallace must have known the attack would come. For more than a year Pegler had been calling on him to affirm or deny his authorship of the Roerich letters and to reveal the nature of his relationship with those to whom they had been sent. By the fall of 1946, Pegler had a copy of the letters in his possession. Fortuitously or otherwise, he then received from Wallace, in October and November of that year, two handwritten letters evidently relating to a charge Pegler was preparing to make that Wallace had avoided military service in World War I. (Wallace explained that his father had sought exemption for him on the ground that he was an essential employee — the father's other two sons were in the armed forces and there was the farm as well as the family paper to run. Moreover, Wallace had pointed out, the father had "had no recourse . . . after my sickness [believed to be tuberculosis] developed.") Pegler had sent the two handwritten letters relating to Wallace's exemption from war service, together with a selection of twenty-two of the Guru letters (several of which were in longhand) to Clark Sellers, an "examiner of questioned documents" in Los Angeles, asking whether they were the work of the same person. Sellers concluded that those letters among the group of twenty-two that were in longhand had been written by Wallace, and his judgment was confirmed by two other experts. He also reported that those letters among the group of twenty-two that were typed had been typed by the same person.[65]

Thus armed, Pegler had begun his campaign to destroy Wallace with a column on 6 May 1947 entitled "Is Henry Wallace a Student of Yoga?" In the course of that campaign the journalist read quite deeply into several mystical belief systems, conducted his own research into the 1934–35 expedition to Mongolia, and interviewed those former members of the Roerich group whom he could locate. He also followed up, with considerable tenacity, some of the more plausible leads contained in a substantial correspondence prompted by his extended series of articles. Whatever one might think of Pegler's style and standards of journalism (in a column released on 21 May 1947 he described Wallace as "this strange fellow with the wet, flapping lips and Hitlerian bang over his eyes"), his research in this instance had been thorough.

Pegler's material could hardly have been more damaging. On 16 May 1947 he wrote that, should the letters in his possession turn out to be authentic, Wallace's "open cordiality to Communists and his current partiality to Soviet Russia could be no more than a momentary political convenience in the aspiration of a messianic fumbler toward an idealistic brotherhood of man and the purification of the whole human race through suffering, philosophy and politics." In succeeding columns he named the three experts who had identified Wallace's handwriting, revealed the identities of some of the persons (FDR, Cordell Hull, and so on) referred to in the correspondence by derisory pseudonyms, made scornful references to the Roerich expedition to Asia, and revealed details of the lawsuit brought by Louis Horch to recover ownership of the Roerich Museum and the manner in which Wallace's name had been kept out of the proceedings. Addressing Wallace through his column of 20 June 1947, Pegler wrote: "For two months I have been calling at your office and telephoning to ask you to declare whether you ever were a disciple or pupil of Nicholas Roerich. . . . I have been trying to corner you to make you answer whether you wrote Roerich a lot of idiotic letters and whether you regarded him as a guru or a supernatural master of mankind." If Wallace would not answer these questions, the columnist warned, he, Westbrook Pegler, would.

In March 1948 Pegler began to publish some of the actual letters in his widely syndicated column. One letter asked, "Have you heard from the horoscope?" Some contained references to "the Flaming One," "the Sour One," "the Tigers," and so on. Still others displayed the strange ethereal language in which much of the early correspondence had been couched: "I look at the locket from out of the past and wonder if I shall see it in the far distant future. Apparently we are fighting always a new battle. Shall our hearts sing at the fighting? Do we never create that sweet land of beauty and justice?" Or again: "Disappointments are frequent and difficulties great, but we hope for much because of the obvious imminency of the times. The earth beat, the Indian rhythm of ancient America, haunts me like a faint fragrance from the past while I strive to center my complete forces on the pressing problems of the day."[66]

Though politically damaging, Wallace's refusal to discuss the letters is understandable. He simply had no answers left. It was hardly reasonable for him to claim that all of the letters were forgeries—Pegler's research could easily give the lie to that; yet for Wallace to admit authorship of some of them would invite intensive scrutiny of those the handwriting experts had validated, and the revelations in them would be sufficient to ruin him. In his later ruminations about the outcome of the crusade on which he was about to embark, he made no reference to this disastrous confrontation with the working press. Yet his silence would have been taken by many of those who read of it as admitting the justice of Pegler's charges. It served to strengthen the long-standing public image of him as an unpredictable mystic, not a reliable man of affairs.

The grim shadow of the Guru letters did not extend to the Convention Hall itself, where all was optimism. On Saturday afternoon the ritual of nomination speeches was followed, although there was only one presidential and one vice-presidential candidate. After the nominations Wallace and Glen Taylor came to the platform and were greeted by a great ovation. That evening was given over to the euphoria of the acceptance speeches, delivered before an audience of thirty-two thousand at a rally in Shibe Park, Philadelphia. When Wallace addressed the great crowd he repeated his pledges of working for the common man, of seeking peace, and of making capitalism progressive. But he also expressed a larger hope. He had always been prone to regard new developments — the social turmoil and suffering that accompanied the Great Depression, the appearance of Nicholas Roerich, the menacing events in Europe, the onset of the nuclear age — as portents of the coming millennium and would speak expansively of the possibility of the social transformation that might soon occur. Now, with the Progressive crusade in prospect, he again allowed himself to believe that the moment may have arrived. Alight with biblical fervor, he made this extempore peroration: "The American dream is the dream of the prophets of old, the dream of each man living in peace under his own vine and fig tree; then all the nations of the world shall flow up to the mountains of the Lord and man shall learn more of the law. We are the generation blessed above all generations, because to us is given for the first time in all history the power to make the dream come true. . . . All you who are within the sound of my voice tonight have been called to serve and to serve mightily, in fulfilling the dream of the prophets and the founders of the American system." [67]

The messianic tone of Wallace's statement — that "all you who are within the sound of my voice tonight have been called to serve" — is revealing. For him, the campaign would be a messianic one; he, too, would deliver a message to the people that might free them from the threat of war and usher in an era of enlightenment and peace.

On Sunday, amendments to the previously distributed draft party platform were to be voted on and the final platform approved. In Wallace's hotel that morning, he, Baldwin, Ted O. Thackrey, editor of the *New York Post* and a member of the Progressive Party, and one or two others discussed a lengthy addendum to the briefly stated call for American-Soviet agreement, which was already in the draft platform. The addition had been drafted and brought to Wallace for his approval that morning by Frederick L. Schuman, a Williams College political scientist, and was a statement supporting the concept of a "world government" operating through the United Nations. This was entirely acceptable to Wallace; it was a concept that was at least implied by his long-term advocacy of one world and his statements about the ideal function of the United Nations.

Schuman's draft went on to argue that a world government was necessary in order to eliminate the prospect of World War III, and continued: "Responsibility for this tragic prospect is an American responsibility insofar as the leaders of the bipartisan foreign policy have placed monopolistic profits and military power ahead of peace in their dealings with other nations. It is a Soviet responsibility insofar as the leaders of the Soviet Union have subordinated the preservation of peace and concord to aggrandizement and power politics. We hope for more political liberty and economic democracy throughout the world."[68] Apportioning blame to both powers was also concordant with many of Wallace's previous statements.

But when the Schuman amendment reached the platform committee, in session at the Convention Hall, it immediately provoked a heated and protracted discussion. Some members would not agree to the inclusion of direct criticism of the Soviet Union. Presumably some of the opposition came from the far Left or fellow travelers, but some also came from liberals who felt that criticism of Russia was yielding to the pressure of the Red-baiting orthodoxy they passionately opposed.

As debate raged on, Thackrey urged Wallace to go to the Convention Hall and speak on behalf of the Schuman amendment, but he refused, insisting that the decision must be made by the platform committee, not by the party leader. Finally Baldwin was permitted to tell the committee meeting that Wallace and Taylor both approved of the world government plank, and so it went in. The final form of the contentious paragraph read: "Responsibility for ending the tragic prospect of war is a joint responsibility of the Soviet Union and the United States."

At about the same time the Schuman amendment reached the platform committee, so did another amendment, this one drafted by two members of the Vermont delegation. It had seemed to these delegates that the original draft program might be considered one-sided, critical only of American foreign policy. They had no way of knowing that the updated version of the program, containing the Schuman amendment, had redressed that balance. The Vermont amendment read: "Although we are critical of the present foreign policy of the United States, it is not our intention to give blanket endorsement to the foreign policy of any nation." This amendment was noted by the platform drafting committee but rejected on the ground that the Schuman amendment seemed to cover the same issue.

Under rules agreed to by the delegates, during the confirmation of the platform both amendments accepted and rejected by the platform committee were read aloud and voted on. The Schuman amendment was readily accepted, but later, when in due course the Vermont delegates' amendment was read as a rejected proposal, heated debate ensued. Highly charged speeches were made for and against it, the main objection being, again, that it would be taken as saying that the Progressive Party dissociated itself from the Soviet Union. Its only motivation appeared to be to bow to the Red-baiting attacks of the party's opponents, and it was anathema to many in the new party to grant those attacks legitimacy. After a half-hour's feverish debate, the amendment was narrowly rejected on a voice vote.

A hostile press could hardly have been presented with a better opportunity. *New York Times* correspondent W. H. Laurence wrote that "with Communists and Fellow Travelers in complete control, the Progressive party approved its 'peace, freedom and abundance' platform at its final session late today after shouting down an attempt to deny formally any blanket endorsement of the Soviet Union's foreign policy." The *Louisville Courier-Journal* noted that "the hard inner core of control in the Progressive party convention showed plainly where its heart lies. Its tender regard for the feelings of Soviet Russia was never so obvious as when the moment came to push through the party's platform declaration on foreign policy."[69] Such reporting served to confirm the suspicion that the party was Communist-dominated and surreptitiously serving Soviet foreign-policy interests.

THE 1948 CAMPAIGN: CIVIL RIGHTS AND COMMUNIST SMEARS

Communists and fellow travelers, as seasoned political workers, did a disproportionate amount of the practical administrative and street-level work of the Progressive Party, though even their experienced efforts could not supply nearly as much doorbell ringing as was needed. The more amateurish liberals had little aptitude for the grating, hard work of garnering votes. Further, as the "Communist" smear took hold,

Wallace addressing an election meeting at Sibley, Iowa, during the 1948 campaign. (Courtesy of the University of Iowa Library)

more and more of them began to drop out of active participation and open identification with the Progressive Party. There was a fear, a quite realistic one as many events showed, of economic disadvantage, job loss, and loss of "respectability" from being known to participate in the party's work. Commenting later on Communist involvement in the movement, Wallace pointed to a crucial distinction between Progressive Party members and the ADA. The latter, he said, "was in effect setting up a kind of Gestapo to make sure that nobody who belonged to them was a Communist. We just didn't believe in setting up a loyalty board and thought that all types of opinion, as long as they believed in our ultimate objective, should be represented in the Progressive Party."[70]

Early in the campaign Wallace went on a speaking tour of the South.

True to the party's support for civil rights, he announced in advance that he would neither address segregated audiences nor stay in segregated hotels. This was virtually a unique political position to take at the time, and it won the movement a good deal of liberal admiration. Historian Leon Litwack, then a student at Berkeley, has explained his admiration for Wallace in just these terms: "I mean, it was hard to believe, but here was a presidential candidate who was really willing to stand steadfastly for civil rights and was prepared to campaign actively in the South and insist on speaking to non-segregated audiences."[71] But there were to be unpleasant, even violent, consequences, as Wallace was soon to discover.

The policy about hotels had been formulated by Benham Baldwin, and evidently Wallace had some misgivings about its practical wisdom —whether it would result in the kind of aggressive confrontation he deplored. "This meant I had to stay in Negro homes everywhere I went, which was really slapping the Southern tradition. It's the kind of thing I wouldn't normally have done. . . . It's one of those things that just happened. You didn't know the policy had been formed, but if you questioned it at that stage of the game, that's too bad. In that respect I'd say that Beanie Baldwin made a mistake in judgment. You can't change the customs of people that fast. They continually shouted, 'Go back to Russia, you nigger-lover.' " This same conflation of segregationist and anti-Communist ideas had led the editor of the *Southern Labor Review* to see the attempt to integrate colleges as "part of a communistic doctrine . . . aimed at America with the intention of provoking revolution."[72]

The southern tour had begun peacefully enough in Virginia, despite the existence in that state of a law banning racially mixed public assemblies. In Norfolk, Suffolk, and Richmond, Wallace spoke to unsegregated and largely receptive audiences. But when the party went on into supposedly more liberal North Carolina, where there was no law against unsegregated meetings, the violence started. A near riot preceded his first address, and a supporter, James D. Harris of Charlotte, was stabbed twice in the arm and six times in the back. The next day there was no bloodshed, but Wallace was subjected to a barrage of eggs and fruit, and the crowd of about five hundred got so completely out of control that he had to abandon his speech. At Hickory, North Carolina, the barrage of eggs and tomatoes and the shouting were so furious that Wallace was prevented from speaking, but he tried to deliver a parting thrust over the public address system: "As Jesus Christ told his disciples, when you enter a town that will not hear you willingly, then shake the dust of that town from your feet and go elsewhere." If they closed their minds against his message, he would, like Jesus Christ, abandon them to their iniquity.[73]

It was not a question of his retreating in fear. There is no doubting the physical and moral courage he showed on this tour. The missile throwing was more than gestural; there are photographs of Wallace with bits of eggshell caught in his hair, going on unshaken, trying to address the crowd. It was a thought-provoking experience for him, to see such primitive hatred, and again he likened his situation to that of Jesus Christ: "It was an experience to see human hate in the raw that I've never been through before, and never care to go through again. I don't know to what extent it does good to confront human hate in that way, *unless you want to be crucified for the sake of somebody 2000 years hence*" (emphasis added). Nevertheless, he was determined to persevere. After the early violence, Baldwin asked him whether they ought to continue. Wallace insisted they must.[74]

The italicized phrase above shows how ready he was to equate his position with that of Jesus Christ, who, according to New Testament teachings, had been crucified for sinners, including those living two thousand years after his death. In Wallace's self-concept it was in almost that spirit that he decided to "go through with it"—to expose himself to the danger of crucifixion for the sake of his ideals. It was not a blasphemous nor yet a schizophrenic idea, but rather a reflection of his earlier Christian beliefs.

After North Carolina the violence worsened. Wallace would stop at a courthouse square or some other public place and attempt to discuss the economic welfare of the South, not, he imagined, a controversial subject, but "I'd get about six sentences along and then they'd begin throwing. They just kept on all the time." He thought it remarkable that no one else was seriously hurt. In at least some areas, local opposition to desegregated audiences was evidently sufficiently strong to overcome Progressive Party principles; a contemporary photograph shows a segregated audience at Montgomery, Alabama, awaiting one of Wallace's campaign speeches.[75] Yet despite the violence and abuse he frequently encountered, Wallace could recall some pleasurable moments of the campaign. "There was always singing," he said. "There was a fellow by the name of Pete Seger [*sic*], with a banjo. . . . I enjoyed the good fellowship when we'd sit around after a meeting was over in a hotel and talk until half past twelve or one in the morning."[76]

Looking back, he speculated about the wisdom of this southern campaign and the efficacy it might have had, again comparing his experiences with those of Christ. "What is the best way to get people to go along with you toward a constructive outcome? It's quite possible that Jesus Christ himself made a serious mistake in the way he handled that kind of a problem. But if it was a mistake, the mistake caused his message to be remembered."[77] In just the same way, Henry Wallace believed that his campaign in the South had left a memorable message about peace and equal rights for all.

His identification with Christ should not surprise us. Brought up in the United Presbyterian church, and a member, later, of Episcopal congregations in Des Moines and then in Washington, Wallace was thoroughly familiar with both Old and New Testaments, as the frequent scriptural allusions in his writings and speeches show. He had come to see Theosophy as a clearer or less-restrictive path to truth, but Theosophy had subsumed Christianity rather than replaced it, so that the historical Jesus remained for him a person of superior enlightenment, highly evolved in the spiritual sense but not necessarily perfect, whose life could serve as an example and whose words could be quoted with genuine approval. The hint of Wallace's unorthodoxy in the passage quoted above comes, of course, in his admission that Jesus may have made a mistake.

As the campaign progressed it became clear that the party's message was eliciting only wavering support. On Wallace's swing through California, audiences were dismally small. It was not the first time the faithful had been called on to attend and empty their pockets, and the biased publicity about the supposed Communist link had begun to raise doubts, if not about Wallace's sincerity, then about the soundness of his judgment. Near the end of the campaign he made a rather despairing speech about the long-term good the party would be shown to have done, whatever the outcome:

> We have gone into the South and held unsegregated political meetings for the first time in American history. We have answered the threats of the Ku Klux Klan with our challenge, "Jim Crow must go." . . .
>
> With our help peace is being declared by the common people of the earth. . . .
>
> Because of us there are still millions in America who know that

Wallace with Paul Robeson during the Progressive Party campaign, 1948.
(Photograph © by Julius Lazarus)

the Bill of Rights guarantees free speech as much for the ideas we hate as for the ideas we favor. Because of the Progressive party this nation will not be turned into a people of ciphers, afraid to speak and afraid to think anything but the words of Wall Street and of Wall Street's press.[78]

There was a good deal of truth in those brave sentences. Not only had Wallace challenged the segregationists of the South, he had also spoken out against the House Un-American Activities Committee, with "those infamous agents of reaction, Mundt and Nixon." A member of that committee, Democrat J. E. Rankin, had demanded on 24 August, a month after the Progressive convention, that Wallace be subpoenaed to explain why he had appointed actively subversive Communists to key positions in the Commerce Department "at a time when our young men were fighting and dying on every battlefield in the world for the protection of this country." This threat was probably provoked by Wallace's public statement of two weeks earlier on the House committee hearings. "The President has aptly termed the proceedings a 'red herring,'" he had said. "Yet there is more involved here than the circus or sideshow. There is a whole pattern of terror and fear-making which has been developing in this free land since the death of Franklin Roosevelt. It is a pattern for which the leaders of both old parties including Mr. Truman bear full responsibility. It is a pattern for the total destruction of civil liberties."[79]

Despite the House committee's bluster, Wallace was never subpoenaed, but several former New Dealers and current members of the Progressive Party were called, including John Abt, Lee Pressman, and Nathan Witt. They pleaded the First, Fifth, and Sixth Amendments in their defense and were not cited for contempt. But for all Wallace's open disdain of the whole apparatus of public opinion manipulation, and his repeated disavowals that he was, ever had been, or was ever likely to be a Communist, the damage had been done.[80] Opinion polling during the run-up to the election showed that at least half of the electorate believed the Progressive Party to be Communist-dominated, and in the end that must have told heavily against it.[81]

By the end of the campaign, the confidence Wallace had felt during the euphoria of the Progressive convention had been largely dispelled by later realistic assessments of the likely vote. He could hardly have been prepared, however, for the debacle that was to come.

10

WHAT IF THE WHOLE WORLD
BE AGAINST ME?

Across the country a mere 1,157,140 votes were recorded for Wallace, only 2.37 percent of the total.[1] At party headquarters on election night, as news of the disastrous result came in, his wife sobbed repeatedly and hysterically, "I told him so all the time. He should never have done it."[2] She had indeed told him so during the campaign, and told reporters that she did not want him to run. She had accompanied him during his speaking tours like a "good sport," Wallace said, but her sympathies were never really with the Progressives, largely because of the presence of suspect Communists, whom she detested.[3] But as Wallace did not discuss his political affairs with his wife, it is not surprising that her forebodings went unheeded.

Those who had gathered at party headquarters tried to minimize the importance of the election. It had only been the first round in a struggle that was to continue. In a short radio address that evening, Wallace predicted that the Republicans' and Democrats' "cup of iniquity" would soon "overflow," and that if they failed to abandon "this bipartisan foreign policy of high prices and war," the Progressive Party would become the nation's leading political force. Progressives would continue to fight for peace and to expose those who used anticommunism as "a cover for the iniquitous machinations of the exploiters and misleaders of the people in the country and abroad." The need for the new party was greater than ever.[4]

For a year or so Wallace helped keep alive the fiction that the Progressive Party was an ongoing, long-term political entity, gathering strength for the 1952 election and thereafter. But many of its more moderate members had deserted it, and his own disenchantment with the extremists had begun as soon as the last remaining hope of substantial electoral support was so humiliatingly extinguished.

He protested later that he felt no bitterness about his defeat, but some of the things that slipped out belie this claim.[5] When the result of the vote became known, John Abt drafted for Wallace a telegram to be sent to Truman, acknowledging his triumph and calling on him to return to the policies of the New Deal. Political advisers said that the message should include a word of personal congratulation, but Wallace was adamant in his refusal to give it. "Under no circumstances," he said, "will I congratulate that son of a bitch."[6]

He admitted later to having been "hurt and baffled" when his old liberal supporters failed to turn back to him after Truman was nominated—"Sometimes," he said, "I think that their only governing motive is that they hate Henry Wallace," and his comments on the electorate's rejection of his message reveal a similar pain.[7] Why, he asked defensively but unconvincingly, should he have felt bitter over the people's "inability . . . to understand the forces at work in the world today"? They would "bring their own penalty upon themselves so you just feel sorry for them. They don't understand, that's all and it's too bad for them as they're the ones that are going to be hurt."[8] The falling away, after he had announced his candidacy, of labor leaders and their followers had also been a keen disappointment, though in speaking of it he was again able to call up Christlike attitudes to muffle the resentment he felt. "My own slant, as these various types of support left, was conditioned by my biblical upbringing—even though I'm all alone I'll go ahead with what I think is right. . . . When it comes to an issue like that [the prevention of an inconceivably terrible war], what if the whole world be against me?"[9]

Despite such disclaimers, the 1948 result must have been a harsh blow. He had given the American people a chance to vote for peace, but they had rejected it. He had presented a vision of a new world order, but they had failed to respond. The general spiritual awakening for which he had hoped now seemed further away than ever, the Century of the Common Man a futile dream. Instead of one world there would now be two, whose leaders would face each other with awesome weapons and inflexible distrust. Henry Wallace, the liberal visionary, may well have been close to despair.

Many factors had combined to turn liberal-minded voters of the middle ground away from Henry Wallace. The relentless propaganda campaign against the Soviet Union, increasingly seen as supported by hard historical facts, combined with the poisonous atmosphere created by the House Un-American Activities Committee inquiries, pushed voters toward conservatism. Anyone who seemed even to be open-minded toward communism, as Wallace did, was liable to be shunned as a security risk. But perhaps the fatal flaw undermining Wallace's credibility was the baseless, philistine yet persistent attribution of "woolly-minded mysticism" that had begun to cling to him even as early as 1940 and had become a real and present political danger with the surfacing of the Guru letters in the 1944 campaign. So much of Wallace's message depended on his personal credibility. Calls for a spiritual awakening that would change life for the millions, promises of boundless abundance in a world at peace, could only be seen as having substance if they came from someone with feet on the ground as well as eyes on the stars. The Guru letters, cabalistic in expression and misguided in content as they were, could be seen as some of the wilder flights of a cosmology and a conception of religion with a lengthy and respectable intellectual provenance, one to which a considerable number of thoughtful, sober-minded American citizens then subscribed. But the mass of the public knew nothing of that context; all that they knew were the distortions and jibes of the media, and as the days went by it became increasingly difficult to believe in and vote for the man thus characterized.

REASSESSMENT AND RECANTATION

Wallace was keen, in retrospect, to exculpate himself from Communist affiliation, accepting that the party had been "more tolerant to the Communists than we should have been," because of the need to avoid Red-baiting. In his conversations in the early 1950s with Dean Albertson of the Columbia Oral History Project he raised the question of how much Benham Baldwin had known of the work of the Communists. "Baldwin was always very close to me personally," he said, "but in action from day to day he was guided and convinced more and more by John Abt. John Abt I think was following the straight Communist line and what he was after was complete control, so it meant that Mr. Baldwin, who was more and more in John Abt's pocket, was not prepared to follow what I believed in. . . . After the fact he claimed that the extremists were the doorbell ringers—that's when I was fighting for a strictly American party."[10]

Wallace had come to feel that he had been deceived, that the party's base had become narrow rather than broad, liberal, and popular. He contrasted the narrow base of the extremists with the "strictly American party," as if he no longer believed that a person could be a Communist and still have American interests at heart. Thus, later on he said that Baldwin was "the most baffling person" of them all to him. "He seems to be following today (1952) the straight Communist line, and yet in the Farm Security Administration he did the meanest job that anybody did in the entire department, did it unflinchingly, faced the guns up on Capital Hill of the most virulent opposition, and fought for what he thought would serve the poor farmers of the South and of the entire nation."[11]

Perhaps affected despite himself by the media's vilification of Communists, Wallace had now come to suspect that a Communist could not be sincerely dedicated to righting a social injustice or to anything else, only to following "the party line." "It may be that Beanie was under some type of Communist influence in those days and was doing it [the Farm Security work] in order to raise hell later on. . . . The Communists act in such curious ways and have had such far-reaching ramifications that, in view of later history, you can't be sure. I just don't know."[12] Later, Wallace would conclude that the Communists in the party had actually worked against him, hoping, through their ostentatious support of his candidacy, to decrease the party's vote and show the world how reactionary the United States had become. Having destroyed Wallace's influence, they could then take over the party machinery they had worked so industriously to build.[13]

Between 1948 and 1950, when he began to record his interviews, Wallace had undergone a profound reversal of attitude toward both American Communists and the Soviet Union. For some time after the Progressives' defeat, he had continued to attack United States policies abroad and to raise questions that few were in a mood to answer. In March 1949, for example, he charged that the proposed North Atlantic Pact would have the effect of replacing the United Nations, an organization aiming at one world, with a military alliance that would split the world in two. "Stripped of legal verbiage," he declared, the pact "gives the United States Army military bases up to the very borders of the Soviet Union." Could anyone believe that, "as they stare across their borders at our jet bombers and our cannon, calm visions of peace will be born in their minds?" Suppose the Soviets were to establish military bases on the borders of Mexico, Canada, or Cuba. Could a treaty that allowed such a thing, one that "put guns in our faces," seriously be termed "a pact of peace"? He had "seen and talked to the common man all over the world"—in Latin America, China, Western Europe, Palestine, and Soviet Asia—and knew of his desire for peace; Stalin himself had indicated a willingness to discuss points of disagreement with the United States, but the State Department and the White House had failed to respond. "The Atlantic Pact, this war alliance, is their reply."[14] But despite these forthright condemnations of his country's anti-Soviet stance, there were increasing signs that Wallace had begun to change his mind.

He began to object to the direction in which the Progressive Party seemed to be heading. Writing to Baldwin in February 1950, he expressed his disquiet over its apparently narrow, pro-Soviet orientation. "With me," he said, "everything hangs on broadening out the party so it will attract all who believe in 'One World at Peace.' Also I want to drive home to the consciousness of people that we want the US to lead the drive for peace—that we are in no sense apologists for either the USSR or Communism."[15] Then, at the second national convention of the Progressive Party, in Chicago on 24 February 1950, Wallace insisted, against strong opposition by some extremists, on the party endorsing the Vermont resolution whose rejection had led to the party's crucifixion by the anti-Communist press in 1948—a clear indication of the firming of his anti-Soviet attitude. Even so, he continued for a time to assail the policies of both the United States and the Soviet Union, calling them "the big brutes of the world." "Each in its own eyes," he said, "rests on high moral principles—but each in the eyes of other nations is guided by force and force alone."[16]

Matters came to a head in the spring. Testimony was given before the House Un-American Activities Committee that some of those who were still running the party were Communists. Wallace had told Baldwin that the party could not employ anyone known to be a Communist, and Baldwin replied that he did not think the persons referred to were such. But, after contacting a member of the committee, Congressman Francis E. Walter, Wallace wrote Baldwin that those in question should go before the committee and testify, and, to show his own position, he sent a copy of the letter to Congressman Walter. That action made Baldwin and John Abt "as sore as hell," and the resulting quarrel was one of the things that entered into Wallace's separation from the Progressive Party.[17]

Concerning Russia's international intentions, Wallace had been given information in 1949 that quite changed his beliefs about the Soviet intervention in Czechoslovakia, the intervention he had so hastily defended the previous year. Personal reports from Czechoslovakia, from Progressive Party members who had visited relatives there, had convinced him that "Russia had a complete grip on Czechoslovakia." He had repeatedly told Progressive Party leaders that "the native communism was being destroyed and Russian communism being imposed in its place," but they would not accept this interpretation.[18]

For Wallace, the outbreak of the Korean War in June 1950 was decisive. When North Korean Communist troops invaded the South, Truman, with the backing of the United Nations Security Council (from which the Soviet Union had withdrawn), opposed them with armed force. Progressive leaders met shortly after this to consider the party's position. Vito Marcantonio opened the discussion by remarking that "everyone here agrees that this is an unjust war." Wallace said firmly, "I don't."[19]

He did not believe that he had been wrong in 1948 and earlier about the Soviet Union's policies, but rather that Soviet policies had changed. For him, this suspicion had been crystallized by Ellis Zacharias's book *Behind Closed Doors*, published in 1950. It reported an alleged meeting in the Kremlin in January 1949 "at which certain plans were made," this report being based on the story of a defector, the secretary of one of the generals who had been present.[20] A couple of years earlier Wallace would have disregarded such hearsay evidence, but this time it fit his own new opinions.

When the Executive Committee of the Progressive Party met on 6 July to formulate its position on Korea, Wallace announced that he would not endorse any statement critical of the United States government in time of war, and that if such a statement were released he would have to issue his own dissenting one. Two days later, he received word that Trygve Lie, secretary general of the United Nations, wished to see him. When Wallace called at Lie's Forest Hills residence, Lie told him that the situation in Korea was grave and that private information available to him had convinced him that the Soviets "had been preparing for this attack for two years and that they expected to be able to over run South Korea in 48 hours." He asked Wallace publicly to condemn the North's aggression. Wallace had already prepared a statement to that effect and read it to Lie, who received it enthusiastically. When Wallace said that "the Russians could stop the fighting in Korea any time they wished" the secretary general "cried out with approval."[21]

As subsequently released, Wallace's statement, altered only slightly as a result of his conversation with Lie, read (in part):

> I want to make it clear that when Russia, the United States and the United Nations appeal to force, I am on the side of the United States and the United Nations. Undoubtedly the Russians could have prevented the attacks by the North Koreans and undoubtedly they could stop the attack any time they wish.
>
> I hold no brief for the past actions of either the United States or Russia but when my country is at war and the United Nations sanctions that war, I am on the side of my country and the United Nations.[22]

Wallace's moral arguments had reached the bottom line: My country (and the United Nations) right or wrong. Syngman Rhee, president of South Korea, had been installed by the United States at the end of World War II as leader of a provisional government, and in a rigged election in 1948 he had retained power by the use of strong-arm squads and after the assassination of moderate opposition leaders. His was exactly the kind of authoritarian regime for the support of which Wallace had castigated the bipartisan foreign policy, but that fact could not stand in opposition to Wallace's patriotism, which had always been, for him, an absolute value. In time of peace he was prepared to criticize, not his country, but his country's foreign policy as laid down by the governmental forces he opposed—it was this and only this that gave rise to the cries of "traitor" when he spoke abroad against that policy. But the continued existence and well-being of the United States itself was for him an imperative not to be questioned.

To some extent it was the fact that his country was engaged in actual physical conflict that swung Wallace's attitude around so wholeheartedly. The aggression that he tried determinedly to control within himself found legitimate vicarious expression when his country was at war. He would do whatever he could to assist a struggle that was right by definition, just as he had in World War II. In August 1950, he declared that he thought it legitimate to use the atomic bomb in Korea if the battlefield situation demanded it, and in November he advocated a large-scale rearmament program for the United States, publicly condemning the Soviet Union as the real aggressor.[23]

His change of heart toward the Soviet Union, his reversion to a conservative, patriotic orthodoxy, is reminiscent of the reversal of his feelings toward Nicholas Roerich when he finally decided that that champion of enlightenment and peace was a cynical, self-aggrandizing adventurer making a mockery of Wallace's finest intentions. The unqualified condemnation, the complete white-to-black switch in which Roerich was now denied any good motives whatever, was brought about by the sudden recognition of how the entire expedition would look if the full story broke in the newspapers. His formerly venerated guru had uncaringly exposed Wallace to the risk of public ridicule and condemnation. Now, on a much larger scale, the country, the Soviet Union, from which he had expected the coming of that economic democracy of his ideal vision, had in turn revealed itself as cynical, self-aggrandizing, and exploitative. Because of his high-minded allegiance to another false idol, Wallace had in fact suffered public humiliation in the press and at the polls, and in his betrayed virtue he turned bitterly against it.

His public statement dissociating himself from Progressive Party policy on Korea provoked a flood of mail. Many who wrote congratulated him on his change of heart, but there were some wounding letters, too, from Progressives who felt bewildered and betrayed. "So you have slipped into the silly little arms of Truman," a Georgia member of the party wrote. "Betrayer! You have set the fight for human rights back 100 years." "There are millions of us," said another, "who would have thought it impossible that YOU would thus renege on the ideals you professed and upheld until recently." What was "especially shocking," another dismayed former follower declared, was "to hear you speak of 'my country.' Do Truman, the Missouri crowd and brass hats in Washington represent your country? Does McArthur speak for you? Can you easily align yourself with Senators Eastland and McCarthy?"[24]

On 9 August Wallace resigned from the Progressive Party, again to bitter recrimination. He had tried to explain his position to Curtis MacDougall, declaring that he had no doubts about the wisdom of his actions since 1946, but now felt that he could better help the cause of peace from outside the party. MacDougall was hardly mollified. "Honestly, Mr. Wallace," he wrote, "I hope you never realize the full effect that your action has had and will have. The remorse will be greater punishment than it would be just for anyone to endure." Having "broken" Wallace, MacDougall said, the Progressives' opponents were "now out for a fast mop-up of the rest of us." He referred to academic colleagues who expected soon to be in jail or were contemplating leaving the United States. In self-defense Wallace claimed that by following so closely the Soviet line the Progressives' leaders had wrecked the party, an outcome for which he refused to accept responsibility, but MacDougall insisted that the effect of Wallace's defection had been to greatly strengthen the forces of reaction, who were now branding those who refused to quit the party with Wallace as traitors to the United States.[25]

Wallace denied that his changed attitude toward the Soviet Union and his support for Truman's actions in Korea indicated wholesale acceptance of U.S. policies, and in some of his correspondence he continued to demonstrate the evenhandedness of earlier times. Referring to the threat to the world from overpopulation, he wrote Harry Weinberg: "I denounce both the Republican and Democratic leaders for having wasted the past six years — for not having the imagination and statesmanship to put before the world a challenging peace program. . . . I denounce the iron curtain dictators for bringing forward phony peace programs of a purely propaganda nature."[26] But more frequently in his statements and actions, his deepening hostility toward the Soviet regime was made plain.

As the international situation became more threatening, Wallace tried to prevent an alliance between Russia and China, and to draw the latter closer to the United States. In an initiative that recalls his open letter to Stalin, he wrote on 30 September 1950 to the Chinese leader Mao Tse-tung, reminding him that both of them were farmers, interested in a peaceful world with "more food and clothing available for the hungry multitudes." Both had played major roles in reforming their countries' agriculture, an achievement Mao would surely not wish to see jeopardized by a continuation of a cold war or the beginning of a hot one. Wallace acknowledged that the Chinese nation would need to remain on friendly terms with the Soviet Union, but pointed out that the United States was its more natural trading partner. "Unless the New China is interested in joining the USSR in an insane drive toward world conquest, it is high time that she consider the fundamentals of a peaceful understanding with the U.S." Such an understanding could help resolve the Korean problem and smooth the way for China's entry to the United Nations, something that Wallace supported but that "my people here in the U.S." had opposed, because sections of the Chinese Communist Party were attempting to make the Chinese people totally subservient to Moscow and because of calls in the Chinese press for military support for North Korea.[27]

Even in relation to the Soviet Union, Wallace thought he might still play a constructive role, this time by appealing not to its leadership but directly to its people. When Helen Rogers Reid of the *New York Herald Tribune* asked, during a conversation with him in February 1951, whether he believed that the Communist regime's hold over the Soviet people could be broken, Wallace replied: "While I had not suggested it to a soul and hoped no one would approach me on it, I was convinced that if I gave talks in Russian over the Voice of America to the Russian people it would have a tremendous effect." He pointed out to Reid that the Russian leadership had refrained from attacking him, almost certainly because they "did not want the Russian people to know how critical I had become of [them]." "I told her of my talks in Russian in Siberia in 1944 and how the Russian press had printed them at that time." Later, when Nikita Khrushchev visited the United States in 1959, Wallace tried unsuccessfully to arrange a meeting with him, stressing to Russian ambassador Mikhail Menshikov his own pioneering work in breeding corn (Khrushchev was to visit a farm in Iowa) and describing the Soviet premier as a man "whose attitude toward both Indian Corn and Peace has interested me greatly."[28] Clearly, Wallace's sense of his own importance and destiny had not diminished at the same rate as his political influence.

As the hunt for domestic subversives intensified, not merely Wallace's stand in 1948 but even many of his wartime actions began to be called into question. Already in 1949 his mission to China in 1944 had come under suspicious scrutiny. In August of that year he complained to Henry Luce that a *Time* article had twisted the meaning of advice he had given to Roosevelt, as summarized in a recent State Department White Paper. One passage in the White Paper had read: "Mr. Wallace referred to the patriotic attitude of the Communists in the United States and said that he could not understand the attitude of the Chinese Communists, as described by President Chiang," but in reporting it *Time* had omitted the words "as described by President Chiang," making it appear not only that Wallace had welcomed the support of United States Communists but also that he had hoped for more whole-hearted support of the Soviet war effort from those in China. In the latter event, the threat to Chiang's embattled regime would have been magnified, a point seized on by Luce in his brusque and sarcastic rejection of Wallace's complaint: "It is evident . . . that you and your friends had determined to work for the overthrow of the government headed by Chiang Kai-shek. Neither the White Paper itself, nor our review of it give you the credit you deserve for your success in this venture."[29]

Attempting to undo the damage, Wallace made public the actual report he had given Roosevelt, but in summarizing its contents, *New York Times* correspondent William S. White pointed out that Wallace had urged Roosevelt to consider Chiang "only as a 'short-term investment,' neither intelligent enough nor politically strong enough for postwar China." Although the United States must for the time being support Chiang, Wallace had told Roosevelt, "the leaders of postwar China will be brought forward by evolution or revolution, and it now seems more likely the latter." These revelations were quickly seized on by congressional Republicans, currently attacking the administration for its refusal to give further aid to Chiang's forces. Wallace's "secret report," Republican senator Homer Ferguson of Michigan now charged, had virtually determined United States policy toward China ever since, a policy designed to " 'coerce or destroy' Generalissimo Chiang to the benefit of the Chinese Communists."[30]

Wallace was soon being attacked on other fronts. In William Henry Chamberlin's book, *America's Second Crusade*, he found himself listed with Alger Hiss, Klaus Fuchs, and others as betrayers of the United States. Chamberlin had based this accusation on a claim by General Leslie Groves, director of the Manhattan Project, that during the war Groves had withheld from Wallace reports on the atom bomb project because he considered Wallace a security risk. Wallace now asked Groves to produce evidence to support his claim and to explain on what grounds, in testimony before the House Un-American Activities Committee, Groves had said that Wallace had facilitated the transfer of nuclear materials to the Soviet Union. "Your name has been connected with so many attacks on me since 1946, first whispers and finally in the press and over the air in mounting crescendo from August of 1948 till December of 1949 that I now give you an opportunity to state clearly and exactly what is your position." Perhaps, Wallace suggested disingenuously, the press had been quoting Groves incorrectly; he certainly hoped that the general had not been involved "in all this smear campaign to destroy my record of helping effectively my country in the winning of World War II."[31]

If the allegation that Wallace had facilitated the transfer of nuclear materials to the Soviet Union upset Wallace, it caused still greater alarm in the FBI. About this time the agency learned that the Internal Security Subcommittee of the Senate Judiciary Committee had "received information that in 1943 or 1944 Wallace met a subversive agent in Philadelphia and . . . the subversive agent asked Wallace for additional data on the atomic bomb." Wallace was "reported to have said to the subversive agent that he had gotten the U235 for the agent and that should be enough." Informed of these allegations, J. Edgar Hoover ordered a thorough investigation, in the course of which "over 2,000 files on Henry Wallace" and "10 cartons of material received from General Groves on a confidential basis in 1946 on Boris Pregal," president of the Canadian Radium and Uranium Company and a friend of Wallace, were scrutinized. Nothing that would substantiate the story was discovered and the matter was dropped. (The agency was alerted again in 1958, when Wallace applied for a passport to visit Europe, and a notation was made in his file: "Mr. Wallace will be 70 years old this fall and is engaged in the plant-breeding business"—as if to suggest that the bureau's long surveillance of Wallace might now safely cease.)[32]

Faced with this growing criticism of his motives and patriotism, Wallace had sought to defend himself before both congressional bodies investigating domestic subversion and the public at large. When a House Un-American Activities Committee report noted that he, Albert Einstein, Thomas Mann, and others had been members at one time of organizations now listed by the attorney general as subversive, he wrote to committee member Francis Walter denying that he had ever knowingly belonged to a subversive organization and stating that if he had ever innocently given talks to such groups, it was likely that those addresses had "included statements not palatable to communists or Russians." Like Einstein, he had refused to sign the Stockholm peace petition after North Korea invaded the South. "But just like Einstein . . . and tens of millions of other decent, highly patriotic Americans I still think the discovery of a firm foundation for peace is supremely important. . . . The FBI and the Committee have performed a useful service in unmasking those who cry peace when there is not peace in their hearts. But surely peace itself is not subversive."[33]

In September 1951, Wallace appeared before the Internal Security Subcommittee of the Senate Judiciary Committee to answer questions about, among other things, his vice-presidential trip to Soviet Asia in 1944. His attitude was cooperative, and when suggestions appeared in the press that he was being treated unfairly by the committee, he emphatically refuted them:

> Senator Smith: . . . I assume you are in sympathy with the over-all objective of this committee's activities in tracking down Communists in the Government if there are any?
>
> Mr. Wallace: Of course. I agree completely that [with] the world situation as it is, it is a very important function indeed. . . .
>
> Senator Smith: Do you feel now from published reports and information you have there are any Communists or Communist sympathizers in America? Is there any doubt in your mind about that?
>
> Mr. Wallace: They seem to have gotten into various places. They even got into the Manhattan project, if you remember. They have a capacity to get around that is altogether astounding and which has been well demonstrated, it seems to me, by documented evidence.
>
> Senator Smith: . . . You feel these Communists as such as you have just mentioned should be tracked down, if possible?
>
> Mr. Wallace: Certainly. If there is real trouble going to break out, there is no question where their allegiance will be. . . .
>
> Senator Smith: You have any personal complaining against the committee either for its subpenaing [sic] you or for its failure to hear you?
>
> Mr. Wallace: As a matter of fact, I wrote Senator Ferguson sometime in early September. I had quite a little correspondence with him in which I indicated if there was any way I could be of service to him personally or through the committee. I would be glad to do so.[34]

Later, Wallace wrote to the chairman of the subcommittee, Senator Pat McCarran, agreeing that testimony such as that given by Elinor Lipper (who had revealed that the "model village" that had so impressed Wallace during his 1944 Siberian trip was actually a slave-labor camp) "should be included in any balanced view of Soviet Asia," but pointing out that there was no way, in 1944, that he could have known the truth.[35]

Even Winston Churchill, of whose imperialistic ambitions, chauvinist conception of Anglo-Saxon superiority, and, as Wallace believed, ill-intentioned wartime attempts to foment disunion between the United States and the Soviet Union Wallace had formerly been so critical, appeared in a new light. "There were times when you and I did not see eye to eye in the past," Wallace wrote to the newly elected British prime minister in October 1951, "but I want you to know that in this time of great crisis I wish you and the Anglo-Saxon peoples the very best as they meet a rising tide of the most cruel barbarism."[36]

In December 1951 Wallace announced publicly that he had been wrong about Russian intentions. When he had run for president in 1948, he said, he had believed that the Soviet Union genuinely wanted peace in order to develop its vast lands. He could now see that it was trying to dominate the world. "Old bubble head has seen the light at last," J. Edgar Hoover commented, when told of the admission, "but all too late."[37] In an article entitled "Where I Was Wrong," published in September the following year, Wallace conceded much that his critics had charged against him. Elinor Lipper was correct in claiming that he had failed to see that the Siberian economic system of which he had written so glowingly in 1944 had been based on slave labor. He ought not, when Russia crushed Czechoslovakia in 1948, to have been blind to Stalin's expansionist aims. He now understood that the Soviets wanted the cold war to go on indefinitely, even if it led to a hot one. If Wallace's enemies had wanted him to recant, they could hardly, by the autumn of 1952, have asked for more.[38]

Wallace's recantation does not seem to have been based on any newly uncovered evidence; rather, it appears to have been a result of his conversion to the clamorous official interpretation of known facts. Even such an independent-minded person as Wallace must have found it hard to remain unaffected by the tremendous anti-Soviet feeling, especially when it implicated him personally. But the admission of error did not save him from continuing charges that his wartime actions assisted nations now hostile to the United States.

In 1945 Wallace and his wife had bought a 115-acre hilltop farm at South Salem, New York, fifty miles northwest of New York City, and after his defeat in 1948, he returned, for solace, to the work in which his competence was unchallenged, and resumed serious experimental genetic work there. He continued with his corn-breeding activities and sought, through extensive crossing, to develop better commercial varieties of chickens and strawberries—chickens that weighed less (with a consequent saving in feed) but produced more eggs, and strawberry plants that were resistant to disease, whose fruit was more suitable for canning and freezing, and which would reach the market at the right time for northern growers. He also developed new strains of gladioli.[39]

The satisfaction he felt in this work can be read clearly in his letters. He inquired of his friend Luis Quintanilla about the possibility of finding land for summer experiments in the mountainous regions of northern Arizona and New Mexico, and explained: "You see, my passion is breeding plants and especially glads and strawberries." To fellow enthusiast Carl Fisher, he wrote: "My seedlings planted this spring look beautiful. . . . Summer Queen was far better than last year. Also Ruffled Dream. Snow Velvet was lovely. . . . Knights Rose looked fine. . . . China Blue is fantastically good."[40]

He kept "farmers' hours," rising early each morning to deal with a very extensive correspondence before breakfasting at seven o'clock. He spent the rest of each day (when he was not attending conferences, inspecting agricultural work elsewhere, or giving occasional lectures) growing plants from seed in his hothouse, transplanting them to numerous experimental plots surrounding his home, and observing their progress. The results of his experiments were recorded in large ledgers. A neighbor would later remember him as "a real dirty-kneed farmer," who could be seen from early in the morning working in the soil, and this serious application earned him the respect and liking of the South Salem folk.[41]

Wallace's experimental work tied in with the family business. In 1926 he had formed a company, which became the Pioneer Hi-Bred Corn Company, to propagate the idea of hybrid corn and to market seed for it. It prospered and his sons had become managers of two of its branches: Henry B. of the Hy-Line Poultry Farms near Johnson, Iowa, and Robert B. of the Wallace Hy-Cross Hatcheries in Doylestown,

Pennsylvania. But, characteristically, Wallace viewed his work at South Salem within a much wider context. One of his aims, he explained to a visiting reporter, was to discover how to transfer the high productivity of temperate regions to tropical lands, where population was rapidly outrunning the food supply. When he had delivered his Century of the Common Man speech in 1942, he said, he had not foreseen the extent to which DDT and public health measures would control human disease, resulting in huge population increases in underdeveloped areas of the world. To help meet this problem he was attempting to develop new varieties of hybrid corn and other crops that would flourish in poorer parts of the hemisphere and in other unpromising climatic conditions. When the reporter then asked whether his gladioli, too, were meant to feed the hungry, Wallace replied with a grin that they were "more for the inner man," and that he was "trying to get enough colors and tints for an artist to paint with."[42]

These activities insulated him to some extent from the slurs to which he was still subjected, but every so often he felt compelled to confront his accusers. In April 1954, for example, he protested loudly, both to the journalist H. V. Kaltenborn and to WNBC station management, over a two-minute television résumé of his life. The program had been largely based, he complained, on the testimony of certain "disgruntled extremists whom I fired" (a reference to the 1935 purge in the Department of Agriculture) and included a discussion of Nicholas Roerich, whom he had also dismissed. Ignoring his many achievements, it had "played him up as a good-natured, futile crank who always follows the Russian line." Wallace also sharply questioned Senator Alben W. Barkley over a claim in his memoirs, which were being serialized by the *Saturday Evening Post*, that in 1940 Barkley "was beginning to be troubled by the symptoms he [Wallace] was displaying of the increasing mysticism which later made it possible for the left wing groups to exploit him." What precisely were these symptoms, Wallace wanted to know, and how could the senator be ignorant of the fact "that all genuine left wingers hate mysticism as the Devil hates Holy Water"?[43]

He felt obliged to assure federal attorney general Herbert Brownell Jr. that he had not known until 1950 that some Progressive Party members were Communists, and that he could find no evidence to support a claim made before the Senate Internal Security Committee by former Department of Justice employee Herbert A. Philbrick that

Philbrick and another Communist had altered one of Wallace's campaign speeches to make it conform more closely to the Moscow line. He pointed out that in Philbrick's book *I Led Three Lives*, the author had stated that the Communists had not liked Wallace in 1948, believing him to he "a social reformer and idle dreamer," and that they had had "no use whatever for my faith in God and in 'Progressive Capitalism.'" In fact, the Communists had actually sought to destroy his influence within the party, and in so doing "broke the hearts of liberal, well meaning people who desperately wanted peace but who hated the force, deceit and intrigue for which Communism stands."[44]

More keenly resented by Wallace was the publication, in October 1955, of extracts from Truman's memoirs. In November 1952, Wallace had been surprised but gratified to be asked to a formal dinner at the White House, given by the outgoing president for former cabinet colleagues. "Everyone seemed quite cordial," he wrote later, "except perhaps Biddle." Truman had spoken to him in a friendly manner, saying that he would like to see him again, and Wallace was glad that he had attended. But now, in recounting in his memoirs the circumstances surrounding his former commerce secretary's dismissal, Truman had written that the two of them had discussed Wallace's Madison Square Garden speech only very briefly, and that his statement to reporters that he approved of the speech implied only that Wallace had his approval to deliver it, not that he endorsed its contents.

The *New York Times* informed Wallace in advance of Truman's comments and he wrote a rebuttal, which the paper published alongside Truman's article. Declaring that the purpose of his statement was to "enumerate only a few of the essential facts, which Mr. Truman has evidently forgotten," Wallace used diary notes made at the time to support his claims that the former president not merely had read carefully through the speech before it was delivered but had stated specifically that it did not conflict with current United States foreign policy.[45] But it seems that for the media in general this story was regarded as dead, and there was no sequel to the exchange.

A few months later Truman sent Wallace a copy of the first volume of his memoirs, saluting him as "the greatest of Secretaries of Agriculture" and offering his "kindest regards," but Wallace had not forgiven him. Not unnaturally, he delayed acknowledging this equivocal gift, and when he did write he reproached Truman for failing to answer an earlier letter in which he had challenged Truman's version of events. "I know how deeply you love your daughter and how you wish to avoid doing anything which will hurt her," he wrote. "Well, I have three children and eleven grandchildren and I feel that in your diary of Sept. 19, 1946 you have left a time bomb which will blow up and hurt my children and grandchildren. You talked one way to me on Sept. 10 and Sept. 18, 1946 and in your diary wrote another way on Sept. 19, 1946." He went on to warn Truman, with a rather desperate optimism, that posterity's verdict would go against him, as the tide of events was now flowing Wallace's, rather than in the former president's, way. "History is coming my way and the press more and more demonstrate this trend. 'The soil bank,' 'Globaloney,' 'Quarts of milk for Hottentots,' TVA's on the Nile if not on the Danube. Even 'peace' and the peaceful use of atomic energy are becoming popular. Peace could have been had with Russia while she was still devastated and before she had the atom bomb. Now a less advantageous peace will be reached after she is strong."[46] But public recognition of the soundness of Wallace's views was a long time coming.

The same month, March 1956, he wrote this letter, Wallace stated publicly that if Republican president Dwight Eisenhower chose to run for a second term he would vote for him. He invested great faith in Eisenhower, seeing him as a man dedicated to peace, who could "tell his generals where to get off—and some of the Republicans, too," and after Eisenhower's reelection he wrote to him from time to time offering advice and support.

Early in his second term, Eisenhower was subject to a good deal of criticism, for "self-righteous moralizing" and other supposed failings. He hit back by advising the Washington press to examine what their predecessors had said about George Washington. Wallace took the comparison much further, writing Eisenhower that the likeness between him and the nation's first president was "more than superficial." Both had "a combined military-agricultural background," but more important was "a profound faith in God innate in your own natures and bequeathed to you by God-fearing ancestors." He enclosed one of Washington's speeches with his letter, expressing the hope that it would give the president courage. Eisenhower replied in the same vein, finding it "humbling" that one "so widely read as yourself should find certain similarities" between Washington and himself, and adding that he had often felt the need for Washington's "clarity of vision in big things, his strength of purpose and his genuine greatness of mind and spirit."

Later that year Wallace told Eisenhower that he, the president, could "lead the whole world into a New Era of freedom and prosperity." [47] Wallace himself never lost hope of this vision, though after the events of 1948 he expressed it less extravagantly, and with noticeably less faith in the common man. Having outlined some suggestions for peace to his friend Harry Weinberg, he conceded rather sourly that "selfish, short-sighted, suspicious, greedy humanity" would never have been inclined to accept any proposals of this kind were it not for growing realization of what another war might mean. Asked, in August 1958, by *Washington Star* reporter Donald Freitel, whether he still believed in the common man, Wallace replied that he did, but (belying the intended meaning of "believe in") added that it was uncertain whether the march of the common man would be in a constructive or a destructive direction. Instead of a vision of peace, he now saw almost inevitable future conflict, which the United States must strive to win. Given the hideously destructive capacity of the weapons both sides now possessed, and the runaway increase in world population, food might become the decisive weapon. The United States could use its huge food surpluses to "woo China away from Russia." It could challenge the Soviet Union to join it in helping to feed "the critical neutral lands" of Asia, Africa, and the Middle East. "This may force Russia into a difficult and resource-draining program if they agree. And if they don't or if they offer only a token, the United States should be prepared to exploit this failure to the fullest extent in psychological warfare." Wallace sounded more like his former charitable self when he went on to suggest that the United States must help now to raise the standard of life for all the peoples of the world, taking over "the job of the former colonial powers, but with a different spirit." Americans, he said, "must do our task under the same ideals of justice, equality and reverence that guided the founding fathers." [48]

Through all these years Wallace proudly maintained his political independence (relatively ineffectual though it may have become), welcoming the freedom it gave him to criticize or endorse whichever party or leader he wished. When reports began to circulate in November 1959 that he was about to rejoin the Democratic Party he denied them, but his agreement to act as a sponsor for a Democratic dinner in honor of Eleanor Roosevelt, which all likely contenders for the presidential

Wallace talking with Dominican Republic farmers, April 1963. (Courtesy of the University of Iowa Library)

nomination would attend, signaled at least a reconciliation with members of his former party. He did not, however, vote in 1960 for John F. Kennedy, whose farm program he thought inferior to Richard Nixon's.[49]

For Lyndon Johnson, on the other hand, Wallace felt a genuine enthusiasm. Writing just after Kennedy's assassination, he expressed to Johnson his confidence that "you will handle your vast powers with both confidence and moderation." Despite the hatred the new president would encounter, Wallace knew that he "would stand straight and strong." Johnson replied in similar vein, declaring that "warm and compassionate" letters such as Wallace's had given him courage, and fondly recalling Wallace's own time in government. "How well I remember . . . the sturdiness of your character," he said, "and your undiminished love for your country."[50]

Wallace's deep interest in the political and economic life of the hemi-

Wallace's last trip to Central America, February 1964. (Courtesy of the University of Iowa Library)

sphere never flagged. Twice in the early months of Johnson's presidency he traveled south, visiting lands whose cultures he so admired and whose people he had repeatedly sought to help—Central America and Mexico in November 1963, and in March 1964, Guatemala and El Salvador, where he attended agricultural conferences and studied the corn-growing techniques of the highland Indians.[51]

Back in the United States, he found the calls on his time heavier than usual. To historian Frank Freidel, who must have sought an interview, he explained that he had only just returned from his Central American trip. "Before me," he said, "is a mountain of mail and I am my own stenographer. Planting time is just coming up. There are many conferences among our chicken breeders. In short time is lacking." Furthermore, "I very much prefer living in the future to living in the past." Wallace scrawled a personal note across the bottom of this letter. In a week's time the family would be gathering to celebrate his and Ilo's golden wedding anniversary. He would enjoy seeing them all, including those of his thirteen grandchildren who were able to come, but on the whole he did not like such occasions, which in effect said: "That was the Life that was."[52]

At seventy-six Henry Wallace looked determinedly forward to the many useful things he still wished to do, and with less inclination than ever before to fashion or refashion the past.

EPILOGUE

Ten years earlier, Henry Wallace had agreed to cast back over his life, for the sake of the historical record. As their long series of conversations drew to a close, Dean Albertson of the Columbia Oral History Project had asked him to assess his achievements, to recall the things of which he was most proud, and Wallace had done so willingly and at some length. Naturally, his answers dealt with the goals he had consciously and successfully striven to achieve. He mentioned first the practical aspects of his endeavors to improve the quantity and quality of food, on which, in significant measure, his vision of abundance rested — specifically, the impetus he had given to the concept of hybrid corn and chickens. He spoke of the Ever-Normal Granary, which had protected the nation against shortages and assisted in winning the war, of his efforts to raise the fertility of the nation's soils, the results of which, whenever he visited the South, gratified him deeply. The farmer committees, organized under the Agricultural Adjustment Administration, through which rural problems were solved at community, county, and state levels, had provided, he claimed, "the first nation-wide example of genuine economic democracy we've ever had."

He was proud of his efforts to promote a good relationship with Latin America, vitally necessary if the United States were to be secure, and of his success, through wartime agencies, in obtaining materials vital to the winning of the war. His Century of the Common Man speech, he believed, would "go down in history as one of the great speeches of this century," though he now realized that the common man could become "barbarous" if misled, and he regretted that the United States, by failing to offer constructive leadership to common people throughout the world, had left a vacuum that others had unfortunately filled.

He reflected with pleasure on his stand for civil liberties, on how he had come out boldly, at the Democratic National Convention in 1944, for the abolition of the poll tax and the provision of equal educational opportunities for all. He spoke of the writings in which he had warned his nation against economic autarky, or offered it a vision of abundance and peace. He was proud of the efforts to convince Truman that an understanding with Russia was at one time possible, and for campaigning vigorously for that understanding as spokesman for the Progressive cause in 1947 and 1948; yet he was also proud that when he finally became convinced of Russia's aggressive intentions, he had publicly admitted his error and condemned a regime that he had come to see as gravely threatening world peace.[1]

As he and Albertson talked, Wallace tried to draw together the strands of his life as he saw it, seeking to identify the ethical calculus that underlay his long career. In the end he returned to the formulation he had arrived at years before, in trying, as a high school youth, to decide the direction his life should take. He had asked himself then what the chief end of our existence on Earth should be, what was ultimately worthwhile, and his conclusion had been that he at any rate should try to promote "the long time good of all mankind." More recently, he had given the same answer to an Iowa college student, who, Wallace was convinced, had genuinely tried to understand his ideas — that that which was valuable above all else was "the end time good of all mankind." "It has long seemed evident to me," he added, elaborating a basic philosophy that seems in many ways to have informed his public life, "that no nation could prosper unless other nations prospered with it. The only security which any nation can find in the long run is the welfare of all nations regardless of race, religion or color." Although "the fundamental morality of the situation was clear," Wallace wrote, the difficulty came in applying that morality "at a given time and place."[2]

Such difficulties arise, of course, when there is a clash of interests and not all parties can achieve their aims. Wallace must have been reflecting ruefully on such issues, remembering, for example, the trust he had so foolishly reposed in Nicholas Roerich, and his insufficiently critical reading of postwar Soviet intentions. Yet even those failures in judgment had come about in the pursuit of his overriding goal, which he had hoped to achieve in the first place through a general spiritual awakening, and in the second through an era of prosperity and peace.

As with all Grail seekers, Henry Wallace's journey had been essentially a solitary one. Time after time, people who in a formal sense had known Wallace and worked with him for years almost without exception said that they did not *really* know him, indeed they felt that no one knew the real Wallace. Prompted by Albertson, Wallace managed to mention a few people to whom he "felt close" — in the Department of Agriculture, he was close to Paul Appleby, Rex Tugwell, M. L. Wilson (whose judgment he valued highly), and Louis Bean ("a lovely character"); while vice president, he "placed considerable reliance on Harold

Young," but "Milo Perkins is about the only one I would put in the category of a close, personal friend." Evidently he drew a distinction between regarding people as reliable colleagues and as being personally close. Even the highly valued M. L. Wilson said: "There wasn't anybody that I know of who could say he knew Henry Wallace intimately."[3] Those with whom Wallace did feel some spiritual closeness were those whose spiritual convictions merged with his own. Louis Bean and Milo Perkins had Theosophical connections, and before Wallace's political career there had been Charles Roos and George W. Russell (the latter described as "one of the loveliest characters I ever knew"), but even on a spiritual plane he did not take directions from these people, or admit their superior authority. Of course, for a brief period, he was greatly swayed by the Roerich clan, but on a closer reading of the letters one sees that he typically asked guidance not from them personally, but from the masters whose advice they would relay to him, and when political embarrassment threatened, he was very quick to shrug off any remaining influence.

Despite his principled and perfectly genuine concern for the common man, Wallace in his personal relationships was introverted and self-defensive. His personal space was inviolable. The most elaborate verbal portrait of him was given by Will Alexander, the former Farm Security Administration head, in his Columbia University interviews. They attended the same dinner party soon after Alexander arrived in Washington. "That evening Henry began to try to find out whether I had any interest in these occult matters or not. He tried to get up a conversation about some minor philosophy he had — some cosmic theories, and so on. I didn't know anything about it. He discovered that I had no interest in those things. Ever after this he never thought I was very worthwhile. . . . That night when I wouldn't talk, he went off out on the verandah and took a nap on the couch off on the porch."

Alexander lists others Wallace worked with who were not interested in the occult — Benham Baldwin, James LeCron, Paul Appleby. "These people were officially close to Henry. You could be officially close to him but not personally close to him. His personality was always veiled in mystery. . . . I always felt that he had no abiding interest in persons — individuals. . . . As long as you were part of the thing he was concerned with and you were contributing to it, he thought of you. But I doubt if he ever thought of you afterwards."

Alexander went on to recall a time when the president had lost control of Congress and someone on the Democratic National Committee proposed that they might as well take a weekend off and go to a country club on Jefferson Island in Chesapeake Bay. Most of the Democratic senators and congressmen spent part of that weekend there, picnicking and boating: "Everybody relaxed. Everybody had a good time. The President was at his best and was surrounded by a little group of those fellas all day long. . . . It was just to establish some sense of fellowship and morale in the party that was represented in the government in Washington. . . . I watched Henry down there. He reminded you of a country dog lost in town. He was doing his best, you could see. He was working awfully hard to be a part of that business. You had a feeling that he just didn't know how to fit in." Alexander spent all of one afternoon out fishing in a boat with Senator Joe Robinson, "a great fisherman and a great sportsman and a great hunter." "We had the grandest time that afternoon. He asked me to go with him. Think of having to spend a whole afternoon on a boat on Chesapeake Bay with Henry Wallace! He'd be miserable, and you would, too." Wallace, Alexander added, was "socially ill at ease. He never was open and free with you. I don't think the Secretary liked human contacts very well. I don't think he liked people except in the abstract. His humanitarian motives were a philosophical thing."[4]

This lack of closeness between Wallace and his colleagues and personal friends obviously puzzled his interviewer, because there is a long section toward the end of the oral history in which Albertson probes this very point. But although Wallace is happy to pay generous tribute to many people, he specifically denies that he was close to any of them except, possibly, Milo Perkins, and never gives the impression that they significantly influenced his policies or attitudes. His general world view had been formed by his early experiences, by his reading, by his observation of social conditions, and by his own intellectual ponderings. The details of political life he left to others.

One part of his story that Wallace never properly told concerned the impact of his unusual spiritual beliefs on his political career. Looking back, we can see how profoundly important this impact had been. His secret past complicated his relationship with Franklin Roosevelt and may even have played some part in denying him the vice-presidential nomination in 1944, and therefore the presidency. It was raised by his enemies just before Roosevelt dismissed him from the Board of Economic Warfare, and again during the crucial period in 1944 when

Roosevelt was deciding whether or not to retain Wallace as his running mate. In the run-up to the 1948 election, Westbrook Pegler used his copy of the Guru letters first to ridicule and then so publicly and damagingly to challenge Wallace that experienced observers all but wrote him off as a serious candidate.

His decisions to seek national political office, to oppose the recognition of the Soviet Union, and most obviously to dispatch the expedition to Mongolia owed something to his spiritual beliefs. In part, too, his notion of a general enlightenment that could transform our lives here on Earth was Theosophically inspired, and, as some of the language he used during his 1948 campaign for the presidency suggests, may have influenced his decision to lead the Progressive Party crusade. In the international field, his vision of, as he would have phrased it, a universal spiritual "brotherhood" of the common man, underlay his economic internationalism and his desire for detente with the Soviet Union.

For whatever reasons, Wallace had always set himself to confront issues he saw as fundamentally important to humankind. He wanted to reconcile science and religion, especially in view of the challenge of Darwinism; to bring about constructive relationships between nations in economic as well as political spheres, thus putting an end to imperialism and to the inequitable distribution of the world's resources that it brought about; and to promote the one world that must come about now that a divided world could destroy itself with atomic weapons. He looked for a new era in which "common" people everywhere could throw off their oppressors and enjoy the rights and freedoms so long denied. If sometimes his efforts had gone awry because of an idealized conception of human potential, nevertheless he had kept his eyes on these larger goals, never allowing himself to be diverted into pettiness or personal abuse, leaving the politicking he so disliked to a Paul Appleby or a Harold Young, or, naively but characteristically, to some in the Progressive Party whose aims he would never have approved.

When intimations of his mortality became marked and imminently threatening, Wallace met them with the courage he had demonstrated in confrontations with human foes. Descending the great pyramid at Huehuetenango in Guatemala, during his trip there in the spring of 1964, he became aware of an unfamiliar sensation in one of his legs. It did not greatly surprise or worry him, for the climb up had been exceedingly steep and he had taken it at his customary strenuous pace. But his discomfiture persisted after he returned to South Salem and members of his family began to notice that he dragged his left leg when he walked, and he himself realized that he could not move around the tennis court as easily as before.[5] Though his overall strength did not seem to be affected ("I have a slightly game left leg," the seventy-six-year-old Wallace reported to his friend Wallace Ashby, "but am still able to do 20 pushups. Did 21 this morning. And then after a 10 minute interval 17 more"),[6] eventually he agreed to have the problem diagnosed, in order, as he lightheartedly put it, "to lift the Mayan curse on my leg."[7] Intensive tests followed at the Danbury Hospital, and then at the Mayo Institute, and after some initial uncertainty he was diagnosed as having amyotrophic lateral sclerosis, a disease that progressively affects cells in the spinal column with consequent loss of muscular control. There was no known cure.

For a time, his illness hardly seems to have interrupted his many activities. He was still busy with his genetic work, he wrote Marshall Bean that December, with "breeding chickens, hybridizing strawberries and gladioli and growing them from seed," and had begun a new project aimed at assisting the highland Indians of Guatemala to grow more corn.[8] He kept up a lively correspondence with numerous friends, as well as with many of those involved in improving the quality of flowers and grain, typing his letters each morning to a background of the classical music he had always loved. "Someone must do a book some time on the therapy of sound," he suggested to Don Murphy of *Wallace's Farmer*. "Why is it that music of this kind often repeated grows on you and heals you more and more?"[9] Though by January 1965 his leg had become much weaker and his speech noticeably impaired, he traveled to the Dominican Republic, Jamaica, and South Florida to inspect corngrowing work there.[10]

Wallace consulted various medical authorities in the United States, and in the winter of 1965 spent several weeks at the Zimmerman Klinik at Starnberg, Germany, where vitamin and enzyme treatments were tried. Even as he searched for possible cures—pretty much a matter of shooting in the dark, as he admitted to a friend—he kept a keen eye on the international political scene as well as attending to the agricultural and genetic projects that he found so fulfilling. While recuperating at his sister's home on the shores of Lake Geneva, he wrote Cyril Clemens that it would be difficult for the United States to extricate itself from Vietnam. Johnson and Humphrey were not to blame. "The wrong turning was taken before them, before Kennedy, before Eisenhower. In fact it was taken when I was getting the hell kicked out of me for suggesting that we were taking on more than we could chew."[11] That was a reference to the Truman Doctrine — that communism must everywhere be contained — a policy that Wallace had so resolutely opposed. To Dr. George Darrow, coauthoring with him a book on strawberries, he wrote that he would do everything he could "to make the book not only a grand success but a labor of love and thing of enduring beauty which will be appreciated 200 years hence."[12]

Back in the United States he continued to go from one medical authority to another until warned against it by Dr. Joseph Belsky of the Danbury Hospital, who had first treated him in this illness. "Your energies are better spent working and writing about the things you know and do very well," Belsky advised. "You probably have a lot of time for any project you want."[13] The prognosis was much too optimistic.

As friends and political associates realized how ill he was they wrote to express sympathy or to pay him tribute. "I just can't accept it's happening to you," Gladys Baker of the Department of Agriculture wrote. The people were now realizing, she told him, that his Century of the Common Man speech had completely anticipated Lyndon Johnson's Great Society program, that John F. Kennedy's New Frontier was "only an echo" of the ideas contained in Wallace's similarly named book. He had been far ahead in his understanding of science and technology, and his 1944 speech nominating Franklin Roosevelt for a fourth term had "demonstrated . . . the most courage and sense of social justice of any I have read." Public addresses that Wallace had given in retirement "made us all realize what a dull place the Department had become since you left."[14]

Arriving at the same time as Gladys Baker's letter was another from Lyndon Johnson. "Your friendship and counsel have always been for me a source of much pride and joy," the president wrote. "May God bless you for all that you have done for this great land of ours."[15] The following month, Johnson invited him to the White House, offering to send a plane to collect him, and a delighted Wallace wrote enthusiastically to Johnson of the matters he hoped they could discuss. He assumed that Johnson wished to talk with him about agriculture, but for his part, he wanted to discuss the question of industrial decentralization and how the new Department for Urban Development and Housing could cooperate with the Department of Agriculture to bring that about. The problem, he explained to Johnson in his letter, was that the relatively shorter hours and higher wages on offer were drawing inefficient farmers to the cities, some of which were becoming "cesspools" on that account. It would be better to relocate marginal farmers within commuting distance of urban centers, so that they could supplement their income without losing contact with the land. He continued: "I do not like to see a situation emphasized which creates a population where less than 10% of the people know what it was to get the hay in out of the rain or cultivate corn in the hot June sun, or fix up the fence so the cows would not break out. 62 years ago I cultivated 5 acres of corn with a single horse cultivator. On that experience was based a million dollar business. As a boy of 14 I was working for my Father not for a Boss. I tremble for the future of the USA even though the cities are made very attractive and the schools are perfect, if 90% of the children have not had some type of farm discipline. I fear we are following the path of Ancient Rome."[16] In this reversion to a traditional agrarianism there was an echo of the idea he had discussed with George W. Russell all those years ago—that contact with the earth was necessary for a people's spiritual health. "I really should not come down to see you," Wallace wrote, "because my voice is so bad." He was, however, "quite willing to keep quiet and listen and speak with the utmost brevity." But the following day he had to write and cancel the trip. Worried that it might completely drain his strength, his wife had consulted Wallace's doctor, who had ruled it out.

In late September 1965 Wallace was admitted to the National Institute of Health at Bethesda, Maryland, for an operation to ease the difficulty he was having in swallowing.[17] Discharged after a month, he returned to his South Salem farm, but on 18 November he was rushed to the Danbury Hospital, where he died a short time later. He was seventy-seven.

Shortly before his death, he had received through the mail a request for a private interview in which he would be asked his views on the current national and international scene. In a courteous reply Wallace explained that, as he now found great difficulty in speaking, he would write his ideas on these subjects down. "First," he said, "we must remember that the Democrats inherited Viet Nam from the Republicans who in turn had inherited their policy from Truman." It was Harry Truman and John Foster Dulles who "took steps which will make the USA bleed from every pore." Wallace could see "enough trouble ahead so that I feel there is even a chance of the Republicans gaining the

Presidency in 1968," but they would merely continue with the foreign policy the Democrats had pursued and "in a short time will be in worse trouble than Johnson now is." The processes of democracy would be too slow to solve the problems of nations whose literacy rates were low and whose populations were rapidly outstripping their food supply. "These people in their pain raise hell and the communists have a free ride." As for the Latin American nations, they were "set to go off like a bunch of fire crackers." The challenge was to find a "constructive substitute" for democracy in these economically depressed areas, and though, in the short run, America's food surplus might help win their people away from communism, in the longer term something more would be needed. Yet "sooner or later," he wrote, venturing one more prediction on a subject that had brought him so much calumny and pain, "Russia will realize she will have to play ball with us. . . . Her interests are with us even though she may not realize it for a long time." [18]

As Henry Wallace looked once more across the international scene, he felt certain that the world stood on the brink of great changes, but the tone of foreboding in these, his final judgments, shows clearly his belief that the new world order of his ideal imaginings was still a great way off.

NOTES

PREFACE

1 Will Alexander interview, Columbia University Oral History Collection, Columbia University, New York (hereafter cited as Oral History), pp. 614, 629; Samuel Bledsoe, Oral History, pp. 125, 162; *Akron (Ohio) Beacon Journal*, 2 July 1943. (Interviews in the Columbia University Oral History Collection are available in transcription, and the page numbers following interview citations refer to these transcripts.)
2 Samuel Bledsoe interview, Oral History, pp. 128–29.
3 See Graham White and John Maze, *Harold Ickes of the New Deal: His Private Life and Public Career* (Cambridge: Harvard University Press, 1985).

CHAPTER ONE

1 Henry A. Wallace, Columbia University Oral History Collection, Columbia University, New York (hereafter cited as Oral History), pp. 1–2.
2 Russell Lord, *The Wallaces of Iowa* (Boston: Houghton Mifflin, 1947), pp. 105, 107.
3 Wallace, Oral History, pp. 2–4.
4 Ibid., pp. 4, 28–29.
5 Ibid., pp. 7, 34.
6 Ibid., pp. 19–27.
7 Ibid., p. 23.
8 T. W. Adorno, Else Frenkel-Brunswik, Daniel J. Levinson, and R. Nevitt Sanford, *The Authoritarian Personality* (New York: Basic Books, 1950); R. M. Henry, *The Psychodynamic Foundations of Morality* (Basel: Karger, 1983).
9 Wallace, Oral History, pp. 27, 34–35.
10 Ibid., pp. 37–38.
11 Ibid., pp. 7–9, 5221.
12 Ibid., pp. 11–17.
13 Ibid., p. 35.
14 Ibid., pp. 45–49.
15 William James, *The Varieties of Religious Experience* (1902; reprint, London: Collins, 1960), pp. 487, 498; George Cotkin, *William James: Public Philosopher* (Baltimore: Johns Hopkins University Press, 1990).
16 Ralph Waldo Trine, *In Tune with the Infinite* (London: G. Bell and Sons, 1960); Wallace, Oral History, pp. 49–50.
17 Wallace, Oral History, pp. 56–57.
18 Ibid., pp. 34–35, 51–57, 62.

19 Edward L. Schapsmeier and Frederick H. Schapsmeier, *Henry A. Wallace of Iowa: The Agrarian Years, 1910–1940* (Ames: Iowa State University Press, 1968), p. 23.

20 Wallace, Oral History, pp. 79–84.

21 Ibid., p. 86.

22 Lord, *Wallaces of Iowa*, pp. 184–85; Wallace, Oral History, p. 87; Lord, *Wallaces of Iowa*, p. 86.

23 Schapsmeier and Schapsmeier, *Agrarian Years*, pp. 24–26; Wallace, Oral History, pp. 89–91, 95–97, 114, 101–2.

24 Wallace to Dan Murphy, 30 September 1961, Correspondence, Henry A. Wallace Papers, University of Iowa, Iowa City.

25 Wallace, "The Aztecs as Geneticists," *Wallaces' Farmer*, 12 December 1908, quoted in Lord, *Wallaces of Iowa*, p. 142.

26 Henry A. Wallace and William L. Brown, *Corn and Its Early Fathers* (Ames: Iowa State University Press, 1988), pp. 87–88, 116–18; untitled publication of Pioneer Hi-Bred Corn Company, 1965, Miscellaneous 1934–65, Henry A. Wallace Papers, University of Iowa, Iowa City.

27 Wallace, Oral History, pp. 4–6.

28 Ibid., pp. 76, 78, 98–99.

29 Ibid., pp. 119, 29–30, 131.

30 Ibid., p. 49.

CHAPTER TWO

1 Edward L. Schapsmeier and Frederick H. Schapsmeier, *Henry A. Wallace of Iowa: The Agrarian Years, 1910–1940* (Ames: Iowa State University Press, 1968), p. 28.

2 John C. Evans to Wallace, 12 January 1929, Correspondence, Henry A. Wallace Papers, University of Iowa, Iowa City (hereafter cited as Wallace Papers, Correspondence).

3 Wallace to John C. Evans, 18 January 1929, ibid.

4 Wallace to Rev. John Jones Smith, 12 January 1929, ibid.

5 Wallace to Westermann Book Co., 14 January 1929, ibid.

6 Wallace to O. S. Bowman, 8 February 1929, ibid.

7 Wallace to Herbert J. Browne, 11 March 1929; Wallace to Rev. John Jones Smith, 18 January 1929; Wallace to Curtis Updegraff, 8 April 1930, ibid.

8 Charles Roos to Wallace, 19 October 1931; Juanita Roos to Wallace, 22 October 1931, ibid.

9 Irving S. Cooper to Wallace, 12 July 1927, ibid.

10 Henry A. Wallace, Columbia University Oral History Collection, Columbia University, New York (hereafter cited as Oral History), pp. 5210–11, 5219–20.

11 Wallace to Paul DeKruiff, 24 October 1931; Juanita Roos to Wallace, 22 October 1931; Wallace to Oliver Ditson Co., 14, 23 October 1931; Juanita Roos to Wal-

lace, [October 1933?]; Wallace to George W. Russell, 22 October 1931; Wallace to L. Edward Johndro, 22 October 1931, Wallace Papers, Correspondence.

12 Wallace to L. Edward Johndro, 22 October 1931, ibid.

13 Wallace to L. Edward Johndro, 24 October 1931, ibid.

14 William H. Dower to Wallace, 14 October 1931, ibid.

15 Charles Roos to Wallace, 12 November 1931, ibid.

16 Wallace to Juanita Roos, 23 November 1931; George W. Russell to Wallace, 6 November 1931, ibid.

17 Wallace to Mark Hyde, 14 July 1930, ibid.

18 Wallace to George W. Russell, 22 December 1930, ibid.

19 Bruce F. Campbell, *Ancient Wisdom: A History of the Theosophical Movement* (Berkeley and Los Angeles: University of California Press, 1980), p. 62.

20 Ibid., p. 63.

21 Charles Roos to Wallace, 10 July 1932, Wallace Papers, Correspondence.

22 Charles Roos to Wallace, 29 July, 3 August 1932, ibid.

23 William H. Dower to Wallace, 1 July 1932, ibid.

24 Charles Roos to Wallace, 3 August 1932, ibid.

25 Wallace to Ruth Muskrat Bronson, 3 July 1932; Wallace to Henry Roe Cloud, 8 July 1932; Wallace to David Owl, 8 July 1932, ibid.

26 Charles Roos to Wallace, 30 August 1932, ibid.

27 Schapsmeier and Schapsmeier, *Agrarian Years*, pp. 121–22.

28 Wallace to Frances Grant, 16 May 1932; Frances Grant to Wallace, 25 October 1929, Wallace Papers, Correspondence.

29 Wallace, Oral History, pp. 5221–23.

30 Campbell, *Ancient Widsom*, p. 66.

31 Ralph Waldo Trine, *In Tune with the Infinite* (London: G. Bell and Sons, 1960), pp. 180, 186; Ralph Waldo Emerson, "The Over-Soul," in Bliss Perry, ed., *The Heart of Emerson's Essays: Selections from His Complete Works* (Boston: Houghton Mifflin, 1933), p. 143.

32 Louis Bean, Oral History, p. 131.

33 Schapsmeier and Schapsmeier, *Agrarian Years*, pp. 101–2.

34 Quoted in ibid., p. 108.

35 David E. Hamilton, *From New Day to New Deal: American Farm Policy from Hoover to Roosevelt, 1928–1933* (Chapel Hill: University of North Carolina Press, 1991), pp. 201–4.

36 Wallace, Oral History, pp. 167, 169.

37 Ibid., pp. 171, 175–77.

38 Wallace to L. Edward Johndro, 19 January 1932; Johndro to Wallace, 21 January, 28 July 1932; Wallace to Charles Roos, 4 February 1932; Roos to Wallace, 9 February, 28 July 1932, Wallace Papers, Correspondence.

39 Wallace, Oral History, pp. 177–78.

40 Ibid., pp. 182–83.

41 Ibid., pp. 189–91.

42 Quoted in Russell Lord, *The Wallaces of Iowa* (Boston: Houghton Mifflin, 1947), pp. 324–25.

43 Wallace, Oral History, pp. 195–98, 200–202.

44 L. Edward Johndro to Wallace, [late 1932?], Wallace Papers, Correspondence.

CHAPTER THREE

1 Russell Lord, *The Wallaces of Iowa* (Boston: Houghton Mifflin, 1947), p. 330.

2 Ibid.

3 Henry A. Wallace, Columbia University Oral History Collection, Columbia University, New York (hereafter cited as Oral History), pp. 5417–18; Lord, *Wallaces of Iowa*, p. 331.

4 Edward L. Schapsmeier and Frederick H. Schapsmeier, *Henry A. Wallace of Iowa: The Agrarian Years, 1910–1940* (Ames: Iowa State University Press, 1968), pp. 170–72.

5 Wallace to Dante Pierce, [March 1933?], Correspondence, Henry A. Wallace Papers, University of Iowa, Iowa City (hereafter cited as Wallace Papers, Correspondence).

6 Wallace, Oral History, pp. 197, 199.

7 Wallace to Franklin D. Roosevelt, 19 April 1933, Wallace Papers, Correspondence.

8 Wallace, Oral History, p. 251.

9 Lord, *Wallaces of Iowa*, pp. 332–33.

10 Ibid., pp. 333–36; Unofficial Observer [J. Franklin Carter], *The New Dealers* (New York: Da Capo Press, 1975), p. 82.

11 Lord, *Wallaces of Iowa*, p. 335.

12 Unofficial Observer, *New Dealers*, pp. 78, 80.

13 Henry A. Wallace diary, 20 December 1939, University of Iowa Library, Iowa City.

14 Kenneth S. Davis, *FDR: The New Deal Years, 1933–1937* (New York: Random House, 1979), p. 271.

15 Ibid., p. 274.

16 Wallace, Oral History, p. 5428.

17 Davis, *FDR: The New Deal Years*, pp. 274–75.

18 Wallace, Oral History, pp. 5167–68.

19 Quoted in Lord, *Wallaces of Iowa*, p. 363.

20 Henry A. Wallace, *Statesmanship and Religion* (London: Williams and Norgate, 1934), pp. 119–20, 118, 120–21.

21 Henry A. Wallace, "Pigs and Pig Iron," in Henry A. Wallace, *Democracy Reborn* (London: Hammond and Hammond, 1945), pp. 99–101.

22 Robert C. Williams, *Russian Art and American Money* (Cambridge: Harvard University Press, 1980), p. 115.

23 Ibid., p. 118.

24 Ibid., p. 121.

25 Ibid., p. 123.

26 Wallace to Frances Grant, 15 April 1929, subject file Wallace, Henry A.—General, Westbrook Pegler Papers, Herbert Hoover Library, West Branch, Iowa (hereafter cited as Pegler Papers).

27 Prentiss Gilbert to Louis L. Horch, 12 April 1930; Special Agent Kinsey to R. C. Bannerman, 2 July 1930; Memorandum on Scientific Standing of Roerich Museum, 26 February 1930; Paul J. Sailly to W. R. Castle, 23 July 1930, General Records of the Department of State, 1930–39, File no. 031.11R62, Roerich Expedition to Central Asia, RG 59, National Archives.

28 Memorandum on Scientific Standing of Roerich Museum, 26 February 1930, ibid. For further unfavorable views on the museum's activities at Naggar, see George F. Waugh to Secretary of State, 30 October 1930; Memorandum, United States Embassy, London, to Secretary of State, 21 March 1932; United States Embassy, London, to William R. Castle Jr., 12 April 1932; Benjamin Thaw, Memorandum of Conversation, 7 April 1932; Louis L. Horch to Secretary of State, 12 April 1932, ibid.

29 L. V. Mitrokhin, "N. K. Roerich: A Great Explorer of the East," in S. N. Verma, ed., *Nicholas K. Roerich, 1874–1974* (Simla, India: Department of Languages, Art and Culture Himachal Pradesh, 1975), pp. 47–48.

30 Frances R. Grant to Wallace, 25 October 1929; Sina Lichtmann to Wallace, 6 June 1930, Wallace Papers, Correspondence.

31 Wallace to Frances Grant, 20 January 1931, ibid.

32 Wallace to Frances Grant, 12 October 1931; Wallace to George W. Russell, 23 November 1931; Wallace to Frances Grant, 22 February 1932, ibid.

33 Wallace to Cordell Hull, 31 August 1933; Wallace to Franklin D. Roosevelt, n.d.; Cordell Hull to Wallace, 29 September 1933, ibid.

34 In a postscript to an appendix to his book, entitled "The Mysticism Legend," Markowitz reports the discovery of these letters and states that "if . . . authentic, they would lend credence to Westbrook Pegler's reproductions although not necessarily to his interpretation." He adds that he "fully accept[s] responsibility for any errors in the appendix." Markowitz, of course, had no opportunity to take account of this new evidence. See Norman D. Markowitz, *The Rise and Fall of the People's Century: Henry A. Wallace and American Liberalism, 1941–1948* (New York: Free Press, 1973), pp. 333–42.

35 Clark Sellers to Westbrook Pegler, 2, 19 May 1947, subject file Wallace, Henry A.—General, Pegler Papers.

36 "G" to "Dear Guru," 12 March 1933, ibid.

37 Nicholas Roerich, *Shambhala* (New York: Frederick A. Stokes, 1930), pp. 2–13.

38 See Nicholas Roerich, *Heart of Asia* (New York: Roerich Museum Press, 1930), pp. 116, 129.

39 Richard Dean Burns and Charyl L. Smith, "Nicholas Roerich, Henry A. Wallace and the 'Peace Banner': A Study in Idealism, Egocentrism, and Anguish," *Peace and Change: A Journal of Peace Research* (Fall 1972): 4.

40 Wallace to Frances Grant, 17 June 1933 (enclosing letter of same date from Wallace to Nicholas Roerich); Wallace to Franklin D. Roosevelt, [August

1933?]; Wallace to Cordell Hull, 31 August 1933; Wallace to Louis Horch, 16 September 1933, Wallace Papers, Correspondence.

41 Cordell Hull to Wallace, 29 September 1933, ibid.

42 Wallace to W. M. Phillips, [late 1933?], ibid.; "G" to "Dear M," n.d.; "G" to "Dear M," 17 January 1934, subject file "Guru Letters" Henry A. Wallace (from copy of these letters in University of Iowa Library), Samuel I. Rosenman Papers, Franklin D. Roosevelt Library, Hyde Park, N.Y. (hereafter cited as Rosenman Papers).

43 Harold L. Ickes diary, 1933–51, Harold L. Ickes Papers, Library of Congress, p. 4981.

44 "HAW" to Nicholas Roerich, 29 October 1933, subject file Wallace, Henry A.— General, Pegler Papers.

45 Quoted in Verma, *Nicholas K. Roerich*, pp. 77–78; quoted in ibid., p. 77.

46 "HAW" to "F.R.G.," n.d., subject file "Guru Letters" Henry A. Wallace, Rosenman Papers.

47 "HAW" to "F," n.d., ibid.

48 Wallace to Cordell Hull, 29 September 1933, Wallace Papers, Correspondence; "G" to "M," n.d., subject file "Guru Letters" Henry A. Wallace, Rosenman Papers.

49 "G" to "M," [n.d.], subject file Wallace, Henry A.—General, Pegler Papers.

50 Wallace, Oral History, pp. 5398, 235.

51 David Eugene Conrad, *The Forgotten Farmers: The Story of Sharecroppers in the New Deal* (Urbana: University of Illinois Press, 1965), p. 28; Davis, *FDR: The New Deal Years*, p. 276.

52 Lord, *Wallaces of Iowa*, p. 339; Arthur M. Schlesinger Jr., *The Coming of the New Deal* (Boston: Houghton Mifflin, 1959), p. 46.

53 Wallace, Oral History, pp. 235–36.

54 Wallace to Dante Pierce, 19 June 1933, Wallace Papers, Correspondence; Wallace, Oral History, pp. 5401–2.

55 Wallace, Oral History, pp. 238–39, 5430, 5404.

56 Conrad, *Forgotten Farmers*, pp. 205, 27.

57 Ibid., pp. 64–65, 52–53.

58 Ibid., pp. 68–73.

59 Ibid., pp. 141–45.

60 Ibid., pp. 146–47; Chester Davis, Oral History, pp. 394, 401–3. Just at this period, when turmoil in department was at its peak, Wallace, using money provided by a supporter, Mary Rumsey, brought George W. Russell to Washington to deliver a series of inspirational talks to bureau chiefs, Extension Service personnel, and the like. In the diary entry for 9 February 1935, four days after the purge, Wallace records that he attended a dinner in honor of Russell at the home of Department of Agriculture statistician Louis Bean. Like Russell, Bean was a Theosophist. See Lord, *Wallaces of Iowa*, pp. 383–84; Wallace diary, 24 January, 9 February 1935.

61 Wallace diary, 7 February 1935.

62 Ibid., 2, 3, 4 February 1935.

63 Ibid., 5 February 1935; Gardner Jackson, Oral History, pp. 621–22; Lord, *Wallaces of Iowa*, pp. 398–99; Wallace, Oral History, pp. 168, 5461.

64 Wallace diary, 11 February 1935; Wallace, Oral History, pp. 5459–64.

CHAPTER FOUR

1 Henry A. Wallace, Columbia University Oral History Collection, Columbia University, New York (hereafter cited as Oral History), pp. 5102–6.

2 Mary Huss to Frances Grant, 8 August 1933; Frances Grant to Wallace, 14 August 1933; Mary Huss to Frances Grant, 11 September 1933; Wallace to Jesse Jones, 25 August 1933, Correspondence, Henry A. Wallace Papers, University of Iowa, Iowa City (hereafter cited as Wallace Papers, Correspondence).

3 Wallace to Franklin D. Roosevelt, 23 December 1933, Franklin D. Roosevelt Library, Hyde Park, N.Y., quoted in Robert C. Williams, *Russian Art and American Money* (Cambridge: Harvard University Press, 1980), p. 137; Williams, *Russian Art and American Money*, p. 137.

4 Wallace to Nicholas Roerich, 16 March 1934; Nicholas Roerich to Wallace, 20 March 1934, Wallace Papers, Correspondence.

5 "G" to "M," March 1934, subject file "Guru Letters" Henry A. Wallace (from copy of these letters in University of Iowa Library), Samuel I. Rosenman Papers, Franklin D. Roosevelt Library, Hyde Park, N.Y. (hereafter cited as Rosenman Papers).

6 United States State Department to American Ambassador in Tokyo, 9 May 1934 (telegram 66), 10 May 1934 (telegram 70), Wallace Papers, Correspondence.

7 Arthur Garrels to Secretary of State, 13 June 1934, General Records of the Department of State, 1930–39, File no. 102.7302, MacMillan, Howard G., and Stephens, James L., RG 59, National Archives; Howard G. MacMillan to Knowles Ryerson, 9 June 1934, Wallace Papers, Correspondence.

8 Arthur Garrels to Secretary of State, 8 June 1934; Cordell Hull to American Embassy, Tokyo, 11 June 1934, General Records of the Department of State, 1930–39, File no. 102.7302, MacMillan, Howard G., and Stephens, James L, RG 59, National Archives.

9 H. G. MacMillan to Knowles A. Ryerson, 9 June 1934, Wallace Papers, Correspondence.

10 H. G. MacMillan to Arthur Garrels, 20 July 1934, ibid.

11 H. G. MacMillan to Knowles A. Ryerson, 11 August 1934, ibid.

12 Knowles A. Ryerson to H. G. MacMillan, 11 August 1934, ibid.

13 Wallace to H. G. MacMillan, 20 September 1934; Wallace to Nicholas Roerich, 20 September 1934; Wallace to George C. Hanson, 27 September 1934; Wallace to Nicholas Roerich, 27 September 1934, ibid.

14 Nicholas Roerich to Wallace, 1 October 1934, ibid.

15 Wallace to Frances Grant, [?] October 1934; Wallace to Frances Grant, [?] October 1934, subject file "Guru Letters" Henry A. Wallace, Rosenman Papers;

Wallace to Knowles Ryerson, 20 October 1934, Wallace Papers, Correspondence.

16 Nicholas Roerich to Wallace, 1 October 1934; Knowles Ryerson to H. G. Mac-Millan, 11 August 1934; Wallace to Nicholas Roerich, 17 October 1934, Wallace Papers, Correspondence; C. E. Gauss to Walter A. Adams, 28 February 1935; Walter A. Adams to Nelson Trusler Johnson, 15 March 1935, General Records of the Department of State, 1930–39, File no. 102.7302, MacMillan, Howard G., and Stephens, James L., RG 59, National Archives; R. Walton Moore to Wallace, 24 August 1935, Wallace Papers, Correspondence; Nelson Trusler Johnson to Secretary of State, 10 April 1935, General Records of the Department of State, 1930–39, File no. 102.7302, MacMillan, Howard G., and Stephens, James L., RG 59, National Archives.

17 Wallace to Frances Grant, n.d., subject file "Guru Letters" Henry A. Wallace, Rosenman Papers.

18 Wallace, Oral History, pp. 82–83.

19 Wallace to "M," n.d.; Wallace to [Frances Grant], n.d.; "G" to "M," n.d., subject file "Guru Letters" Henry A. Wallace, Rosenman Papers.

20 Wallace to Grant, February 1935, ibid.

21 Wallace to Grant, n.d., ibid.

22 Quoted in *Pan American Union Bulletin* (May 1935): 359–60; Wallace to Bernard Hansen, 16 April 1935, Wallace Papers, Correspondence.

23 Wallace to Nicholas Roerich, 3 July 1935; Wallace to Louis Horch, 3 July 1935, Wallace Papers, Correspondence.

24 E. N. Bressman to Nicholas Roerich, 9 July 1935, ibid.

25 Wallace to Nicholas Roerich, 15 August 1935; George Roerich to Wallace, 19 August 1935; Wallace to George Roerich, 19 August 1935, ibid.

26 R. Walton Moore to Wallace, 24 August 1935, ibid.

27 Wallace to F. D. Richey, 30 August 1935, ibid.

28 Wallace to George Roerich, 4 September 1935; Wallace to Nicholas Roerich, 24 September 1935; F. D. Richey to "Roerich," 23 September 1935, ibid. The Roerichs despatched a considerable quantity of seeds and roots to the Bureau of Plant Industry, but apparently these were not in such an order or of such a nature that anything useful could be done with them. There is no mention of them in the official department literature, save for a note saying: "Brought in 435 plant specimens, either in form of seeds or plants . . . 170 herbarium specimens of various genera and species. Trunk-full of drug plant materials. No one knew what to do with them. Trunk is in the attic. They have a list of plants included—roots, etc. It's never been opened." Quoted in Thomas D. Isern, "The Erosion Expeditions," *Agricultural History* 52, no. 2 (1985): 190.

29 Wallace to Louis Horch, 18 September 1936, Wallace Papers, Correspondence.

30 "'Spy' Rumor Ends Roerich Expedition," press clipping, ibid.; see, for example, Wallace to Oswaldo Aranha, 23 October 1935, ibid.

31 Wallace to Guy T. Halvering, 1 October 1935, ibid.

32 Wallace to Herbert H. Lehman, 18 January 1936, ibid.

33 Wallace to Winthrop Aldrich, 29 January 1936; Wallace to Vincent Bendix, 29 January 1936; Wallace to Henry Ford, 29 January 1936, ibid.

34 Sumner Welles, Memorandum of Conversation with the British Ambassador, Sir Reginald Lindsay, 21 February 1938, United States State Department General Records, 865D.01/385, quoted in Williams, *Russian Art and American Money*, p. 143.

35 Torbjorn Sirevag, *The Eclipse of the New Deal: And the Fall of Vice-President Wallace, 1944* (New York: Garland, 1985), pp. 523, 675.

36 Wallace, Oral History, pp. 5104, 5106–7.

37 Wallace to Knowles Ryerson, 11 October 1935; Wallace to Howard G. MacMillan, 6 November 1935; Wallace to James L. Stephens, 19 November 1935, Wallace Papers, Correspondence.

CHAPTER FIVE

1 Henry A. Wallace, Columbia University Oral History Collection, Columbia University, New York (hereafter cited as Oral History), pp. 302–3.

2 Ibid., p. 420.

3 Henry A. Wallace, *New Frontiers* (New York: Reynal and Hitchcock, 1934), p. 242; Wallace, Oral History, pp. 421–22.

4 Wallace, Oral History, pp. 421–22.

5 Ibid., pp. 355–56.

6 Ibid., pp. 351–54.

7 Russell Lord, *The Wallaces of Iowa* (Boston: Houghton Mifflin, 1947), p. 466.

8 Wallace, Oral History, pp. 5479–80.

9 Lord, *Wallaces of Iowa*, p. 460.

10 Quoted in ibid., pp. 460–61.

11 Quoted in ibid., p. 462.

12 Wallace, Oral History, p. 5482.

13 Will Alexander, Oral History, pp. 628–29.

14 Wallace, Oral History, pp. 5482–83, 5422.

15 Lord, *Wallaces of Iowa*, pp. 462–63.

16 Wallace, Oral History, pp. 394–98.

17 Ibid., p. 398.

18 Ibid., pp. 394–95.

19 Ibid., pp. 5487–91, 5467, 5471–72, 5442–43.

20 Ibid., pp. 464–65, 469.

21 Ibid., pp. 407, 531, 533.

22 Ibid., p. 560.

23 Ibid., pp. 407–8, 472.

24 Ibid., pp. 479–81, 502–3.

25 Ibid., pp. 79, 101.

26 Ibid., pp. 264–68.

27 Wallace to Franklin D. Roosevelt, 22 December 1937. See copy in Wallace, Oral History, p. 493.

28 Wallace to Franklin D. Roosevelt, 24 March 1938. See copy in Wallace, Oral History, pp. 508–11.

29 Wallace to Franklin D. Roosevelt, 25 March 1938. See copy in Wallace, Oral History, pp. 513–14.

30 Wallace, Oral History, pp. 407–8, 552.

31 Chester Davis, Oral History, pp. 344–45, 423.

32 Paul Appleby, Oral History, pp. 163–64.

33 Wallace, *New Frontiers*, pp. 174–79.

34 J. Samuel Walker, *Henry A. Wallace and American Foreign Policy* (Westport, Conn.: Greenwood Press, 1976), p. 60. Walker's treatment of the Guru letters largely agrees with ours; however, he misses the concealed references to the possible abode of the masters, and so does not see that Wallace had a motive for promoting the expedition over and above the search for drought-resistant grasses. Nor does he explore Wallace's spiritual history in the pre–New Deal period, without an understanding of which the entire Roerich episode remains unintelligible; Edward L. Schapsmeier and Frederick H. Schapsmeier, *Henry A. Wallace of Iowa: The Agrarian Years, 1910–1940* (Ames: Iowa State University Press, 1968), p. 254.

35 Paul Appleby, Oral History, pp. 163–64.

36 Paul Appleby to R. M. Evans, 28 December 1936, United States Department of Agriculture Papers, Appleby (Personal) 1936, RG 16, National Archives.

37 R. M. Evans, Oral History, pp. 141–42.

38 Paul Appleby, Oral History, pp. 210–12.

39 Samuel I. Rosenman, *Working with Roosevelt* (New York: Harper and Brothers, 1952), p. 206.

40 Samuel Bledsoe, Oral History, pp. 130–36.

41 Wallace, *New Frontiers*, pp. 7–8.

42 Quoted in Lord, *Wallaces of Iowa*, pp. 475–76.

43 Ibid., p. 476.

44 Paul Appleby, Oral History, pp. 35–36; Gardner Jackson, Oral History, pp. 572–73; Harold L. Ickes diary, 1933–51, 7, 17 December 1934, Harold L. Ickes Papers, Library of Congress.

45 Wallace, Oral History, p. 989.

46 Ibid., pp. 1074–75.

47 Henry A. Wallace diary, 24 May 1940, University of Iowa Library, Iowa City.

48 Wallace, Oral History, pp. 1218–19.

49 Ibid., p. 1242.

50 Paul Appleby, Oral History, pp. 213–15.

51 Ibid.

52 Quoted in Rosenman, *Working with Roosevelt*, p. 213.

53 James A. Farley, *Jim Farley's Story*, extract reproduced in Wallace, Oral History, pp. 1236–37; James Farley interview, James Farley Papers, Library of Congress, p. 11.

54 George Martin, *Madame Secretary* (Boston: Houghton Mifflin, 1976), p. 434; L. Taber, Oral History, p. 361.

55 Rosenman, *Working with Roosevelt*, p. 216.

56 Lord, *Wallaces of Iowa*, p. 480.

57 Roger Biles, *A New Deal for the American People* (De Kalb: Northern Illinois University Press, 1991), p. 70.

58 Wallace, Oral History, pp. 5164–69.

59 Mordecai Ezekiel to Louis Bean, 15 August 1940; James Jardine to Bean, 15 August 1940; E. N. Bressman to Louis Bean, 16 August 1940; Dillon S. Meyer to Bean, 23 August 1940; Gove Hambidge, "Four Qualities of Henry Wallace the Man," Correspondence, Henry A. Wallace Papers, University of Iowa, Iowa City.

60 *New York Times*, 3 November, 29, 18 October, 30 August, 26 September, 23 October, 29 September, 19, 31 October 1940.

61 *New York Times*, 30 August 1940.

62 *New York Times*, 16, 31 August 1940.

63 *New York Times*, 27 October, 1 November 1940.

64 Wallace, Oral History, pp. 1259–60.

65 *New York Journal American*, 23 March 1948.

66 Robert H. Ferrell, ed., *Truman in the White House: The Diary of Eben A. Ayres* (Columbia: University of Missouri Press, 1991), pp. 176–77; Samuel I. Rosenman, Summary of Events Relating to the "Guru" Letters, subject file "Guru Letters" Henry A. Wallace, Samuel I. Rosenman Papers, Franklin D. Roosevelt Library, Hyde Park, N.Y. (hereafter cited as Rosenman Papers); Paul Appleby, Oral History, p. 244; Paul Appleby to Samuel I. Rosenman, 24 June 1949, 7 February 1950, subject file "Guru Letters" Henry A. Wallace, Rosenman Papers.

67 Wallace, Oral History, p. 5107.

68 For a discussion of the dispute over the Forest Service, see Graham White and John Maze, *Harold Ickes of the New Deal: His Private Life and Public Career* (Cambridge: Harvard University Press, 1985), chap. 5. Wallace fought hard, and eventually successfully, to prevent Ickes from moving the Forest Service from the Department of Agriculture to the Department of the Interior, without showing any of the fanaticism that this issue aroused in his cabinet colleague.

69 Wallace, Oral History, pp. 433–34, 307–8, 674–75.

70 Wallace to Franklin D. Roosevelt, 24 March 1938, quoted in Wallace, Oral History, pp. 508–12.

71 Wallace, Oral History, pp. 462, 354.

CHAPTER SIX

1 Henry A. Wallace, Columbia University Oral History Collection, Columbia University, New York (hereafter cited as Oral History), pp. 5211–12.

2 Chester Davis, Oral History, pp. 344–45, 423.

3 Wallace, Oral History, p. 5169.

4 Ibid., pp. 5179–80.

5 Ibid., pp. 1286–87.

6 J. Samuel Walker, *Henry A. Wallace and American Foreign Policy* (Westport, Conn.: Greenwood Press, 1976), p. 76; Russell Lord, *The Wallaces of Iowa* (Boston: Houghton Mifflin, 1947), pp. 484–85.

7 Avila Camacho to Wallace, 3 January 1941, Correspondence, Henry A. Wallace Papers, University of Iowa, Iowa City (hereafter cited as Wallace Papers, Correspondence).

8 Wallace, Oral History, pp. 1286–94; SAC, San Antonio to Director FBI, 2 August 1944, Henry A. Wallace file, FBI Papers, University of Iowa Library, Iowa City (hereafter cited as FBI Papers).

9 *New York Times*, 16 March 1941; *Amarillo (Texas) News*, 15 February 1941; *Miami Herald*, 5 February 1941; *Baltimore Sun*, 15 February 1941.

10 *Boston Globe*, 17 February 1941; *Lancaster (Pennsylvania) Intelligencer-Journal*, 4 February 1941; Wallace, Oral History, pp. 1300–1301.

11 *Birmingham News*, 26 July 1941; *Washington Evening Star*, 20 March 1942.

12 Frank Ryhlick, "Wallace—New Kind of Vice President," *New York Daily Worker*, 20 September 1942.

13 *Washington Merry-Go-Round*, 2 May 1941; *Birmingham News*, 26 July 1941; Wallace, Oral History, pp. 1322, 1319; *New York Times*, 16 March 1941.

14 John Morton Blum, *V Was for Victory: Politics and American Culture during World War II* (New York: Harcourt, Brace, Jovanovich, 1976), p. 782.

15 *Atlantic Monthly*, January 1942, quoted in Lord, *Wallaces of Iowa*, p. 490.

16 Henry A. Wallace, "Veblen's 'Imperial Germany and the Industrial Revolution,'" *Political Science Quarterly* 55 (1940): 435–45.

17 Wallace, Oral History, pp. 1373–75.

18 Ibid., p. 1376.

19 Ibid., pp. 1359–60.

20 Ibid., p. 1785.

21 Blum, *V Was for Victory*, p. 282.

22 Ibid.; Norman D. Markowitz, *The Rise and Fall of the People's Century: Henry A. Wallace and American Liberalism, 1941–1948* (New York: Free Press, 1973), pp. 69–70.

23 Blum, *V Was for Victory*, p. 283.

24 Wallace, Oral History, pp. 1449–51.

25 Ibid., p. 1478.

26 Ibid., pp. 1455–56.

27 Ibid., p. 1478.

28 Ibid., pp. 1480–81.

29 Martin Dies to Wallace, 28 March 1942, Wallace Papers, Correspondence; Wallace, Oral History, p. 1472.

30 Wallace, Oral History, p. 1505.

31 Henry A. Wallace diary, 19 May 1942, University of Iowa Library, Iowa City.

32 Markowitz, *Rise and Fall of the People's Century*, pp. 9, 14–15.

33 Henry A. Wallace, Speech to Free World Association, 8 May 1942, *Congressional Record*, 77th Cong., 2d sess., 21 April–24 July 1942, pp. A1675–76.

34 Wallace, Oral History, pp. 1608–9.

35 Ibid., pp. 1996, 1998.

36 Ibid., pp. 1966–68, 1996.

37 *Congressional Record*, Senate Committee on Banking and Currency, 77th Cong., pp. 5–6, 19.

38 Wallace, "Rubber and the New Isolationism," *New York Times Magazine*, 19 July 1942.

39 Wallace, Oral History, p. 2020.

40 Ibid., p. 2024.

41 *Congressional Record*, Senate Committee on Banking and Currency, 77th Cong., pp. 65–66, 77–78.

42 Wallace, Oral History, p. 2040.

43 Wallace to William M. Jeffers, 12 January 1943, Wallace Papers, Correspondence; Wallace diary, 10 February 1943.

44 "Reception of Vice President Wallace in Latin America (Second Report)"; "Visit of Vice President Henry A. Wallace to Peru—Political," 21 April 1943, Henry A. Wallace file, FBI Papers.

45 Drew Pearson, "South America Sends Back Word Wallace Is Top Man There," *Washington Post*, 16 May 1943.

46 "Visit of Vice President Henry A. Wallace to Peru—Political," 21 April 1943, Henry A. Wallace file, FBI Papers; Wallace, Oral History, pp. 2443–44q.

47 Wallace, Oral History, p. 2446.

48 Ibid., p. 1956.

49 Ibid., pp. 2450–51.

50 Ibid., p. 2453.

51 Ibid., pp. 2508–12.

52 Ibid., p. 2540.

53 Markowitz, *Rise and Fall of the People's Century*, p. 71; Wallace, Oral History, pp. 2540–41.

54 Wallace, Oral History, p. 2551.

55 Wallace diary, 30 June 1943; Wallace, Oral History, pp. 2553–54.

56 Wallace, Oral History, p. 2563.

57 Ibid., pp. 2565–66.

58 Ibid., pp. 2568, 2574.

59 Ibid., p. 2779.

60 *New York Sun*, 16 July 1943; *New York Herald Tribune*, 18 July 1943; Wallace, Oral History, p. 2493; Lord, *Wallaces of Iowa*, p. 513; Wallace, Oral History, p. 2543.

61 Markowitz, *Rise and Fall of the People's Century*, p. 71.

62 Wallace, Oral History, p. 4020.

63 Walker, *Wallace and American Foreign Policy*, pp. 94–95; Wallace diary, 25 June 1943.

64 Nathan Robertson, "New Dealers Rally to Support of Wallace," *PM*, 18 July 1943.

CHAPTER SEVEN

1 Henry A. Wallace, "What We Fight For," in Henry A. Wallace, *Democracy First* (London: Oxford University Press, 1944), pp. 11, 12ff.
2 *Congressional Record*, Senate Committee on Patents, 77th Cong., pp. 3279, 3311, 4676ff.
3 Henry A. Wallace, Columbia University Oral History Collection, Columbia University, New York (hereafter cited as Oral History), p. 4020.
4 *New York Times*, 23 July, 4 August, 12 September 1943.
5 *New York Times*, 5 September 1943; "Heard in Washington," 26 October 1943, Correspondence, Henry A. Wallace Papers, University of Iowa, Iowa City (hereafter cited as Wallace Papers, Correspondence).
6 Roy Armes, *A Critical History of British Cinema* (London: Cinema Two, 1978), pp. 163–64; Henry A. Wallace diary, 15 December 1942, 11 January 1943, University of Iowa Library, Iowa City; Andrew R. Kelley, "Wallace Ideals Planned as Motion Picture Story," *Washington Times-Herald*, 11 January 1943; Gabriel Pascal to Charles E. Marsh, 30 December 1942, Charles E. Marsh to Gabriel Pascal, 3 January 1943, Wallace to Gabriel Pascal, 9 January 1943, Gabriel Pascal to Wallace, 20 January 1943, Wallace to Gabriel Pascal, 10 July 1943, Gabriel Pascal to Wallace, 5 November 1943, Gabriel Pascal to Wallace, 11 April 1944, Wallace to Gabriel Pascal, 20 April 1944, Wallace Papers, Correspondence; H. K. Girvetz, *From Wealth to Welfare: The Evolution of Liberalism* (Stanford, Calif.: Stanford University Press, 1950), pp. 276–78.
7 Wallace to Franklin D. Roosevelt, 25 April 1940, vol. 257; Transcript of phone conversation between Wallace and Henry Morgenthau Jr., 29 May 1940, Volume 267, Henry Morgenthau Diaries, Roosevelt Library, Hyde Park, N.Y., cited by J. Samuel Walker, *Henry A. Wallace and American Foreign Policy* (Westport, Conn.: Greenwood Press, 1976), p. 71.
8 Wallace diary, 3, 17 November 1943.
9 Ibid., 18 November 1943.
10 Wallace, Oral History, pp. 3040–41; Wallace diary, 23 January 1944.
11 *New York Times*, 10 February 1944; Wallace, Oral History, p. 3062.
12 Wallace, Oral History, p. 3153.
13 Ibid., p. 3198.
14 Ibid., p. 3091; Wallace diary, 12 November 1942.
15 Wallace diary, 3 January 1944; on expressions of support for Wallace, see, for example, ibid., 1, 16 February 1943; *Washington Post*, 5 March 1944.
16 Wallace diary, 8 January, 17 October 1943, 3, 10 January 1944.
17 Ibid., 14 March 1944.
18 Wallace, Oral History, p. 3207.
19 Ibid., pp. 1342–43; Wallace diary, 22 May 1943.

20 Wallace diary, 18 January, 4 February 1943.

21 Wallace, Address to Congress of Soviet-American Friendship, 12 November 1942, *Congressional Record*, 77th Cong., 2d sess., p. A3952; Henry A. Wallace, "Practical Religion in the World of Tomorrow," in Henry A. Wallace et al., *The Christian Bases of World Order* (Nashville: Abingdon-Cookesbury Press, 1943), pp. 10–20, quoted in Norman D. Markowitz, *The Rise and Fall of the People's Century: Henry A. Wallace and American Liberalism, 1941–1948* (New York: Free Press, 1973), pp. 165–66; Henry A. Wallace, "Two Peoples, One Friendship," *Survey Graphic*, February 1944.

22 Henry A. Wallace, *Soviet Asia Mission*, with the collaboration of Andrew J. Steiger (New York: Reynal and Hitchcock, 1946), p. 19; Harriman to the President and the Secretary, 20 June 1944, President's Secretary's file, Franklin D. Roosevelt Papers, Franklin D. Roosevelt Library, Hyde Park, N.Y.

23 Wallace, *Soviet Asia Mission*, pp. 44, 59–60, 84, 85, 90, 93.

24 William L. O'Neill, *A Better World: The Great Schism: Stalinism and the American Intellectuals* (New York: Simon and Schuster, 1982), p. 151.

25 Robert Conquest, *The Great Terror: Stalin's Purge of the Thirties* (London: Macmillan, 1968), preface.

26 Wallace, Oral History, p. 3345; Wallace diary, 8 May 1944.

27 Wallace, Oral History, p. 3351.

28 Wallace, *Soviet Asia Mission*, pp. 19, 156.

29 Wallace, Oral History, p. 3358.

30 Ibid., p. 5483.

31 Ibid., pp. 3356, 3362–63.

32 Ibid., p. 3364.

33 Ibid., p. 3366.

34 Wallace diary, 1 August 1944.

35 Wallace, Oral History, pp. 3373–74.

36 Ibid., pp. 3409–10.

37 Ibid., p. 3411. For a full discussion of the machinations involved in the dumping of Wallace, see Robert L. Messer, *The End of an Alliance: James F. Byrnes, Roosevelt, Truman, and the Origins of the Cold War* (Chapel Hill: University of North Carolina Press, 1980), pp. 17–30.

38 Jake Moore to Wallace, 18 July 1944, Wallace Papers, Correspondence.

39 *Washington Post*, 19 July 1944.

40 Charles Van Devander and William O. Player Jr., "Thunderous Reception for Wallace," *New York Post*, 24 July 1944.

41 Quoted in Russell Lord, *The Wallaces of Iowa* (Boston: Houghton Mifflin, 1947), p. 533.

42 Wallace, Oral History, p. 3421.

43 Ibid., p. 3425; Markowitz, *Rise and Fall of the People's Century*, p. 111.

44 Wallace, Oral History, p. 3384.

45 Frank McNaughton and Walter Hehmeyer, *This Man Truman* (London: George G. Harrap, 1946), p. 122.

46 Wallace, Oral History, p. 3404.

47 John Morton Blum, *V Was for Victory: Politics and American Culture during World War II* (New York: Harcourt, Brace, Jovanovich, 1976), pp. 290–91.
48 Wallace diary, 3 August 1944.
49 Ibid., 8 August 1944; Henry A. Wallace, *Our Job in the Pacific*, quoted in Wallace, Oral History, p. 3494.
50 Wallace, Oral History, pp. 3497, 3495.
51 Wallace diary, 6 October 1944.
52 Wallace, Oral History, p. 3419.
53 Lord, *Wallaces of Iowa*, p. 537.
54 Wallace diary, 8 August 1944; James Reston, "Roosevelt to Hold Post for Wallace," *New York Times*, 10 August 1944.
55 Wallace diary, 29 August 1944.
56 Wallace, Oral History, p. 3489.
57 Jack Santino, *Miles of Smiles, Years of Trouble: Stories of Black Pullman Porters* (Urbana: University of Illinois Press, 1989), pp. 87–88.
58 Wallace diary, 10 November 1944.
59 "The Department of Commerce," 29 November 1944, Wallace Papers, Correspondence; Wallace diary, 20 December 1944.
60 Samuel I. Rosenman, Oral History, p. 204.
61 Lord, *Wallaces of Iowa*, p. 545.
62 Ibid.
63 Jonathan Daniels, interview with Truman, 12 November 1949, Jonathan Daniels Papers, University of North Carolina, quoted in Harold F. Gosnell, *Truman's Crises: A Political Biography of Harry S. Truman* (Westport, Conn.: Greenwood Press, 1980), p. 210.
64 Gosnell, *Truman's Crises*, pp. 210–11; Harry S. Truman, *Memoirs*, vol. 1, *Year of Decisions* (New York: Signet Books, 1955), p. 220; Robert H. Ferrell, ed., *Truman in the White House: The Diary of Eben A. Ayres* (Columbia: University of Missouri Press, 1991), p. 239.
65 Lord, *Wallaces of Iowa*, pp. 548–49.
66 *Under the Surface in Washington*, vol. 3, no. 3, 5 February 1945, Wallace Papers, Correspondence.
67 Among those who congratulated him was a Chippewa Indian priest, minister of St. Patrick's Church, Centuria, Wisconsin, who wrote: "The Great High Spirit, the Kitchi Manitou—may he keep you ever and ever. This is the prayer of your innumerable friends. . . . Poseyemo." Rev. Philip Gordon to Wallace, 7 March 1945, ibid.
68 Wallace diary, 14–15 April 1945.

CHAPTER EIGHT

1 Henry A. Wallace diary, 27 April 1945, University of Iowa Library, Iowa City.
2 Henry A. Wallace, Columbia University Oral History Collection, Columbia University, New York (hereafter cited as Oral History), p. 3698.

3 Norman D. Markowitz, *The Rise and Fall of the People's Century: Henry A. Wallace and American Liberalism, 1941–1948* (New York: Free Press, 1973), p. 142.

4 Wallace to Kenneth Payne, 10 March 1945, enclosing article "Planning for Freedom," Correspondence, Henry A. Wallace Papers, University of Iowa, Iowa City (hereafter cited as Wallace Papers, Correspondence).

5 Henry A. Wallace, *Sixty Million Jobs* (London: William Heinemann, 1946), pp. 1–17, 51, 59, 83, 117–18, 166.

6 Wallace diary, 21 September 1945; Markowitz, *Rise and Fall of the People's Century*, p. 174.

7 *New York Daily Mirror*, 26 September 1945; *New York Times*, 22 September 1945.

8 Wallace to Harry S. Truman, 24 September 1945, see Wallace diary, 21 September 1945.

9 Wallace, Oral History, pp. 4140–43.

10 David Dietz, *Atomic Energy in the Coming Era* (New York: Dodd, Mead, 1945), p. 155, quoted in Jim Falk, *Global Fission: The Battle over Nuclear Power* (Melbourne: Oxford University Press, 1982), pp. 18–19.

11 Wallace diary, 15, 19, 24 October 1945.

12 Wallace, Oral History, p. 4845.

13 Wallace diary, 31 July 1946.

14 Harry S. Truman diary, 17 September 1946, quoted in Robert H. Ferrell, ed., *Off the Record: The Private Papers of Harry S. Truman* (New York: Harper and Row, 1980), p. 94.

15 Wallace diary, 31 July 1946.

16 Ibid., 11 December 1942, 29 December 1945.

17 Wallace, Oral History, p. 4955.

18 John C. O'Brien, "Wallace and Pepper Organization Alarmed[;] Rallying Independents[;] Personal Following Building for 1948," *Philadelphia Enquirer*, 28 August 1946.

19 Truman diary, 17 September 1946, quoted in Ferrell, *Off the Record*, p. 94.

20 Wallace diary, 10 September 1946; Wallace, Oral History, p. 4953.

21 Wallace, Oral History, p. 4966.

22 "An Address by Henry A. Wallace, Secretary of Commerce," 12 September 1946. Speech is in Wallace diary following entry for 20 September 1946.

23 James F. Byrnes, *Speaking Frankly* (New York: Harper and Brothers, 1947), p. 95.

24 Ibid., p. 203.

25 Wallace, Oral History, p. 4966.

26 *New York Times*, 13 September 1946.

27 Wallace, Oral History, p. 4975.

28 Harry S. Truman, *Memoirs* (Stoughton, N.Y.: Hodder and Stoughton, 1955–56), vol. 1, p. 498.

29 Ibid., pp. 492–93.

30 Wallace, Oral History, pp. 4983, 4984.

31 Ibid., p. 4983; Wallace diary, 16 September 1946.

32 Wallace, Oral History, p. 4988.

33 James Forrestal, *The Forrestal Diaries*, ed. Walter Millis (New York: Viking Press, 1951), p. 154; Byrnes, *Speaking Frankly*, p. 239.

34 Byrnes, *Speaking Frankly*, p. 240.

35 Wallace diary, 18 September 1946.

36 Truman diary, 17 September 1946, quoted in Ferrell, *Off the Record*, p. 95. In his memoirs, Truman omitted any reference to Ross's call directing Wallace to await his final decision, and Wallace's agreement to do so. See Truman, *Memoirs*, vol. 1, p. 613. On the release of the letter, Wallace received the following note from Albert Einstein: "I cannot refrain from expressing to you my high and unconditional admiration for your letter to the President of July 23rd. There is a deep understanding concerning the factual and the psychological situation and the far-reaching perception of the fateful consequences of present Administration foreign policy. Your courageous intervention deserves the gratitude of all of us who observe the present attitude of our government with grave concern." Einstein to Wallace, 18 September 1946, Wallace Papers, Correspondence.

37 Wallace, Oral History, pp. 4999–5000.

38 Wallace diary, 18 September 1946.

39 Ibid.; Wallace, Oral History, p. 5005.

40 Wallace, Oral History, pp. 5004, 5007.

41 Byrnes, *Speaking Frankly*, pp. 241–42.

42 Truman diary, 19 September 1946, quoted in Robert L. Messer, *The End of an Alliance: James F. Byrnes, Roosevelt, Truman, and the Origins of the Cold War* (Chapel Hill: University of North Carolina Press, 1980), p. 211.

43 Wallace, Oral History, pp. 5028, 5030, 5026.

44 Wallace diary, 29 July 1946.

45 Wallace, Oral History, p. 4985.

CHAPTER NINE

1 *New York Times*, 21 September 1946; Henry A. Wallace, Columbia University Oral History Collection, Columbia University, New York (hereafter cited as Oral History), pp. 5033–34.

2 *New York Times*, 25 October 1946.

3 *Washington Post*, 31 October 1946.

4 *New York Times*, 7 November 1946.

5 Quoted in Curtis D. MacDougall, *Gideon's Army* (New York: Marzani and Munsell, 1965), p. 106.

6 Quoted in ibid., p. 106.

7 *New York Times*, 30 December 1946.

8 Quoted in MacDougall, *Gideon's Army*, pp. 121–22.

9 *New York Times*, 23 January 1947.

10 MacDougall, *Gideon's Army*, p. 130; J. C. Strickland to D. M. Ladd, 11 April 1947, Henry A. Wallace file, FBI Papers, University of Iowa Library, Iowa City (hereafter cited as FBI Papers).

11 Quoted in MacDougall, *Gideon's Army*, p. 131.

12 Wallace, Oral History, p. 5071.

13 Wallace, "The Fight for Peace Begins," *New Republic*, 24 March 1947, pp. 12–13.

14 Henry A. Wallace, *Speeches in Britain* (London: Reynolds News, by arrangement with New Statesman and Nation, 1947), pp. 2, 21, 23.

15 Ibid., pp. 24, 25.

16 Ibid., p. 26.

17 Ibid., pp. 26–27.

18 Ibid., p. 34.

19 *Washington Evening Star*, 15 April 1947; *Congressional Record*, 80th Cong., 1st sess., 2 April–12 June 1947, pp. A1694–95; Norman D. Markowitz, *The Rise and Fall of the People's Century: Henry A. Wallace and American Liberalism, 1941–1948* (New York: Free Press, 1973), p. 240; Wallace, Oral History, p. 5074; *Congressional Record*, 80th Cong., 1st sess., 13–26 June 1947, p. A3249; *New York Times*, 26 April 1947; Robert H. Ferrell, ed., *Truman in the White House: The Diary of Eben A. Ayres* (Columbia: University of Missouri Press, 1991), pp. 176–77.

20 MacDougall, *Gideon's Army*, p. 155.

21 *New York Times*, 20 May 1947; *Minneapolis Times Herald*, 13 May 1947; Markowitz, *Rise and Fall of the People's Century*, p. 242.

22 Henry A. Wallace, "Report from the Middle West," *New Republic*, 26 May 1947; "Report from the Southwest," ibid., 2 June 1947; "Report from California," ibid., 9 June 1947; "Report from the Northwest," ibid., 16 June 1947; "Report from Oregon," ibid., 23 June 1947; "Report on the Farmers," ibid., 30 June 1947; "Report from Iowa," ibid., 7 July 1947.

23 *Baltimore Sun*, 10 September 1947; Boston Agency to J. Edgar Hoover, 18 October 1947; Atlanta Agency to Hoover, 24 November 1947, Henry A. Wallace file, FBI Papers.

24 Wallace, Oral History, p. 5079.

25 MacDougall, *Gideon's Army*, p. 42.

26 Quoted in ibid., p. 185; Henry A. Wallace, "My Commitments," *Vital Speeches* 14 (1 August 1948): 620–23.

27 *New York Times*, 1 September 1947.

28 *New York Times*, 12 September 1947.

29 Wallace, Oral History, pp. 5065, 5080–81, 5089.

30 Quoted in MacDougall, *Gideon's Army*, p. 186.

31 Quoted in ibid., p. 207. See also, for example, "Wallace Insists Truman Give Date," *New York Times*, 11 October 1947.

32 MacDougall, *Gideon's Army*, p. 201.

33 Quoted in ibid., p. 204.

34 Quoted in ibid., p. 207.

35 *New York Herald Tribune*, 30 December 1947.

36 Wallace, Oral History, p. 5115.

37 Quoted in MacDougall, *Gideon's Army*, p. 82.

38 Quoted in ibid., pp. 248–49.

39 Quoted in ibid., p. 303.

40 Quoted in ibid., p. 279; Wallace, Oral History, pp. 5067–69.

41 MacDougall, *Gideon's Army*, p. 335. Wallace discusses this in Oral History, pp. 5140–41.

42 Harry S. Truman, "Special Message to the Congress on the Threat to the Freedom of Europe," 17 March 1948, in *Public Papers of the Presidents of the United States: Harry S. Truman* (Washington, D.C.: United States Government Printing Office, 1964), pp. 183–86.

43 Ibid., pp. 186–90.

44 William Hillman, *Mr. President: The First Publication from the Personal Diaries, Private Letters, Papers and Revealing Interviews of Harry S. Truman, Thirty-Second President of the United States of America* (New York: Hutchinson, 1952), p. 135, cited in Robert A. Divine, "The Cold War and the Election of 1948," *Journal of American History* 59, no. 1 (June 1972): 98.

45 Quoted in MacDougall, *Gideon's Army*, p. 251.

46 Quoted in ibid., pp. 351–52.

47 *Congressional Record*, 80th Cong., 2d sess., 12 May–2 June 1948, pp. 5686–87.

48 *New York Times*, 18 May 1948.

49 MacDougall, *Gideon's Army*, p. 360.

50 Ibid., pp. 360–61. Wallace also denied to his oral history interviewer that he had ever sent the letter; see Wallace, Oral History, p. 5058.

51 *Congressional Record*, 80th Cong., 2d sess., 12 April–11 May 1948, pp. 5186–88.

52 D. M. Ladd to J. Edgar Hoover, 5 March 1948, Henry A. Wallace file, FBI Papers.

53 FBI Agent (Costa Rica) to J. Edgar Hoover, 5 April 1943; "Report of Vice Presidential Visit to Peru," 8 April 1943; "Bolivian Communistic Influence over Vice President Wallace," 21 April 1943; J. Edgar Hoover to Francis Biddle, 3 May 1943, Henry A. Wallace file, FBI Papers.

54 FBI Agent to J. Edgar Hoover, 15 February 1944, "Reception for Wallace"; R. B. Hood to J. Edgar Hoover, 15 February 1944, ibid.

55 D. M. Ladd to J. Edgar Hoover, 12 May 1944, ibid.

56 New York Office of FBI to J. Edgar Hoover, 24 July 1944; J. C. Strickland to D. M. Ladd, 31 January 1945; K. K. Conroy to J. Edgar Hoover, 24 February 1945, ibid.

57 J. C. Strickland to D. M. Ladd, 3 April 1945, "Henry A. Wallace: Information Concerning," ibid.

58 E. G. Fitch to D. M. Ladd, 19 August 1947, ibid.

59 SAC Atlanta to J. Edgar Hoover, 24 November 1947; J. Edgar Hoover to Francis Biddle, 8 December 1947; SAC Boston to J. Edgar Hoover, 24 April 1948; Hoover Directive, 3 June 1947; Hoover to Major General Harry Hawkins Vaughan, 18 August 1947, ibid.

60 FBI report, 12 April 1948, ibid.

61 J. Edgar Hoover to Francis Biddle, 18, 20 May 1948, ibid.

62 Quoted in MacDougall, *Gideon's Army*, p. 357.

63 Quoted in ibid., p. 519.

64 Quoted in ibid, p. 498.

65 Wallace to Westbrook Pegler, 18 October 1946; Clark Sellers to Pegler, 2, 19 May 1947, subject file Wallace, Henry A.—General, Westbrook Pegler Papers, Herbert Hoover Library, West Branch, Iowa (hereafter cited as Pegler Papers).

66 See subject file Wallace, Henry A.—General, Pegler Papers, for copies of Pegler's columns.

67 *Congressional Record*, 80th Cong., 2d sess., 9 August 1948, pp. A5362–65; MacDougall, *Gideon's Army*, p. 533.

68 MacDougall, *Gideon's Army*, p. 565.

69 Ibid., p. 571.

70 Wallace, Oral History, pp. 5131–32.

71 Leon F. Litwack, interview with Shane White and Ian Hoskins, University of Sydney, Australia, 27 August 1991.

72 Wallace, Oral History, p. 5123; *Southern Labor Review*, 7 April 1948, quoted in Robin D. G. Kelley, *Hammer and Hoe: Alabama Communists during the Great Depression* (Chapel Hill: University of North Carolina Press, 1990), p. 226.

73 MacDougall, *Gideon's Army*, pp. 717–18; quoted in Karl M. Schmidt, *Henry A. Wallace: Quixotic Crusade* (Syracuse: Syracuse University Press, 1960), p. 206.

74 Wallace, Oral History, pp. 5123–24.

75 Ibid., pp. 5121–24; see Kelley, *Hammer and Hoe*, p. 229.

76 Wallace, Oral History, pp. 5124–25.

77 Ibid., p. 5128.

78 Quoted in MacDougall, *Gideon's Army*, pp. 837–38.

79 Quoted in ibid., p. 685.

80 Wallace, Oral History, pp. 5091–92.

81 Schmidt, *Henry A. Wallace*, p. 260.

CHAPTER TEN

1 Norman D. Markowitz, *The Rise and Fall of the People's Century: Henry A. Wallace and American Liberalism, 1941–1948* (New York: Free Press, 1973), p. 295.

2 Curtis D. MacDougall, *Gideon's Army* (New York: Marzani and Munsell, 1965), p. 603.

3 Henry A. Wallace, Columbia University Oral History Collection, Columbia University, New York (hereafter cited as Oral History), p. 5142.

4 MacDougall, *Gideon's Army*, pp. 881–82.

5 Wallace, Oral History, p. 5143.

6 MacDougall, *Gideon's Army*, p. 882.

7 James Wechsler, "My Ten Months with Wallace," *Progressive* 12 (November 1948): 4–8.

8 Wallace, Oral History, p. 5143.

9 Ibid., p. 5118.

10 Ibid., pp. 5131–32.

11 Ibid., p. 5213.

12 Ibid.

13 Edward A. Lahey, "The Chicken Raiser—A Man Who Used to Be Mr. Henry Wallace," *New York Herald Tribune*, [? date partly obscured; see Correspondence, Henry A. Wallace Papers, University of Iowa, Iowa City (hereafter cited as Wallace Papers, Correspondence), for this clipping] April 1951; Wallace to Harry Weinberg, 20 February 1951, Wallace Papers, Correspondence.

14 *Congressional Record*, 81st Cong., 1st sess., 14 March–19 May 1949, p. A1866. Wallace repeated many of these arguments in a letter to every member of the Senate, as that body prepared to consider the new alliance; see Wallace Papers, Correspondence, April 1949–July 1950.

15 Wallace to C. B. Baldwin, 15 February 1950, Wallace Papers, Correspondence.

16 *New York Times*, 25 February 1950.

17 Wallace, Oral History, pp. 5133–34.

18 Press clipping, Wallace Papers, Correspondence, August 1950–January 1951; Wallace, Oral History, pp. 5135, 5137.

19 Wallace, Oral History, pp. 5144–45.

20 Ibid., pp. 5138–39.

21 Wallace memorandum, "Korea, Trygve Lie and the Progressive Party from July 6 to 12, 1950," Miscellaneous 1934–65, Henry A. Wallace Papers, University of Iowa, Iowa City (hereafter cited as Wallace Papers, Misc. 1934–65).

22 *New York Times*, 16 July 1950.

23 *New York Times*, 11 August, 13 November 1950.

24 Ethel Beckwith, "Wallace Expects to Run Again in 1952; Korea Split Doesn't End His Ties," n.d. (see Wallace Papers, Correspondence, for this clipping); C. H. Doyle to Wallace, 17 July 1950; Marcia K. Freeman to Wallace, 17 July 1950, Wallace Papers, Correspondence.

25 Wallace to Curtis MacDougall, 8 August 1950; Curtis MacDougall to Wallace, 11, 15, 19 August 1950, Wallace Papers, Correspondence.

26 Wallace to Henry Weinberg, 20 February 1951, ibid.

27 Wallace to Mao Tse-tung, 30 September 1950, ibid.

28 Wallace, "Summary of Conversation with Helen Reid at Herald Tribune Building," 21 February 1951, Wallace Papers, Misc. 1934–65; Wallace to Mikhail Menshikov, 28 September 1959, Wallace Papers, Correspondence.

29 Wallace to Henry Luce, 17 August 1949; Henry Luce to Wallace, 19 August 1949, Wallace Papers, Correspondence. See also Wallace to Luce, 24 August 1949, ibid.

30 William S. White, "Chiang Too Weak for Postwar Rule, Wallace Advised," *New York Times*, 19 January 1950, p. 1. The text of Wallace's report is on p. 3 of this issue.

31 Wallace to Leslie R. Groves, 7 March 1951, Wallace Papers, Correspondence.

32 L. B. Nichols to Clyde A. Tolson, 17 October 1951, Henry A. Wallace file, FBI Papers, University of Iowa Library, Iowa City (hereafter cited as FBI Papers); Tom Knudson, "Hoover's FBI Spied on Iowan Wallace," *Des Moines Register*, 4 September 1983.

33 Wallace to Francis Walter, 10 April 1951, Wallace Papers, Correspondence. See also Wallace to Francis Walter, 18 May 1951, ibid.

34 *Congressional Record*, 82d Cong., 1st sess., 3 January–23 October 1951, p. 13562.

35 Wallace to Pat McCarran, 22 October 1951, Wallace Papers, Correspondence.

36 Wallace to Winston S. Churchill, 22 October 1951, ibid.

37 "Henry A. Wallace Believes the United States Faces Its Gravest Period from Russia's Ambition to Dominate the World," *Washington City News Service*, 11 December 1951, Henry A. Wallace file, FBI Papers.

38 *New Leader* 35, no. 37 (15 September 1952), based on article in *This Week*, 7 September 1952.

39 Donald Feitel, "A Visit with Henry Wallace," *Washington Sunday Star Magazine*, 3 August 1958, Wallace Papers, Correspondence.

40 Wallace to Luis Quintanilla, 19 January 1954; Wallace to Carl Fisher, 28 August 1958, ibid.

41 Thomas Buckley, "Residents of South Salem Grew to Like Wallace," *New York Times*, 19 November 1965.

42 Cabell Phillips, "At 75, Henry Wallace Cultivates His Garden," *New York Times Magazine*, 6 October 1963, pp. 47, 104–6.

43 Wallace to H. V. Kaltenborn, 23 April 1954; Wallace to Hamilton Shea, 25 May 1954; Wallace to Alben W. Barkley, 21 May 1954, Wallace Papers, Correspondence.

44 Wallace to Herbert Brownell Jr., 23 October 1954; Wallace to Herbert A. Philbrick, 25 November 1954, ibid.

45 Wallace memorandum, "The Last Cabinet Dinner, December 4, 1952: The End of an Era," Wallace Papers, Misc. 1934–65; Wallace to Arthur H. Sulzberger, 1 October 1955, Wallace Papers, Correspondence. (The extracts from Truman's memoirs and Wallace's rebuttal are in the *New York Times*, 28 October 1955, p. 27.) Wallace to Harry S. Truman, 10 March 1956, Wallace Papers, Misc. 1934–65.

46 Wallace to Harry S. Truman, 10 March 1956, Wallace Papers, Correspondence.

47 George Humphrey to Wallace, 7 March 1956, enclosing press clipping "Wallace Will Vote for Ike If He Runs"; Wallace to Dwight D. Eisenhower, 26 November 1956, 19 February 1957; Eisenhower to Wallace, 22 February 1957; Wallace to Eisenhower, 31 December 1957, ibid.

48 Wallace to Harry Weinberg, 20 February 1951; Donald Feitel, "A Visit with Henry Wallace," *Washington Sunday Star Magazine*, 3 August 1958, ibid.

49 Markowitz, *Rise and Fall of the People's Century*, p. 318.

50 Wallace to Lyndon Baines Johnson, 24 November 1963; Lyndon Baines Johnson to Wallace, 4 December 1963, Wallace Papers, Correspondence.

51 Wallace to George Darrow, 11 December 1963, ibid.
52 Wallace to Frank Freidel, 13 March 1964, ibid.

EPILOGUE

1 Henry A. Wallace, Columbia University Oral History Collection, Columbia University, New York (hereafter cited as Oral History), pp. 5164–76.
2 Wallace to Lynn W. Ely, 5 June 1951, Correspondence, Henry A. Wallace Papers, University of Iowa, Iowa City (hereafter cited as Wallace Papers, Correspondence).
3 Wallace, Oral History, p. 5474; J. Samuel Walker, *Henry A. Wallace and American Foreign Policy* (Westport, Conn.: Greenwood Press, 1976), p. 35.
4 Will Alexander, Oral History, pp. 623–24, 629–32, 613–20.
5 Wallace to Joseph Belsky, 10 October 1964, Wallace Papers, Correspondence.
6 Wallace to Wallace Ashby, 22 October 1964, ibid.
7 Wallace to Don Murphy, 31 October 1964, ibid.
8 Wallace to Marshall Bean, 17 December 1964, ibid.
9 Wallace to Don Murphy, 28 December 1964, ibid.
10 Wallace to Cyril Clemens, 18 February 1965, ibid.
11 Wallace to Cyril Clemens, 1 April 1965, ibid.
12 Wallace to George Darrow, 14 April 1965, ibid.
13 Joseph Belsky to Wallace, 28 June 1965, ibid.
14 Galdys Baker to Wallace, 16 July 1965, ibid.
15 Lyndon Baines Johnson to Wallace, 16 July 1965, ibid.
16 Wallace to Lyndon Baines Johnson, 12 August 1965, ibid.
17 *New York Herald Tribune*, 12 October 1965.
18 Wallace to James Pappathanasi, 4 July 1965, Wallace Papers, Correspondence.

lenges Wallace over "Guru letters,"
271
Pepper, Claude, 204, 225, 256
Perkins, Frances, 71, 72, 136
Perkins, Milo, 156, 157, 160, 161, 165,
166, 168, 169, 174, 176, 177, 217,
307
Peter, Agnes, 132
Philadelphia Inquirer, 225
Philbrick, Herbert A., 298, 299
Phillips, W. M., 68
Pierce, Dante, 46, 76
Pioneer Hi-Bred Corn Company, 14,
16, 297
PM, 236
Potash, Irving, 258
Powell, Adam Clayton, Jr., 267
Pregal, Boris, 294
Pressman, Lee, 75, 79, 81, 116, 282
Preston, Georgiana, 177
Progressive Citizens of America
(PCA), 243, 250
Progressive Party, 276, 279, 283, 287,
288, 309; attacks on potential sup-
porters of, 265–66; formation of,
270, 274–76; and 1948 campaign,
276–82

Quintanilla, Luis, 297

Rank, J. Arthur, 185
Rankin, John R., 249, 282
Raper, Arthur, 111
Rayburn, Samuel, 176, 191, 203, 206
Readers Digest, 218
Reconstruction Finance Corporation
(RFC), 156, 166, 168, 174, 176, 178,
213
Reid, Helen Rogers, 292
Remarque, Erich Maria, 183
Resettlement Administration, 111,
114
Reston, James, 208, 230, 231
Reuther, Walter, 258
Richey, F. D., 100

Richie, L. R., 210
Robeson, Paul, 267
Robinson, Edward G., 267
Robinson, Joseph, 308
Roerich, George, 57, 62, 85, 87, 89, 90,
91, 99, 100
Roerich, Helena, 57, 59, 66, 73, 103,
143
Roerich, Nicholas, 56, 59, 60, 64, 66,
67, 69, 73, 84, 86, 87, 88, 89, 92, 93,
94, 95, 96, 98, 99, 100, 101, 102,
124, 125, 131, 142, 144, 148, 239,
273, 274, 290, 298, 306; early career,
57; activities in United States, India,
and Soviet Union, 57–62; interest
in Theosophy and Buddhism, 58;
leads first expedition to Asia, 59;
promotes Roerich Pact and Banner
of Peace, 60–61, 89; establishes
Urusvati, Himalayan Research
Institute, 62; leads Department of
Agriculture expedition to Mongolia, 83–84; activities as leader of
expedition, 87–100
Roerich, Svetoslav, 57, 62
Roerich Museum, 31, 58, 59, 83, 143
Roos, Charles, 15, 19–21, 22, 23, 24,
25, 28, 29, 30, 63, 124, 131, 307
Roos, Juanita ("Nita"), 19–20, 22, 122
Roosevelt, Eleanor, 71, 136, 188, 191,
210, 245
Roosevelt, Franklin D., x, 1, 28, 38, 42,
49, 64, 67, 71, 72, 93, 117, 123, 131,
132, 133, 134, 143, 145, 147, 159,
160, 161, 165, 166, 173, 176, 177,
182, 186, 187, 188, 189, 200, 202,
203, 205, 208, 211, 214, 241, 272,
282, 307, 308, 311; appoints Wallace
secretary of agriculture, 39–41;
dissociates himself from Nicholas
Roerich, 103; develops closer relations with Wallace, 118–21; resolves
doubts over Wallace's mysticism,
131–33; insists on Wallace as running mate, 135–37; reservations

Wagner, Robert, 167

Walker, James, 60

Walker, J. Samuel, 126

Wallace, Annabelle, 4

Wallace, Henry ("Uncle Henry"), 2, 6

Wallace, Henry A.: contradictory qualities of, ix; Samuel Bledsoe's assessment of, ix–x; political philosophy of, xi, xii–xiii, 9, 51, 53–54, 124, 178–79, 199, 306; and new world order, xi, xiii–xiv, 51, 53, 55–56, 63–64, 124–25, 126, 183, 221, 224, 274, 301, 313; oral history interview, xi–xii, 2, 285, 305; political diary, xii; spiritual quest, xiii, 15, 43; interest in agricultural experimentation, 2; early life, 2–6; influence of "Uncle Henry" on, 3, 6, 8, 10; origins of political attitudes, 3–5, 6; attitude toward father, 5, 14–15, 33; influence of mother on, 5–6, 15; influence of William James on, 6, 8–9; develops interest in Theosophy and Native American religion, 8, 9, 10, 11, 21–31, 27–28; 32–35; experiments with diet, 9; influence of Ralph Waldo Trine on, 9; distinguished academic record, 10; meets George W. Russell ("A.E."), 10–11; applies scientific methods to agriculture, 11; develops tuberculosis, 11; marries Ilo Browne, 11; promotes development of hybrid corn, 13–14; early political ideas, 14; disdains political processes, 14–15, 42–43; contributes to plant and animal genetics, 16; writings of, 16, 37, 53, 107, 124, 194, 195, 207, 218; interest in astronomical and astrological influences on the weather, 17–19; meets Charles and Juanita Roos, 19–21; seeks religious keynote of the new age, 23; first contacts with the Roerich group, 31–32, 60–61, 62–63; views on value of agricultural life, 35–36; alienation from Republican Party, 37; supports Voluntary Domestic Allotment Plan, 37–38; becomes secretary of agriculture, 38–41; first impressions of Franklin D. Roosevelt, 39–40, 41, 42, 43; and Agricultural Adjustment Act, 44–46; opposes cuts to Department of Agriculture budget, 46, 48; scientific expertise, 49; orders cotton plow-under and piglet slaughter, 50; resists regimentation of farm program, 51; supports National Industrial Recovery Act, 55; supports Reorich Pact, 60–61, 64–73; appoints Nicholas Roerich to head expedition to Mongolia, 62, 83–84; hostility toward leaders of Soviet Union, 72; purges liberals from Department of Agriculture, 79–81; claims Roosevelt suggested expedition to Mongolia, 82; and secret aims of expedition, 84–85; dismisses expedition's botanists, 91, 92–93; seeks funds to establish industrial enterprise in Mongolia, 94–96; nominates Nicholas Roerich for Nobel Peace Prize, 97; signs Roerich Pact and Banner of Peace, 97; terminates Roerich expedition and dissociates himself from Roerich, 97–102; reluctance to admit blame for expedition's failure, 104; circumvents invalidation of Agricultural Adjustment Act, 105–7; promotes economic democracy, 108, 110; criticizes Roosevelt's economic thinking and administrative competence, 109–10; tours areas of rural poverty in South, 111–13; establishes Farm Security Administration, 113–16; opposes court-packing plan, 117; opposes purge of Congressional Democrats,

117–18; develops closer relations with Roosevelt, 118–21; interest in international affairs, 119; urges more cooperative approach by Roosevelt, 119–20; develops wider political ambitions, 121–24; gains support of African Americans, 129–31; strengths and weaknesses as vice-presidential candidate, 129–31; influence of 1936–37 trip to the South, 130–31; tributes to, on resignation as secretary of agriculture, 137–38; denies authenticity of "Guru letters," 144–45; critical of Roosevelt's performance, 145–46; liberalism of, 147–49, 153–54, 156, 158, 162–64, 165, 183–86, 204; attitude toward Catholic church, 149, 156, 193–94, 206, 224; tours Latin America, 149–51; studies Spanish language, 150, 153; vice-presidential style of, 152–53; devotion to physical fitness, 152; wartime disputes with Jesse Jones, 152–64, 172–79, 180; heads Board of Economic Warfare, 153; delivers "Century of Common Man" speech, 162–64, 298, 305; interest in postwar world, 165–66, 179, 186, 189; popular reception of, on second Latin American trip, 170–71; warns against economic imperialism in Latin America, 171–73; attacks agreement between I. G. Farbenindustrie and Standard Oil of New Jersey, 181–82; attacks reactionary groups, 183–84; attempts to mobilize liberal opinion, 186–88; visits Soviet Union and China, 189, 194–99; assesses chances of retaining vice presidency, 190–92; suspects aims of British policy, 193, 207; urges cooperation with Soviet Union, 194, 219; arouses ire of British government, 198–99, 207;

loses vice-presidential nomination, 199–206; assesses character of Harry Truman, 206; pressures Roosevelt to maintain liberal goals, 208–9; outlines aims as secretary of commerce, 211; confirmed as secretary of commerce, 213–14, 330 (n. 67); advocates full employment, 218; attempts to heal rift between United States and Soviet Union, 222–23; challenges United States foreign policy, 224–31; seeks Truman's approval for Madison Square Garden speech, 225–27; dismissal by Truman, 236–39; attacks federal loyalty program, 245; becomes editor of *New Republic*, 245; opposes Truman Doctrine, 246–48; attacks on, in United States, 248–49; denounces loyalty program, 250; attacks J. Edgar Hoover and FBI, 251; becomes Progressive Party candidate, 257; reviled as Communist dupe, 257–58, 261–62; writes open letter to Stalin, 262–63; surveillance of, by FBI, 266–69; challenged by Westbrook Pegler over "Guru letters," 271–73; leads Progressive Party campaign of 1948, 276–82; tours South during campaign, 277–80; identifies himself with Jesus Christ, 278, 280, 284; seeks to exculpate himself from Communist affiliation, 285–86; reverses attitude toward Soviet Union, 286, 288–90, 291; breaks with Progressive Party, 287–91; suffers continuing attacks on patriotism, 292–94; defends himself before congressional committees, 294; returns to farming and plant breeding, 297; rebuts further attacks on credibility, 298–300; favorable attitude toward Dwight Eisenhower, 300–301; favorable attitude toward Lyndon B. Johnson, 302; visits Latin America, 303; assessment of achievements, 305–6; aspects of character discussed, 306–8; impact of spiritual beliefs on career, 308; contracts amyotrophic lateral sclerosis, 309–10; tributes paid to, 311; death of, 312

Wallace, Henry B., 11, 297

Wallace, Henry C., 2, 3, 5, 12–13, 14, 27, 28, 33, 36, 41, 81

Wallace, Ilo, 136, 205, 283, 297. *See also* Browne, Ilo

Wallace, James, 4

Wallace, Jean, 11

Wallace, John, 4

Wallace, May, 2

Wallace, Robert B., 11, 297

Wallaces' Farmer, 3, 10, 11, 12, 13, 19, 29, 31, 32, 37, 38, 62, 310

Wallaces' Farmer and Iowa Home-stead, 31, 41, 46

Walsh, J. Raymond, 258

Walter, Francis E., 287, 294,

War Production Board (WPB), 156, 164, 167, 180

Washington Evening Star, 152, 249

Washington Post, 157

Washington Star, 301

Washington Times-Herald, 177

Watson, Edwin M, 199

Weinberg, Harry, 301

Welles, Sumner, 102, 161

White, William S., 293

Wickard, Claude, 134

Williams, Robert C., 57, 58

Willkie, Wendell, 140, 144

Wilson, M. L., 38, 76, 80, 306, 307

Witt, Nathan, 282

Woodin, William, 42, 83,

Young, Harold, 307, 309

Zacharias, Ellis, 288